The Economics of Decarbonized Transport:

AI Technologies, Market Mechanisms, and Policy Innovation

Mohamed Amine Frikha
https://orcid.org/0000-0002-6737-1370

King Faisal University, Saudi Arabia

IGI Global
Scientific Publishing
Publishing Tomorrow's Research Today

Vice President of Editorial Melissa Wagner
Director of Acquisitions Mikaela Felty
Director of Book Development Jocelynn Hessler
Production Manager Mike Brehm
Cover Design Jose Rosado

Published in the United States of America by
IGI Global Scientific Publishing
701 East Chocolate Avenue
Hershey, PA, 17033, USA
Tel: 717-533-8845 | Fax: 717-533-7115
Website: https://www.igi-global.com E-mail: cust@igi-global.com

Library of Congress Cataloging-in-Publication Data

Names: Frikha, Mohamed Amine, 1982- editor
Title: The economics of decarbonized transport : AI technologies, market mechanisms, and policy innovation / edited by Mohamed Amine Frikha.
Description: Hershey, PA : IGI Global Scientific Publishing, [2026] | Includes bibliographical references and index. | Summary: "This book advances understanding of the economic foundations of transport decarbonization by integrating artificial intelligence (AI) technologies, market-based mechanisms, and policy innovation within a unified analytical framework"-- Provided by publisher.
Identifiers: LCCN 2026012254 (print) | LCCN 2026012255 (ebook) | ISBN 9798337390031 hardcover | ISBN 9798337390048 paperback | ISBN 9798337390055 ebook
Subjects: LCSH: Transportation--Environmental aspects | Carbon dioxide mitigation | Transportation | Transportation--Technological innovations | Transportation and state
Classification: LCC HE147.65 .E266 2026 (print) | LCC HE147.65 (ebook)
LC record available at https://lccn.loc.gov/2026012254
LC ebook record available at https://lccn.loc.gov/2026012255

British Cataloguing in Publication Data
A Cataloguing in Publication record for this book is available from the British Library.

Table of Contents

Preface xiv

Acknowledgement xx

Chapter 1
Artificial Intelligence and Machine Learning Applications in Decarbonized Transport 1
Deepak Gupta, Institute of Technology and Management, Gwalior, India
Anorgul Ashirova, Mamun University, Khiva, Uzbekistan
Abdusamatov Mamayusup, Termez University of Economics and Service, Termez, Uzbekistan
Mukimov Askar Shukhratovich, Ifraganus University, Tashkent, Uzbekistan
Bobojonov Azizjon, Tashkent State University of Economics, Tashkent, Uzbekistan
Dilshojon Urinov, Fergana State University, Fergana, Uzbekistan
Temur Khudayberganov, Urgench State University Named After Abu Raykhan Beruni, Urgench, Uzbekistan

Chapter 2
AI-Driven Logistics, Data Governance, and Sustainability: A Critical Analysis of India's Digital Personal Data Protection Act 2023 33
Vijeta Verma, Christ University, India
Shashank Solanki, Christ University, India
Vijaishree Dubey Pandey, Christ University, India
Sheetal Singh, Christ University, India
Rituraj Sinha, Christ University, India

Chapter 3
Governance by Investment: How Emerging Economy OFDI Drives the Green Transition? 81
R. Sukanya, Christ University, India

Chapter 4
From Emissions Targets to Market Behavior: Evaluating Policy-Driven Decarbonization Pathways in Road and Freight Transport Systems 113
Shoyimkulov Asror, Termez University of Economics and Service, Termez, Uzbekistan
S. Aarthi, Marwadi University, Rajkot, India
R. N. Ravikumar, Marwadi University, Rajkot, India
Jabbarov Umarbek, Mamun University, Khiva, Uzbekistan
Kurbonov Jasurbek Pozilovich, Alfraganus University, Tashkent, Uzbekistan

Chapter 5
Decision Frameworks for Sustainable Urban Transport Systems 147
Sena Kumcu, Department of Industrial Engineering, Faculty of Engineering, Gazi University, Ankara, Turkey
Beste Desticioğlu Taşdemir, Department of Operations Research, Alparslan Defence Sciences and National Security Institute, National Defence University, Ankara, Turkey & Department of Econometrics, Erasmus School of Economics, Erasmus University Rotterdam, Rotterdam, The Netherlands

Chapter 6
Digital Twins and Data-Driven Infrastructure Management 173
Atul Kumar, Dnyaan Prasad Global University, India
Shaturaev Jakhongir, Termez University of Economics and Service, Termez, Uzbekistan
Jabbarov Umarbek, Mamun University, Khiva, Uzbekistan
Muzaffar Shojonov, Urgench State University, Urgench, Uzbekistan
Allambergenova Mukhabbat Khasanbaevna, Nukus State Pedagogical Institute, Uzbekistan
Abdullayev Abdulla Fayzulla Ugli, Tashkent State University of Economy, Tashkent, Uzbekistan

Chapter 7
Economic Signals and Artificial Intelligence for Sustainable Transport and Low-Carbon Logistics Systems 213
Turdiev Abdullo Sagdullaevich, Alfraganus University, Tashkent, Uzbekistan
S. Aarthi, Marwadi University, Rajkot, India
R. N. Ravikumar, Marwadi University, Rajkot, India
Shoyimkulov Asror, Termez University of Economics and Service, Termez, Uzbekistan
Jabbarov Umarbek, Mamun University, Khiva, Uzbekistan

Chapter 8
Cost-Benefit Analysis of Low-Carbon Mobility Solutions 247
Deepak Gupta, Institute of Technology and Management, Gwalior, India
Ergashev Nuriddin Gayratovich, Karshi State Technical University. Karshi, Uzbekistan
Mirzaev Abdullaevich, Tashkent State University of Economy, Uzbekistan
Davlatova Toshpulatovna, Termiz State University of Engineering and Agrotechnology, Termiz, Uzbekistan
Yarmatov Sharofiddin, Termez University of Economics and Service, Termez, Uzbekistan
Begimov Uktam, Alfraganus University, Tashkent, Uzbekistan

Chapter 9
Green Finance, AI-Enabled Investment Strategies, and Renewable Energy for Decarbonizing Transport Infrastructure in Emerging Economies 275
Aarohi Kumari, Vivekananda Global University, India
Gautam Jha, Vivekananda Global University, India
Vikas Rana, Vivekananda Global University, India
Pratishtha Singh, Vivekananda Global University, India
Pratyush Sinha, Vivekananda Global University, India

Chapter 10
Reimagining Logistics Systems for Sustainable Supply Chain Transformation 313
A. Priscila, Saveetha School of Management, Saveetha Institute of Medical and Technical Sciences, Chennai, India
R. Durai Pandian, Saveetha School of Management, Saveetha Institute of Medical and Technical Sciences, Chennai, India
M. Siva Sarswathi, Saveetha School of Management, Saveetha Institute of Medical and Technical Sciences, Chennai, India
V. Selvalakshmi, Saveetha School of Management, Saveetha Institute of Medical and Technical Sciences, Chennai, India

Compilation of References 345

About the Contributors 375

Index 383

Detailed Table of Contents

Preface xiv

Acknowledgement xx

Chapter 1
Artificial Intelligence and Machine Learning Applications in Decarbonized Transport 1
Deepak Gupta, Institute of Technology and Management, Gwalior, India
Anorgul Ashirova, Mamun University, Khiva, Uzbekistan
Abdusamatov Mamayusup, Termez University of Economics and Service, Termez, Uzbekistan
Mukimov Askar Shukhratovich, Ifraganus University, Tashkent, Uzbekistan
Bobojonov Azizjon, Tashkent State University of Economics, Tashkent, Uzbekistan
Dilshojon Urinov, Fergana State University, Fergana, Uzbekistan
Temur Khudayberganov, Urgench State University Named After Abu Raykhan Beruni, Urgench, Uzbekistan

The transportation sector accounts for approximately 24% of global energy-related carbon dioxide emissions, making it a critical domain for decarbonization efforts. Artificial intelligence and machine learning technologies have emerged as transformative tools for achieving sustainable transport systems through intelligent optimization of energy management, traffic flow, route planning, and predictive maintenance. This chapter provides a comprehensive examination of AI and ML applications across multiple transport modalities, including electric vehicles, autonomous driving systems, urban traffic management, and multimodal logistics. Through systematic analysis of recent innovations in reinforcement learning, deep neural networks, and predictive analytics, the chapter demonstrates how these technologies enable significant reductions in energy consumption and emissions while improving operational efficiency.

Chapter 2
AI-Driven Logistics, Data Governance, and Sustainability: A Critical Analysis of India's Digital Personal Data Protection Act 2023 33
Vijeta Verma, Christ University, India
Shashank Solanki, Christ University, India
Vijaishree Dubey Pandey, Christ University, India
Sheetal Singh, Christ University, India
Rituraj Sinha, Christ University, India

This paper is a critical overview of the blowout of artificial intelligence (AI)-empowered logistics, cross-border data governance, and sustainability regulation as the Digital Personal Data Protection Act, 2023 (DPDP Act) of India. It addresses the ways AI-based logistic systems (including the predictive routing or digital twins systems and emission tracking systems) rely on the smooth flow of transnational data, and how the regulatory uncertainty of the DPDP Act affects the efficiency of operations, compliance, and climate governance. The study places the Indian framework in a global frame using doctrinal analysis and comparative legal analysis against global regimes of EU GDPR, OECD Privacy Guidelines and APEC CBPR system. The results underscore a regulatory paradox: Reconciling data sovereignty, AI-trade efficiencies, and sustainability imperatives. The article posits that in order to match the global data protection law with the decarbonization and digital trade agenda in India, interoperable, risk-based, and technologically adaptive governance frameworks are necessary.

Chapter 3
Governance by Investment: How Emerging Economy OFDI Drives the Green Transition? 81
R. Sukanya, Christ University, India

The dynamics between FDI and environmental sustainability have been conceptualized within the North-South framework, in which MNEs from upper-middle-income economies are said to transfer superior technologies to low- and middle-income countries. This perspective neglects the growing importance of outward FDI originating from emerging economies in shaping the global shift towards sustainability. TFirstly, it redefines the transmission of sustainability as a multidirectional, institutionally influenced process rather than a regular North-to-South flow. Secondly, it incorporates reverse spillovers and regulatory requirements into the emerging OFDI landscape of the emerging economy. Thirdly, establish a policy-relevant governance structure that connects sectoral carbon intensity, institutional capacity for absorption, and regulatory accord to the outcomes. Using India's OFDI trend from 2021-2025 as a representative illustration of carbon-intensive practices, thereby affecting the sustainability and governance frameworks.

Chapter 4
From Emissions Targets to Market Behavior: Evaluating Policy-Driven Decarbonization Pathways in Road and Freight Transport Systems 113
Shoyimkulov Asror, Termez University of Economics and Service, Termez, Uzbekistan
S. Aarthi, Marwadi University, Rajkot, India
R. N. Ravikumar, Marwadi University, Rajkot, India
Jabbarov Umarbek, Mamun University, Khiva, Uzbekistan
Kurbonov Jasurbek Pozilovich, Alfraganus University, Tashkent, Uzbekistan

The decarbonization of road and freight transport depends not only on emissions reduction targets, but on how these targets are translated into economic and regulatory signals that shape market behavior. This chapter examines policy-driven decarbonization pathways by analyzing the transmission of emissions targets into pricing instruments, standards, incentives, and procurement mechanisms, and the resulting behavioral responses of transport and logistics actors. Using comparative case studies from advanced and emerging economies, the chapter demonstrates that strong, credible, and recurring policy signals induce more immediate operational and investment responses, while fragmented or constrained policy environments yield uneven outcomes. The analysis highlights the roles of institutional capacity, policy credibility, and actor heterogeneity in determining effectiveness. The chapter contributes a market-behavioral framework to support coherent, efficient, and resilient transport decarbonization policy design.

Chapter 5
Decision Frameworks for Sustainable Urban Transport Systems 147
Sena Kumcu, Department of Industrial Engineering, Faculty of Engineering, Gazi University, Ankara, Turkey
Beste Desticioğlu Taşdemir, Department of Operations Research, Alparslan Defence Sciences and National Security Institute, National Defence University, Ankara, Turkey & Department of Econometrics, Erasmus School of Economics, Erasmus University Rotterdam, Rotterdam, The Netherlands

The rapid pace of urbanization, combined with mounting environmental concerns, has necessitated a strategic shift toward sustainable urban transport systems. Electric buses and high-speed rail (HSR) represent two of the most promising technologies in decarbonizing the transport sector. This chapter develops a structured selection criteria–based framework to support decision-making in evaluating these systems. Through this decision-making approach, the research seeks to fill a gap in comparative sustainability evaluations of urban transport technologies. Furthermore, the chapter highlights the relevance of applying multi-criteria decision-making (MCDM) models for robust planning under uncertainty. Drawing on performance indicators, the chapter provides a structured analysis to guide policymakers and stakeholders in prioritizing infrastructure investments with long-term climate and sustainability objectives.

Chapter 6
Digital Twins and Data-Driven Infrastructure Management 173
Atul Kumar, Dnyaan Prasad Global University, India
Shaturaev Jakhongir, Termez University of Economics and Service, Termez, Uzbekistan
Jabbarov Umarbek, Mamun University, Khiva, Uzbekistan
Muzaffar Shojonov, Urgench State University, Urgench, Uzbekistan
Allambergenova Mukhabbat Khasanbaevna, Nukus State Pedagogical Institute, Uzbekistan
Abdullayev Abdulla Fayzulla Ugli, Tashkent State University of Economy, Tashkent, Uzbekistan

Digital twins represent transformative technology for decarbonized transport infrastructure management, integrating real-time data analytics, artificial intelligence, and predictive modeling. This chapter examines the convergence of digital twin technology and data-driven decision-making in sustainable transportation systems, exploring economic implications, market mechanisms, and policy innovations driving decarbonization. Through comprehensive analysis of current applications, technological frameworks, and implementation strategies, this work demonstrates how digital twins enable optimized infrastructure performance, reduced carbon emissions, and enhanced operational efficiency. Key findings reveal that integrating AI-powered digital twins with IoT sensors, machine learning algorithms, and cloud computing platforms creates intelligent transportation systems capable of real-time monitoring, predictive maintenance, and adaptive control.

Chapter 7
Economic Signals and Artificial Intelligence for Sustainable Transport and Low-Carbon Logistics Systems 213
Turdiev Abdullo Sagdullaevich, Alfraganus University, Tashkent, Uzbekistan
S. Aarthi, Marwadi University, Rajkot, India
R. N. Ravikumar, Marwadi University, Rajkot, India
Shoyimkulov Asror, Termez University of Economics and Service, Termez, Uzbekistan
Jabbarov Umarbek, Mamun University, Khiva, Uzbekistan

Supply chains involve transport and logistics systems that are significant sources of global carbon emission and thus their decarbonization is a key sustainability issue. This chapter discusses how economic indicators and Artificial Intelligence

(AI) may be combined to promote low-carbon transport and logistic systems. It takes a conceptual and analytical approach based on recent case studies on urban transport and freight logistics. The paper shows that the optimization through AI, when accompanied by the emissions-based pricing and incentives, could be an effective way of enhancing the efficiency of the supply chain and minimizing logistics-related emissions. The chapter makes a contribution because it suggests a single framework that interconnects economic indicators, AI-based decision-making, and regulatory policies. The results indicate that efficient transport decarbonization involves collaborative signal planning to provide sustainable, efficient and scalable mobility and logistics networks.

Chapter 8
Cost-Benefit Analysis of Low-Carbon Mobility Solutions 247
Deepak Gupta, Institute of Technology and Management, Gwalior, India
Ergashev Nuriddin Gayratovich, Karshi State Technical University. Karshi, Uzbekistan
Mirzaev Abdullaevich, Tashkent State University of Economy, Uzbekistan
Davlatova Toshpulatovna, Termiz State University of Engineering and Agrotechnology, Termiz, Uzbekistan
Yarmatov Sharofiddin, Termez University of Economics and Service, Termez, Uzbekistan
Begimov Uktam, Alfraganus University, Tashkent, Uzbekistan

Transport is responsible for approximately 24% of global CO2 emissions, making it a critical sector for decarbonization. This chapter presents a comprehensive cost-benefit analysis (CBA) of low-carbon mobility solutions, including battery electric vehicles (BEVs), hydrogen fuel cell vehicles (FCEVs), public transit systems, and active transport modes such as cycling and walking. Drawing on life-cycle assessment (LCA) methodologies, total cost of ownership (TCO) models, and estimates of the social cost of carbon (SCC), the analysis quantifies both the private and social returns to low-carbon investment. Evidence suggests that BEVs and public transit deliver benefit-cost ratios significantly above unity when externalities are monetized, while active transport yields some of the highest co-benefits through reduced congestion, improved public health, and lower infrastructure costs.

Chapter 9
Green Finance, AI-Enabled Investment Strategies, and Renewable Energy for Decarbonizing Transport Infrastructure in Emerging Economies 275
Aarohi Kumari, Vivekananda Global University, India
Gautam Jha, Vivekananda Global University, India
Vikas Rana, Vivekananda Global University, India
Pratishtha Singh, Vivekananda Global University, India
Pratyush Sinha, Vivekananda Global University, India

Due to urbanization, the increase in income, and the expanding infrastructure within cities are all contributing to an increase in CO_2 emissions from transportation. This research looks at 23 years of data on the emission levels of 143 developing countries for the purpose of assessing whether renewable energy sources and green financing can reduce transportation emissions. The results of our analysis indicate that renewable energy does have a positive impact on reducing emissions, but an increase in income will cause an increase in the number of vehicles being used. Pollution is expected to follow an inverted-U pattern, and infrastructure 'locked' into the emission-producing behavior of vehicles will continue to produce emissions, indicating that sustainable transportation investment must be made for the long-term.

Chapter 10
Reimagining Logistics Systems for Sustainable Supply Chain Transformation 313
A. Priscila, Saveetha School of Management, Saveetha Institute of Medical and Technical Sciences, Chennai, India
R. Durai Pandian, Saveetha School of Management, Saveetha Institute of Medical and Technical Sciences, Chennai, India
M. Siva Sarswathi, Saveetha School of Management, Saveetha Institute of Medical and Technical Sciences, Chennai, India
V. Selvalakshmi, Saveetha School of Management, Saveetha Institute of Medical and Technical Sciences, Chennai, India

Logistics is a major contributor to greenhouse emissions and environmental degradation which calls for a shift to a more sustainable and decarbonized model of operation. This chapter explores the significance of green logistics in the attainment of sustainable development goals, with a focus on the mediating effect of environmental performance. This chapter presents a conceptual framework that combines eco efficient transportation, warehousing, reverse logistics and digitalization to sustainability. This is based on institutional theory, which explains how supportive policies, market forces, digitalization and firm competences reform green logistics adoption. This chapter presents real life examples of the application of sustainable logistics strategies. This chapter concludes that a supportive environment, innovation and firm competences enable logistics firms to effectively balance economic and environmental sustainability.

Compilation of References 345

About the Contributors 375

Index 383

Preface

INTRODUCTION

Technological advancement, market design, and public policy reduce transport emissions while maintaining efficient mobility systems. AI optimizes routes, improves energy efficiency, and enables smarter infrastructure for electric and autonomous vehicles. Market mechanisms like carbon pricing, emissions trading systems, and green subsidies reshape incentives for organizations and consumers. Policy innovation accelerates this transition by aligning regulatory frameworks with climate goals and fostering investment in sustainable transport solutions. Together, these forces redefine cost structures, competitiveness, and long-term value creation in the global transportation sector.

The Economics of Decarbonized Transport: AI Technologies, Market Mechanisms, and Policy Innovation examines how digital intelligence, economic instruments, and progressive policy frameworks transform mobility and logistics systems toward full decarbonization. It explores the integration of AI, including machine learning, optimization models, and digital twins, with transport economics, green finance, and climate policy. This book covers topics such as digital technology, pollution control, and climatology, and is a useful resource for engineers, business owners, policymakers, academicians, researchers, and scientists.

Coverage:

The many academic areas covered in this publication include, but are not limited to:

- Artificial Intelligence (AI)
- Climatology
- Decarbonization
- Digital Technology
- Economics & Economic Theory

- Emissions Reduction
- Environmental Science
- Green Finance
- Marketing & Communications
- Policymaking
- Pollution Control
- Transportation Systems

CHAPTER OVERVIEW

Chapter 1: Artificial Intelligence and Machine Learning Applications in Decarbonized Transport

The transportation sector accounts for approximately 24% of global energy-related carbon dioxide emissions, making it a critical domain for decarbonization efforts. Artificial intelligence and machine learning technologies have emerged as transformative tools for achieving sustainable transport systems through intelligent optimization of energy management, traffic flow, route planning, and predictive maintenance. This chapter provides a comprehensive examination of AI and ML applications across multiple transport modalities, including electric vehicles, autonomous driving systems, urban traffic management, and multimodal logistics. Through systematic analysis of recent innovations in reinforcement learning, deep neural networks, and predictive analytics, the chapter demonstrates how these technologies enable significant reductions in energy consumption and emissions while improving operational efficiency.

Chapter 2: AI-Driven Logistics, Data Governance and Sustainability – A Critical Analysis of India's Digital Personal Data Protection Act 2023

This paper is a critical overview of the blowout of artificial intelligence (AI)-empowered logistics, cross-border data governance, and sustainability regulation as the Digital Personal Data Protection Act, 2023 (DPDP Act) of India. It addresses the ways AI-based logistic systems (including the predictive routing or digital twins systems and emission tracking systems) rely on the smooth flow of transnational data, and how the regulatory uncertainty of the DPDP Act affects the efficiency of operations, compliance, and climate governance. The study places the Indian framework in a global frame using doctrinal analysis and comparative legal analysis against global regimes of EU GDPR, OECD Privacy Guidelines and APEC CBPR system. The results underscore a regulatory paradox: Reconciling data sovereignty, AI-trade efficiencies, and sustainability imperatives. The article posits that in order to match the global data protection law with the decarbonization and digital trade agenda in India, interoperable, risk-based, and technologically adaptive governance frameworks are necessary.

Chapter 3: Governance by Investment how Emerging Economies OFDI Drives the Green Transition?

The dynamics between FDI and environmental sustainability have been conceptualized within the North-South framework, in which MNEs from upper-middle-income economies are said to transfer superior technologies to low- and middle-income countries. This perspective neglects the growing importance of outward FDI originating from emerging economies in shaping the global shift towards sustainability. TFirstly, it redefines the transmission of sustainability as a multidirectional, institutionally influenced process rather than a regular North-to-South flow. Secondly, it incorporates reverse spillovers and regulatory requirements into the emerging OFDI landscape of the emerging economy. Thirdly, establish a policy-relevant governance structure that connects sectoral carbon intensity, institutional capacity for absorption, and regulatory accord to the outcomes. Using India's OFDI trend from 2021-2025 as a representative illustration of carbon-intensive practices, thereby affecting the sustainability and governance frameworks.

Chapter 4: From Emissions Targets to Market Behavior-Evaluating Policy-Driven Decarbonization Pathways in Road and Freight Transport Systems

The decarbonization of road and freight transport depends not only on emissions reduction targets, but on how these targets are translated into economic and regulatory signals that shape market behavior. This chapter examines policy-driven decarbonization pathways by analyzing the transmission of emissions targets into pricing instruments, standards, incentives, and procurement mechanisms, and the resulting behavioral responses of transport and logistics actors. Using comparative case studies from advanced and emerging economies, the chapter demonstrates that strong, credible, and recurring policy signals induce more immediate operational and investment responses, while fragmented or constrained policy environments yield uneven outcomes. The analysis highlights the roles of institutional capacity, policy credibility, and actor heterogeneity in determining effectiveness. The chapter contributes a market-behavioral framework to support coherent, efficient, and resilient transport decarbonization policy design.

Chapter 5: Decision Frameworks For Sustainable Urban Transport Systems

The rapid pace of urbanization, combined with mounting environmental concerns, has necessitated a strategic shift toward sustainable urban transport systems. Electric buses and high-speed rail (HSR) represent two of the most promising technologies in decarbonizing the transport sector. This chapter develops a structured selection criteria–based framework to support decision-making in evaluating these systems. Through this decision-making approach, the research seeks to fill a gap in comparative sustainability evaluations of urban transport technologies. Furthermore, the chapter highlights the relevance of applying multi-criteria decision-making (MCDM) models for robust planning under uncertainty. Drawing on performance indicators, the chapter provides a structured analysis to guide policymakers and stakeholders in prioritizing infrastructure investments with long-term climate and sustainability objectives.

Chapter 6: Digital Twins and Data-Driven Infrastructure Management

Digital twins represent transformative technology for decarbonized transport infrastructure management, integrating real-time data analytics, artificial intelligence, and predictive modeling. This chapter examines the convergence of digital twin technology and data-driven decision-making in sustainable transportation systems, exploring economic implications, market mechanisms, and policy innovations driving decarbonization. Through comprehensive analysis of current applications, technological frameworks, and implementation strategies, this work demonstrates how digital twins enable optimized infrastructure performance, reduced carbon emissions, and enhanced operational efficiency. Key findings reveal that integrating AI-powered digital twins with IoT sensors, machine learning algorithms, and cloud computing platforms creates intelligent transportation systems capable of real-time monitoring, predictive maintenance, and adaptive control.

Chapter 7: Economic Signals and Artificial Intelligence for Sustainable Transport and Low-Carbon Logistics Systems

Supply chains involve transport and logistics systems that are significant sources of global carbon emission and thus their decarbonization is a key sustainability issue. This chapter discusses how economic indicators and Artificial Intelligence (AI) may be combined to promote low-carbon transport and logistic systems. It takes a conceptual and analytical approach based on recent case studies on urban transport and freight logistics. The paper shows that the optimization through AI, when accompanied by the emissions-based pricing and incentives, could be an effective way of enhancing the efficiency of the supply chain and minimizing logistics-related emissions. The chapter makes a contribution because it suggests a single framework that interconnects economic indicators, AI-based decision-making, and regulatory policies. The results indicate that efficient transport decarbonization involves collaborative signal planning to provide sustainable, efficient and scalable mobility and logistics networks.

Chapter 8: Cost–Benefit Analysis of Low-Carbon Mobility Solutions

Transport is responsible for approximately 24% of global CO2 emissions, making it a critical sector for decarbonization. This chapter presents a comprehensive cost-benefit analysis (CBA) of low-carbon mobility solutions, including battery electric vehicles (BEVs), hydrogen fuel cell vehicles (FCEVs), public transit systems, and active transport modes such as cycling and walking. Drawing on life-cycle assessment (LCA) methodologies, total cost of ownership (TCO) models, and estimates of the social cost of carbon (SCC), the analysis quantifies both the private and social returns to low-carbon investment. Evidence suggests that BEVs and public transit deliver benefit-cost ratios significantly above unity when externalities are monetized, while active transport yields some of the highest co-benefits through reduced congestion, improved public health, and lower infrastructure costs.

Chapter 9: Green Finance, AI-Enabled Investment Strategies, and Renewable Energy for Decarbonizing Transport Infrastructure in Emerging Economies

Due to urbanization, the increase in income, and the expanding infrastructure within cities are all contributing to an increase in CO2 emissions from transportation. This research looks at 23 years of data on the emission levels of 143 developing countries for the purpose of assessing whether renewable energy sources and green financing can reduce transportation emissions. The results of our analysis indicate that renewable energy does have a positive impact on reducing emissions, but an increase in income will cause an increase in the number of vehicles being used. Pollution is expected to follow an inverted-U pattern, and infrastructure 'locked' into the emission-producing behavior of vehicles will continue to produce emissions, indicating that sustainable transportation investment must be made for the long-term.

Chapter 10: Reimagining Logistics Systems for Sustainable Supply Chain Transformation

Logistics is a major contributor to greenhouse emissions and environmental degradation which calls for a shift to a more sustainable and decarbonized model of operation. This chapter explores the significance of green logistics in the attainment of sustainable development goals, with a focus on the mediating effect of environmental performance. This chapter presents a conceptual framework that combines eco efficient transportation, warehousing, reverse logistics and digitalization to sustainability. This is based on institutional theory, which explains how supportive policies, market forces, digitalization and firm competences reform green logistics adoption. This chapter presents real life examples of the application of sustainable logistics strategies. This chapter concludes that a supportive environment, innovation and firm competences enable logistics firms to effectively balance economic and environmental sustainability.

Acknowledgement

Funding: this work was supported by the Deanship of Scientific Research, Vice Presidency for Graduate Studies and Scientific Research, King Faisal University, Saudi Arabia [Grant No. KFU261821]

Chapter 1

Artificial Intelligence and Machine Learning Applications in Decarbonized Transport

Deepak Gupta
http://orcid.org/0000-0003-3929-1362
Institute of Technology and Management, Gwalior, India

Anorgul Ashirova
Mamun University, Khiva, Uzbekistan

Abdusamatov Mamayusup
Termez University of Economics and Service, Termez, Uzbekistan

Mukimov Askar Shukhratovich
Ifraganus University, Tashkent, Uzbekistan

Bobojonov Azizjon
Tashkent State University of Economics, Tashkent, Uzbekistan

Dilshojon Urinov
Fergana State University, Fergana, Uzbekistan

Temur Khudayberganov
Urgench State University Named After Abu Raykhan Beruni, Urgench, Uzbekistan

ABSTRACT

The transportation sector accounts for approximately 24% of global energy-related carbon dioxide emissions, making it a critical domain for decarbonization efforts. Artificial intelligence and machine learning technologies have emerged as transformative tools for achieving sustainable transport systems through intelligent optimization of energy management, traffic flow, route planning, and predictive maintenance. This chapter provides a comprehensive examination of AI and ML applications across multiple transport modalities, including electric vehicles,

DOI: 10.4018/979-8-3373-9003-1.ch001

autonomous driving systems, urban traffic management, and multimodal logistics. Through systematic analysis of recent innovations in reinforcement learning, deep neural networks, and predictive analytics, the chapter demonstrates how these technologies enable significant reductions in energy consumption and emissions while improving operational efficiency.

1. INTRODUCTION

The global transportation sector stands at a critical juncture in human history, facing unprecedented challenges related to climate change, environmental degradation, and sustainability. According to recent assessments, transportation contributes approximately 24% of direct carbon dioxide emissions from fuel combustion globally, with road vehicles accounting for nearly three-quarters of transport emissions. The urgency of addressing these emissions has catalyzed a fundamental transformation in how societies conceptualize, design, and implement transportation systems.

Artificial intelligence and machine learning technologies have emerged as powerful enablers of this transformation, offering sophisticated tools for optimizing energy consumption, reducing emissions, and enhancing the efficiency of transportation networks. These computational approaches leverage vast quantities of real-time and historical data to make intelligent decisions that would be impossible through traditional optimization methods. From managing battery systems in electric vehicles to coordinating traffic signals across entire metropolitan areas, AI-driven solutions are fundamentally reshaping the landscape of sustainable mobility.

The convergence of multiple technological trends—including advances in sensor technology, computational power, communication networks, and algorithmic sophistication—has created an environment where intelligent transportation systems can operate with unprecedented effectiveness. Machine learning algorithms can now process complex patterns in traffic flows, predict maintenance requirements before failures occur, optimize routing decisions in real-time, and coordinate the operation of thousands of vehicles simultaneously. These capabilities represent a quantum leap beyond the rule-based systems that characterized earlier generations of transportation technology (Saki & Soori, 2024).

This chapter contributes to The Economics of Decarbonized Transport by providing a structured analysis of how AI and ML technologies translate into economic outcomes across the transport value chain. Rather than treating technological capabilities as ends in themselves, the analysis situates each application within a cost-benefit framework, examining efficiency gains, externality pricing, investment incentives, and market design implications. The chapter addresses five interconnected domains—electric vehicle energy management, autonomous driving systems, traffic optimization, predictive maintenance, and smart city integration—and for each assesses not only what AI can do technically, but what it costs, what it saves, and what policy conditions are required to unlock its full economic potential. This dual technological-economic lens constitutes the chapter's distinctive contribution to the broader book.

1.1 The Imperative for Transportation Decarbonization

Transportation's contribution to global greenhouse gas emissions extends beyond simple carbon dioxide release. The sector generates significant quantities of nitrogen oxides, particulate matter, and other pollutants that affect air quality, public health, and ecosystem integrity. Urban areas, where transportation density is highest, experience particularly severe impacts, with traffic-related emissions contributing substantially to respiratory diseases, cardiovascular problems, and premature mortality. The economic costs of these health impacts run into hundreds of billions of dollars annually across developed nations alone.

Traditional approaches to reducing transportation emissions have focused primarily on improving fuel efficiency, transitioning to cleaner fuels, and promoting modal shifts from private vehicles to public transportation. While these strategies remain important, they have proven insufficient to achieve the dramatic emission reductions required to meet international climate targets. The Paris Agreement's goal of limiting global temperature increase to well below two degrees Celsius necessitates transformative changes in transportation systems that go far beyond incremental improvements in conventional technologies.

The transportation sector's energy intensity varies significantly across different modes and regions. Aviation and maritime shipping, while representing smaller shares of total passenger and freight movement, contribute disproportionately to emissions due to limited alternatives to fossil fuels. Road transport, particularly in developing economies experiencing rapid motorization, represents the fastest-growing source of transportation emissions. Urban freight delivery, driven by explosive growth in e-commerce, compounds congestion and local air quality challenges while contributing to overall emission trends.

Decarbonization of transportation requires a comprehensive approach that addresses multiple dimensions simultaneously: transitioning vehicle fleets to zero-emission powertrains, optimizing the efficiency of existing infrastructure, reducing overall vehicle-miles traveled through smart planning, and integrating renewable energy sources into transportation systems. Each of these dimensions presents complex optimization challenges involving multiple variables, dynamic conditions, and competing objectives. From an economic standpoint, these challenges are compounded by persistent market failures—including the underpricing of carbon externalities, split-incentive problems between vehicle manufacturers and fleet operators, and positive network externalities in charging infrastructure deployment that are systematically under-supplied by private markets. Artificial intelligence and machine learning technologies are well-suited to navigating these high-dimensional problem spaces, and their deployment can be meaningfully accelerated by well-designed carbon pricing regimes, public procurement standards, and technology-neutral performance regulations that reward efficiency outcomes rather than prescribing specific technical solutions (Szczepański et al., 2025).

Table 1. AI/ML Technologies and Their Applications in Decarbonized Transport

AI/ML Technology	Application Domain	Key Benefits	Emission Reduction
Deep Reinforcement Learning (DRL)	EV energy management, autonomous vehicle control, traffic signal optimization	Adaptive decision-making, real-time optimization, learns from experience	15-30% in EVs, 20-35% in traffic systems
Convolutional Neural Networks (CNN)	Autonomous driving perception, infrastructure monitoring, pothole detection	Superior object detection, real-time processing, multi-modal sensor fusion	10-25% through safety improvements and efficiency
Recurrent Neural Networks (RNN/ LSTM)	Traffic flow prediction, energy demand forecasting, route optimization	Temporal pattern recognition, accurate prediction, sequential decision support	12-22% through predictive routing and demand management
Random Forests / Gradient Boosting	Predictive maintenance, battery health estimation, failure prediction	High accuracy, interpretability, robust to outliers, feature importance	5-15% through optimized maintenance and vehicle lifecycle
Autoencoders	Anomaly detection in vehicle systems, traffic pattern analysis	Unsupervised learning, early fault detection, compressed representations	8-18% through proactive maintenance and system optimization
Graph Neural Networks (GNN)	Network-level traffic optimization, multi-vehicle coordination	Spatial relationship modeling, network-wide optimization, scalability	18-28% in urban networks through coordination
Multi-Agent Reinforcement Learning	Cooperative autonomous driving, platoon formation, fleet management	Distributed intelligence, emergent cooperation, scalable coordination	25-40% through vehicle cooperation and aerodynamic benefits

1.2 Evolution of AI Technologies in Transportation

The application of artificial intelligence in transportation has evolved through several distinct phases, each characterized by progressively more sophisticated capabilities and broader scopes of application. Early systems, developed in the 1980s and 1990s, relied primarily on expert systems and rule-based logic to address specific problems such as traffic signal timing and route optimization. These systems demonstrated value in controlled environments but lacked the adaptability and learning capabilities required for complex real-world applications.

The emergence of machine learning techniques in the 2000s marked a significant advancement, enabling systems to learn patterns from historical data and make predictions about future conditions. Support vector machines, decision trees, and early neural networks found applications in traffic prediction, incident detection, and demand forecasting. However, these approaches still required extensive feature engineering and struggled with the high dimensionality and non-linearity characteristic of many transportation problems.

The deep learning revolution of the 2010s fundamentally transformed the field by enabling end-to-end learning from raw sensor data without manual feature engineering. Convolutional neural networks achieved remarkable success in computer vision tasks essential for autonomous driving, while recurrent neural networks and their variants demonstrated superior performance in sequential prediction tasks such as traffic forecasting. Perhaps most significantly, reinforcement learning algorithms began to show promise in sequential decision-making tasks, opening new possibilities for intelligent control of complex transportation systems (Zhao et al., 2024; Sahoo & Varadarajan, 2025).

Contemporary AI applications in transportation leverage combinations of these techniques, often integrating deep learning for perception and prediction with reinforcement learning for decision-making and control. The availability of massive datasets from connected vehicles, infrastructure sensors, and mobile devices, combined with dramatically increased computational power through cloud computing and specialized hardware accelerators, has enabled the deployment of increasingly sophisticated AI systems in real-world transportation applications. Table 1 provides a comprehensive comparison of major AI and machine learning technologies currently deployed in decarbonized transport applications, highlighting their specific use cases, key advantages, and demonstrated emission reduction capabilities. To organize the economic analysis that follows, this chapter employs a three-tier conceptual framework linking AI technologies to economic outcomes. At the first tier, AI generates direct efficiency gains—reduced energy consumption, lower maintenance costs, and fewer accidents—that translate into private cost savings for operators and users. At the second tier, these efficiency improvements produce emission reductions that constitute positive externalities for society, whose value can be monetized using social cost of carbon estimates (currently USD 50–200 per tonne CO_2e across major economies). At the third tier, the cumulative deployment of AI across the transport sector drives structural market transformation—reshaping industry cost curves, enabling new business models, and shifting competitive dynamics in ways that produce economy-wide productivity effects. This framework guides the cost-benefit assessments and policy prescriptions developed throughout the chapter.

Figure 1. Comprehensive AI/ML Framework for Decarbonized Transportation Systems

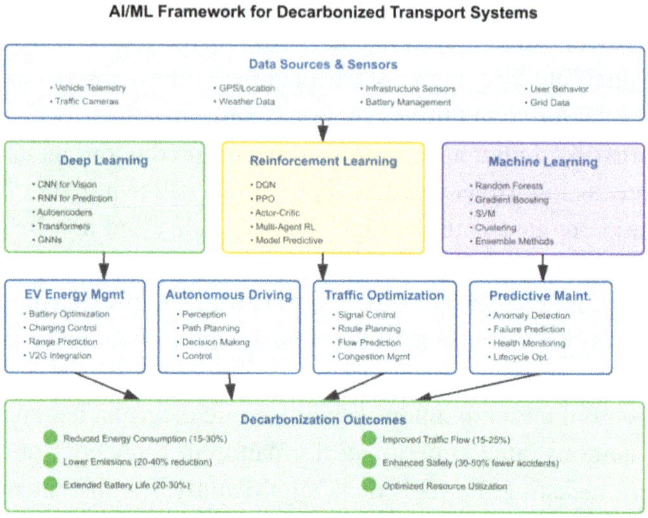

Figure 1 illustrate multi- layer framework data sources, AI/ML technologies, application domains, and quantified decarbonization outcomes. Emission reduction potential: 15-64% across different applications.

2. AI-DRIVEN ELECTRIC VEHICLE ENERGY MANAGEMENT SYSTEMS

Electric vehicles represent a cornerstone technology in the transition toward decarbonized transportation, offering the potential for zero-emission operation when powered by renewable electricity sources. However, the effectiveness of electric vehicles in reducing emissions and their practical viability for consumers depend critically on efficient energy management. Battery systems, which store and deliver electrical energy for vehicle propulsion, face complex challenges related to capacity limitations, charging infrastructure availability, degradation over time, and optimal usage patterns under varying operating conditions.

Artificial intelligence and machine learning technologies have emerged as essential tools for addressing these challenges, enabling sophisticated energy management systems that optimize battery usage, extend vehicle range, predict maintenance requirements, and coordinate charging patterns to minimize grid impact and maximize renewable energy utilization. The application of AI to electric vehicle systems represents one of the most mature and impactful areas of intelligent transportation technology, with numerous successful deployments demonstrating substantial improvements in efficiency and user experience.

The complexity of electric vehicle energy management stems from the interaction of multiple dynamic factors including driver behavior, route characteristics, traffic conditions, weather, battery state, and auxiliary system demands. Traditional rule-based control strategies, while computationally simple, cannot adequately account for these interdependencies and often fail to achieve optimal performance across diverse operating scenarios. Machine learning approaches, by contrast, can learn complex non-linear relationships from data and adapt their strategies to specific contexts, delivering superior performance in real-world applications.

2.1 Reinforcement Learning for Energy Optimization

Reinforcement learning has proven particularly effective for energy management in electric vehicles because it can learn optimal control policies through interaction with the environment without requiring explicit models of complex system dynamics. Recent research has demonstrated the application of deep reinforcement learning algorithms, including Deep Q-Networks, Proximal Policy Optimization, and Actor-Critic methods, to various aspects of electric vehicle energy management. These algorithms learn to make sequential decisions about power distribution, regenerative braking, and auxiliary system operation to minimize energy consumption while maintaining performance and comfort requirements (Ananganó-Alvarado et al., 2025).

The power of reinforcement learning lies in its ability to discover non-obvious strategies through exploration and to adapt to changing conditions over time. For instance, RL agents can learn to anticipate upcoming road conditions based on GPS data and historical patterns, adjusting energy management strategies preemptively rather than reactively. They can balance competing objectives such as minimizing travel time, maximizing range, and reducing battery degradation, finding Pareto-optimal solutions that would be difficult to specify through traditional control approaches. Moreover, these systems can personalize their behavior to individual driving styles and preferences, continuously improving performance through ongoing experience. From an economic perspective, the value proposition of RL-based energy management is substantial: studies report energy consumption reductions of 10–20% compared to rule-based baselines, translating directly into lower per-kilometer operating costs. For commercial fleet operators, these savings compound across large vehicle counts, often yielding payback periods of two to four years on the software investment. At the aggregate level, the associated emission reductions represent a monetizable externality benefit—one that carbon pricing mechanisms can internalize to further strengthen the business case for adoption.

Hybrid electric vehicles present particularly complex energy management challenges because they must coordinate operation between internal combustion engines and electric powertrains, deciding when to use each power source, when to charge the battery through regenerative braking or engine operation, and how to distribute power between the two systems. Deep learning-based model predictive control has shown exceptional performance in these applications, combining neural network predictions of future driving conditions with optimization algorithms to make real-time control decisions that minimize fuel consumption and emissions (Cao & Zhou, 2024).

Implementation of reinforcement learning for energy management requires careful consideration of reward function design, state representation, and safety constraints. The reward function must appropriately balance immediate energy efficiency with long-term objectives such as battery health preservation and trip completion reliability. State representations must capture relevant information about vehicle status, environment, and route while remaining computationally tractable. Safety constraints ensure that learned policies do not compromise vehicle safety or violate physical limitations of battery and powertrain systems.

2.2 Battery Life Optimization Through Machine Learning

Battery degradation represents one of the most significant challenges for electric vehicle adoption, affecting both the economic viability and environmental sustainability of these vehicles. Lithium-ion batteries, which power most contemporary electric vehicles, experience capacity fade and power capability reduction over time due to complex electrochemical processes influenced by temperature, charge-discharge rates, state-of-charge levels, and usage patterns. Understanding and mitigating these degradation mechanisms requires sophisticated analytical approaches that can model the intricate relationships between operating conditions and battery health.

Machine learning algorithms have demonstrated remarkable capability in predicting battery degradation, estimating remaining useful life, and optimizing charging strategies to extend battery longevity. Techniques including random forests, gradient boosting machines, and deep neural networks can learn complex non-linear relationships between operational variables and degradation rates from historical data. These models enable proactive battery management strategies that adapt charging profiles, limit operation in degradation-accelerating conditions, and provide accurate predictions of battery replacement timing (Karthick et al., 2024).

Advanced machine learning approaches integrate multiple data sources including battery management system telemetry, environmental sensors, vehicle usage patterns, and laboratory degradation studies to build comprehensive models of battery behavior. Transfer learning techniques enable these models to adapt quickly to new battery chemistries or vehicle platforms by leveraging knowledge gained from related systems. Ensemble methods combine predictions from multiple models to improve accuracy and provide uncertainty quantification, essential for making reliable maintenance and replacement decisions.

The integration of battery life optimization with energy management systems creates synergies that enhance overall vehicle performance. By considering both immediate energy efficiency and long-term battery health in decision-making, these integrated systems can achieve superior outcomes compared to approaches that optimize each objective independently. Recent research has demonstrated that machine learning-based optimization of charging patterns can extend battery life by 20-30% while maintaining user convenience and minimizing charging costs (Ren, 2025).

State-of-health estimation, a critical component of battery management, has benefited significantly from advances in machine learning. Traditional methods based on electrochemical models require extensive calibration and struggle with the variability inherent in real-world conditions. Data-driven approaches can learn patterns directly from operational data, adapting to individual battery characteristics and usage patterns. Explainable AI techniques provide insights into which factors most significantly influence degradation, informing both user behavior and vehicle design decisions. The economic stakes are considerable: battery packs represent 30–40% of EV purchase price, and premature degradation imposes significant costs on both consumers and manufacturers. Accurate state-of-health estimation enables more precise residual value pricing in secondary markets, reduces warranty exposure for manufacturers, and supports the emergence of battery-as-a-service business models where pack longevity directly determines revenue. These market design implications—from insurance pricing to battery leasing contracts—illustrate how AI-generated technical information reshapes economic incentives across the EV supply chain.

2.3 Intelligent Charging Infrastructure and Grid Integration

The widespread adoption of electric vehicles presents both opportunities and challenges for electrical grid infrastructure. On one hand, vehicle batteries represent significant distributed energy storage capacity that could provide valuable grid services including demand response, frequency regulation, and renewable energy integration. On the other hand, uncontrolled charging of large numbers of electric vehicles could create problematic demand peaks, require expensive infrastructure upgrades, and increase reliance on fossil fuel power generation during peak periods.

Artificial intelligence technologies enable intelligent coordination of electric vehicle charging to maximize benefits while minimizing challenges. Machine learning algorithms can predict charging demand patterns, optimize the timing and rate of charging to align with renewable energy availability, and coordinate vehicle-to-grid services to support grid stability. These systems must balance multiple competing objectives including minimizing charging costs for users, avoiding grid stress, maximizing renewable energy utilization, and ensuring vehicles are adequately charged when needed (Boudmen et al., 2024).

Deep reinforcement learning has shown particular promise for managing distributed charging systems because it can learn effective coordination strategies without requiring detailed models of user behavior or grid dynamics. These algorithms can adapt to seasonal variations in energy supply and demand, respond to real-time electricity price signals, and accommodate the stochastic nature of vehicle arrival and departure times. Federated learning approaches enable privacy-preserving coordination across multiple charging locations while maintaining user anonymity and data security (Kumar et al., 2024).

Vehicle-to-grid integration represents an emerging application area where bidirectional power flow enables electric vehicles to serve as mobile energy storage resources. During periods of high renewable generation or low demand, vehicles can charge their batteries; during peak demand or low renewable availability, they can discharge power back to the grid. Coordinating these activities across thousands of vehicles while respecting individual user constraints requires sophisticated optimization algorithms that can handle uncertainty, scale to large fleets, and respond rapidly to changing conditions. The economic architecture underpinning V2G is equally important as the technical one: dynamic time-of-use tariffs and real-time electricity pricing signals are prerequisite market mechanisms that create the incentive structures AI systems need to allocate charging and discharging optimally. Without appropriate pricing design, the social value of distributed battery storage remains largely uncaptured. Regulatory frameworks that define aggregator roles, liability for grid services, and revenue-sharing between vehicle owners and grid operators are therefore critical complements to the AI technology itself. Early V2G pilots in Denmark, the Netherlands, and Japan suggest that well-designed market structures can enable vehicle owners to earn USD 300–500 annually from grid services, materially improving EV total cost of ownership and accelerating adoption.

3. AUTONOMOUS DRIVING SYSTEMS AND DEEP LEARNING

Autonomous driving represents one of the most ambitious applications of artificial intelligence, with the potential to fundamentally transform transportation systems and contribute significantly to decarbonization efforts. While the direct emission reduction benefits of autonomous vehicles depend on their powertrain technology, autonomous driving systems enable numerous indirect pathways to reduced emissions including optimized driving behaviors, improved traffic flow, reduced congestion, enhanced vehicle sharing and utilization, and integration with public transportation systems. Moreover, the perception, prediction, and planning technologies developed for autonomous driving find applications across the broader transportation ecosystem.

Deep learning has emerged as the dominant paradigm for autonomous driving, enabling unprecedented capabilities in environmental perception, situation understanding, and behavior prediction. Contemporary autonomous vehicles employ multiple deep neural networks operating in concert to process data from diverse sensors including cameras, lidar, radar, and ultrasonic sensors. These networks perform tasks ranging from low-level perception such as object detection and semantic segmentation to high-level reasoning about traffic participant intentions and appropriate vehicle responses (Sahoo & Varadarajan, 2025).

Figure 2. Deep Reinforcement Learning Architecture for Autonomous Vehicle Decision-Making and Control

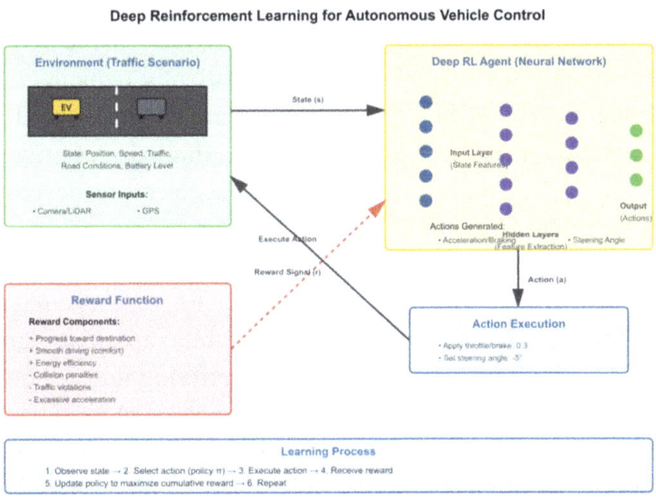

Figure 2 illustrates Detailed DRL architecture showing environment-agent interaction loop, neural network structure, reward function components, and the complete learning process for autonomous vehicle control.

3.1 Computer Vision and Environmental Perception

Environmental perception forms the foundation of autonomous driving, requiring robust and accurate interpretation of complex visual scenes under diverse conditions including varying illumination, weather, and traffic situations. Convolutional neural networks have revolutionized computer vision for autonomous driving, achieving human-level or superior performance in tasks such as object detection, classification, tracking, and semantic segmentation. Modern architectures including ResNet, EfficientNet, and Vision Transformers process camera imagery to identify vehicles, pedestrians, cyclists, traffic signs, lane markings, and other relevant environmental features with remarkable accuracy.

The integration of multiple sensor modalities through deep learning fusion techniques provides robustness superior to any single sensing approach. Lidar sensors offer precise three-dimensional spatial information but struggle with adverse weather conditions, while cameras provide rich semantic information but are sensitive to lighting variations. Radar sensors excel at detecting objects in poor visibility but offer limited resolution. Deep neural networks can learn to optimally combine information from these complementary sensors, leveraging the strengths of each while compensating for individual weaknesses (Almalioglu et al., 2022).

Recent advances in self-supervised and semi-supervised learning have addressed one of the major challenges in developing perception systems: the need for massive quantities of labelled training data. These techniques enable networks to learn useful representations from unlabelled data, dramatically reducing the annotation burden. Additionally, synthetic data generation using advanced rendering engines and domain adaptation techniques allows networks trained primarily on simulated imagery to perform well on real-world data, further accelerating development cycles and improving coverage of rare but important scenarios.

Temporal integration of perceptual information across multiple frames enables more robust object tracking and scene understanding. Recurrent neural networks and temporal convolutional networks can maintain persistent representations of dynamic objects, predicting their future trajectories and identifying unusual behaviours that might indicate hazardous situations. Multi-object tracking algorithms built on deep learning foundations achieve unprecedented accuracy in maintaining consistent identities for numerous simultaneous actors in crowded urban environments.

3.2 Deep Reinforcement Learning for Motion Planning and Control

Motion planning and control represent perhaps the most challenging aspects of autonomous driving, requiring systems to make split-second decisions in complex, dynamic environments with incomplete information and substantial uncertainty. Traditional approaches based on hierarchical planning with predefined behaviour primitives struggle to handle the full complexity of real-world driving scenarios, particularly in dense urban environments with numerous interacting agents. Deep reinforcement learning offers an alternative paradigm that can learn sophisticated driving behaviours end-to-end through experience rather than explicit programming.

Recent research has demonstrated the effectiveness of deep reinforcement learning for autonomous driving across multiple levels of the control hierarchy. At the tactical level, RL algorithms learn high-level decisions such as when to change lanes, how aggressively to merge into traffic, and how to navigate complex intersections. At the operational level, they learn low-level control policies for steering, acceleration, and braking that execute chosen manoeuvres smoothly and safely. Multi-agent reinforcement learning approaches can even learn cooperative behaviours that improve overall traffic flow and safety through implicit coordination between vehicles (Han & Shen, 2024; Zhao et al., 2024).

One of the most significant contributions of deep reinforcement learning to autonomous driving safety is the development of comprehensive testing and validation methodologies. Traditional testing approaches that rely on real-world test drives or limited simulation scenarios cannot adequately cover the vast space of possible driving situations, particularly rare but critical safety scenarios. Dense reinforcement learning techniques systematically explore the space of possible scenarios, identifying edge cases and challenging situations that might be missed by conventional testing. This capability enables more thorough safety validation and helps identify potential weaknesses in perception and control systems before deployment (Feng et al., 2023).

Sim-to-real transfer represents a crucial challenge for deploying reinforcement learning in autonomous vehicles. Policies learned in simulation must generalize to real-world conditions despite inevitable differences in sensor characteristics, dynamics, and environmental variability. Domain randomization techniques that expose learning agents to diverse simulated conditions improve robustness to real-world variations. Progressive training curricula that gradually increase task difficulty enable more efficient learning of complex behaviours. Model-based approaches that learn explicit world models can reduce sample complexity and improve data efficiency.

3.3 Robustness, Safety, and Adversarial Challenges

The deployment of autonomous vehicles in real-world environments raises critical questions about the robustness and safety of AI-based perception and control systems. Deep neural networks, despite their impressive performance on benchmark datasets, can exhibit unexpected failures when confronted with inputs that differ from their training distribution. Adversarial examples—inputs deliberately crafted to fool neural networks—have demonstrated that small, imperceptible perturbations to images can cause misclassification with high confidence. In the context of autonomous driving, such vulnerabilities could have catastrophic consequences.

Recent research has identified numerous potential attack vectors against autonomous vehicle systems, including physical adversarial patches that can cause stop sign misclassification, sensor spoofing attacks that inject false objects into perception systems, and GPS manipulation that could misdirect navigation. Understanding these vulnerabilities and developing robust defenses represents a critical research priority. Defensive techniques including adversarial training, input validation, ensemble methods, and runtime monitoring have shown promise in improving system resilience, though no single approach provides complete protection (Ibrahum et al., 2024; Chen et al., 2025).

Beyond adversarial robustness, autonomous vehicles must handle a wide range of challenging environmental conditions including poor weather, unusual lighting, construction zones, and novel object types not represented in training data. Achieving the level of reliability required for widespread deployment demands comprehensive validation across diverse scenarios, continuous monitoring and updating of deployed systems, and graceful degradation strategies that ensure safe operation even when individual components fail. The integration of multiple redundant perception modalities, explicit uncertainty quantification, and human oversight mechanisms provides defense-in-depth against potential failures.

Formal verification methods adapted for neural networks offer promising approaches to providing mathematical guarantees about system behaviour. Techniques such as abstract interpretation, satisfiability modulo theories solving, and reachability analysis can verify that networks satisfy specific safety properties within bounded input domains. While computational limitations currently restrict verification to relatively small networks, ongoing research aims to scale these methods to the large, complex networks deployed in real autonomous vehicles.

4. TRAFFIC OPTIMIZATION AND SMART CITY INTEGRATION

Urban traffic congestion represents one of the most significant sources of transportation-related emissions and energy waste, with vehicles consuming fuel while making minimal progress toward their destinations. Congestion also imposes enormous economic costs through lost productivity, wasted fuel, and increased vehicle wear. Traditional approaches to traffic management based on fixed signal timing or simple responsive strategies have proven inadequate for managing the complexity of modern urban transportation networks. Artificial intelligence and machine learning offer powerful tools for optimizing traffic flow, reducing congestion, and minimizing emissions through intelligent coordination of traffic control systems and dynamic routing of vehicles.

The integration of transportation systems with broader smart city infrastructure creates additional opportunities for optimization. Sensors embedded throughout the urban environment provide rich real-time data about traffic conditions, air quality, public transportation usage, and other relevant variables. Internet of Things technologies enable communication between vehicles, infrastructure, and central management systems. Cloud computing platforms process vast quantities of data and execute sophisticated optimization algorithms. Together, these technologies enable coordinated management of transportation networks at unprecedented scales (Zhao & Chen, 2025).

Figure 3. Projected Transportation Emissions Reduction Through AI/ML Technologies (2020-2030

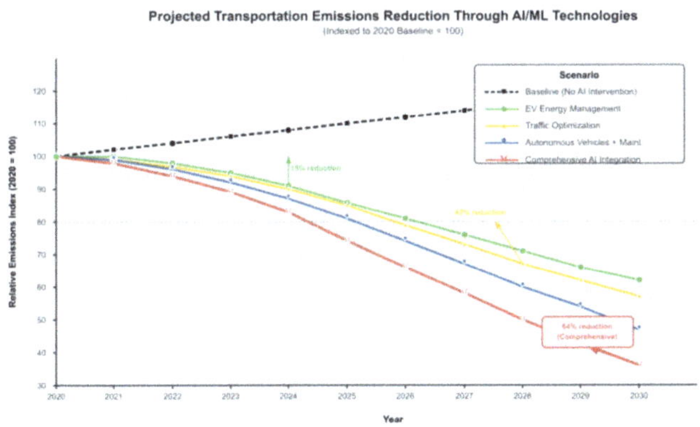

Figure 3 illustrate Time-series comparison showing baseline scenario vs. multiple AI intervention strategies. Demonstrates up to 64% emission reduction potential through comprehensive AI/ML integration by 2030

4.1 AI-Driven Traffic Signal Control

Traffic signal control represents one of the most impactful applications of AI in urban transportation, with the potential to significantly reduce congestion, travel times, and emissions through optimized coordination of signal timings across road networks. Traditional traffic signal systems rely on fixed timing plans or simple adaptive strategies that respond to immediate local conditions. These approaches fail to account for network-wide effects, temporal patterns in traffic demand, or complex interactions between signals. Machine learning, particularly deep reinforcement learning, enables more sophisticated control strategies that optimize system-wide performance.

Recent research has demonstrated remarkable success using reinforcement learning for traffic signal control. The CoLight algorithm, which learns network-level cooperation between signals, achieved substantial improvements over conventional methods by enabling signals to implicitly coordinate their timing decisions to facilitate traffic progression through arterial roads and reduce unnecessary stops. Deep Q-Networks and actor-critic methods have shown similar success, learning policies that adapt to changing traffic patterns throughout the day and respond effectively to special events or incidents (Wei et al., 2019).

The environmental benefits of AI-driven traffic signal control extend beyond simple congestion reduction. By minimizing stop-and-go driving patterns, these systems reduce fuel consumption and emissions associated with frequent acceleration and deceleration. They can prioritize public transportation vehicles to improve transit service reliability and attractiveness, encouraging modal shifts away from private vehicles. Integration with air quality sensors enables signals to respond dynamically to pollution levels, adjusting timing to reduce exposure in sensitive areas. Field deployments have demonstrated emission reductions of 15-25% in optimized corridors, with proportionally larger benefits during congested periods (Yao et al., 2025).

Scalability to large urban networks presents both technical and institutional challenges. Centralized control architectures face computational and communication bottlenecks as network size increases, while fully distributed approaches may struggle to achieve system-wide coordination. Hierarchical and federated learning architectures offer potential solutions by partitioning control across multiple scales while maintaining coordination. Institutional barriers including fragmented authority, legacy infrastructure, and procurement processes often impede adoption of advanced traffic control technologies despite their demonstrated benefits. A rigorous cost-benefit analysis of AI-driven signal control must account for deployment costs—typically USD 15,000–50,000 per intersection for hardware and software upgrades—against quantified gains in fuel savings, reduced idling emissions, lower accident rates, and productivity improvements from reduced delay. Studies from cities including Pittsburgh (Surtrac system) and Hangzhou (City Brain) indicate benefit-to-cost ratios of 3:1 to 8:1 over ten-year horizons, providing a strong economic case that municipalities can present to budget authorities and bond markets. Performance-based procurement contracts that tie vendor payments to verified emission and congestion reductions offer a promising mechanism for aligning private innovation incentives with public decarbonization goals.

4.2 Intelligent Route Optimization and Navigation

Route optimization and navigation represent another critical application area where AI technologies deliver substantial benefits for transportation efficiency and environmental sustainability. Traditional navigation systems compute shortest-path routes based on static road network models and historical average speeds. While useful, these approaches fail to account for real-time traffic conditions, future congestion patterns, or the collective impact of routing decisions on overall system performance. Machine learning enables more sophisticated navigation that considers multiple objectives including travel time, fuel consumption, emissions, and system-wide traffic distribution.

Deep neural networks have demonstrated exceptional capability in predicting future traffic conditions, a crucial prerequisite for effective route optimization. Recurrent neural networks, particularly Long Short-Term Memory architectures and their variants, can learn complex temporal patterns in traffic flow and make accurate predictions minutes to hours into the future. Graph neural networks leverage the network structure of road systems to propagate information spatially, capturing how congestion propagates through connected roadways. These predictive models enable proactive route planning that anticipates future conditions rather than merely reacting to current states (Liyanage et al., 2025).

Eco-routing, which optimizes routes specifically to minimize fuel consumption and emissions rather than simply travel time, represents an important application of AI-based navigation. Machine learning models can learn relationships between route characteristics, driving conditions, and vehicle emissions, enabling selection of routes that minimize environmental impact even if they require slightly longer travel times. For electric vehicles, range-aware routing that considers battery charge state, available charging infrastructure, and expected energy consumption provides essential functionality for long-distance travel. Multi-objective optimization approaches balance user preferences for time, cost, and environmental impact (Dikshit et al., 2023).

System-optimal routing that considers network-wide effects represents a more challenging problem than user-optimal routing that focuses solely on individual trip efficiency. When large numbers of vehicles follow individually optimal routes, the collective result can be worse for all users due to congestion concentration—the Braess paradox demonstrates this counterintuitive phenomenon. Mechanism design approaches that provide appropriate incentives can align individual and collective interests, though implementation faces practical challenges related to user acceptance, privacy, and fairness. Congestion pricing—where road users pay charges that reflect the marginal external cost they impose on other travelers and on air quality—is the economically efficient instrument for internalizing these externalities. AI systems that integrate real-time pricing signals into routing decisions enable a virtuous cycle: prices that reflect true social costs guide AI to system-optimal routes, which in turn reduce the congestion and emissions that necessitate the charges. Revenue from congestion pricing can be hypothecated to fund public transport improvements or low-income travel subsidies, addressing distributional concerns that frequently impede political acceptance of pricing reforms. This intersection of market design, pricing strategy, and AI routing optimization represents a particularly fertile area for policy innovation in urban transport economics.

4.3 Multimodal Transportation Coordination

Achieving truly sustainable urban transportation requires seamless integration of multiple transport modes including private vehicles, public transit, bicycling, walking, and emerging mobility services such as ride-sharing and micro-mobility. Each mode has distinct characteristics regarding capacity, flexibility, environmental impact, and user experience. Artificial intelligence enables intelligent coordination across these modes, helping travelers make optimal mode choices and facilitating smooth transfers between modes. Such integration can dramatically reduce reliance on private vehicle use, with corresponding environmental benefits.

Machine learning models can predict demand for different transportation modes based on time of day, weather conditions, special events, and other factors, enabling dynamic allocation of resources to match expected needs. For public transit, these predictions inform scheduling decisions, vehicle assignments, and service adjustments that improve reliability and reduce wait times. For shared mobility services, they enable efficient positioning of vehicles to minimize customer wait times while maximizing utilization. Reinforcement learning approaches can optimize these dynamic resource allocation decisions, learning effective strategies through experience (Mohsen, 2025).

Integration with Internet of Things infrastructure enables real-time coordination between transportation modes. Connected vehicles can communicate their locations and destinations, allowing transit systems to adjust schedules to facilitate connections. Mobile applications provide travelers with comprehensive multimodal routing that considers all available options and presents optimal combinations based on user preferences for time, cost, convenience, and environmental impact. Blockchain technologies can provide secure, transparent coordination of payments and incentives across different operators, reducing friction in multimodal travel (Villegas-Ch et al., 2023; Moraga et al., 2025).

Mobility-as-a-Service platforms that integrate multiple transportation providers under unified interfaces represent the culmination of multimodal coordination efforts. These platforms leverage AI for demand prediction, dynamic pricing, resource allocation, and personalized recommendations. Success requires not only technical integration but also appropriate business models, regulatory frameworks, and governance structures that balance interests of different stakeholders including operators, users, and public authorities.

5. PREDICTIVE MAINTENANCE AND LIFECYCLE OPTIMIZATION

Vehicle maintenance represents a significant contributor to the total environmental impact of transportation systems, both through the direct emissions and resource consumption associated with repair and replacement activities and through the indirect effects of degraded vehicle performance on efficiency and emissions. Traditional maintenance approaches based on fixed service intervals or reactive repairs after failures occur are inefficient, often performing unnecessary maintenance while missing critical developing problems. Predictive maintenance, enabled by artificial intelligence and machine learning, offers a fundamentally superior approach that optimizes maintenance timing based on actual vehicle condition and predicted future needs.

The proliferation of sensors in modern vehicles, combined with connectivity that enables continuous data transmission, creates unprecedented opportunities for monitoring vehicle health and predicting maintenance requirements. Engine control units, brake systems, suspension components, electrical systems, and numerous other subsystems generate continuous streams of telemetry data that reflect their operational status. Machine learning algorithms can analyze these data streams to detect subtle patterns indicative of developing problems, often identifying issues long before they would be apparent to human operators or traditional diagnostic systems (Mahale et al., 2025).

5.1 Anomaly Detection and Failure Prediction

Anomaly detection forms the foundation of predictive maintenance, identifying deviations from normal operating patterns that might indicate developing problems. Unsupervised learning techniques including autoencoders, isolation forests, and one-class support vector machines can learn representations of normal vehicle behavior from historical data and flag unusual patterns for further investigation. These approaches are particularly valuable for detecting novel failure modes not represented in training data, a common challenge in complex mechanical systems with numerous potential failure mechanisms.

Once anomalies are detected, supervised learning models can classify their likely causes and predict remaining useful life of affected components. Random forests, gradient boosting machines, and deep neural networks achieve high accuracy in failure prediction tasks by learning complex relationships between sensor measurements, operating conditions, maintenance history, and component failures. Time series models including recurrent neural networks and temporal convolutional networks can capture temporal dependencies in degradation processes, improving prediction accuracy for gradual failure modes (Ucar et al., 2024).

The application of these techniques extends across all vehicle systems and transportation modes. In electric vehicles, they monitor battery health, motor performance, and power electronics. In conventional vehicles, they track engine wear, transmission condition, and brake system degradation. For commercial fleets and public transportation, they enable proactive maintenance scheduling that minimizes downtime while ensuring safety and reliability. Maritime transportation has seen particularly significant benefits from AI-driven predictive maintenance, with systems monitoring propulsion systems, auxiliary equipment, and structural integrity to optimize maintenance timing and reduce unexpected failures (Tsekouras et al., 2024).

Integration of predictive maintenance with broader vehicle management systems enables optimization across multiple objectives including safety, reliability, cost, and environmental impact. Maintenance scheduling can consider parts availability, technician capacity, and vehicle utilization patterns to minimize disruption. Prognostic information can inform decisions about vehicle replacement, route assignment, and operational strategies. Real-time health monitoring enables dynamic adjustment of operating parameters to mitigate degradation and extend component life.

5.2 Computer Vision for Infrastructure Monitoring

Transportation infrastructure including roads, bridges, tunnels, and rail systems requires continuous monitoring and maintenance to ensure safety and operational efficiency. Traditional inspection methods relying on manual visual assessment are labor-intensive, subjective, and often miss critical defects. Computer vision powered by deep learning enables automated infrastructure monitoring at scale, detecting and characterizing defects with superhuman consistency and coverage. Mobile sensors mounted on vehicles can collect imagery during normal operations, enabling continuous monitoring without dedicated inspection activities.

Convolutional neural networks trained on large datasets of infrastructure imagery can detect various defect types including cracks, potholes, spalling, rutting, and structural damage with high accuracy. Semantic segmentation models provide pixel-level classification of defect extent and severity, enabling quantitative assessment of infrastructure condition. The integration of these visual assessments with other data sources including structural sensors, weather information, and traffic loading patterns provides comprehensive understanding of infrastructure health and degradation trajectories (Khan et al., 2024).

The environmental benefits of infrastructure maintenance extend beyond the immediate impact of repair activities. Well-maintained road surfaces reduce vehicle rolling resistance, improving fuel efficiency and reducing emissions. Timely repair of minor defects prevents their progression to major failures that require resource-intensive reconstruction. Optimized maintenance scheduling concentrates activities temporally and spatially, minimizing traffic disruption and associated congestion emissions. Machine learning-based prioritization of maintenance activities ensures that limited resources focus on locations where they deliver maximum benefit for safety, efficiency, and longevity.

Advanced imaging technologies including thermal cameras, ground-penetrating radar, and lidar provide complementary information about infrastructure condition that cannot be assessed through visible-light imagery alone. Deep learning fusion approaches can integrate these diverse data sources to build comprehensive assessments of infrastructure health. Digital twin technologies that combine physical sensor data with simulation models enable prediction of future condition trajectories under different maintenance strategies, supporting long-term asset management planning.

6. CHALLENGES, LIMITATIONS, AND FUTURE RESEARCH DIRECTIONS

While artificial intelligence and machine learning have demonstrated remarkable capabilities in transportation applications, numerous challenges and limitations must be addressed to realize their full potential for enabling decarbonized transport systems. These challenges span technical, economic, social, and ethical dimensions, requiring interdisciplinary collaboration and sustained research investment. Understanding these challenges and developing effective solutions represents a critical priority for the field.

6.1 Data Requirements and Privacy Concerns

The effectiveness of machine learning systems depends fundamentally on the availability of large, high-quality datasets for training and validation. Transportation applications often involve sensitive personal information including location trajectories, travel patterns, and behavioral data. Collecting, storing, and processing such data raises significant privacy concerns that must be carefully addressed. The tension between data utility for model development and privacy protection presents a fundamental challenge for AI-enabled transportation systems.

Federated learning and differential privacy offer promising approaches to reconcile these competing requirements. Federated learning enables model training on distributed data without centralized aggregation, allowing individual users or organizations to maintain control over their data while still contributing to collective learning. Differential privacy provides mathematical guarantees about the information revealed by model outputs, enabling quantifiable privacy protection. However, both approaches involve trade-offs between privacy protection and model accuracy that require careful calibration based on application requirements and stakeholder preferences.

Beyond privacy, data quality and representativeness present significant challenges. Training datasets may not adequately represent diverse populations, geographic regions, or edge cases, leading to biased or unreliable model performance in underrepresented scenarios. Ensuring fairness and equity in AI-enabled transportation systems requires careful attention to dataset composition, validation across diverse conditions, and ongoing monitoring of deployed system performance across different population segments — challenges that mirror broader concerns about algorithmic exclusion and the digital disenfranchisement of marginalised communities (Gupta et al., 2026). Active learning and adaptive sampling techniques can help identify and address data gaps, but require sustained commitment to inclusive system development.

6.2 Computational Requirements and Energy Consumption

Advanced AI systems, particularly deep learning models, require substantial computational resources for both training and inference. Large language models and computer vision systems may consume megawatt-hours of energy during training, with associated carbon emissions depending on the electricity generation mix. Real-time inference on edge devices in vehicles demands energy-efficient hardware and optimized algorithms to avoid negating the environmental benefits these systems are intended to provide. This creates a paradox where the tools designed to enable transportation decarbonization themselves contribute to energy consumption and emissions.

Addressing these challenges requires multi-pronged approaches including algorithmic efficiency improvements, specialized hardware accelerators, and sustainable computing practices. Model compression techniques including pruning, quantization, and knowledge distillation can reduce computational requirements by orders of magnitude with minimal accuracy loss. Neuromorphic computing and other novel hardware architectures promise dramatic improvements in energy efficiency for neural network inference. Training infrastructure powered by renewable energy and careful scheduling to coincide with periods of clean energy availability can minimize the carbon footprint of model development.

Life cycle assessment of AI-enabled transportation systems must account for the full environmental impact including manufacturing of specialized hardware, energy consumption during operation, and end-of-life disposal. Holistic optimization that considers these factors alongside operational benefits ensures that AI applications genuinely contribute to sustainability goals rather than merely shifting environmental burdens to different parts of the system or lifecycle. Transparency about computational costs and environmental impacts of AI systems enables informed decision-making about their deployment.

6.3 Integration and Standardization

The transportation ecosystem involves numerous stakeholders including vehicle manufacturers, infrastructure operators, service providers, and regulatory agencies, each with their own systems, standards, and objectives. Achieving the full benefits of AI-enabled transportation requires unprecedented levels of integration and coordination across these diverse entities. The lack of common standards for data formats, communication protocols, and system interfaces presents a significant barrier to realizing network-level optimizations and enabling seamless multimodal transportation.

Developing and implementing appropriate standards requires balancing multiple considerations including technical feasibility, security requirements, competitive dynamics, and regulatory constraints. Open standards that enable interoperability without stifling innovation represent the ideal, but achieving consensus among stakeholders with competing interests remains challenging. Progressive harmonization approaches that start with limited interoperability and gradually expand scope as trust and experience develop may offer practical pathways forward.

Legacy infrastructure and systems present additional integration challenges, as most transportation networks include equipment and systems with decades-long lifespans. Retrofitting existing infrastructure with AI-enabled capabilities requires careful consideration of technical compatibility, cost-effectiveness, and operational disruption. Incremental deployment strategies that demonstrate value in limited contexts before broader rollout can help manage risks and build stakeholder confidence. Modular architectures that enable gradual capability enhancement without wholesale replacement of existing systems offer practical paths to modernization.

6.4 Regulatory and Ethical Considerations

The deployment of AI systems in safety-critical transportation applications raises profound ethical and regulatory questions. Who bears responsibility when autonomous vehicles are involved in accidents? How should AI systems make decisions in unavoidable collision scenarios? What level of safety is sufficient for autonomous vehicle deployment? How can we ensure that AI-enabled transportation systems serve all segments of society equitably? These questions lack clear answers and require ongoing dialogue among technologists, policymakers, ethicists, and the public.

Regulatory frameworks must evolve to address the unique characteristics of AI-based systems including their opacity, potential for emergent behaviors, and continuous evolution through learning. Traditional regulatory approaches based on prescriptive requirements and type certification may be inadequate for systems that adapt and improve over time. Performance-based regulation that focuses on outcomes rather than specific implementations, combined with robust monitoring and ongoing validation requirements, may better suit the dynamic nature of AI systems.

Ensuring algorithmic fairness and preventing discrimination in AI-enabled transportation services demands careful attention throughout system design, development, and deployment. As AI automates increasingly complex technical tasks, concerns about the deskilling of human professionals and the erosion of domain expertise also warrant attention (Gupta et al., 2026). Machine learning systems can inadvertently perpetuate or amplify existing societal biases present in training data or encoded in optimization objectives. Explicit fairness constraints, diverse development teams, participatory design processes involving affected communities, and transparency about system capabilities and limitations all contribute to more equitable outcomes. Ongoing monitoring and auditing of deployed systems help identify and address fairness issues that emerge in practice. From an economic welfare standpoint, these fairness imperatives are not merely ethical desiderata but conditions for efficient market outcomes: transportation systems that exclude or underserve population segments generate allocative inefficiency and suppress the full social return on infrastructure investment. Public economics theory suggests that where distributional outcomes are inadequate, corrective instruments—such as subsidized mobility credits for low-income households, universal service obligations on AI-managed transit platforms, or income-contingent congestion charge rebates—are more economically efficient than compromising the technical optimization of the AI system itself. Designing such instruments requires close coordination between transport economists, AI architects, and regulators, illustrating the interdisciplinary governance challenge at the heart of equitable and efficient AI deployment in transport.

6.5 Future Research Priorities

Advancing AI applications in decarbonized transport requires sustained research across multiple frontiers. Sample efficiency remains a critical challenge, as many reinforcement learning approaches require enormous amounts of experience to achieve competent performance. Transfer learning and meta-learning techniques that enable rapid adaptation to new tasks or environments could dramatically reduce the data and time requirements for developing effective policies. Sim-to-real transfer methods that leverage simulation for the bulk of training while efficiently adapting to real-world conditions offer another promising direction.

Explainability and interpretability of AI decision-making processes require continued attention, particularly for safety-critical applications. While deep neural networks achieve impressive performance, their internal representations often lack clear semantic meaning that humans can understand and verify. Developing architectures and training procedures that produce interpretable models without sacrificing performance, or creating effective post-hoc explanation methods for existing models, would enhance trust and enable better validation of system behavior.

Multi-agent coordination and collective intelligence represent another important research frontier. Most current AI systems operate independently, missing opportunities for cooperation that could improve overall system performance. Developing communication protocols, learning algorithms, and incentive mechanisms that enable beneficial coordination between autonomous agents while maintaining robustness to strategic manipulation or malicious actors presents significant challenges. Success in this area could unlock dramatic improvements in traffic flow, energy efficiency, and safety through cooperative behaviors.

Integration of AI with emerging technologies including quantum computing, advanced materials, and biotechnology may enable capabilities beyond those possible with current approaches. Quantum machine learning could solve optimization problems intractable for classical computers. Advanced battery materials discovered through AI-guided materials science could extend electric vehicle range and lifespan. Bio-inspired algorithms could enable more robust and adaptive transportation systems. Exploring these synergies represents an exciting frontier for future research that may unlock transformative advances in sustainable transportation.

7. CONCLUSION

Artificial intelligence and machine learning technologies have emerged as indispensable tools in the global effort to decarbonize transportation systems, generating economic value alongside environmental benefits. This chapter has examined the diverse applications of these technologies across electric vehicle energy management, autonomous driving, traffic optimization, predictive maintenance, and smart city integration, situating each within a cost-benefit framework that links technological capability to economic outcomes. The evidence demonstrates that AI-enabled solutions can deliver substantial reductions in energy consumption and emissions while improving operational efficiency, safety, and user experience across multiple transportation modalities—and that the economic returns from these improvements, properly measured to include externality values, are strongly positive across a wide range of deployment contexts.

The success of reinforcement learning in optimizing electric vehicle energy management illustrates how AI systems can discover effective strategies through experience, adapting to individual usage patterns and operating conditions to maximize efficiency and battery longevity. Deep learning's transformative impact on autonomous driving demonstrates the power of end-to-end learning from raw sensor data, enabling unprecedented capabilities in environmental perception and decision-making. AI-driven traffic signal control and route optimization showcase how intelligent coordination at network scales can dramatically improve traffic flow and reduce congestion-related emissions. Predictive maintenance applications highlight the value of continuous monitoring and data-driven decision-making in extending vehicle and infrastructure lifespans while optimizing resource utilization.

Despite these impressive achievements, significant challenges remain to be addressed before AI-enabled transportation can fully realize its potential for enabling sustainable mobility. Data requirements, privacy concerns, computational demands, integration complexities, and regulatory uncertainties all present substantial barriers that require continued research and development efforts. The ethical implications of deploying AI in safety-critical transportation applications demand ongoing attention from technologists, policymakers, and society at large. Ensuring that AI-enabled transportation systems serve all segments of society equitably while protecting individual privacy and autonomy represents a fundamental responsibility that must be embedded in system design and governance from the outset.

The path forward requires sustained collaboration across disciplines, sectors, and stakeholder groups. Researchers must continue advancing the fundamental capabilities of AI systems while addressing critical challenges in robustness, efficiency, and interpretability. Industry must translate research advances into practical deployments that deliver real-world benefits while maintaining safety and reliability standards. Policymakers must develop regulatory frameworks that enable innovation while ensuring safety, equity, and accountability. The public must engage in informed dialogue about the role of AI in shaping future transportation systems and the values that should guide its development and deployment.

Looking ahead, the integration of AI with emerging technologies including quantum computing, advanced materials, and next-generation communication networks promises to unlock capabilities beyond those achievable with current approaches. The convergence of autonomous vehicles, intelligent infrastructure, and coordinated mobility services enabled by AI has the potential to fundamentally transform how people and goods move through urban and rural environments. Achieving this vision will require sustained investment, thoughtful governance, and commitment to ensuring that technological advancement serves broader societal goals of sustainability, equity, and human wellbeing.

The journey toward decarbonized transportation represents one of the defining economic and environmental challenges of our time. Artificial intelligence and machine learning provide powerful tools for addressing this challenge, but technology alone is insufficient. The analysis presented in this chapter underscores that the full economic potential of AI in transport is realized only when technological capability is paired with appropriate market mechanisms—carbon pricing that internalizes emission externalities, dynamic tariff structures that align private decisions with social optima, and regulatory frameworks that reward performance rather than prescribing solutions. Policymakers should prioritize market design interventions that create durable economic incentives for AI adoption, while researchers must continue developing robust cost-benefit methodologies that capture the full social value of decarbonization. By embracing this comprehensive economic perspective alongside technological innovation, society can harness AI's transformative potential to build mobility systems that are not only cleaner and more efficient, but also economically sustainable and equitable for future generations.

REFERENCES

Almalioglu, Y., Turan, M., Trigoni, N., & Newman, P. (2022). Deep learning-based robust positioning for all-weather autonomous driving. *Nature Machine Intelligence*, *4*(9), 749–760. DOI: 10.1038/s42256-022-00520-5 PMID: 37790900

Ananganó-Alvarado, G., Umaña-Morel, I., & Keith-Norambuena, B. (2025). Reinforcement learning in electric vehicle energy management: A comprehensive open-access review of methods, challenges, and future innovations. *Frontiers in Future Transportation*, *6*, 1555250. DOI: 10.3389/ffutr.2025.1555250

Boudmen, K., El ghazi, A., Eddaoudi, Z., Aarab, Z., & Rahmani, M. D. (2024). Electric vehicles, the future of transportation powered by machine learning: A brief review. *Energy Informatics*, *7*(1), 80. DOI: 10.1186/s42162-024-00379-3

Cao, Y., & Zhou, M. (2024). Energy management optimization of hybrid electric vehicles based on deep learning model predictive control. *Intelligent Decision Technologies*, *18*(4), 2451–2472. DOI: 10.3233/IDT-240298

Chen, S., Liao, Y., Wang, F., Wang, G., Wang, L., Wang, Y., & Zhu, X. (2025). Toward the robustness of autonomous vehicles in the AI era. *Innovation (Cambridge (Mass.))*, *6*(3), 100780. DOI: 10.1016/j.xinn.2024.100780 PMID: 40098668

Dikshit, S., Atiq, A., Shahid, M., Dwivedi, V., & Thusu, A. (2023). The use of artificial intelligence to optimize the routing of vehicles and reduce traffic congestion in urban areas. *EAI Endorsed Transactions on Energy Web*, *10*, e4. DOI: 10.4108/ew.4613

Feng, S., Sun, H., Yan, X., Zhu, H., Zou, Z., Shen, S., & Liu, H. X. (2023). Dense reinforcement learning for safety validation of autonomous vehicles. *Nature*, *615*(7953), 620–627. DOI: 10.1038/s41586-023-05732-2 PMID: 36949337

Gupta, D., Azizbek, I., Suxrob, P., & Abdullaeva, I. Ravshan kizi, B. M., Abdukabilovna, T. D., & Jumayev, U. (2026). Digital Hoboism. In E. Kaygisiz (Ed.), Digital Ideologies in the Age of Algorithmic Culture (pp. 307–338). IGI Global Scientific Publishing. DOI: 10.4018/979-8-3373-4531-4.ch010

Gupta, D., Xusniddin, R., Jumaniyazova, N., Sherbek, S., Rajabova, N., Shavkat, R., & Dilorom, O. (2026). Developer Confidence, Competence, and Self-Efficacy in the Age of AI. In Le, H. (Ed.), *AI Impacts on Deskilling and Reskilling Software Engineers* (pp. 27–60). IGI Global Scientific Publishing., DOI: 10.4018/979-8-3373-8450-4.ch002

Han, D., & Shen, S. (2024). Deep reinforcement learning for autonomous driving with multi-scenario fusion: A unified reward function approach. In *Proceedings of the 2024 7th International Conference on Machine Learning and Machine Intelligence (MLMI)* (pp. 83-89). ACM. DOI: 10.1145/3696271.3696284

Ibrahum, A. D. M., Hussain, M., & Hong, J. (2024). Deep learning adversarial attacks and defenses in autonomous vehicles: A systematic literature review from a safety perspective. *Artificial Intelligence Review*, *58*(1), 11014. DOI: 10.1007/s10462-024-11014-8

Karthick, K., Ravivarman, S., & Priyanka, R. (2024). Optimizing electric vehicle battery life: A machine learning approach for sustainable transportation. *World Electric Vehicle Journal*, *15*(2), 60. DOI: 10.3390/wevj15020060

Khan, M., Raza, M. A., Abbas, G., Othmen, S., Yousef, A., & Jumani, T. A. (2024). Pothole detection for autonomous vehicles using deep learning: A robust and efficient solution. *Frontiers in Built Environment*, *9*, 1323792. DOI: 10.3389/fbuil.2023.1323792

Kumar, K. B. N., Pratyusha, D., Sravanthi, B., & Reddy, E. J. (2024). Recent AI applications in electrical vehicles for sustainability. *SSRG International Journal of Mechanical Engineering*, *11*(3), 50–64. DOI: 10.14445/23488360/IJME-V11I3P106

Liyanage, S., Abduljabbar, R., & Dia, H. (2025). Machine learning traffic flow prediction models for smart and sustainable traffic management. *Infrastructures*, *10*(7), 155. DOI: 10.3390/infrastructures10070155

Mahale, Y., Kolhar, S., & More, S. A. (2025). A comprehensive review on artificial intelligence driven predictive maintenance in vehicles: Technologies, challenges and future research directions. *Discover Applied Sciences*, *7*(4), 243. DOI: 10.1007/s42452-025-06681-3

Mohsen, M. M., & Mohsen, M. (2025). Reducing emissions through AI-driven multimodal transport optimization in IoT-connected environments. *International Journal of Energy Research*, *2399288*(1), 2399288. Advance online publication. DOI: 10.1155/er/2399288

Moraga, A., de Curtò, J., de Zarzà, I., & Calafate, C. T. (2025). AI-driven UAV and IoT traffic optimization: Large language models for congestion and emission reduction in smart cities. *Drones (Basel)*, *9*(4), 248. DOI: 10.3390/drones9040248

Ren, H. (2025). Optimization method of electric vehicle energy system based on machine learning. *Frontiers of Mechanical Engineering*, *11*, 1597558. DOI: 10.3389/fmech.2025.1597558

Sahoo, L. K., & Varadarajan, V. (2025). Deep learning for autonomous driving systems: Technological innovations, strategic implementations, and business implications - a comprehensive review. *Complex Engineering Systems*, *5*(1), 11. DOI: 10.20517/ces.2024.83

Saki, S., & Soori, M. (2024). Artificial intelligence, machine learning and deep learning in advanced transportation systems, a review. *Multimodal Transportation*, *4*(2), 100242. DOI: 10.1016/j.multra.2025.100242

Szczepański, E., Żochowska, R., Izdebski, M., & Jacyna, M. (2025). Decision-making problems in urban transport decarbonization strategies: Challenges, tools, and methods. *Energies*, *18*(15), 3970. DOI: 10.3390/en18153970

Tsekouras, G. E., Chatzisavvas, K. C., Triantos, D., Mitsikas, G., Christopoulos, L., & Dialynas, E. (2024). AI-driven predictive maintenance in modern maritime transport—Enhancing operational efficiency and reliability. *Applied Sciences (Basel, Switzerland)*, *14*(20), 9439. DOI: 10.3390/app14209439

Ucar, A., Karakose, M., & Kırımça, N. (2024). Artificial intelligence for predictive maintenance applications: Key components, trustworthiness, and future trends. *Applied Sciences (Basel, Switzerland)*, *14*(2), 898. DOI: 10.3390/app14020898

Villegas-Ch, W., Govea, J., & Jaramillo-Alcazar, A. (2023). Advances in the optimization of vehicular traffic in smart cities: Integration of blockchain and computer vision for sustainable mobility. *Sustainability (Basel)*, *15*(22), 15736. DOI: 10.3390/su152215736

Wei, H., Xu, N., Zhang, H., Zheng, G., Zang, X., Chen, C., Zhang, W., Zhu, Y., Xu, K., & Li, Z. (2019). CoLight: Learning network-level cooperation for traffic signal control. In *Proceedings of the 28th ACM International Conference on Information and Knowledge Management* (pp. 1913-1922). ACM. DOI: 10.1145/3357384.3357902

Yao, R., Tripathi, S., Bayen, A., & Poolla, K. (2025). Big-data empowered traffic signal control could reduce urban carbon emission. *Nature Communications*, *16*(1), 1701. DOI: 10.1038/s41467-025-56701-4 PMID: 40016199

Zhao, R., Li, Y., Fan, Y., Gao, F., Tsukada, M., & Gao, Z. (2024). A survey on recent advancements in autonomous driving using deep reinforcement learning: Applications, challenges, and solutions. *IEEE Transactions on Intelligent Transportation Systems*, *25*(12), 19482–19503. DOI: 10.1109/TITS.2024.3452480

Zhao, Z., & Chen, J. (2025). Application of artificial intelligence technology in the economic development of urban intelligent transportation system. *PeerJ. Computer Science*, *11*, e2728. DOI: 10.7717/peerj-cs.2728 PMID: 40134871

KEY TERMS AND DEFINITIONS

Artificial Intelligence (AI): The simulation of human intelligence by computer systems. It involves programming machines to perform complex tasks such as reasoning, problem-solving, and decision-making. AI acts as the "brain" behind modern innovations, processing vast datasets to mimic cognitive functions and automate sophisticated workflows.

Autonomous Driving: Technology that enables vehicles to sense their environment and navigate without human intervention. Using a combination of sensors, cameras, and AI, self-driving systems aim to increase road safety, optimize traffic flow, and provide greater mobility for those unable to drive themselves.

Decarbonization: The process of reducing or eliminating carbon dioxide emissions from the economy, particularly from energy production and industry. This involves transitioning to renewable energy sources and improving efficiency to mitigate climate change and achieve a carbon-neutral footprint globally.

Electric Vehicles (EVs): Vehicles powered entirely or partially by electricity stored in rechargeable batteries rather than internal combustion engines. By replacing fossil fuels with electric power, EVs significantly reduce greenhouse gas emissions and noise pollution, serving as a cornerstone of modern green energy transitions.

Machine Learning (ML): A subset of AI focused on building systems that learn from data to improve performance over time without explicit programming. By identifying patterns and correlations, ML algorithms make predictions and adapt to new information, powering everything from recommendation engines to diagnostic tools.

Sustainable Transportation: Low-impact transit methods that balance environmental, social, and economic needs. This includes public transit, cycling, and walking, as well as high-tech solutions. The goal is to move people and goods efficiently while minimizing pollution, congestion, and the consumption of non-renewable resources.

Chapter 2

AI-Driven Logistics, Data Governance, and Sustainability:

A Critical Analysis of India's Digital Personal Data Protection Act 2023

Vijeta Verma
http://orcid.org/0000-0001-9255-9132
Christ University, India

Shashank Solanki
http://orcid.org/0009-0002-5923-0516
Christ University, India

Vijaishree Dubey Pandey
http://orcid.org/0000-0003-3207-7814
Christ University, India

Sheetal Singh
http://orcid.org/0000-0002-7266-8910
Christ University, India

Rituraj Sinha
http://orcid.org/0000-0001-5790-9571
Christ University, India

DOI: 10.4018/979-8-3373-9003-1.ch002

ABSTRACT

This paper is a critical overview of the blowout of artificial intelligence (AI)-empowered logistics, cross-border data governance, and sustainability regulation as the Digital Personal Data Protection Act, 2023 (DPDP Act) of India. It addresses the ways AI-based logistic systems (including the predictive routing or digital twins systems and emission tracking systems) rely on the smooth flow of transnational data, and how the regulatory uncertainty of the DPDP Act affects the efficiency of operations, compliance, and climate governance. The study places the Indian framework in a global frame using doctrinal analysis and comparative legal analysis against global regimes of EU GDPR, OECD Privacy Guidelines and APEC CBPR system. The results underscore a regulatory paradox: Reconciling data sovereignty, AI-trade efficiencies, and sustainability imperatives. The article posits that in order to match the global data protection law with the decarbonization and digital trade agenda in India, interoperable, risk-based, and technologically adaptive governance frameworks are necessary.

1. INTRODUCTION

1.1 From Physical Trade Corridors to Data-Driven Logistics Infrastructures

A change in structure of global logistic systems occurs. The logistics networks before were largely concentrated on the physical infrastructure through the form of ports, warehouses, shipping fleets and the custom checkpoints. The modern logistics, however, however, is becoming more data-driven and algorithm-driven, via digital supply chains, which are becoming integrated (Balboni & Francis, 2023). This change is possible due to the rapid convergence of artificial intelligence (AI), advanced analytics, and control of digital platforms and can be used to support real-time decision-making between trade corridors geographically located. This change in infrastructure towards data-driven logistics, especially in cross-border trade support, customs reform, and the creation of regional sustainable trade corridors is specifically relevant because all of them rely on the interoperability of digital data infrastructure across borders (Balboni & Francis, 2023).

AI has substituted predictive, structural and adaptive functions that used to be carried out manually in AI-based logistical applications. The predictive logistics and demand-sensing technologies are founded on the historical and real-time data to predict the changes in the market and optimize the place of the inventory and minimize the needless transportation operations (Barr, 2023). Automated port and customs clearance systems are becoming more popular, and machine learning models that can determine the risks and accelerate the process of being cleared, and minimize the level of congestion in international trade flows, are required. At the same time, AI-based data optimization models are embraced to compute the fuel efficiency, less-emission paths, and to assist in meeting the environmental reporting needs (Burri and Kugler, 2024).

The cross-border interoperable data flows work these artificial intelligence-based logistics systems. This type of systems needs inexorable connectivity to information across multiple jurisdictions, such as shipment tracking data, sensor information, Internet of Things (IoT) information, workforce information, and operating information, and information on trade operations (Chang, 2024). Cross-border flows of data are directly influenced by interruption of the operational scalability, predictive efficiency and environmental performance of logistics networks, especially in cases of regulatory fragmentation. In turn, a more competitive and sustainable governance has become reliant on data governance as a crucial factor in the global competitiveness (Hettler et al., 2024).

Technologically, it is urgent to make a border between categories of AI-based logistics solutions on the sensitivity of the information and the degree of regulatory risk. One of the least risk applications of AI is predictive routing, automated warehouse systems, and fuel optimization systems, which are largely based on anonymized data about operations. The medium-risk systems include systems of customs risk assessment and supply chain transparency tools that could deal with minor quantities of personal or commercially sensitive information. The high risk AI application is workforce surveillance, biometric authentication, and behavioral analytics as they are typified by the massive processing of personal data. Such a classification emphasizes the need to implement various regulatory strategies to the AI-based logistics governance.

1.2 Data Protection Law as a New Trade and Sustainability Regulator

This new logistics world has led to the broadening of the traditional role of the data protection law in providing individual privacy. It is gradually turning into a control system in digital trade, supply chain management and sustainability outcomes. The law regulating the collection, processing, and transmission of the data that falls outside the jurisdiction of the countries have assumed the forefront in the establishment of the technology infrastructure in the international logistic systems, and risk distribution systems between the parties involved.

The cross-border data transfer, with regard to the trade governance, demonstrates that the policies have a direct impact on the viability of digitally integrated supply chain operation. International transfer of data restrictions can end up dividing the logistics processes, localizing data in a high cost and minimize the efficiency benefits achieved with AI-based optimization technologies. On the one hand, data protection frameworks are realized within the institutional governance viewpoint that regulates the relations between logistics operators and technology suppliers and, on the other hand, the public regulatory bodies (Richey et al., 2023).

In the aspect of sustainability, data is one of the key infrastructures and can be employed to oversee emissions, perform environmental reporting and decarbonization. The cross-border data governance regimes are fragmented to result in what may be termed to be a hidden cost of carbon. The mismatch of regulation lowers the quality of AI-based optimization in the supply chain, where the compliance procedures are repeated, non-functional routing functions and excess fuel consumption are witnessed. In addition, the ambiguity in the rules of data cross-border transportation adds even more risk of compliance and indirectly compromises climate governing activities in the sustainable logistics networks (Yalçıntaş, 2022).

Social sustainability within logistics include worker safety, fair labour and ethics in the supply chain. Compliance systems using AI can support labour rights monitoring by providing digital audit trails, automated occupational safety monitoring, and ethical sourcing monitoring. Data governance frameworks should also consider the social aspect of ESG by facilitating lawful workforce data processing in a manner that safeguards the privacy of individuals as well as the rights of the workers in the relevant labour law (Richey et al., 2023). Transparent regulatory reporting systems and corporate accountability mechanisms also promote the sustainability of governance and strengthen the trust of stakeholders in digital supply chains.

It is important to note that the concept of sustainability governance in logistics must be construed in an Environmental, Social, and Governance (ESG) approach which is generalized. In addition to reducing the amount of carbon emissions into the environment, AI-based logistics could be viewed as socially sustainable because it keeps the workers safe by predicting the risks and putting the supply chain to a higher level of transparency to conduct ethical sourcing. Compliance monitoring systems and real-time regulatory reporting systems as well as digital audit trails are useful in raising sustainability of governance. Data protection regulation, in its turn, has an impact on sustainability in all of the three pillars of ESG.

1.3 DPDP Act, 2023, in India: Strategic Bottleneck or Regulatory Turning Point?

India is very strategic on the world trade and logistic network. The nation is also in the process of further development of its port operation, production, and utilization of the digital economy, and therefore its regulatory decisions regarding the data governance can be highly transnational (Bradford, 2023). The Digital Personal Data Protection Act, 2023 (DPDP Act) can be seen as a shift to the piecemeal regime of the privacy law established by the Information Technology Act, 2000, to a more comprehensive regime of data protection in statute.

Nevertheless, the DPDP Act presents complicated regulatory challenges in terms of its interface with international logistics, which is based on AI. Although the Act is likely to enhance the personal data protection and develop the idea of data sovereignty, it is rather liberal in terms of outbound data transfer that will enable the data cross-border transfer to the destinations announced by the executive government. The Act does not have up-to-date elaborated adequacy standards and homogenized transfer protection like the familiar international models.

The regulatory decisions available in India in the DPDP Act, 2023 have direct implications on its involvement in regional trade integration processes, such as the ASEAN -India digital trade corridor, logistics connectivity with the Bay of Bengal Initiative under Multi-Sectoral Technical and Economic Cooperation (BIMSTEC), and WTO e-commerce disciplines in its ongoing Joint Statement Initiative negotiations. Disorganized or hesitant data governance may hinder the incorporation of India into regional sustainable trade areas that rely on digital logistics systems that are interoperable (Ciuriak et al., 2023).

The laws that are already in existence within DPDP Act, specifically those that deal with data transfer processes across the borders are in the development stage as at the turn of 2026. Even though policy consultations have been done on draft rules, final regulatory guidelines on adequacy assessment model, exemptions in the sector and level of data classification have not been declared completely. This regulatory ambiguity will make the multinational logistics operators, using AI-based optimization and emissions-monitoring framework, less certain about these regulations.

Thus, DPDP Act is an embodiment of a regulatory balancing paradox that is grounded on three policy goals that contradict each other, i.e., data sovereignty, efficiency in AI-trades, and promises of climate sustainability. The ambiguity of the compliance requirements on the cross-border basis may deter the adoption of the state of the art AI-based infrastructure of logistics and even the inclusion of India in the global digital supply chains (Burri and Kugler, 2024). DPDP Act, thus, may or may not be a progressive model of regulation that will facilitate sustainable digital trade, or a strategic portal that will make technological and environmental optimization shorter.

1.4 Research Objectives and Questions

This regulatory, and technological context will be critically analyzed against this regulatory and technological background in relation to the DPDP Act, 2023 of India critically in the context of AI-enabled global logistics governance and sustainability regulation. This analysis will be located in the main research question that will be the following:

Does the DPDP Act, 2023 of India assist in the creation of sustainable logistics under AI and across-border or does it create regulatory ambiguity, which does not respond to the global digital trade and climate governance agenda?

The following secondary questions were used to answer this central research question in the chapter:

1. What does the India data transfer regulations in cross-border data transfers look like in comparison to the principles of the world data transfer rules like EU GDPR adequacy regime, OECD on privacy governance, and the APEC Cross-Border Privacy Rules system?
2. What are legal, operational, and compliance risk of AI based optimization and emissions-monitoring technology of multinational logistics operators under the DPDP regulatory framework?
3. What should be the redesign of the data governance models in order to reach all three objectives, i.e., decarbonization, data protection, and regulatory sovereignty?

The research methodology used in this chapter is mainly conceptual and doctrinal with some support by comparative legal research and secondary empirical data in terms of published industry reports, logistics case studies and international regulatory instruments. It is not based on primary data collection; it is rather a synthesis of the current literature, policy reports and organizational case examples to assess the regulatory consequences of the DPDP Act on AI-based sustainable logistics. The strategy aligns with the exploratory research in legal and governance that aims to chart regulatory voids and suggest reform directions (Bradford, 2023).

The chapter will be preoccupied with the legally founded and policy-grounded analysis of AI governance by defining the data protection regime in India in the general context of the global discourse of climate responsibility, AI governance, and regulation of digital trade (Ciuriak et al., 2023).

2. THEORETICAL AND CONCEPTUAL FRAMEWORK

The paper relies on the interdisciplinary approach of theoretical basis that embraces the regulatory governance theory, technology governance scholarship, and sustainability-oriented literature on supply chain governance. The law of data protection is conceptualized in the framework as the foundation of governance infrastructure of the digital trade and environmentally friendly logistics conditions (Eyo-Udo, 2024).

2.1 Theoretical Anchors

2.1.1 Regulatory Interoperability Theory

The regulatory interoperability theory offers a critical analytical framework of exploring cross-border data governance of globalized logistic networks. According to the theory, mutual recognition, functional compatibility, and institutional trust in regulation systems are emphasized over the one that is stricter (Holloway, 2024).

The AI-based logistics technologies, such as smart ports, predictive supply chain analytics, and emissions tracking systems, work at simultaneous when they are implemented across the jurisdictions. Data transfer regulations, which are jurisdiction-specific or fragmented, disrupt predictive modelling accuracy and increase compliance complexity, which have a detrimental impact on AI-driven operational efficiencies (Jusić, 2022).

The transfer authorization model of jurisdiction-based transfer prescribed within the DPDP Act, under this theoretical approach, is capable of causing interoperability problems unless it comes with a declaration of adequacy or a standardized transfer protection. These mechanisms of interoperability may be effective including regulatory equivalence agreements, certification systems, template contractual protection and multi-stakeholder compliance monitoring mechanisms. Without such mechanisms, Indian logistics networks will be threatened with the possibility of being partially integrated into global digital trade systems.

On a multilateral level, the Joint Statement Initiative on e-commerce by the WTO and the OECD work on regulatory coherence in digital trade can be seen as indicative of an increasing appreciation that the only way to have efficient, sustainable and inclusive digital trade is to ensure regulatory interoperability in data governance (WTO, 2022). The interaction of India with these frameworks or its non-adherence will influence the working environment of AI-based logistics within cross-border trade routes.

2.1.2 Risk-Based Data Governance

The risk-based data governance proponents offer a proportionality of the regulations based on the sensitivity of data and situations under which it is processed and the potential effect on the harm (Körner et al., 2025). The model has also been used prominently in the EU GDPR that on the basis of risk assessment and type of processing segregates compliance requirements.

The AI-based logistics systems frequently use a combination of hybrid datasets of personal data, data of operational supply chains and machine generated predictive information. Several sustainability-focused logistics applications are mainly dealing with low-risk or anonymized operational data. Risk-based governance allows regulators to be different in their exploitation of personal data that can be categorized as high-risk or the processing of data that can be considered as low-risk and sustainability-oriented.

The relative uniformity of the transfers restrictions in cross-border transfers, under the DPDP Act, devoid of risk-setting regulatory difference, may create an overreach in compliance. Such regulatory rigidity may be particularly applicable to climate optimization technologies, which are based on a regular stream of information and are unlikely to violate personal privacy.

2.1.3 Co-Evolution of Law and Technology.

The law and technology co-evolution theory recognizes the fact that legal systems, as well as the technological advancement, are in a never-ending form of each other. Technology design decisions are affected by regulatory systems, and new technologies disclose the restrictions of regulatory systems and necessitate legal changes (Richey et al., 2023).

Artificial intelligence-powered logistics applications such as digital twin modelling, predictive analytics engines and automated customs clearance applications are organized around regulatory principles of data mobility. The lack of clear AI specific processing guidelines in the DPDP Act shows a possible regulatory lag, which could impede the technological innovation and adaptive sustainability governance (UNECE, 2024). The management of data privacy will most probably clash with the climate-driven logistics innovation unless dynamical and technologically open systems of governance.

2.1.4 Sustainable Supply Chain Governance Theory

The theory of sustainable supply chain governance is aimed at integrating environmental, social, and governance objectives in the logistics decision making. Sustainability is not seen as a by-product but as a form of governance that is part of the contractual obligations, compliance standards as well as management of digital infrastructure.

It is also through intelligent logistics systems, which enable real-time tracking of emission, efficient transportation route, and resource efficiency supply chain co-ordination that are facilitated by AI. This is on the basis of the unceasing cross-border data flows (Chang, 2024). The data protection regimes that happen due to accident in such technological infrastructure may not only derail global climate policy, but also occur (Toorajipour et al., 2020).

One social aspect of sustainable supply chain governance is adherence to international labour standards, which are summarized in the International Labour Organization (ILO) core conventions, and national labour laws that regulate the workforces in the logistics and warehousing sectors. With transparent data structures, AI-enabled monitoring systems can improve the implementation of fair labour practices, occupational hazard reduction, and the implementation of ethical sourcing. Supply chain ethics, such as anti-corruption, responsible procurement, and human rights due diligence are becoming formalized by reporting standards such as Global Reporting Initiative (GRI) Standards, Sustainability Accounting Standards Board (SASB) framework, and Task Force on Climate-related Financial Disclosures (TCFD) (Hettler et al., 2024). These governance mechanisms affirm the perception that data regulation must be used to promote complete ESG accountability as opposed to being a hindrance.

Social sustainability indicators such as labor protection, supply chain transparency, upholding ethical sourcing, etc. must also be part of sustainable logistics governance. The AI-assisted compliance reporting and electronic accountability boosts the sustainability of governance. Within the specified framework, the concept of cross-border data governance is a multidimensional regulation issue that entails privacy protection, facilitation of trade, and environmental sustainability outcomes.

2.2 Conceptual Linkages

The conceptualization of the research is a causal and effectual relationship between AI-enabled logistical systems, cross-border data flows, predictability of the regulation and the result of the emission reduction based on the above theoretical frameworks. AI-based logistics demand constant transnational data flows in order to keep the predictability and optimization of operations. These rules of data transfer across borders can be consistent and transparent and can assist logistics operators to adopt such technologies on large scale without the high risk of being exposed to compliance risks (Hettler et al., 2024).

Regulatory uncertainty, on the other hand, especially in discretionary or opaque data transfer authorization regimes, creates a cost of operation, fragmentation of compliance and risk-averse technology adoption. These inefficiencies are experienced in the form of inefficient transport routing, increased fuel consumption, and reduced emissions monitoring facilities, which cripple the decarbonization process in the world (Kelly, 2024). Empirical observations in the industry also help in supporting this relationship. To illustrate, the European logistics operators have reported an increase in the compliance costs and inconveniences in processing intermediary data, following the Schrems II decision that suggests how judicial encroachments on the regulation of data can create operational turbulence. Similarly, shipping firms that are multinational and have implemented AI-powered fuel optimization software have reported that they have saved between 5-15 percent of their fuel consumption, which shows how data-driven shipment optimization can benefit the environment. Nevertheless, the technology of the type needs robust international data transfer systems in order to be operationally efficient.

Other jurisdictions such as Singapore and Brazil have also found it difficult to reconcile data sovereignty and enabling trade and, unlike India, have shown regulatory complexity in data regulation across borders is not only an Indian governance problem but also a worldwide issue in governance. Hence, data protection regulation will be facilitating governance infrastructure in which it promotes interoperability, regulation transparency and proportional enforcement. On the contrary, uncertain and disjointed information governance systems could serve as institutional bottlenecks diminishing the integration of digital trade and the promotion of sustainability (Bhandari and Singh, 2023).

Figure 1. Integrated Framework for Sustainable Global Logistics

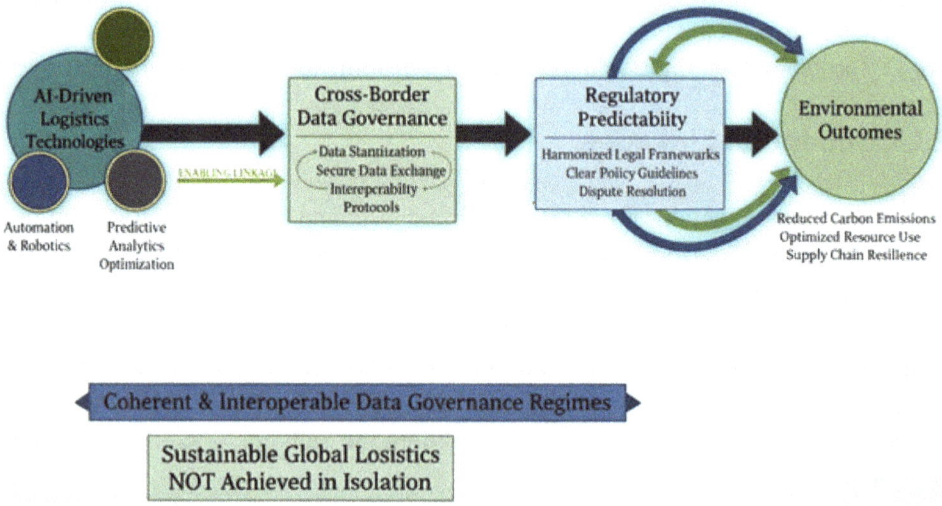

This is an integrated framework that is represented by mapping the interdependences of AI-based logistics technologies, cross-border data governance, regulatory predictability and environmental outcomes. The framework highlights the main premise that it is impossible to have sustainable global logistics without standard regimes of global governance uniform and interoperable by data.

3. METHODOLOGY AND RESEARCH DESIGN

The research design of this chapter is a multi-layered, conceptual-doctrinal, which incorporates doctrinal legal research design, comparative regulatory research design, a technology governance research design, and a sustainability/ESG research design. The research is not empirical; it is analytical and normative in nature and it relies on secondary sources of information, i.e. published literature, including legal tools, policy reports and case studies of the industry, as well as scholarly literature. This methodological framework is suitable to this type of governance studies that aim to evaluate regulatory gaps, chart the comparative regulatory frameworks, and suggest policy reform trajectories in a highly dynamic regulatory space (Bradford, 2023). The sources of data are statutory texts, judicial rulings, legislative history, policy-making documents by WTO and OECD, sustainability reports in the industry, and empirical studies available in peer-reviewed journals and institutional working papers.

3.1 Doctrinal Legal Analysis

The main part of the study is an analysis of the Digital Personal Data Protection Act, 2023 (DPDP Act) in India, through the prism of a doctrinal approach to law. It includes a thorough analysis of the statutory requirements of the consent architecture, data processing requirements, fiduciary liability, and mechanisms of cross-border data transfer (DPO India, 2024). The area of executive discretion to limit the outbound data flows and the lack of codified adequacy assessment standards to the Act are given particular attention.

The constitutional and administrative legal principles such as proportionality, reasonableness, legality and non-arbitrariness are also included in the doctrinal analysis. These principles are examined to assess whether the cross-border data transfer model in the DPDP Act is consistent with the developing constitutional privacy jurisprudence in India and sufficiently limits executive power of regulation.

Furthermore, it also includes a new assessment of the level of implementation of the DPDP regulatory framework. Although the DPDP Act, 2023 is already in force, various working rules are in place to regulate cross-border data transfers, data fiduciary and specific compliance standards in the sector, yet are still being progressively developed. This implementation transition period adds to compliance ambiguity to multinational logistics operators, thus supporting the necessity of the in-depth doctrinal analysis.

3.2 Comparative and Transnational Legal Method

To put the regulatory framework in India into perspective, the paper will use a comparative legal approach to analyse the internationally-based data governance regimes such as the European Union General Data Protection Regulation (GDPR) adequacy regime, the OECD Privacy Guidelines, the APEC Cross-Border Privacy Rules system, and the latest WTO digital trade governance norms.

The comparative analysis measures the best practices in terms of regulatory transparency, transfer protection mechanisms, institutional oversight mechanisms, and cross-border compliance frameworks interoperability. Notably, the research uses a more balanced comparative approach in its approach since it understands that regulatory issues associated with the cross-border data management are not exclusive to India. The European Union and other jurisdictions like the European Union have complexities of implementation after judicial interventions (Schrems II) and other countries, such as Singapore, Brazil, and China have also followed different forms of data localisation and regulation.

This comparative mapping allows the study to find both regulatory strengths as well as the structural constraints in the DPDP framework in India, especially in its discretionary cross-border transfer regime, and lack of clearly operationalised adequacy assessment criteria applicable to AI-enabled logistics operators that participate in international trade (EY India, 2025).

3.3 Technology Governance Lens

The study also embraces a technology governance lens that acknowledges that legal rules exist in larger technological ecosystems (Latham & Watkins, 2023). This framework examines how the data protection regulation and AI system lifecycle interrelate in logistics infrastructure, such as data collection, training, algorithm deployment, predictive analytics, and system optimisation.

In an effort to improve conceptual clarity, the study has divided AI-driven applications in logistics based on regulatory risk and sensitivity of the data:

1. Operational AI Systems: predictive routing, warehouse automation and supply chain optimization tools, which mostly employ operational and sensor-generated data.
2. Compliance-Oriented AI Systems - The systems of automated evaluation of customs risks and fraud detection working with operational and personal data.
3. Sustainability and ESG AI Systems Carbon accounting, emissions forecasting, and climate monitoring solutions that combine cross-jurisdictional data.

The analysis also includes data dependency mapping to show the degree to which AI-supported logistics infrastructure will rely on the ongoing real-time cross-border data movement. This methodology allows analysing the impacts of regulatory constraints on technology performance, operational robustness and environmental optimisation performance.

3.4 Sustainability and ESG Lens

In the research, the analytical approaches of sustainability and Environmental, Social, and Governance (ESG) are combined to understand the impact that data governance frameworks have on environmental and corporate responsibility outcomes. Although one of the key areas of analytical focus is environmental sustainability, especially a decrease in carbon emissions, ESG evaluation is also extended in the study to include:

- Social sustainability indicators like labour monitoring, supply chain transparency, human rights compliance.
- Indicators of governance such as corporate accountability, regulatory transparency, and algorithms oversight mechanisms.

This multi-dimensional ESG lens places cross-border data governance in the context of more global climate and trade policy goals. The review supports the main argument that the efficient data protection systems should be structured so that they could support the global decarbonisation programs and global supply chains governance systems (Matthan, 2023).

The ESG reporting standards that were consulted in this chapter are: GRI Standards (GRI 305 in particular, the Emissions and GRI 308/414 in particular, the Supplier Environmental and Social Assessments) and the SASB Transportation sector standards and the TCFD recommendations on climate-related disclosures. The sources that are used in the industry reports are international chamber of shipping publications, global logistics council publications, and WTO e-commerce working papers. They are the frameworks that give the normative standards based on which the compatibility of the DPDP Act with the ESG obligations is evaluated.

4. AI-ENABLED LOGISTICS AND THE LEGAL SIGNIFICANCE OF DATA FLOWS

The modern global logistics is being structured around the architecture of artificial intelligence-based decision-making systems that are placed on the platforms of unceasing, bulk and transnational streams of data. Compared to the traditional logistics networks, which were more of asset-based (and labour-based) systems, the AI-based logistics networks are more data-based networks, the performance of which in the case of the efficiency of the operations, compliance with regulations and sustainability is optimised through an algorithm (Bhandari and Singh, 2023). Therefore, the cross-border data flow regulation turned out to be one of the determinants of the performance, stability and environment friendliness of the logistics systems of the world.

4.1 AI Use-Cases in Cross-Border Logistics

The whole global supply chain is being applied to AI technologies, both in the upstream planning and production projections, and the downstream optimisation of the delivery and regulatory control.

One of the most general uses of AI that is implemented is predictive routing and optimisation of fuel. These systems use the real time traffic scenario, weather pattern, the fuel price and the records of the port traffic in coming up with the optimal transportation routes. As the empirical study concerning the industry has already found out, AI-based, route optimisation algorithms have already cut down about 10-15 percent of the fuel used in the global shipping procedures, which has already contributed to the reduction in emissions and cost-effectiveness (Jia et al., 2021). Nonetheless, the optimisation models entail integrating permanent information across jurisdictions across the borders.

The other important area of application is the digital twin infrastructure development where the physical modelling of the virtual logistics resources, which include ports, warehouses and intermodal transport hubs, is done. Digital twins is a combination of historical performance and real-time sensor analysis to facilitate predictive maintenance, prediction of traffic and resource allocation efficiency. Implementation of digital twins is said to have increased the effectiveness of the operations in the major international ports by more than 20 percent. The nature of this kind of systems pre-conditions the need to integrate vessel tracking systems, customs databases, environmental sensor networks in jurisdictions, which further indicates even more clearly the legal relevance of cross-border data mobility.

The third notable application of AI usage to international trade is automated customs risk assessment systems which help in streamlining international trade process to be made efficient. Such machine learning systems are used to process shipment records, trade records and behavioural risk factors to automate the customs clearance procedures. In fact, it has been empirically proven that the introduction of automated customs in a number of jurisdictions around the globe has resulted in as much as 30 percent of time saved on clearance, which, in its turn, has indirectly led to a decrease in the number of emissions caused by idling cargo and delays in storage (European Parliament, 2021). These systems however touch on personal information of sensitive nature such as the exporters, drivers and logistics intermediaries and pose complex compliance issues when laws on data protection are put in force.

Lastly, the emergence of AI-related emissions forecasting and ESG reporting tools has turned into a crucial component of the realm of sustainable management of logistics. The systems allow multinational enterprises to estimate the Scope 1, Scope 2 and Scope 3 emissions, the carbon footprint that was predicted and responded to the newly introduced policy of disclosure of ESG. These systems are also the main prerequisites of the centralized international data and another factor that contributes to the structural interdependence of the data flow and climate accountability (Van Ooijen and Vrabec, 2019).

Within the Indian context, a number of logistics operators and cross-border data flows, as well as sustainability, are demonstrated in several logistic operators and public infrastructure projects. The largest container port in India, Jawaharlal Nehru Port Trust (JNPT) has implemented AI-enabled cargo tracking and customs risk assessment technology, which involves real-time data integration by shipping lines, customs bodies, and logistics agents across jurisdictions. In a similar manner, Dedicated Freight Corridor Corporation of India (DFCC) is adopting data-driven freight optimization systems, which rely on cross-border integration with the Southeast Asia and Middle East supply chain partners. Such infrastructure projects highlight the real-world urgency of a foreseeable cross-border data governance framework to the competitiveness of logistics in India.

One example of AI logistics applications being directly integrated into the goals of customs reform and trade facilitation is in the form of automated customs clearance systems, a key feature of the TradeConnect and ICEGATE platforms in India. The limitations of cross-border data transfer may hinder the real-time transfer of information between the customs administrations that such systems need, thus, impacting clearance times, compliance costs, and competitiveness of Indian logistics corridors within regional trade networks (Chang, 2024).

4.2 Legal Characterisation of Logistics Data

The logistics datasets created by AI are a legal category heterogeneous, which can not be imposed on a single data classification system (CJEU, 2020).

Firstly, the logistics operations are likely to deal with the personal data such as the data on the employees, drivers, customs agents, and clients. This data will be directly attractive to the data protection regime requirements such as consent, limitation of purpose, minimisation of data and lawful processing.

Second, the logistic systems produce big data of operating data, such as shipment plans, shipment routing analytics, inventory statistics and sensor performance. Although operation datasets are typically considered to be non-personal data, they can be subject to the data protection regulation in either case, by being aggregated with identifiable datasets, or by the AI algorithms providing inferences on an individual basis (GDPR, 2016).

Third, the logistics systems developed by using AI lead to derived or predictive datasets, i.e., the risk score, efficiency rating, and the emissions performance indices. Such outputs of the machine are in regulatory grey zone, especially when the predictive analytics are a direct prediction of people or business organizations. The existing global regimes on data protection are yet to be harmonised on the regulation standards on inferred forms of data that results to ambiguity in adherence to the multinational logistic actors.

The fact that it can transform unintelligent raw data into intelligent information created by algorithms is just going to make the traditional data classification of legal data more difficult. One of the causes of the higher level of regulatory uncertainty and the potential of simplistic compliance problems in the sphere of logistics among multinational players is the lack of clear legislative indicators of the deliverables of AI.

4.3 Sustainability Implications of Data Disruptions

The cost of compliance delay/legal ambiguity resulting in the interruption of cross-border data flows can cause numerous important environmental and operational sustainability costs. The working principle of logistic systems related to AI has been the availability of real-time data to ensure that the accuracy of prediction will be provided. In this manner data losses result in inefficiency in the optimisation, and hence, sub-optimal routing, and higher consumption of fuel.

Based on the findings, released by the European logistics research agencies, in the form of the empirical supply chain simulation, it is noted that over 24 hours of data transfer can raise the fuel consumption by about 5-8 percent of integrated shipping networks (European Commission, 2023). These kinds of outcomes suggest that the issues of regulation of data governance can be directly translated into inefficiency with regard to carbon.

The result of such phenomenon is a paradox to global governance of trade-environment regulation. As much as data protection regulations are aimed at safeguarding the privacy rights of the individuals, the current cross-border data regulation regime is still yet to be put into pieces and therefore, the impacts of climate mitigation measures may therefore be undermined unless the regulatory considerations are technological and environmental.Moreover, the collapse of the data transfer can affect the quality of the ESG reporting, break the system of emissions monitoring, and decrease scalability of the green logistics technologies. Proper data governance mechanisms should hence be trade off in privacy protection and systemic requirements of data mobility required to have sustainable trade infrastructure (K&L Gates, 2023).

The impact of sustainability goes beyond individual logistics operators to the trade corridors on a regional level. The disjointed governance of data along the India-Middle East-Europe Economic Corridor (IMEEC) - one of the key projects of the G20 New Delhi Declaration - can hamper AI-enhanced emissions monitoring and green logistics compliance in various jurisdictions involved into the program. Such alignment of data governance frameworks is an imperative of trade policies and climate governance rather than a technical issue (UNECE, 2024).

5. INDIA'S DPDP ACT, 2023: STATUTORY ANALYSIS AND COMPLIANCE IMPLICATIONS

India Digital Personal Data Protection Act, 2023, is a historic in the history of legislations of the governments regarding personal data. Although providing a vast array of rights-based data protection architecture, the architecture of the cross-border data transfer system provided by the Act comes with a lot of issues concerning predictability of the legal aspects, regulation of predictability, and practicality of the AI-based logistic systems (TrustArc, 2024).

5.1 Legislative Objectives and Governance Philosophy

The most important law-based groundwork of the processing of personal data is individual consent. The data protection through consent is a model of DPDP Act and therefore the most significant law. It is a practice that does not violate privacy standards practiced on a global scale, but on the other hand, it significantly vests a lot of regulatory authority on the executive (Fieganbaum Solutions, 2025). The Central Government enjoys wide freedom of exemptions in the sector, establish minor regulations and determine what the jurisdictions of cross-border data transfer are. The normative-right and normative-executive model of regulation are established by this kind of government.

The institutional level of the Act has instituted the Data Protection Board of India whose functions are mostly adjudicatory. Nevertheless, the lack of a regulatory authority that would be compulsive in developing its own regulations is an obstacle to developing special purpose compliance standards in the technologically advanced industries like AI-based logistics. The Act also fails to entrench the principles of constitutional proportionality or necessity as principles of operational decision-making in form which could limit the check of rights balancing in judicial executive regulatory action.

The governance structure of the DPDP Act has a direct bearing on the trade facilitation obligations of India under the WTO Trade Facilitation Agreement (TFA) which obligates the expedited customs procedures and electronic data exchange between the customs administrations. The restrictions on data localization or random transfer prescribed by the DPDP model may contradict Article 10 of the TFA in which the processing of information related to trade should be carried out prior to arrival. The compliance requirements of India with the TFA thus present another normative framework to formulating the cross-border data transfer regime of the DPDP Act operationally consistent with digital custom and trade facilitation system (Ciuriak et al., 2023).

5.2 Cross-Border Data Transfer Architecture

DPDP Act also allows cross-border transfer of personal data, but subject to restrictions, which are specified by the government in respect of particular jurisdictions. Unlike this framework that seems to be liberal in theory, individuals lack a systematic review of adequacy and transparency in regulation in identification of constrained jurisdictions.

DPDP does not presuppose the homogeneity of the criteria of evaluating legal protection or institutional regulation or surveillance provisions in destination countries as is the case with GDPR adequacy regime (Burri and Kugler, 2024). The Act also lacks standardised transfer instruments which are in existence at the time e.g. Standard Contractual Clauses or Binding Corporate Rules. This trade gap poses regulatory problems to multinational logistics business ventures which are based on intra-group transfer and assimilation of supply chain across the borders. This would require firms to have a fragmented and mosaic compliance policy, which exposes them to more regulatory risk and higher transaction cost.

It is also important to note that the compliance problems have also been noted to arise in other jurisdictions. In the Schrems II case decision, indicatively, the European multinational companies were highly disrupted in their compliance initiatives, due to an uncertainty on their data transfer activities under the GDPR. On the same note, LGPD in Brazil and data localisation systems in China have cross-border data constraints that are sector-specific and this proves that the issue of cross-border data regulation is not Indian-specific one.

Under ESG governance, there is uncertainty amongst multinational logistics operators that are required to report Scope 3 supply chain emissions in the frameworks of GRI 305 or the CDP Supply Chain program due to the lack of standardised cross-border transfer mechanisms under the DPDP Act. Integrated emissions reporting necessitates legal processing and transfers of operational and environmental information of suppliers, transport operators and logistics agents in various jurisdictions. Reputational and compliance risks of public listed logistics operators may arise due to regulatory uncertainty regarding the legality of data transfer due to the compromise of the integrity and comparability of ESG disclosures (Hettler et al., 2024).

5.3 Legal Uncertainty and Compliance Burdens

The lack of the adequacy evaluation criteria, the discretion of the executive, and the non-presence of the standardised transfer protective measures, puts the multinational logistics operators under a lot of regulatory uncertainty. Companies implementing AI-based logistics cannot be confident in the long-term that cross-border data transfer is accepted, especially in the cases where the activities involve the actions in a regulatory jurisdiction in more than one country.

These signs of regulatory uncertainty incidents within the industry are the proof that a few multinational logistics companies have resorted to data localisation policy or information-processing fragmentation. Although such strategies decrease the exposure to compliance, they affect the performance of AI and optimisation of sustainability. According to the studies, predictive analytics might not be as accurate in integrated logistics networks, up to 12 percent of predictive analytics in the case of decentralised data structure, which limits the opportunities to optimise emissions (Ciuriak & Fay, 2024).

These results suggest that compliance strategies with a high level of risks can unintentionally elude technological change and uptake of sustainability. As a result, the DPDP Act is an illustration of how the data protection regimes that lack well-tuning to their technological and environmental factuality can subvert the sustainable logistics governance innovation unintentionally.

6. COMPARATIVE INTERNATIONAL DATA TRANSFER REGIMES

The factors that determine the viability, scalability and sustainability of the AI-powered global logistics systems are the cross-border data transfer regimes. The data flows are no longer the support components of the trade in the context of the current supply chains but since they are the core infrastructure of which predictive analytics, real-time tracking, automated customs clearance, and emissions optimisation are developed (European Commission, 2021). Therefore, the discrepancies of the international systems of data governance directly influence the credibility of the AI-based logistics and decarbonisation goal of AI, in general.

In this case, they provide analogies with some of the most well-known international data transfer frameworks and review the Digital Personal Data Protection Act, 2023 (DPDP Act) of India in the context of the ever-varying global regulation landscape (Eyo-Udo, 2024). Comparative model unveils that within the framework of the increasing reliance of the established jurisdictions on the data protection as the phenomenon of trusted data flows, the regulation habit in the Indian context is largely normatively ambiguous and highly executive discretionary.

In this chapter we conceptualise the clarity to achieve AI-based logistics by dividing the three functional levels of risks:

- Major risk AI applications - warehouse automation analytics, route optimisation application, fuel consumption prediction.
- Medium risk AI applications- predictive demand modelling, real time shipment monitoring systems.
- Unsafe AI implementation - autonomous freight scheduling, computerization of customs, which is associated with individual and commercial information, and integration systems across jurisdictions data.

This categorization reveals that the regulatory stability is becoming a critical problem in a gradual manner in case the data sensitivity and the degree of automation increase.

6.1 GDPR Adequacy and Structured Safeguards

The most institutionalized and broadest document on the regulation of using personal data transfer between the countries is the General Data Protection Regulation (GDPR) of the European Union. Articles 44-49 imply a gradual system of compliance, and even the latter will not allow transferring data to third countries unless they offer the same or even better standard of protection as one ensured within the EU (European Commission, 2021).

This may be determined by the parallelism shown below:

- Standard Contractual clauses (SCCs).
- There are some Binding Corporate Rules (BCRs) that are binding.
- Decisions of adequacy of the European Commission are formal

Clearly normative character of the GDPR and effective judicial control has become its characteristic feature of power. The principles of adequacy are founded on the publicly debated principles, i.e. rule-of-legal principles, defence of fundamental rights, implementation means and access to judicial redress. It should be mentioned that the power of such executive determinations can be re-examined by the Court of Justice of the European Union (CJEU) as well, and, thus, restrict regulatory discretion due to constitutional accountability (UNECE, 2024). Even the practice of jurisprudence that arose due to the Schrems litigation especially Schrems II, made the governance of transfer of GDPR even stronger. One of the demands of Transfer Impact Assessments provided by CJEU is to assess the efficiency of safeguards in practice in the context of the practice of foreign surveillance (Balboni and Francis, 2023). This will be needed to make the compliance more difficult, but increase the overall trust in EU data governance.

The AI-based sustainable logistics has a relatively stable legal framework as the protection guaranteed by GDPR is well-structured. With harmonised contractual and organisational protection, the multinational logistics operators will be able to implement ongoing information flows required to implement the forecasts of emissions, ESG disclosure and supply chain optimisation. Although the concept of sustainability is rather vaguely defined, as a GDPR goal, regulatory certainty indirectly enables efficient logistics to flow in the environment, by alleviating the pressure of fragmentation and localisation on compliance (EDPB, 2021).

However, not only implementation issues are related to GDPR. The small logistics companies are also vulnerable to paying compliance fees, renewing of SCC contracts may lead to delays in an operation and sufficiency evaluation may be subject to geopolitical factors. All these issues reinforce an argument that even advanced regulatory regimes cannot cross over the issues to implementation which, in its turn, allows concluding that comparative analysis process must be conducted in unison

6.2 OECD and APEC Models: Interoperability-Focused Governance

The OECD Privacy Guidelines and the APEC Cross-Border Privacy Rules (CBPR) system assume the soft-law/trade-facilitative system of governance in comparison with rights-oriented GDPR model. OECD model has the issue of interoperability, accountability, proportionality and economic efficiency and accepts that overly restricting data will be a deterrent to both innovation and inter-border trade.

The principles of APEC CBPR system are applied by implementing a certification based system in which the respective enterprises pledge the minimum privacy standards by being subject to scrutiny by the assigned responsible agencies. The system is used especially in multi-jurisdictional supply chains that are complex as it minimizes the regulatory fragmentation and business can prove as it has adhered to the system as it is and no single approval is given to a jurisdictions by the system (OECD, 2022).

These frameworks are not binding yet flexible and this is the biggest weakness as it does not have a judicial check. However, the OECD and APEC paradigms in AI-based logistics is a good trade-off between data privacy and flexibility of operation (Hettler et al., 2024). The fact that the international logistics networks requires the continuous real-time optimisation and minimisation of emissions is also consistent with their interoperability orientation.The frameworks though only have an indirect role in the objectives of sustainability. The environmental, social and governance (ESG) issues too are mostly on the periphery and as such, they lack efficiency in the handling of the entire sustainable logistics governance.

6.3 Emerging Comparative Models: Singapore, China, and Brazil

The recent regulatory trends in the international sphere suggest that the approach to escaping the mentality of data sovereignty versus digital trade can take a variety of forms.

The Personal Data Protection Act (PDPA) of Singapore talks about pragmatic interoperability. The transfers across the borders are allowed with contractual forces that are enforceable by law and provide similar protection rates. Singapore will combine trade promotion and information security and provide a hybrid regime that facilitates innovation in AI regarding logistics.

Personal Information Protection Law (PIPL) of China is a sovereignty-based model that also presupposes high localisation and security checks rate of the data transfer to the outside. The PIPL system has compliance barriers to multinational logistics networks based on integrated world information systems since it promotes national control.

Brazil's General Data Protection Law (LGPD) follows the examples of the inspirational approach of the GDPR, but is more flexible with additional provisions of administrative guidelines. The Brazilian framework is typified by the conflict of the emerging economy in trying to strike a balance between the interoperability internationally and regulation nationally.

In addition to Singapore, China, and Brazil, South Africa, Indonesia, and Vietnam data governance experiences are other comparative sources of information that can offer India a point of reference. The Protection of Personal Information Act (POPIA) of South Africa has a risk-based adequacy model that is consistent with the general concepts of GDPR but allows trade-facilitative data processing to have sectoral exemptions. The Personal Data Protection Law (2022) of Indonesia contains an agreement on the government-monitored transfer cross-border agreements aimed at balancing the sovereignty with online trade integration. The Cybersecurity Law in Vietnam also similarly requires data localisation on some of the critical sectors but allows transfers subject to regulation. These comparative experiences underscore that emerging economies are converging to hybrid forms of governance that blend the data control of sovereignty with pragmatic accommodation of international trade and logistics needs - a direction that the DPDP implemented rules in India may be useful in following (Bradford, 2023).

As the comparative systems reveal, there is not the Indian problem but the global problem, i.e., the problem of regulatory tensions which are present between the sovereignty, trade facilitation and sustainability

6.4 India's Normative Divergence and DPDP Implementation Status

The Indian DPDP Act, 2023 perceives the data transfer across the borders in a different manner. Section 16 authorizes transfer of default of the international information but these cases are restricted by reporting them to the constrained jurisdictions by the Central Government. The Act, however, does not have any substantive adequacy requirements in place, or procedural protection or systematic review procedures in place. Moreover, it does not attach importance to the existing transfer tools like SCCs, BCRs or certification based systems (Maume, 2023). Policies in all aspects of measuring the variables of transfers across the borders are comprehensive in policy that is yet to be adopted. Even though the negative-list approach has been demonstrated by the government towards the limited jurisdiction, absence of operating guidelines leaves the regulations in uncertainty.

It is a type of executive model and poses a great degree of uncertainty to the AI-driven logistics operators. The automated data flows in large volumes and continuous nature of risky AI systems are a challenge to the compliance planning (Holloway, 2024). India poses a threat to the normative difference of the global data ecosystems in terms of digital trade. This uncertainty in regulation can thus compromise the decarbonisation technologies made possible by the AIs which will be founded on the availability of international data.

In the future, the regulatory path illustrated in India indicates that there will be a slow integration with the international digital trade standards, as long as it is conditional to domestic political economy factors. The active involvement of the Indian government in the negotiations of WTO Joint Statement Initiative along with bilateral agreements on digital economy with the United States (iCET framework), the United Kingdom and the UAE form institutional incentives to the increased regulatory transparency of the cross-border data governance. With the implementation of rules under the DPDP Act gradually publicized, one might anticipate that the government will assume a negative-list adequacy model - defining limited jurisdictions as opposed to listed ones - with sector-specific frameworks of transfer in critical infrastructure, logistics, and financial services. This direction, aligned with WTO digital trade disciplines and international interoperability standards, would decrease the uncertainty of compliance among AI-driven logistics operators and would help India to become a part of sustainable digital trade corridors (Liu, Gang, Yu, and Zhang, 2022).

Table 1. Comparative Analysis of Cross-Border Data Transfer Frameworks

Jurisdiction	Transfer Mechanism	Legal Certainty	AI Compatibility	Sustainability Alignment
European Union (GDPR)	Adequacy decisions; Standard Contractual Clauses (SCCs); Binding Corporate Rules (BCRs)	High	Moderate–High	Emerging
OECD Privacy Framework	Interoperability- and accountability-based principles (non-binding)	Medium	Medium	Indirect
APEC CBPR System	Certification-based accountability and organizational compliance framework	Medium	Medium	Indirect
India (DPDP Act, 2023)	Executive notification model with discretionary restrictions on cross-border transfers	Low	Low	Weak

7. JUDICIAL INTERVENTION AND TRANSNATIONAL DATA GOVERNANCE: DOCTRINAL AND PRACTICAL ANALYSIS

The interface between the state regulation and individual rights, as well as international flows of data, is shaped by judicial institutions more and more. Courts have perceived data governance as not just a technical regulation issue, but as a constitutional, economic and trade-related issue with significant implications to digital supply chains and technological innovation (Körner et al., 2025).

7.1 Justice K.S. Puttaswamy v. Union of India

The Supreme Court of India acknowledged privacy as a basic constitutional right based on personal liberty and human dignity in the case of Justice K.S. Puttaswamy (Retd.) v. Union of India. The court decision provided the conceptual framework that obliges the state data governance activities to comply with the requirements of legality, necessity, and proportionality.

The Court pointed out that the executive intrusion into informational privacy should be justified by a clear statutory authorisation and be followed by the procedural protection (Burri and Kugler, 2024). The implementation of these concepts to DPDP Act gives great constitutional concerns. General executive authority to limit international transfers without clear conditions or reviewing mechanisms might not pass proportionality tests especially when existent limitations to legitimate commercial transactions or public-interest AI uses to sustain environmental sustainability and efficiency in trade.

7.2 Schrems II and Global Data Transfer Accountability

The Schrems II case by the CJEU is a transnational data regulation historical precedent. The nullification of the EU-US Privacy Shield enabled the Court to repeat the point that the adequacy test should be applied in a substance-based manner by considering the institutional safeguards and not on the informal regulatory commitments.

The decision posed an increased burden on regulators and non-governmental participants in that they would have to constantly review the legal systems of third countries. The decision, regarding international logistics and AI, points to the vulnerability of centralised data processing models to the issue of regulatory divergence in particular in the jurisdictions with strong surveillance regimes and weak institutional protection (Körner et al., 2025).

7.3 Practical Lessons from Schrems II for AI-Driven Logistics Governance

Factual Context

Schrems II was a case against Facebook since it had been transferring EU personal data to the United States through its Privacy Shield program. The applicant alleged that the surveillance authorities in the US had violated the adequate standards of data protection.

Judicial Reasoning

The Court found that adequacy imposes enforceable rights and workable institutional protections as opposed to token regulatory guarantees (Richey et al., 2023).

Although SCCs were sustained, the applicability of the same was conditional on risk measurements provided by data exporters.

Operational Implications for AI Logistics

The decision brings into the limelight the fact that cross-border data outages can have a direct impact on AI-enabled efficiency of the supply chain. International data flows interruption may:

- Minimize predictive analytics performance.
- Break the real time monitoring of emissions.
- Put off automated route optimisation.
- Increase use of operating fuel.

7.4 Empirical and Industry Illustrations

The relationship between data governance and logistics sustainability has the empirical evidence of recent changes in the industry.

Data Transfer Disruption in the EU-US

After Schrems II, a number of logistics providers suffered compliance delays in the course of re-organizing the transfer mechanisms. Reporting in the industry shows that there are short-term inefficiencies in operations and high administrative expenses related to compliance reorganization (Balboni & Francis, 2023).

Smart Freight Systems with AI-Based Emission Reduction

Multinational freight operators that have deployed AI-driven route optimisation platforms have shown a range of fuel savings (between 8–15 percent) which further shows that uninterrupted cross-border data analytics benefits the environment (European Commission, 2021).

APEC CBPR-Certified Supply Chain Networks

The engagement of logistics firms that were implemented on the CBPR models also claimed better cross-border data interoperability and reduced time spent on compliance processing and reflected the positive effect of harmonised governance models in their activities (Hettler et al., 2024).

7.5 ESG Dimensions of Data Governance

Despite the fact that the existing regulatory discourses are very carbon emissions-based, the problem of sustainable logistics governance would entail a broader incorporation of ESG:

Environment: Emissions monitoring using AI, fuel optimisation, and supply chains that are energy efficient:

Social: Data protection structures engage with labour law by defining the extent to which AI-based workforce management, automated scheduling, and biometric access control in the logistics process can be allowed. According to international labor standards, such as ILO Convention No. 190 on violence and harassment, and the ILO principles on digital labour platforms, the rights of workers to data security against intrusive algorithmic surveillance are intact. The cross-border data transfer of workforce data should thus be in compliance with both data protection regulation and other provisions of labour law. Ethics requirements in supply chains, like transparency reporting under the UK Modern Slavery Act and compulsory human rights due diligence under the EU Corporate Sustainability Due Diligence Directive, also necessitate the legal processing of supplier and workforce information across borders (Richey et al., 2023).

Governance: Open information systems will enhance corporate accountability, regulatory and investor trust.

7.6 Regulatory Interoperability as a Compliance Mechanism

The regulatory interoperability may take the shape of mutual adequacy recognition, inter-jurisdictional certification system, standard instruments of compliance contracts and international standards of sustainability data disclosure. These mechanisms allow AI-based logistics systems to be operationally coherent across jurisdictions without being regulatory-dispersed, and have strong privacy-guaranteed mechanisms.

8. DETAILED LEGAL CASE STUDY

8.1 Case Study: Schrems II and Its Lessons for AI-Driven Logistics Governance

8.1.1 Factual Matrix

The issue of transfer of the personal information of the EU to the United States via Facebook Privacy Shield led to the case of Schrems II being initiated. The applicant cited a concern over the sufficiency of the US data protection in the perception of such extensive surveillance capability of intelligence agencies.

8.2.1 Legal Issues

Whether the Privacy Shield ensured an essentially similar level of protection, whether SCCs could counter insufficiencies of third-country law, and whether fundamental rights were owed by private actors in cross-country transfers were the key questions before the CJEU.

8.3.1 Arguments and Judicial Reasoning

The Court believed that adequacy did not mean that the promises had to be solely formal but rather had to be efficient and working rights (Richey et al., 2023). The SCCs have been supported in theory but their sanity was conditional on risk-contextual assessments. Such an argument is an indication of the change in formality compliance to functional protection, and its consequences on the industries dependent on AI are monumental.

8.4.1 Implications for AI-Based Supply Chains

The decision, as observed in the case of AI-based logistics, shows how weak data-intensive architectures are as far as regulatory risk is concerned. Interruptions in cross-border data may disrupt predictive analytics, real-time optimisation and emissions monitoring, and sabotage sustainability goals.

8.5.1 Applicability to India's DPDP Framework

The Schrems II case has brought up the importance of the existence of transparent adequacy standards, institutional control and joint responsibility. Introducing these principles into the Indian DPDP paradigm would improve its constitutional capacity, the regulatory confidence, and help India to be integrated into AI-enhanced, low-carbon global logistical systems.

8.6.1 Case Illustration: AI-Enabled Customs and Logistics in India — JNPT and ICEGATE

Factual Context

A domestic example of AI-controlled logistics governance can be found in Jawaharlal Nehru Port Trust (JNPT) in Maharashtra and the Indian Customs Electronic

Data Interchange Gateway (ICEGATE). JNPT has already implemented container tracking and risk evaluation systems, combined with international shipping operators platform, which necessitates the exchange of real-time shipment and individual information with foreign logistics partners. ICEGATE handles customs declarations with data of importers, exporters and freight forwarders across jurisdictions.

Regulatory Significance

The cross-border transfer framework of the DPDP Act has a direct impact on data transfers in the legality of data transactions between them with foreign logistics equivalents. Without explicit adequacy tests or standardised transfer tools, system operators have a grey area in compliance on which jurisdictions are trusted destinations and whether current data sharing agreements with foreign customs administrations are still legal under the new regime.

Lessons for Policy

The urgency of the regulatory reform suggestions in Section 10 is practical, as evident in this case. A predictable and transparent cross-border data governance regime should support customs and logistics systems that support India in her commitments of trade facilitation under the WTO TFA (Ciuriak et al., 2023).

9. DATA GOVERNANCE, AI, AND DECARBONIZATION: REGULATORY MISALIGNMENTS

Regulation uniformity of data protection and trade facilitation norms and climate governance objectives plays a vital role in the functionality of AI-based sustainable logistics systems (Balboni and Francis, 2023). The current logistics systems are getting increasingly dependent on the real-time trans-national information sharing that supports the predictive analytics, emissions measurement, and automatization of the supply chains. Nonetheless, contemporary data governance models, especially those implementing discretionary or fragmented strategies to cross-border data transfers, often overlook the environmental externalities that arise because of the design of regulations.

An illustration of this regulatory imbalance in guaranteeing the sovereign control of the data flows, not necessarily adapting to the operational realities of AI-based low-carbon logistics ecosystems in their entirety, is the Digital Personal Data Protection Act, 2023 (DPDP Act) of India. As of the start of 2026, the DPDP Act is already in force, but some of its regulations remain in the stage of regulation development, in particular, the ones related to the mechanisms of cross-border transfers and the criteria of adequacy assessment (High, 2022). This regulatory uncertainty presents compliance ambiguity to multinational logistic operators using real-time global data integration.

Here, the author talks about this sector where limitations or imprecision in the regulation of data transfer may threaten the optimality of AI, distortion of ESG systems, and establishment of normative contradictions between the trade law and climate requirements.

Figure 2. Regulatory Impact Pathway – Data Restrictions and Carbon Inefficiency

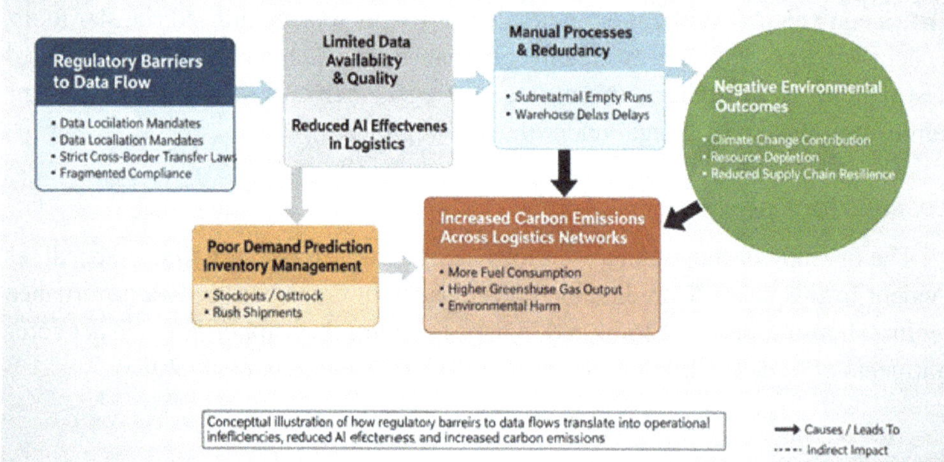

The conceptual representation in Figure 2 shows that regulatory barriers of data flows become operational inefficiencies, decreased AI functionality, and augmented carbon emissions in logistics networks.

9.1 Disruption of AI Optimization

The logistics AI systems highly depend on the enormous and real-time merging of cross-country information. These systems comprise optimization algorithms of routes, predictive maintenance models, simulations of a digital twin supply chain, and autonomous fleet management systems.

Different technologies have a wide difference in the regulatory risk and sensitivity of data. Applications of AI that are high-risk, such as autonomous vehicle coordination, require an ongoing personal and operational data fusion, and less risky AI applications, such as warehouse energy optimization systems, generally work with anonymized operational data.The uncertainty in regulation concerning the cross-border data transfers in the DPDP Act can interfere with these AI systems, as it will force companies to localize the data processing, fragment the datasets or resort to redundant compliance infrastructure (Bradford, 2023). Scattered datasets reduce predictive accuracy and lead to sub-optimality in the routing, fuel wastage, and idle time in ports, warehouses and transportation routes.

The impact is supported by empirical data of the global logistics firms (Ghaffari and Kimiagari, 2023). An example is that multinational shipping organizations reported that the localization of data in at least some jurisdictions can cause quantifiable inefficiencies, including delays in predictive maintenance planning and 3-7 percent increase in operational fuel consumption due to incomplete AI routing data sets. Similarly, digital merging of European logistics corridors also demonstrates that the co-ordinated cross-border data transfer models have resulted in measurable reductions in the level of fleet emissions through the joint model of route optimization and predictive demand models (Richey et al., 2023).

The DPDP Act lacks a well-written system of assessment similar to that of the GDPR Standard Contractual Clauses (SCCs) and adequacy decisions, but relies on executive notifications. As a result, the data protection law, which is aimed at protecting the rights of individuals, can even unintentionally interfere with technologies aimed at decreasing emissions and increasing the sustainability of logistics.

9.2 ESG Reporting and Emissions Accounting Failures

The Environmental, Social and Governance (ESG) compliance has become a fundamental regulatory and contractual law of large international logistician companies. ESG reporting is becoming more and more based on AI-powered analytics that combine data between jurisdictions, vendors, and transport hubs to quantify Scope 1, Scope 2, and Scope 3 emissions (Bhandari and Singh, 2023).Lacking unified cross-border data governance may decrease the integrity of ESG reporting in a number of ways: missing emissions of pollutants, late sustainability reporting, lack of uniform methodologies of measurement in jurisdictions, and reduced visibility into coordinator compliance control.

The increasing requirements of the formal ESG reporting frameworks are to have logistics operators disclose supply chain emissions and social performance metrics based on consolidated cross-jurisdictional data. GRI 305 standard necessitates reporting of Scope 1, 2 and 3 greenhouse gases with Scope 3 largely reliant on supplier-based data aggregation across borders. The SASB Road Transportation and Air Freight and Logistics standards also mandate standardised disclosures of sustainability, which rely on harmonised cross-border disclosures. Disruption of data transfer governance may compromise the credibility and auditing of an organisation to make credible and verifiable ESG disclosures, creating investor relations risks and possible liability under compulsory disclosure regimes like the EU Corporate Sustainability Reporting Directive (CSRD) (Hettler et al., 2024).

Besides the spheres of environmental measures, social sustainability measures implemented in ESG compliance also comprised labour rights and supply chain disclosure and data integration of occupational safety. Governance includes aspects of corporate responsibility, regulatory transparency and compliance audit systems. Additional effects that limits on data transfer policies may have on the long-term sustainability governance are thus possible, in addition to carbon accounting.An example of this is the case of logistics operators utilizing Southeast Asian networks in which they reported that there were major compliance problems when attempting to integrate worker safety and emissions reporting information across multiple jurisdictions that are regulated under various data transfer regulations. These disjointed compliance requirements increased the cost of reporting, and minimized the effectiveness of the sustainability reporting. The existing provisions that the DPDP Act has made regarding AI are minimal and narrow with references to data processing as concerned with sustainability. This regulatory ambiguity complicates the compliance process because the organizations are not aware of how the data on operational emissions, vendor data, and personal workforce information can be processed and transferred across jurisdictions and in a legal manner.

Comparatively, digital regulation is being coupled with sustainability reporting requirements in new global regulatory trends, particularly in the European Union, which is reflective of the growing awareness that data governance frameworks must be applied to complement climate accountability frameworks, but not restrict them (Burri & Kugler, 2024).

9.3 Trade Law vs Climate Commitments

The regulatory controversy between data protection and international trade has a direct impact on climate governance. Liberalization of data is emerging as a requirement and a new area of WTO talks and digital trade agreements since it is the sole means to have efficient and sustainable global trade systems (Ciuriak et al., 2023).

Bans on AI-based logistics because of localization of data or even discretionary exchange may lead to the unintentional increase of the carbon-intensive trade business by the destabilization of digitally-managed supply chains. This presents a kind of regulatory paradox: states are pursuing lofty climate goals and at the same time taking up data governance models that limit technologies that can fulfill these goals.

Although the Indian DPDP framework portrays valid interests in the areas of data sovereignty and protection of data privacy, the same conflicting regulation is evident in each of the other nations in the world. Indicatively, the European Union struggles to run the GDPR and the cross-border digital trade requirements in line with the Schrems II decision. The Personal Data Protection Act of Singapore has been keen on ensuring interoperability in the country although it still requires data transfer protection in the high-risk sectors. The Chinese Personal Information Protection Law (PIPL) has a tight data export security assessment that has an effect on the coordination of logistical operations of multinational corporations. The General Data Protection Law (LGPD) in Brazil contains the aspects of adequacy and contractual transfer but still faces an issue of the consistency of the enforcement. Such comparative experiences demonstrate that regulatory fragmentation is not an India-only problem but also a broader issue across the world of reconciling data sovereignty and sustainable trade integration.

Disciplines on cross-border data flows as a part of digital trade governance are explicitly considered in the 2022 Work Programme on e-commerce by the WTO and in the ongoing negotiations of the Joint Statement Initiative. The members of WTO who are promoting the role of data flow provisions in trade agreements, such as the Comprehensive and Progressive Agreement on Trans-Pacific Partnership (CPTPP), the Digital Economy Partnership Agreement (DEPA), and the Australia-Singapore Digital Economy Agreement, point out that trade-distortive effects of restrictions to cross-border data flows are similar to those of tariff barriers on goods (WTO, The current version of the DPDP Act in India may be objected because it is not a tariff measure, and is therefore contrary to the digital trade disciplines in bilateral and plurilateral agreements that India is or may join. It is thus a regulatory, as well as a trade policy priority to design the DPDP cross-border transfer framework with an understanding of such implications of the trade law.

9.4 Implementation Status of the Digital Personal Data Protection Act, 2023

The Digital Personal Data Protection Act, 2023 is the paradigm shift in the Indian system of data governance, in the sense that it establishes an inclusive legislative framework of data protection of personal data and regulation on the cross-border transfer of data. But the working effectiveness of the Act is open to the issue of the announcement of detailed subordinate regulations and administrative directions. The DPDP Act to date provides a broad statutory framework, which extensively relies on executive notifications to specify the list of trusted jurisdictions, the transfer protection measures, and compliance necessities of data fiduciaries.This is transitional regulatory risk, particularly to multinational logistics and supply chain business which depends on real-time and continuous cross-border data flows. The precise applicability of this uncertainty to AI-based logistics systems is that it is founded on integrated data on activities, environmental situations, and transportation across various jurisdictions. Without adequacy assessment processes that are systematically written or standard contractual transfer systems, logistics operators have to use internal compliance risk assessment models, which may result in increased operations costs and complexity of compliance (Matthan, 2023; Bradford, 2023).

The international regulation frameworks such as the General Data Protection Regulation (GDPR) of the European Union put the cross-border data transfers into practice by way of detailed adequacy assessment framework, Standard Contractual Clauses (SCCs), and Binding Corporate Rules (BCRs). These give regulatory assurance and predictability to global logistics operators. On the other hand, the DPDP regime in India is still in the phase of regulation transition whereby it is expected that procedural clarity shall be achieved as a part of the delegated rule-making processes. Until these implementing rules are completely notified, AI-enabled cross-border logistics activities in India are exposed to an interpretative uncertainty, which may indirectly affect the outcomes of technological innovation and optimization of sustainability.

9.5 Empirical Evidence on AI-Driven Sustainable Logistics

9.5.1 AI-Based Route Optimization and Emission Reduction

Empirical studies demonstrate that AI-based logistics optimization systems exhibit a significant reduction in transportation emissions in case they are supported by cross-country data ecosystems. Logistics companies all over the world have installed AI-powered systems of route optimization on the basis of real-time traffic analytics, information about the functioning of warehouses, and environmental observations programs. These AI systems dynamically re-optimize the route of delivery, reduce the amount of downtime, and optimize the use of vehicles.

It is also discovered that AI-based logistic optimization systems have demonstrated a decrease in emissions of 15-25 percent through fuel consumption reduction and a higher route efficiency (Richey et al., 2023). The multi-jurisdictional data, including customs clearance data, weather analytics, cargo tracking data, and transportation infrastructure data, is needed to achieve the functionality of these systems. The lack of coordinated analytics models due to disjointed information control or transfer restrictions across borders may cause such coordinated analytics models to break down, resulting in unproductive routing decisions and increased carbon intensity in supply chain operations (Cha & Koo, 2020).

9.5.2 Predictive Maintenance and Energy Efficiency in Transportation Systems

One more empirical example of using AI to improve the sustainability of AI-based logistics infrastructure is predictive maintenance technologies. Sensors using AI to monitor maritime transportation ships, aircraft logistics and rail transportation networks allow the analysis of equipment in real time and reveal mechanical inefficiency in the initial stages of its formation. The study in the maritime logistics industry demonstrates that anticipatory maintenance would save approximately 10-20 percent of the fuel and equipment downtime through the anticipation of maintenance planning and re-calibration of the operations (Jia et al., 2021).

These predictive systems are used to implement continuous cross-border transfer of operational data of sensor-based operation. Data locality or fragmentary transfer regimes can impair predictive modelling accuracy and, depending on this, may also increase energy consumption and inefficiency in the transportation networks.

9.5.3 AI-Integrated ESG Reporting and Scope-3 Emission Tracking

The compliance of Environmental, Social, and Governance (ESG) is also becoming dependent on AI-powered systems of emissions accounting particularly, Scope-3 supply-chain emissions, which refer to emissions by third-party suppliers in more than one jurisdiction. Empirical-based supply chain analytics, which is an integrated AI, can improve the precision of the emission reporting by nearly 30 percent to that of the traditional approaches (Bhandari and Singh, 2023).

However, the constraints of data transfer across countries may impact on the quality of reporting and integrity of data. Fragmented data governance regimes may result in a lack of consistency in sustainability reporting practices across jurisdictions, which impacts the regulatory exposure, reputational risk, and uncertainty in compliance of multinational logistics enterprises.

9.6 Comparative Cross-Jurisdictional Data Governance Models

Although the sovereign data governance priorities have been identified in the DPDP Act of India, the regulatory concerns that data protection and enabling digital trade are a global governance challenge. The European Union GDPR provides a systematic transfer procedures and continues to face operational compliance problems following the Schrems II case, in particular, regarding the sustainability of adequacy and transfer impact assessment overheads (Van Ooijen and Vrabec, 2019).

The Personal Data Protection Act in Singapore is, relatively speaking, facilitative in nature with its emphasis on transfer processes across boundaries which are accountability based. Organizations can also prove the same degree of privacy protection through the provision of compliance systems in the form of contracts and the certification based on accountability (Bertoni, 2020). The model is less restrictive to the regulation without undermining the privacy protection standards, which makes it possible to effectively send the logistics data cross-border (Burri and Kugler, 2024).

Similarly, the Personal Information Protection Law of China implies stringent conditions of data localization to the operators of the critical infrastructure, but also has a conditional procedure of security evaluation permitting controlled cross-border data transfer. The General Data Protection Law of Brazil adheres to a hybrid model of governance that is a combination of adequacy based assessment of jurisdiction as well as a framework of contractual protection. These comparative regulatory approaches indicate that there is nothing unique about India and data sovereignty-facilitating digital trade that is a global regulatory problem.

9.7 Risk-Based Classification of AI Applications in Logistics

AI applications implemented in logistics ecosystems present a large range of regulatory risk exposure and sensitivity of data. Risk-based classification model can assist the regulators strike a balance between the objectives of ensuring sustainability, privacy protection and technological innovation.The low-risk AI applications are operation optimization technologies (such as warehouse robots, inventory optimization, and route optimization algorithms) are low-risk. The systems are primarily founded on anonymized or aggregated operational datasets, and typically pose minimal risk of exposure of personal data.

Predictive maintenance analytics, workforce scheduling systems and supply chain demand forecasting systems are moderate-risk AI applications. These technologies partly handle personal or operational data and therefore, need to have enhanced data reduction policies and accountability measures. The biometric workforce monitoring and real-time employee monitoring systems, and behavioral analytics platforms are high-risk applications of AI that process sensitive personal data. These applications need to be subjected to more regulation, need to be impact assessed and be more transparent. Risk-based classification would ensure regulatory compliance is commensurate and enable the use of AI-based sustainability without undue compliance expenses.

9.8 Key Takeaways

Cross-border data governance is the key to sustainable logistics systems driven by AI. Uncertainty of regulations in cross-border transfers systems may disequilibrate the emissions optimization technologies, deter the quality of ESG reporting, as well as reduce the efficiency of global supply chains. International models of regulations show that a medium-level of solution is provided by interoperability-based governance between privacy protection and digital trade facilitation. The classification of AI governance based on risk and empirical validation of the sustainability outcomes also contribute to climate-aligned regulatory design. There must be a balance between the protection of privacy, the ease of trade and environment sustainability in terms of regulations integration.

Figure 3. Integrated Governance of AI, Data Protection, Trade, and Sustainability

The proposed mind map illustrates the supportive regulatory ecosystem that is mutually supporting to execute sustainable global logistics with Sustainable Logistics Governance in the centre. This governance model is the result of active interaction of various legal and technological planes and is applied to optimise, automate and minimise supply chain emissions. The working core is the AI systems that enable AI-supported, low-carbon logistics; any fragmentation at any of the nodes can lead to inefficiencies, and regulatory conflict.

10. POLICY AND REGULATORY REFORM FRAMEWORK

The cross border data governance in India requires systematic and principle oriented reform to create a balance between data protection of privacy and demands of digital trade, and decarbonization. The following roadmap shows the most critical loopholes in the regulatory provisions of the DPDP Act, and proposes certain legal and institutional solutions.

Table 2. Reform Roadmap for India's Cross-Border Data Governance

Reform Area	Existing Gap under DPDP Act, 2023	Proposed Legal / Regulatory Solution	Expected Impact on AI-Driven Sustainable Logistics
Adequacy Framework	Absence of defined criteria or procedural safeguards for determining "trusted" jurisdictions	Introduction of transparent, objective, and reviewable adequacy assessment standards aligned with global benchmarks (e.g., GDPR-inspired principles)	Enhanced legal certainty; increased confidence for cross-border data-dependent logistics operations
Cross-Border Transfer Mechanisms	Lack of standardized transfer instruments such as contractual or organizational safeguards	Formal recognition of Standard Contractual Clauses (SCCs), Binding Corporate Rules (BCRs), and certification-based mechanisms	Improved scalability and continuity of AI-enabled logistics systems across jurisdictions
AI-Specific Governance	No sector-specific or risk-based guidance on AI-driven data processing in logistics and supply chains	Adoption of risk-based AI governance frameworks aligned with sustainability and ESG objectives	Greater environmental efficiency through reliable AI optimization, emissions tracking, and reporting
International Regulatory Cooperation	Fragmented and ad hoc engagement in global digital trade and data governance initiatives	Participation in digital trade agreements, mutual recognition frameworks, and structured regulatory cooperation mechanisms	Facilitation of carbon-efficient global supply chains and development of low-emission logistics corridors

10.1 Transparent Adequacy and Review Mechanisms

Among the key reform points is the creation of transparent and publicly declared principles on the establishment of trusted jurisdictions (Matthan, 2023). Objective evaluation criteria like the privacy protection equivalence, performance capacity, and institutional accountability should be added in the determination of adequacy. The periodic review mechanism mechanisms are to create flexibility of regulation and cut executive discretion. Such alterations would make the logistics operators more predictable, and closer to the global data governance standards, the Indian framework.

10.2 Recognition of Interoperable Transfer Tools

Immediate compliance routes would be provided to multinational logistics companies based on the official endorsement of interoperable transfer systems such as Standard Contractual Clause, Binding Corporate Rules and certification-based transfer systems. These processes achieve regulatory interoperability of making legitimate data transfer and privacy protection. Transfer Impact Assessments and accountability-based compliance models could also be used to supplement risk management frameworks of cross-border AI systems.

10.3 AI-Specific Sustainability-Aligned Governance

As AI has already become a key ingredient of the emission reduction and optimization of logistics programs, AI-specific regulatory directives through risk-based classification should be applied in the DPDP framework. The regulatory standards should provide a boundary between the high-risk AI systems, which involve personal or behavioural-related data, medium-risk AI applications, which involve both operational and commercial data, and the sustainability optimization tools that have low risks, which are based on anonymized information. The imbalance in this risk-based AI governance would not restrict the advantages of the environmental technologies, but rather strike a balance between the data protection needs.

10.4 International Cooperation and Green Trade Corridors

Carbon-efficient global supply chains can be pillared by India active participation in digital trade and mutual regulatory recognition agreements. Specific pathways of reforms include:

(i) ASEANDigital Trade Corridor: India ought to negotiate a data governance interoperability during ASEAN-India free trade area negotiations, which builds on the ASEAN Model AI Governance Framework and ASEAN Digital Masterplan 2025.

(ii) IMEEC Data Governance Protocol: The India-Middle East-Europe Economic Corridor offers a chance to set up a multilateral data governance protocol to logistics and trade data, based on the common data spaces initiative within the EU.

(iii) WTO JSI Engagement: India must become part of the WTO Joint Statement Initiative on e-commerce with a proposal to create interoperability based data flow disciplines that would take into consideration the data sovereignty concerns of developing countries and allow it to facilitate sustainable digital trade.

(iv) GRI/SASB Alignment: DPDP should align the domestic ESG disclosure rules with the GRI, SASB criteria, and the rules should explicitly permit cross-border transmission of sustainability and emissions data which are necessary to report internationally recognised ESG (Bhandari and Singh, 2023).

10.5 Operationalizing Regulatory Interoperability

As a form of implementing regulatory interoperability rather than complete legal harmonization, institutional cooperation and compliance mechanisms of contracts can be employed. To reduce duplication of privacy protection protections to multinational logistics operators, the authorities can get into mutual recognition agreements that allow jurisdictions to recognize a similar privacy protection safeguard.

Development of transfer structures via certification provides standard compliance checks via sustainability audit and data governance audit structures. Also, regulatory sandbox settings enable logistics companies to pilot AI-enabled operational technologies in regulated compliance settings, which will enable responsible technological innovation (Barr, 2023). These work interoperability systems allow conducive regulatory avenues to balance the privacy protection with digital trade-facilitation and climate regulatory objectives.

11. CONTRIBUTION TO SCHOLARSHIP AND PRACTICE

This chapter contributes to the new interdisciplinary literature of AI governance, digital trade law, and sustainable logistics in three novel ways:

First, it develops an integrated analytical framework - never before systematically presented in the literature - that visualizes the causal interdependences between the data protection law, AI logistics infrastructure, facilitation of cross-border trade, and climate sustainability outcomes. This conceptualization goes beyond the traditional privacy law analysis to assert data governance as a determining variable in sustainable digital trade governance.

Second, it offers the initial systematic doctrinal and comparative examination of the cross-border data transfer architecture of the DPDP Act in the particulars of AI-enabled logistical systems, customs reform and regional trade integration. The main focus of previous research concerning the DPDP Act has been the privacy law or technology regulation approach; this chapter repackages the discussion in terms of trade facilitation law, ESG governance, and climate policy.

Thirdly, it suggests a reform agenda that responds to the identified regulatory gaps identified during the comparative and doctrinal analysis, i.e., the lack of adequacy assessment criteria, standardised transfer instruments, and AI-specific sustainability-mindful guidance, and puts the reforms into the context of Indian international trade and climate commitments (Balboni and Francis, 2023).

11.1 Academic Contribution

The Chapter adds to Interdisciplinary Scholarship in Three Key Aspects

To begin with, it creates an integrative analytical framework involving the connection of data protection regulation, AI regulation, and climate-oriented logistics regulation, which traditionally have been reviewed separately (Burri & Kugler, 2024). The paper demonstrates that AI-supported logistics systems, in particular, the ones that focus on optimization of emissions and efficiency of the supply chain are structurally dependent on cross-border data flows.

Second, the chapter expands the current literature on the nexus of digital trade environment by theorizing the cross-border data restrictions as regulatory frictions yielding measureable environmental externalities. A comparative analysis of data transfer regimes in the world like GDPR, OECD Privacy Guidelines and the APEC CBPR system can assist in realizing that different regulatory models can indirectly impede the operation of climate-efficient logistics.

Third, the chapter provides a normative analysis of the frameworks of discretionary data regulation within a new digital economy. The Indian constitutional jurisprudence-supported study, supported by comparative regulatory analysis, contributes to the rule-of-law discourse of technology regulation based on the ideas of legal certainty, proportionality, and accountability (Hettler et al., 2024).

11.2 Practitioner Contribution

The chapter can be of use to the legal practitioners, compliance professionals and policy-makers involved in the AI-driven relationships in logistics and in international trade operations.

It defines the compliance risks that are due to the regulatory uncertainties as per the DPDP Act particularly when it comes to the outbound data transfer. Since the research systematically reviews the gaps in the adequacy standards, transfer mechanisms, and AI-specific processing guidance, it can be utilized by practitioners to predict regulatory exposure and operational uncertainty (Balboni and Francis, 2023). The chapter also provides some comparative information on contracts and compliance in accordance with the world-approved frameworks, such as GDPR-approved transfer mechanisms, Transfer Impact Assessments and AI-based compliance governance. These insights inform organizations to form vendor contracts, AI service contracts, and intra-group transfer arrangements in various jurisdictions.

Finally, the research also has a value in the regulatory policy formulation as it demonstrates how the organization of interoperability and regulation of risk-based classifications can make the governance of data protection oriented towards sustainability.

12. CONCLUSION AND RECOMMENDATIONS

This chapter has also shown how the cross-border data governance is not just a privacy law issue but a determinant of sustainable digital trade, AI-enhanced logistics performance, customs reform, and regional trade integration.

Key Findings of This Chapter are as Follows

First, the DPDP Act, 2023 is a large legislative stride towards a comprehensive data protection in India, but the current model of cross-border transfer, in which the executive holds discretion, codified adequacy criteria are absent and the instruments of transfer are not standardized, leaves compliance questionable, which does not align with the performance demands of AI-driven, globally integrated logistics systems.

Second, this regulatory uncertainty has real environmental expenses. The continuous cross-border data flows are needed to support AI-based route optimisation, emissions monitoring, and predictive maintenance systems, which empirical evidence indicates can help cut logistics emissions by 15-25 percent. These sustainability technologies are directly affected by compliance-driven data fragmentation.

Third, the chapter lays down that the DPDP framework implicates the customs reform commitments of India under the WTO Trade Facilitation Agreement and integrates it into regional trade networks like the IMEEC and ASEANIndia digital logistics networks. The uncertainties in data governance along these corridors are a trade policy and climate governance question, rather than a domestic regulatory question.

Fourth, the comparative analysis establishes that regulatory fragmentation of cross-border data governance is a worldwide issue, yet jurisdictions that have implemented transparent and interoperability-based models, such as Singapore and some of the APEC members, experience a superior trade-off between data sovereignty, ESG sustainability results, and facilitating digital trade.

Based on these findings, the chapter makes three main recommendations: (i) transparent, objective adequacy assessment standards, which are regularly reviewed, should be codified under the DPDP framework in India in the form of standardised cross-border transfer instruments, such as SCCs and certification-based instruments; and (ii) AI-focused, sustainability-oriented regulatory guidance should be designed to ensure that the DPDP framework facilitates, and not

Going forward, the trends of India becoming more aligned with the WTO digital trade disciplines and international interoperability are promising as a more reliable way of developing a reformed DPDP cross-border transfer framework that benefits India as a data-sovereign emerging economy, a global trade partner, and a signatory to the Paris Agreement (Richey et al., 2023; Ciuriak et al., 2023; UNECE, 2024).

REFERENCES

Balboni, P., & Francis, K. (2023). *Data protection as a corporate social responsibility: Integrating privacy, cybersecurity and sustainability*. Edward Elgar Publishing., DOI: 10.4337/9781035314164

Barr, N. A. (2023). The evolution of substantive protection in EU international investment agreements: Taking stock of the EU's early Treaty-Making practice. *European Business Law Review*, *34*(3), 415–436. DOI: 10.54648/EULR2023025

Bertoni, E. (2020). Convention 108 and the GDPR: Trends and perspectives in Latin America. *Computer Law & Security Review*, *40*, 105516. DOI: 10.1016/j.clsr.2020.105516

Bhandari, V., & Singh, R. (2023). Understanding India's new data protection law. Carnegie Endowment for International Peace Working Paper. https://carnegieendowment.org/research/2023/10/understanding-indias-new-data-protection-law

Bradford, A. (2023). *Digital empires: The global battle to regulate technology*. Oxford University Press., DOI: 10.1093/oso/9780197649268.001.0001

Burri, M., & Kugler, K. (2024). Regulatory autonomy in digital trade agreements. *Journal of International Economic Law*, *27*(3), 397–423. DOI: 10.1093/jiel/jgae025

Cha, Y., & Koo, M. G. (2020). Who embraces technical barriers to trade? the case of European REACH regulations. *World Trade Review*, *20*(1), 25–39. DOI: 10.1017/S1474745620000130

Chang, Q. (2024). The legal and regulatory issues of AI technology in cross-border data flow in international trade. Transactions on Economics. *Business and Management Research*, *8*, 111–117. DOI: 10.62051/cyw9y102

Ciuriak, D., Dadkhah, A., & Xin, D. (2023). Trade in a digital interoperability era. Brookings Institution Policy Brief. https://www.brookings.edu/articles/trade-in-a-digital-interoperability-era/

Ciuriak, D., & Fay, R. (2024). Trade agreements and data governance: Pathways to interoperability. Centre for International Governance Innovation Policy Brief, No. 195. https://www.cigionline.org/articles/trade-agreements-and-data-governance/

European Commission. (2021). Commission implementing decision on standard contractual clauses for the transfer of personal data to third countries (C(2021) 3972 final). https://eur-lex.europa.eu/eli/dec_impl/2021/914/oj

European Commission. (2023). Commission implementing decision on the adequate protection of personal data under the EU-U.S. Data Privacy Framework. Official Journal of the European Union, C/2023/4745. https://commission.europa.eu/document/fa09cbad-dd7d-4684-ae60-be03fcb0fddf

European Data Protection Board (EDPB). (2021). Recommendations 01/2020 on measures that supplement transfer tools to ensure compliance with the EU level of protection of personal data (Version 2.0). https://edpb.europa.eu/our-work-tools/our-documents/recommendations/recommendations-012020-measures-supplement-transfer_en

European Parliament. (2021). *Exchanges of personal data after the Schrems II judgment (Study No. 694678). Directorate-General for Internal Policies.* Policy Department for Citizens' Rights and Constitutional Affairs., DOI: 10.2861/95877

Eyo-Udo, N. L. (2024). Examining the integration of artificial intelligence in supply chain management from Industry 4.0 to 6.0: A systematic literature review. *Frontiers in Artificial Intelligence*, *7*, 1477044. Advance online publication. DOI: 10.3389/frai.2024.1477044 PMID: 39902380

Ghaffari, N., & Kimiagari, S. (2023). The Paradoxical Roles of State-Ownership in EMNE Internationalization: OFDI case. *Journal of World Trade*, *57*(4), 609–642. DOI: 10.54648/TRAD2023028

Hettler, B., Cordeiro, J. J., & Schuetz, P. (2024). Corporate scope 3 carbon emission reporting as an enabler of supply chain decarbonization: A systematic review and comprehensive research agenda. *Business Strategy and the Environment*, *33*(2), 1277–1299. DOI: 10.1002/bse.3486

High, A. (2022). Book Discussion: Response to comments by Anna High. *Asian Journal of Law and Society*, *9*(3), 526–530. DOI: 10.1017/als.2022.15

Holloway, D. (2024). Digital transformation in supply chains: Improving resilience and sustainability through AI, blockchain, and IoT. *Frontiers in Sustainability*, *6*, 1584580. Advance online publication. DOI: 10.3389/frsus.2025.1584580

India, D. P. O. (2024). Impact of the Digital Personal Data Protection (DPDP) Act on cross-border data transfers. Data Protection & Privacy Journal, 2(4), 187–204. https://www.dpo-india.com/Blogs/impact-dpdpa-cross-border/

Jia, J., Jin, G. Z., & Wagman, L. (2021). The short-run effects of the General Data Protection Regulation on technology venture investment. *Marketing Science*, *40*(4), 661–684. DOI: 10.1287/mksc.2020.1271

Jusić, M. (2022). The application of GDPR in blockchain technology. *Journal of Emerging Technologies in Accounting*, *19*(1), 47–59. DOI: 10.2308/JETA-2020-065

Kelly, A. (2024). Impact of artificial intelligence on supply chain optimization. *The Journal of Supply Chain Management*, *60*(2), 234–256. DOI: 10.1111/jscm.12298

K&L Gates. (2023). New EU-U.S. Data Privacy Framework—Reliable solution for transatlantic data transfers or gateway to Schrems III? Global Privacy & Data Security Law Blog. https://doi.org/DOI: 10.5281/zenodo.8142367

Körner, M. F., Bauer, D., Keller, R., Rösch, M., Schlereth, A., Simon, P., Bauernhansl, T., & Fridgen, G. (2025). Bridging carbon data's organizational boundaries: Toward automated data sharing in sustainable supply chains. *Electronic Markets*, *35*(1), 13. Advance online publication. DOI: 10.1007/s12525-025-00779-7

Latham & Watkins. (2023). India's Digital Personal Data Protection Act 2023 vs. the GDPR: A comparison. Data Protection & Privacy Practice, White Paper Series. https://www.lw.com/admin/upload/SiteAttachments/Indias-Digital-Personal-Data-Protection-Act-2023-vs-the-GDPR-A-Comparison.pdf

Liu, Z., Gang, L., Yu, B., & Zhang, H. (2022). The routing problem for school buses considering accessibility and equity. *Transportation Research Part D, Transport and Environment*, *107*, 103299. DOI: 10.1016/j.trd.2022.103299

Matthan, R. (2023). Understanding India's new data protection law: An analysis. Carnegie Endowment for International Peace Working Paper. https://carnegieendowment.org/research/2023/10/understanding-indias-new-data-protection-law

Maume, P. (2023). The Regulation on Markets in Crypto-Assets (MICAR): Landmark codification, or first step of many, or both? *European Company and Financial Law Review*, *20*(2), 243–275. DOI: 10.1515/ecfr-2023-0014

Oecd. (2022). OECD Framework for the Classification of AI systems. OECD Digital Economy Papers. Regulation (EU) 2016/679 of the European Parliament and of the Council of 27 April 2016 on the protection of natural persons with regard to the processing of personal data and on the free movement of such data, and repealing Directive 95/46/EC (General Data Protection Regulation). Official Journal of the European Union, L 119/1. https://eur-lex.europa.eu/eli/reg/2016/679/ojDOI: 10.1787/20716826

Richey, R. G.Jr, Chowdhury, S., Davis-Sramek, B., Giannakis, M., & Dwivedi, Y. K. (2023). Artificial intelligence in logistics and supply chain management: A primer and roadmap for research. *Journal of Business Logistics*, *44*(4), 532–549. DOI: 10.1111/jbl.12364

Schrems, M. (2020). Data Protection Commissioner v Facebook Ireland Limited and Maximillian Schrems (Case C-311/18). Court of Justice of the European Union. https://curia.europa.eu/juris/liste.jsf?num=C-311/18

Toorajipour, R., Sohrabpour, V., Nazarpour, A., Oghazi, P., & Fischl, M. (2020). Artificial intelligence in supply chain management: A systematic literature review. *Journal of Business Research*, *122*, 502–517. DOI: 10.1016/j.jbusres.2020.09.009

TrustArc. (2024). How the Schrems II decision changed privacy law. Privacy Compliance Resources. https://trustarc.com/resource/schrems-ii-decision-changed-privacy-law/

United Nations Economic Commission for Europe (UNECE). (2024). White paper on data governance for trade facilitation. United Nations. https://unece.org/sites/default/files/2024-11/WhitePaper-DataGovernanceTradeFacilitation.pdf

Van Ooijen, I., & Vrabec, H. U. (2019). Does the GDPR enhance consumers' control over personal data? An analysis from a behavioural perspective. *Journal of Consumer Policy*, *42*(1), 91–107. DOI: 10.1007/s10603-018-9399-7

Yalçıntaş, D. (2022). Invoking the nullity of non-compete agreements in Employment Law: A comparison of Turkish and Belgian law. *International Journal of Comparative Labour Law and Industrial Relations*, *38*(3), 331–358. DOI: 10.54648/IJCL2022015

Chapter 3
Governance by Investment:
How Emerging Economy OFDI Drives the Green Transition?

R. Sukanya
http://orcid.org/0000-0002-4356-3407
Christ University, India

ABSTRACT

The dynamics between FDI and environmental sustainability have been conceptualized within the North-South framework, in which MNEs from upper-middle-income economies are said to transfer superior technologies to low- and middle-income countries. This perspective neglects the growing importance of outward FDI originating from emerging economies in shaping the global shift towards sustainability. TFirstly, it redefines the transmission of sustainability as a multidirectional, institutionally influenced process rather than a regular North-to-South flow. Secondly, it incorporates reverse spillovers and regulatory requirements into the emerging OFDI landscape of the emerging economy. Thirdly, establish a policy-relevant governance structure that connects sectoral carbon intensity, institutional capacity for absorption, and regulatory accord to the outcomes. Using India's OFDI trend from 2021-2025 as a representative illustration of carbon-intensive practices, thereby affecting the sustainability and governance frameworks.

1. INTRODUCTION

The growing global obligation to achieve low-carbon governance requires a comprehensive review of the relationship between cross-border investment and interna-

DOI: 10.4018/979-8-3373-9003-1.ch003

tional climate governance frameworks. FDI has been widely advocated within policy circles as a principal catalyst for disseminating superior environmental practices, advanced clean technologies, and sophisticated management systems for decades. The traditional narrative portrays the flow of sustainability knowledge, typically focusing on upper-middle-income countries, usually the global North, as the exclusive source and, on the other hand, low and middle-income countries as the passive recipients, usually the global South. However, the existing dominant paradigm is increasingly insufficient for explaining the complex reality of the contemporary global investment landscape. OFDI from low and middle-income economies and emerging economies, especially those in the Global South, is becoming more significant. This structural shift has profoundly changed the global production network and also introduced new, theoretically under, and underexplored environmental complexities. This article systematically addresses the conceptual gap by adopting a governance-centric analytical framework to evaluate the inherent Global North Bias embedded within investment-environmental models and to propose the reframing of OFDI. Instead of viewing OFDI as a multidirectional transfer, the article conceptualized it as a bidirectional mechanism for the transfer of sustainability practices. This restructuring is essential as it explicitly incorporates the potential for 'Reverse Spillovers', where environmental standards, regulatory pressures, or innovations originate in the host economy and substantially influence home-country practices.

This article disproves the cause and effect assumptions about the environmental impact of OFDI from emerging economies by introducing a new and well conceptualized multidimensional governance framework, challenging the theoretical basis, and affirms that environmental and sustainability spillovers are neither predetermined nor inherent to the capital flow, but are institutionally mediated and sectorally dependent outcomes that are rooted in the border, multilayered architecture of global climate and environmental governance at four levels: (1) International Treaties and regimes (like the Paris Agreement); (2) Bilateral and Multilateral Investment Agreements; (3) National Regulatory Environment, including both the home and host country outbound investment screening, regulations and enforcement; and (4) Non-state government Mechanisms like the CSR[1] initiatives, Industry Standards and certifications, and Civil Society Oversight and Stakeholder Activities. These four levels of governance allow a dynamic analysis of how regulatory alignment, institutional capacity, and stakeholder pressure interact to shape whether OFDI from emerging economies serves as a force for environmental betterment or an agent of degradation in the host economy. Incorporating these institutional and sectoral contingencies provides a refined, predictive framework and a policy-relevant perspective for discerning the capacity of emerging economies' OFDI to accelerate global climate resilience and the low-carbon transition. Specifically, the transport sector, it constitutes one of the largest contributors to global carbon emissions, has emerged as a crucial area for decarbonization efforts. OFDI from emerging economies is progressively being allocated to electric vehicle ecosystems, sustainable logistics infrastructure, and AI-enabled mobility systems. These trends underscore the increasing confluence of international capital, digital advancements, and the transition toward low-carbon transport modalities. This chapter adopts a qualitative and conceptual research design, supported by secondary data analysis. It integrates insights from existing literature, global investment reports (UNCTAD, World Bank), and policy documents to develop a governance-oriented analytical framework. The study also uses India's OFDI trends (2021–2025) as an illustrative case to examine how emerging economy investments interact with sustainability and decarbonization outcomes.

1.1 The Changing Nature of Global Investment

Over the past three decades, the structure of global investment has changed dramatically. During the 1990s and early 2000s, most cross-border investment came from upper-middle-income economies such as the US, Japan, Germany, and the UK. MNEs from these economies dominated global production and global market networks. However, rapid economic growth in emerging economies has transformed this landscape, with countries such as India and China experiencing significant industrial expansion, technological advancement, and capital accumulation. As a result, firms from these economies have developed the capacity to expand internationally. Today, multinational companies from emerging economies operate across multiple continents, with investments spanning a wide range of sectors, including manufacturing, information technology, pharmaceuticals, renewable energy, infrastructure, and financial services. These investments are driven by several motivations: first, companies invest abroad to access new markets, expanding internationally to increase their customer base and strengthen their global presence; second, they invest to acquire new technologies and capabilities, learning from advanced technologies and business practices in economies with sophisticated research systems and skilled labour forces; and third, they invest abroad to diversify risk and increase resilience by reducing dependence on a single domestic economy. These changing patterns of investment have important environmental implications, as companies operating across different countries interact with diverse regulatory systems, environmental standards, and social expectations, creating both opportunities and risks; while some companies may shift pollution-intensive activities to countries with weaker environmental standards, many firms also upgrade their practices when operating in highly regulated environments, therefore, the environmental consequences of OFDI depend largely on how companies respond to these regulatory environments and institutional pressures.

1.2 OFDI and Decarbonized Transport Systems

OFDI has emerged as a strategic mechanism through which firms and countries actively participate in the global transition toward decarbonized transport systems. In contrast to traditional efficiency-seeking or market-seeking investments, contemporary OFDI increasingly reflects sustainability-driven rationales. Under this paradigm, firms engage in internationalization not solely to access markets and resources but also to secure green technologies, integrate into low-carbon value chains, and facilitate a climate-aligned industrial transformation.

1.2.1 OFDI and Electric Vehicle (EV) Supply Chains

The widespread adoption of electric transport systems has fundamentally altered global production networks, leading to the establishment of highly specialized and geographically fragmented Electric Vehicle (EV) supply chains. OFDI is instrumental in facilitating the integration of firms, particularly those originating from emerging economies into these dynamic and evolving ecosystems. Firms undertake OFDI to procure essential upstream resources, such as lithium, cobalt, and rare earth elements, which are indispensable for battery production. Concurrently, investments in technologically advanced host nations grant access to state-of-the-art battery technologies, energy storage systems, and vehicle electrification capabilities. For example, Indian enterprises directing investments towards Southeast Asia and Africa frequently prioritize regions abundant in minerals, whereas investments in Europe or East Asia typically center on fostering technological collaboration and engaging with innovation ecosystems. Also, OFDI facilitates vertical integration throughout the Electric Vehicle (EV) value chain, encompassing raw material extraction, battery production, assembly, and distribution. This integration mitigates supply chain vulnerabilities while simultaneously bolstering sustainability outcomes through enhanced traceability and rigorous environmental governance. Consequently, OFDI significantly contributes not only to the competitive advantage of firms but also to the worldwide dissemination of clean mobility technologies.

1.2.2 OFDI and Smart Logistics Ecosystems

Decarbonized transport systems are intrinsically linked with the evolution of intelligent logistics, characterized by the convergence of efficiency, digitalization, and sustainability. OFDI facilitates the development of such ecosystems by enabling firms to invest in cross-border logistics infrastructure, digital platforms, and multimodal transport systems. OFDI facilitates firms' acquisition of sophisticated logistics capabilities, encompassing real-time tracking, optimized route planning, automated warehousing, and unified supply chain management systems. Such investments hold particular importance in digitally advanced regions, enabling firms to assimilate superior methodologies and subsequently deploy them in their domestic or alternative host markets. Smart Logistics Systems (SLS) reduce carbon emissions by minimizing fuel consumption, optimizing load capacity, and enabling modal shifts toward greener alternatives such as rail and inland waterways. OFDI driven logistics investments support the development of green corridors and sustainable trade routes, thereby aligning international business operations with global climate objectives. Moreover, internationalization of logistics capabilities enhances resilience against disruptions encountered during global supply chain crises while concurrently promoting environmental sustainability.

1.2.3 OFDI, AI, and Transport Innovation

Artificial Intelligence (AI) plays a pivotal role in the decarbonization of transport systems, and OFDI serves as a crucial channel for the acquisition and deployment of AI-driven innovations. Enterprises engaged in foreign investment obtain AI capabilities encompassing predictive analytics, autonomous systems, energy optimization, and intelligent transport management. The integration of AI into the transport sector encompasses dynamic route optimization, demand projection, fleet administration, and anticipatory maintenance. These applications collectively contribute to the mitigation of emissions and the enhancement of operational efficacy. For instance, AI-driven systems are capable of optimizing logistics routes instantaneously, consequently diminishing fuel consumption and the associated carbon footprint. OFDI in advanced economies facilitates collaboration with innovation hubs to accelerate AI adoption. Alternatively, investment in emerging markets allows deployment of scalable, cost-effective AI solutions, democratizing access to sustainable transport technologies. Crucially, the integration of AI serves to enhance not only environmental performance but also economic efficiency, thereby yielding a dual advantage that strengthens the strategic justification for sustainability-focused OFDI. Artificial intelligence plays a critical role in optimizing transport systems by enabling route optimization, predictive maintenance, and real-time emissions monitoring. Indian IT firms are increasingly integrating AI-driven solutions into logistics and mobility systems, thereby enhancing transport efficiency and reducing carbon footprints.

1.2.4 OFDI and Emissions Reduction Strategies

The core objective of decarbonized transport systems is the systematic reduction of greenhouse gas emissions, a goal to which OFDI contributes through various mechanisms. First, OFDI facilitates the transfer of technology, enabling enterprises to implement cleaner production methodologies, energy-efficient transportation infrastructures, and low-emission technologies across national boundaries. Second, corporations investing in jurisdictions with rigorous environmental statutes are frequently obligated to comply with elevated sustainability criteria, which may subsequently be integrated and disseminated throughout their worldwide operations. Third, OFDI facilitates the establishment of green infrastructure, encompassing charging networks for electric vehicles, the integration of renewable energy sources within transport systems, and sustainable urban mobility solutions. These investments are instrumental in cultivating environments conducive to low-carbon transport transitions, both regionally and globally. Furthermore, OFDI facilitates engagement in global carbon markets and sustainability initiatives, thereby providing a stronger incentive for emissions reduction. By harmonizing investment strategies with established climate objectives, firms not only enhance their environmental performance but also strengthen their legitimacy and competitiveness within a progressively sustainability-conscious global economy.

The nexus between OFDI and decarbonized transport systems signifies an evolution in the underlying rationale of international business. This shift moves beyond mere profit maximization to encompass value creation that integrates economic, environmental, and technological imperatives. OFDI serves as a crucial channel for the global dissemination of green technologies, the integration of sustainable supply chains, and the advancement of digital and AI-driven transport solutions. For policymakers, this underscores the importance of creating enabling environments that attract and guide OFDI toward sustainable sectors. For firms, it highlights the strategic necessity of aligning internationalization decisions with decarbonization imperatives. Ultimately, OFDI emerges not merely as an economic activity but as a transformative force shaping the future of sustainable global mobility. For policymakers, this emphasizes the criticality of establishing supportive frameworks that both attract and direct OFDI toward ecologically sustainable sectors. For enterprises, it underscores the strategic imperative of harmonizing international expansion strategies with decarbonization objectives. Ultimately, OFDI transcends its definition as a mere economic endeavor to become a pivotal, transformative catalyst for shaping the future of sustainable global activity.

2. THEORETICAL FRAMEWORK

International businesses are shifting their focus from just making a profit to a more sustainable approach to environmental and societal impact. Earlier, OFDI was viewed through a North-South lens, in which firms from upper-middle-income countries expanded their operations into emerging markets. However, today, the firms from emerging economies are increasingly investing in upper-middle-income countries. This outward expansion is no longer focusing on market seeking but is a strategic mechanism for acquiring sustainability capabilities. An in-depth understanding of this transformation requires transcending the restrictions with a single theory; therefore, the four theoretical frameworks, like the OLI paradigm, the institution-based view (IBV), GVC governance theory, and the reverse spillover theory, are integrated to explain how internalization helps environmental upgrading and the reverse spillovers of sustainability practices back to the home country.

The Eclectic (OLI) Paradigm comprises Ownership, Location, and Internalization advantages, reinterpreted to explain sustainability-oriented OFDI from emerging economies (Dunning, 1988). Ownership advantages range from traditional assets to green capabilities developed by investing in economies with strict environmental standards, transforming environmental competencies into a strategic competitive advantage. Locational advantage moves from cheap resources to regulatory refinement and green technologies. Internalization prevents green competencies from degrading through outsourcing and ensures the newly acquired technologies are distributed and maintained throughout the global subsidiaries (Dunning, 2000). The Institutional Based View is presented as a complement to the OLI framework, focusing in the institutional rules and asymmetric information faced by the emerging economy firms in the upper middle income countries markets with stricter environmental standards create legitimacy pressure of these firms to pursue either regulatory Arbitrage or upgrading, which is mandatory, given the stakeholder pressures from activities, investors, and communities in host countries (Peng et al., 2008; Peng, 2023).

The traditional Ownership advantage, like IP, focuses on sustainability-specific assets and capabilities. Emerging-economy firms are strategically investing in green OFDI under strict regulations (upper-middle-income economies) to acquire, adopt, and internalise advanced green technologies, sustainable operational practices, and sophisticated environmental management systems. By gaining environmental expertise, companies fulfill compliance and gain the key competitive edge. Enabling them to meet stricter environmental rules in the home and host economy. Location Advantage - Companies usually invest abroad to gain the benefits of cheap labour, natural resources, and large markets. However, when it comes to green investments, firms are mainly attracted to countries having strong environmental enforcement. This allows firms to advance their green technologies and skilled expertise. Countries with expertise in sustainable engineering, environmental cosnulting, and circular economy practices provide valuable support in a more environmentally responsible way. Companies gain an Internalization advantage by retaining their green technology and sustainability expertise within the organisation rather than sharing or outsourcing it. This strategic decision protects their innovations and competitors from accessing them. By maintaining internal control, companies ensure consistent application of green technology and practices across all their global operations.

Table 1. Core Theoretical Pillars of Global Green Investment

Theoretical Lens	OLI Paradigm	Institution-Based View	GVC Theory	Reverse Spillover
Traditional Focus	Cost efficiency	Regulatory compliance	Operational efficiency	One-way technology transfer
Sustainability-Oriented Focus	Acquisition of green technologies	Upgrading for legitimacy	Environmental performance	Bidirectional knowledge flow
Strategic Outcome	Development of "green" ownership advantages	Global reputation and risk mitigation	Lead firm influence on sustainable logistics	Domestic industrial modernization

Source: Author's compilation

While the OLI framework explains the company's ability and motivation to invest abroad, the Institutional-Based View (IBV) focuses on the external environments that influence its decisions. It primarily examines how rules, regulations, and social expectations across countries shape firms' strategies. Especially when the firms from emerging economies invest in upper-middle-income countries and wealthier economies, they often face strict environmental laws and high public expectations. On the other hand, it's a pressure on firms to prove their responsiveness and trustworthiness in business. Firms either move to weaker environmental rules to reduce the cost or upgrade themselves to meet these standards. In sustainability-focused investments, firms choose to upgrade by leveraging FDI opportunities. This not only helped them meet the regulations but also improved their performance and reputation, and gained acceptance in the global market. The OLI framework explains the firm's capabilities and motivations, while the IBV framework explains the external pressures that push firms to adopt sustainable practices when investing overseas.

Figure 1. Theoretical frameworks - Sustainability in OFDI from emerging economies.

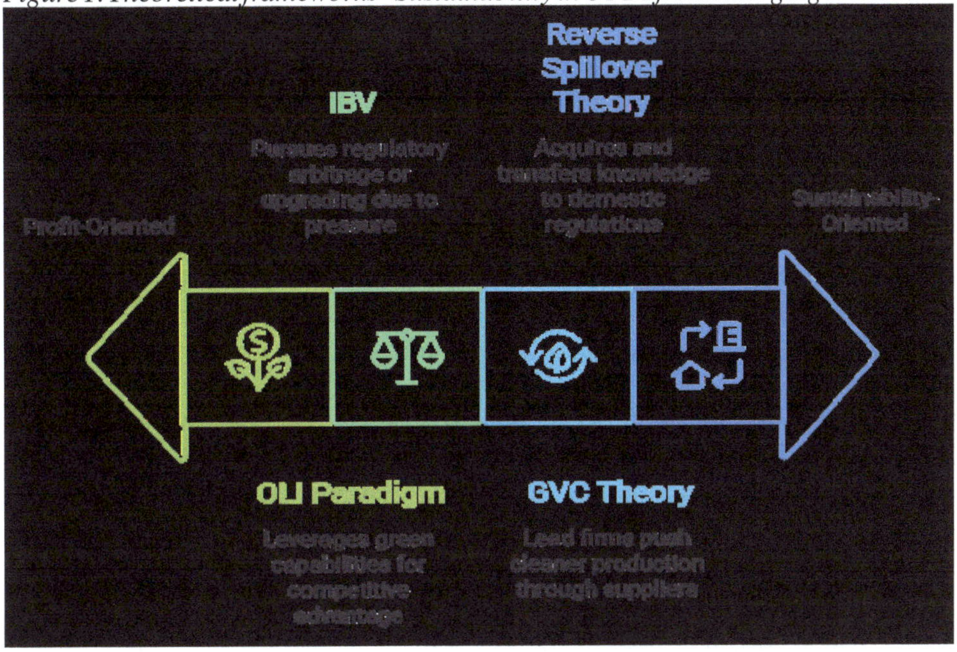

Source: Author's compilation

Global Value Chains (GVCs) determine the organization of modern production across various nations, with each production phase located in the most optimal location. Especially large firms that control brands and markets play a crucial role in guiding these chains' operations. They often encourage or require suppliers to adopt cleaner technologies and more sustainable practices, thereby improving their environmental performance across their supply networks.

At the same time, firms also focus on improving how products are produced, designed, and delivered by strengthening their technical skills and SCM[2] capabilities. These changes influence the industry standards, consumer and social group pressure, and government regulations on labour and environment. Companies invest in more environmentally advanced locations within their networks to spread better sustainability practices throughout their operations. The GVC allocates production stages across economies, while governance theories describe how power and systems are determined within GVCs. Environmental upgrading is driven by lead firms that push cleaner production and greater adoption of sustainable practices through their suppliers. Functional upgrading involves governance in design and logistics. GVCs' governance includes private standards, social pressures, and public regulation, and firms invest in environmentally advanced nodes to internalize and diffuse high sustainability standards within their networks (Gereffi & Fernandez-Stark, 2011).

OFDI from emerging economies to upper-middle-income countries facilitates a "reverse spillover" effect, in which firms acquire and transfer knowledge and support domestic environmental regulations (Awate et al., 2015).

2.1 OFDI From Emerging Economies

The past two decades have witnessed a fundamental, transformative shift that has redefined the global economy: the rise of emerging economies as major sources of Outward Foreign Direct Investment (OFDI). Historically, these nations were primarily recipients of capital from developed countries, but they are now actively dispatching their own funds across borders, establishing themselves as powerful global investors. This trend is perhaps most evident in China, which has established itself as the leading global source of OFDI. Its capital is financing significant international undertakings, particularly extensive infrastructure and energy projects across various continents. Importantly, this investment paradigm is evolving, characterized by a heightened strategic focus on sectors essential for future progress, such as solar power generation and the manufacture of electric vehicle components.

The strategic investment pattern observed in China is mirrored in other emerging economies. Brazil is exporting its expertise and capital in sustainable energy, particularly biofuels. South Korea is investing heavily in high-tech sectors such as advanced electronics, semiconductors, and energy storage, thereby cementing its pivotal role in the Fourth Industrial Revolution. Moreover, financial centers like Singapore are indispensable, functioning as global capital hubs and specifically championing "green finance" to underwrite sustainable infrastructure initiatives worldwide. The investment strategy of enterprises from developing economies is fundamentally shifting from basic resource- and market-seeking Outward Foreign Direct Investment (OFDI) to a more sophisticated pursuit of "strategic asset-seeking investments." This contemporary approach focuses on systematically acquiring high-value intangible assets—including advanced knowledge and intellectual property, proprietary technology, modern management techniques, and skilled personnel—by establishing R&D centers or by acquiring foreign firms in technologically advanced regions. By using OFDI as a strategic instrument for this asset acquisition, these firms are actively pursuing integration into global innovation networks (GINs), a process vital to boosting their internal capabilities, accelerating learning, and ultimately securing a sustainable competitive advantage against established multinational corporations on the global stage.

The increasing engagement of enterprises from emerging economies in global innovation and supply networks presents a significant opportunity to elevate worldwide environmental performance by compelling these entities to adopt advanced green technologies and adhere to international sustainability standards. However, the outward foreign direct investment (OFDI) from these same economies exhibits a complex duality: while strategic capital flow towards low-carbon sectors like renewable energy and sustainable transport is crucial for accelerating the green transition, a substantial portion is regrettably directed toward environmentally damaging ventures, including new fossil fuel projects and carbon-intensive heavy industries, risking the lock-in of high emissions for decades. This tension necessitates an urgent, balanced approach to maximize the beneficial capital while mitigating its inherent environmental hazards, demanding a strategic shift from broad assessments to a highly granular, project-specific evaluation that meticulously scrutinizes the initiative's precise character, the governance structures in recipient nations, and the contractual embedment of rigorous, independently verified sustainable practices and enforceable environmental liability clauses.

2.2 India's OFDI Trajectory

India has established itself as a significant force in the international investment landscape, a trajectory marked by rising OFDI. The period from 2021 to 2025 witnessed a persistent increase in capital employed by MNEs in overseas markets, with investment strategically focused on upper-middle-income countries. The continuous and increasing OFDI demonstrates that the country's strategic deployment of capital globally strengthens its economic benefits and enhances its competitiveness. Indian MNEs use OFDI to secure the critical resources, diversify the revenue streams, access specialised skills, and integrate complex global value chains. Sectors like IT, pharmaceuticals, and manufacturing dominate and tend towards investments in sustainability and renewable energy, aligning with the green economy transition goals. However, the overall environmental consequences remain sector-specific. The period immediately succeeding the global pandemic marked a significant turning point for overseas investment. Post-COVID-19, Indian MNEs expanded into overseas markets through strategic asset acquisitions and market penetration. This post-pandemic reflects the increasing confidence and financial strength of Indian MNEs to compete and invest globally.

Table 2. India's Phases of Outward FDI (2021-2025)

Year	Investment (USD Billion)	Growth Phase
2021	15	Post-pandemic recovery
2022	18	Sectoral expansion
2023	20	Diversification of interests

continued on following page

Table 2. Continued

Year	Investment (USD Billion)	Growth Phase
2024	24	Seeking strategic assets and technology
2025	28–30	Deep penetration into advanced markets

Source: Authors' compilation. Data from UNCTAD, 2025; World Bank, 2024.

2.2.1 The Evolving Landscape of Indian Outward Foreign Direct Investment (OFDI): 2021-2025

The period between 2021 and 2025 marks a pivotal and dynamic phase in India's Outward Foreign Direct Investment (OFDI), displaying a strategic shift from immediate post-pandemic recovery to aggressive, technology-focused global expansion. This evolution exhibited the growing maturity and ambition of Indian MNEs in the world market.

2.2.2 Post-Pandemic Consolidation and Resilience (2021)

Following the immediate economic shock of the COVID-19 pandemic, Indian OFDI was primarily defined by consolidation and strategic reinforcement. The primary objective was to strengthen the existing overseas subsidiaries, ensuring operational efficiency and optimizing the global supply chain. Investments are directed towards highly resilient and growth sectors during a crisis, especially into IT and pharmaceuticals. This strategic allocation strengthened the core competencies and captures the rising global demand for digital services and healthcare services.

Figure 2. Evolution of India's OFDI (2021-2025)

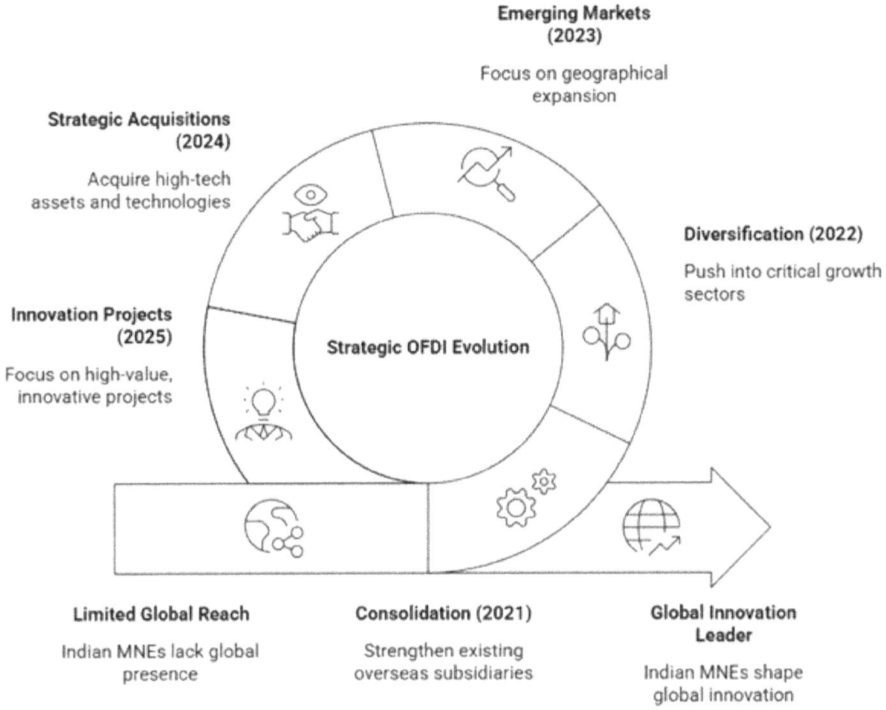

Source: Author's Compilation

2.2.3 Sectoral diversification and future forward investments (2022)

By 2022, the strategic narrative broadened beyond the core sectors as Indian MNEs began to push into critical areas for future economic growth, indicating a commitment to sectoral diversification. The key investment areas included renewable energy, stake acquisitions, and development projects in solar, wind, and green hydrogen technologies, aligned with global climate goals and India's energy transition targets. Simultaneously, invested in the global logistics and supply chain, warehousing and cold chain manufacturing to de-risk and optimize the international trade flow. Also, the expansion into digital infrastructure, covering data centres, cloud computing services, and telecommunications infrastructure to support the global digital economy.

2.2.4 Emerging market focus and strategic Mergers and Acquisitions (2023)

The year 2023 witnessed a strong emphasis on geographical expansion and mergers and acquisitions (M&A), especially in the high-growth emerging markets in Southeast Asia, Africa, and parts of Eastern Europe. These M&A were driven by a dual strategy where initially they gain immediate market access by acquiring established local entities, thereby overcoming the entry barriers and securing the existing distribution network and customer base; followed by securing critical IP through acquisitions of firms possessing proprietary technology or IP, which directly enhance the product offerings and competitive advantage, signaling a strategic shift towards external growth.

2.2.5 Acquisition of Strategic Assets and Advanced Technologies (2024)

The M&A drive intensified in 2024, with a major focus on strategic high-tech acquisitions to close technological gaps and position Indian MNEs at the cutting edge of global innovation. Semiconductors, Advanced Manufacturing, and Artificial Intelligence (AI) are identified as the key sectors. Investments were directed to design firms, fabrication capabilities, and material science companies in Semiconductors to secure a place in the critical global supply chain; specialized capabilities in robotics, automation, and precision engineering in Advanced Manufacturing; and AI startups and research firms to integrate machine learning and data analytics capabilities across all business operations.

2.2.6 Focus on High-Value, Innovation-Driven Projects

By 2025, a new trend emerged in OFDI by Indian MNEs, as their focus shifted towards high-value, innovative, and proprietary projects. Rather than merely allocating capital for production expansion, they began strategically selecting investments to acquire superior technology and secure a sustainable competitive advantage. This transformation signifies the full maturity of Indian overseas investment into a sophisticated, technology-centric global strategy, with Indian multinational corporations now proactively shaping the global innovation landscape instead of simply participating in it.

Table 3. Destinations of India's OFDI

Destination	Approximate Share (%)	Primary Driver
Singapore	22.6%	Regional hub and tax efficiency
United States	15.4%	Technology and market access
UAE	9.1%	Energy and strategic logistics
Mauritius	10.9%	Financial services hub
Netherlands	9.6%	European market entry and tax efficiency

Source: Author's compilation. Data from Reserve Bank of India, 2025

Table 4. Sectoral composition of India's OFDI

Sector	Nature of Investment	Sustainability Impact
Manufacturing	Mixed (Heavy and High-Tech)	Conditional, moving toward clean-tech
Financial Services	Banking, Insurance, and Business	Supports green finance ecosystems
Energy	Renewable (Hydrogen/Solar) vs. Fossil	High potential for "green" upgrading
Technology	Software, AI, and Digital Infrastructure	Enhances efficiency and reduces waste

Source: Author's compilation. Data from Reserve Bank of India, 2025

Indian MNEs have focused their investments on a few key hubs. Singapore remains the top destination because it is a gateway to the rest of Asia and offers a very stable business environment. Other major destinations include the USA, the UAE, the UK, Mauritius, and the Netherlands. More than half of these investments flow through 'Low tax jurisdictions" like Singapore and the Netherlands, where companies use to manage their global taxes more effectively while they expand. Indian firms majorly focus on investing and expanding themselves into two main categories. On one hand, there are "sustainability-enhancing" investments in technology and renewable energy. India's National Manufacturing Mission has encouraged firms to invest in clean technologies such as EV batteries and green hydrogen infrastructure. On the other hand, many firms' investments remain in "carbon-intensive" sectors like traditional heavy manufacturing and certain parts of the energy sector. This shows that while India is becoming a green leader in certain areas, its overall environmental impact depends on which sectors grow the fastest.

India's OFDI investment trajectory from 2021-2025 illustrates the "Integrated Theoretical Proposition" in action. By moving into sophisticated markets like the U.S and the Netherlands, Indian firms are "upgrading" their capabilities and bringing new standards back home. However, the continued presence in carbon-intensive sectors reminds us that the journey towards sustainability is a work in progress, shaped by the pressure of global rules and regulations and by firms' ability to learn and adapt.

3. MAJOR INDIAN MNEs & THEIR INVESTMENT STRATEGY

Outward Foreign Direct Investment (OFDI) by major Indian corporations is experiencing a pronounced increase. This trend is fundamentally driven by the extensive domestic growth of India's largest multinational corporations (MNCs), prompting a strategic shift toward global expansion. These corporations operate across a diverse spectrum of sectors, including complex manufacturing, Information Technology and software, conventional and clean energy, large-scale infrastructure development, and the rapidly evolving automotive industry. Their foreign investment is motivated by several sophisticated strategic imperatives. Primarily, they aim to penetrate new markets, acquire new customer bases, and enhance operational efficiency through economies of scale. Furthermore, they are actively pursuing access to advanced technologies and superior operational methodologies to maintain a competitive advantage. Securing essential natural resources, particularly energy and minerals, constitutes another key objective. Crucially, these investments represent a deliberate effort to achieve greater integration into global supply chains, thereby optimizing cross-border production and logistics.

In the contemporary, dynamic global economic landscape, these enterprises are increasingly aligning their investment strategies with broader sustainability objectives and transitioning toward operating models that minimize carbon emissions. Indian multinational corporations recognize that sustained long-term financial viability necessitates robust performance in Environmental, Social, and Governance (ESG) criteria. Consequently, their foreign capital deployment is increasingly channeled into projects that support green technology development, expand renewable energy capacity, create energy-efficient buildings and infrastructure, and promote responsible resource management. This concerted effort demonstrates a tangible commitment to contributing to the development of a global "green economy." This sophisticated integration of commercial goals with critical environmental considerations signifies a mature, forward-looking phase in India's international investment posture.

3.1 Tata Group

The Tata Group employs a comprehensive global investment strategy focused on strategic acquisitions, securing frontier technologies, and expanding market presence across its diversified portfolio, including steel, automotive, IT, and hospitality. This approach is exemplified by the 2008 acquisition of Jaguar Land Rover (JLR), which provided Tata Motors with immediate access to advanced R&D and international markets, while simultaneously compelling significant investments in electric vehicle technologies and sustainable mobility solutions to comply with stringent European regulations. Similarly, the expansion of Tata Steel in Europe mandated substantial capital expenditure in cleaner production methods, such as carbon capture, to adhere to regional emissions standards. Beyond these sector-specific examples, the group's operations are increasingly bolstered by cross-sector investments in renewable energy and smart infrastructure, underscoring a deep commitment to environmental, social, and governance (ESG) factors. This holistic strategy demonstrates how international investment serves as a crucial catalyst, effectively compelling Indian multinational enterprises like the Tata Group to integrate sophisticated, sustainable practices into their core business strategies, ultimately raising global standards for responsible corporate growth.

3.2 Reliance Industries

Reliance Industries Limited (RIL) is undergoing a significant strategic transformation, moving away from its traditional petrochemical and hydrocarbon focus to establish global leadership in renewable energy and advanced digital infrastructure, aligning its vision with India's national priorities for the future economy. This pivot is anchored by two core strategies: first, a massive, integrated investment to achieve Net Carbon Zero by 2035 through its New Energy complex, which involves building gigafactories for solar manufacturing, developing advanced energy storage and green hydrogen ecosystems, and investing in decentralized renewables to secure a definitive position in the clean energy transition. Second, the RIL-owned Jio platform is driving India's digital revolution by rapidly deploying next-generation 5G connectivity, building hyperscale cloud infrastructure, deeply integrating Artificial Intelligence across its ecosystem, and expanding its integrated digital platforms like JioMart and Jio Financial Services. By aggressively dominating both the foundational low-carbon energy space and the critical high-technology digital domain, RIL is systematically constructing a resilient, future-proof business model designed for long-term global competitiveness and a multifaceted contribution to India's accelerated economic growth and technological sovereignty.

3.3 Adani Group

The Adani Group has established itself as a global conglomerate, commanding a major presence across essential sectors including global infrastructure, logistics, and energy markets. The strategic direction of the group's international investment activities, particularly its OFDI, is intrinsically linked to the development of critical physical assets like port infrastructure, the expansion of renewable energy capacity, large-scale mining operations, and the establishment of robust transportation networks. A cornerstone of the Adani Group's global expansion strategy is its aggressive push into the renewable energy sector. The company has committed substantial capital to developing and implementing large-scale solar and wind energy projects, not only within its home base of India but also across international jurisdictions. These significant investments are fundamentally driven by a dual mandate: to actively support the global transition toward cleaner, more sustainable energy systems, and simultaneously to cement and expand the company's competitive footprint within the rapidly evolving global energy markets. Adani Green Energy Limited (AGEL), a core subsidiary of the Adani Group, stands as a critical vehicle for these ambitions. AGEL has been instrumental in the conception, financing, and execution of numerous large-scale renewable energy facilities. These projects directly contribute to international efforts aimed at mitigating climate change and achieving meaningful reductions in global carbon emissions. The company's capacity for rapid scale-up in renewable energy generation has been facilitated through a combination of crucial strategic partnerships with global technology providers and securing complex international financing arrangements from multilateral and private institutions. Concurrently, the Adani Group's substantial international investments in port infrastructure and sophisticated logistics networks serve a pivotal, complementary economic function. These developments are vital for streamlining global trade flows and deepening international supply chain integration. By consistently developing and modernizing port and logistics infrastructure systems in various parts of the world, the Adani Group assumes an increasingly important role in linking emerging economies, which often lack cutting-edge infrastructure, more seamlessly and efficiently with the broader global marketplace. This integrated approach ensures that the group not only contributes to green energy but also facilitates the physical movement of goods that underpins global commerce.

3.4 Infosys

Infosys has become a world leader in IT, but not by following the old path of manufacturing. Instead, it's grown globally by focusing sharply on offering smart, high-quality services that rely on knowledge. This means the company is always ahead of the curve, creating advanced digital systems and building vast, connected networks of innovation around the world. This smart way of working lets Infosys grow quickly and change direction easily, keeping pace with the fast-moving tech world. You can see its strength in its huge global presence, which includes top-notch delivery centres, research labs, and creative hubs located in key markets like North America, Europe, Asia, and Australia. Being so deeply rooted in different tech communities isn't just about logistics; it allows Infosys to work hand-in-hand with clients, crafting solutions that fit their exact needs. Plus, this local presence gives them direct access to the newest ideas, emerging technology, and the best talent and specialized partners globally. Beyond its main business, Infosys is actively shaping the future as a champion for building sustainable digital systems. The company has made serious promises to reduce the harm it does to the environment through various actions. These include strict programs to cut down its total carbon emissions, using less energy in all its buildings, and aggressively switching to renewable energy, all with the clear goal of achieving complete neutrality on carbon globally. At the same time, Infosys uses its powerful digital tools—like cloud technology, artificial intelligence, data analysis, and the Internet of Things—not only for its own sustainability but also to help its many clients. By using these digital aids, Infosys helps clients accurately track, review, and significantly decrease their own environmental impact and how much they consume. This dual approach—caring for its own planet-friendly practices while also powering its clients' green efforts—solidifies Infosys's role as a leading tech company and a crucial driver in the worldwide shift toward a clean and sustainable economy.

3.5 Mahindra Group

The Mahindra Group, a major Indian company with business in cars, renewable energy, farm equipment, and computers, is focusing its international investments on a simple idea: making things that are good for the planet, like cleaner transportation, green energy, and responsible manufacturing. They're not just talking about it; they are putting money into it all over the world. A big part of this plan is electric vehicles, mainly through Mahindra Electric Mobility Ltd. This company is heavily investing in research to make better electric cars and improved batteries. They want to be a leader in the global shift to electric vehicles, offering practical, sustainable ways to get around in the future. To grow internationally and get new technology, the Group buys and partners with companies in key places like Europe, North America, and Asia. These partnerships are crucial for getting top-notch car engineering knowledge and for securing a spot in the fast-changing electric car world. These collaborations help them share technology, create new vehicle platforms together, and manufacture locally, which makes Mahindra more competitive globally. Working alongside their clean transport efforts is a strong commitment to clean energy, managed by Mahindra Susten, the Group's clean technology division. Mahindra Susten invests a lot in solar power projects—including huge solar farms and smaller rooftop systems—to increase the amount of clean energy available. These projects not only help build a strong, worldwide clean energy network but also improve the Mahindra Group's reputation as a major champion of corporate responsibility and environmental care on the international stage. This complete approach ensures that as the Group grows, it also creates a positive impact on the environment and society.

4. INDIA'S GREEN INVESTMENT INITIATIVES AS OFDI STRATEGY

As the global community increasingly prioritizes addressing climate change and promoting environmental sustainability, Indian multinational enterprises (MNEs) are progressively embedding 'green' investment strategies into their international expansion blueprints. This strategic shift reflects a broader commitment to sustainable development and is driven by both regulatory pressures and growing market demand for environmentally responsible practices. Several key areas of outward foreign direct investment (OFDI) clearly illustrate this profound transition toward more sustainable and responsible international business models. This integration of green investment is manifesting across various sectors. For instance, there is a notable rise in OFDI directed towards renewable energy projects, such as solar and wind farms, in various host countries. Indian MNEs are leveraging their expertise to establish and operate these clean power generation assets, contributing to the global energy transition. Furthermore, investments in environmentally-friendly infrastructure, including smart grids, sustainable urban development projects, and green transportation systems, are becoming more common. Beyond core infrastructure, this green focus is also evident in technology and manufacturing, with companies investing in R&D and production facilities abroad that specialize in energy-efficient technologies, waste management solutions, and circular economy initiatives. This holistic approach signals a maturation of Indian OFDI, moving beyond traditional resource-seeking or market-seeking motives to embrace a more sustainable, value-driven, and environmentally conscious international footprint.

4.1 Renewable Energy

Renewable energy has emerged as a cornerstone of green investment for Indian MNEs, reflecting a strategic pivot toward sustainable international expansion. Driven by ambitious global climate commitments and the escalating worldwide demand for clean energy, Indian firms are aggressively augmenting their footprint across solar, wind, and nascent renewable energy technologies. These enterprises are not merely investing; they are spearheading the development of large-scale, transformative projects globally. This includes the establishment of vast solar parks, significant wind energy installations, and cutting-edge energy storage systems across various international jurisdictions. This outward flow of capital, or Outward Foreign Direct Investment (OFDI), into the green sector serves a dual purpose. Primarily, it offers substantial support to global decarbonization efforts, aligning India's corporate sector with international environmental goals. Secondarily, these ventures act as vital conduits for technological acquisition, enabling Indian companies to absorb, adapt, and refine advanced capabilities in renewable energy development and project execution, thereby enhancing their long-term competitiveness. Furthermore, this surge in renewable energy OFDI is fundamentally crucial for national and global energy security. By diversifying energy sources internationally, these investments play a critical role in reducing the world's collective dependence on volatile fossil fuels, which mitigates geopolitical risks and stabilizes energy markets. As renewable technologies continue their rapid cost-curve decline, becoming increasingly competitive with conventional power generation, Indian MNEs are strategically integrating these clean energy solutions into the core of their entire international operational framework. This holistic approach ensures that their global supply chains and manufacturing bases become progressively more sustainable, cementing their role as key players in the global green economy transition.

4.2 Electric Vehicle Supply Chains

The global automotive sector is undergoing a profound and swift transformation, principally driven by rigorous environmental policies aimed at reducing carbon emissions, positioning Electric Vehicles (EVs) as the cornerstone technology for sustainable mobility. Indian multinational enterprises (MNEs), most notably Tata Motors and Mahindra & Mahindra, are vigorously engaging in this worldwide EV shift through significant outward foreign direct investment (OFDI). These strategic investments are comprehensive, covering the entire EV ecosystem, encompassing EV manufacturing operations, the crucial development and production of next-generation battery technologies, and the deployment of necessary charging infrastructure networks. By forging international alliances and partnerships, these Indian corporations are successfully acquiring access to advanced technologies, such as solid-state batteries and sophisticated electronic systems, thereby substantially boosting their global competitive standing. These outward investments are dual-purposed: they materially contribute to the worldwide effort for cleaner transportation systems while simultaneously unlocking considerable new economic opportunities for the Indian corporate sector, effectively establishing these firms as essential, forward-looking players in the future landscape of automotive technology.The global automotive industry is undergoing a rapid and profound transformation, principally driven by rigorous environmental policies aimed at reducing carbon emissions, positioning Electric Vehicles (EVs) as the central technology for sustainable mobility. Indian multinational enterprises (MNEs), most notably Tata Motors and Mahindra & Mahindra, are vigorously engaging in this worldwide EV shift through significant outward foreign direct investment (OFDI). These strategic investments are comprehensive, covering the entire EV ecosystem, encompassing EV manufacturing operations, the crucial development and production of next-generation battery technologies, and the deployment of necessary charging infrastructure networks. By forging international alliances and partnerships, these Indian corporations are successfully acquiring access to advanced technologies, such as solid-state batteries and sophisticated electronic systems, thereby substantially boosting their global competitive standing. These outward investments are dual-purposed: they materially contribute to the worldwide effort for cleaner transportation systems while simultaneously unlocking considerable new economic opportunities for the Indian corporate sector, effectively establishing these firms as essential, forward-looking players in the future landscape of automotive technology.

4.3 Green Hydrogen Development

Green hydrogen is a promising way to power industries that are hard to clean up with just regular renewable energy. It's made by using clean electricity to split water, and it can be used as a clean fuel for things like big factories, transport, and storing energy. Big Indian companies, such as Reliance Industries and the Adani Group, are putting a lot of money into green hydrogen, working with international experts, technology companies, and energy firms. These projects need major investments in solar and wind farms, the equipment to make the hydrogen (electrolyzers), and storage systems. By investing in these projects abroad and forming international partnerships, Indian businesses are becoming key players in the growing worldwide hydrogen market. This push into green hydrogen shows how Indian companies investing overseas can help bring about new technologies and a cleaner environment.

5. REGULATORY CONDITIONING, REVERSE SPILLOVERS, AND SUSTAINABILITY CONVERGENCE

The regulatory environment of the host country is a powerful and compelling force that influences the operational behavior and strategic decisions of investing firms, and in the case of MNEs from emerging economies investing in upper-middle-income countries with developed, stringent environmental laws, the regulatory conditioning effect (i.e., the need to comply with measures such as mandatory ESG reporting, strict emission standards, and carbon pricing mechanisms) compels them to adapt their internal operational and governance practices (IMF, 2024). High standards are not just a legal obligation; they are a force for modernization and innovation, which requires firms to integrate sophisticated environmental management systems into their global governance frameworks, and to align them with global best practices (OECD, 2020). The Institutional-Based View (IBV) emphasizes a strategic dilemma for emerging-economy firms: they can either seek to engage in regulatory arbitrage (i.e., they move pollution-intensive activities to jurisdictions with weaker rules to reduce the cost of compliance) or they can upgrade their sustainability capabilities, which is often the case with green-focused outward foreign direct investment (OFDI) in order to gain market acceptance and legitimacy in overseas markets (Peng et al., 2008; Peng et al., 2023), which further strengthens their competitive advantage and the transfer of advanced green technologies back home.

This reverse spillover process, where subsidiary companies from emerging economies operating within more developed host economies gather cutting-edge environmental knowledge, the best tools, and leading sustainability practices, including practical improvements such as more efficient use of energy, sophisticated Environmental, Social, and Governance (ESG) reporting, and real-time digital pollution tracking, is then repatriated and back to the home country operations, and, more importantly, to its domestic supply chain partners and local suppliers (Sarker and Serieux, 2022). The knowledge transfer that results can spark a major upgrade in the sustainability profile of the home economy, but the successful diffusion and integration of this green knowledge is not a foregone conclusion, and is dependent on two factors: the absorptive capacity of the home country (the institutional and organizational capacity of local firms and public bodies to recognize, assimilate, and apply the repatriated knowledge), and the type of industry in which the investment is made (the effect of reverse spillovers is most significant in the most carbon-intensive industries, such as heavy manufacturing, where the need for clean technology is most pressing, and OFDI provides a link to high-standard foreign markets that can drive a broader, more extensive tran

6. POLICY FRAMEWORK FOR GOVERNING EMERGING ECONOMIES OUTWARD FDI

Economic growth is being seen more and more as an integrated part of environmental protection and sustainable development. The amount of money flowing across borders through overseas investment has grown dramatically, as companies from fast-growing economies invest more abroad, and overseas investment can support key global objectives like clean energy, climate action, sustainable infrastructure, and responsible resource use, but without adequate guidance, overseas investment can cause environmental harm, strain local resources, and create social issues for host countries. There is no single set of strong and clear rules governing the operations of companies abroad, even though most countries have environmental laws in place that apply to companies operating within their borders. This, in turn, can lead to some businesses investing in areas where environmental rules are weaker or poorly enforced, resulting in gaps in responsibility, and companies also claiming that their projects are environmentally friendly even when the environmental benefits are less than substantial. The solution is to establish clearer guidelines for businesses operating overseas, requiring them to carefully evaluate the potential environmental and social effects of their projects before operations start and to prevent or minimize damage to ecosystems and local communities.

At the same time, countries and international organizations should cooperate to establish universal global standards that promote responsible business practices and ensure that companies abide by sound environmental standards wherever they invest. Governments can also encourage companies to invest in renewable energy, green technologies, sustainable transport, and climate-resilient infrastructure through financial incentives, tax breaks, and more accessible green funding. Equally crucial is transparency, and companies should publicly disclose the environmental footprint of their overseas projects so that governments, communities, and other stakeholders can determine whether these investments actually contribute to sustainable development. Moreover, agreements between countries to promote trade and investment should include firm commitments to environmental protection and fair labor practices so that economic cooperation does not lead to the degradation of nature or exploitation of people. In the end, the best way to ensure that international investment serves the world's needs is to strengthen rules, encourage responsible investments, improve transparency, and promote cooperation between countries, so that investment can be a source of economic growth as well as environmental health for the future.

6.1 Alignment with Climate Commitments

The first, and most fundamental, foundation to align global investment with sustainability is to formally and explicitly link a country's OFDI strategy to its national climate objectives. Governments around the world, and especially those representing the largest emerging economies, including India, have made meaningful and aspirational pledges, often through Net Zero targets or Nationally Determined Contributions (NDCs) under the Paris Agreement. These official, high-level directives are more than just political speeches; they're powerful commands, often legally required or at least strategically essential. When a nation clearly announces a mandatory date for significant cuts in carbon emissions and shares a detailed plan for specific sectors to move toward a low-carbon, circular economy, it sends a clear, unmistakable message to the market. This message targets all domestic companies, especially the big Multinational Enterprises (MNEs) thinking about or already undertaking overseas expansion. This strong focus pushes MNEs to completely rethink their strategies and focus on "green" investments in their foreign projects, like building renewable energy facilities, sustainable transportation systems, clean manufacturing and technology, and circular economy programs. When a country commits to a climate goal, it completely changes the game. Environmental responsibility is no longer just a voluntary "nice thing to do" (like a Corporate Social Responsibility project); instead, it becomes an absolute **must-have for business success** and a core part of a company's survival strategy. This commitment forces the government and all its major financial players—like development banks, export-import banks, and even sovereign wealth funds—to change how they invest. They must start using a "climate check" for all their investment decisions, meaning they are required to actively favor, financially support, or reduce the risk for any investments that clearly support the country's long-term climate goals. In short, it weaves green principles directly into the fabric of global money flow.

6.2 Sectoral diversification

Since not all fund flows affect the environment equally, we can't use the same rules for everyone. This second main idea, called "Sectoral Differentiation," means we need different policies for different types of industries. Some industries, like making steel, petrochemicals, and getting traditional energy, naturally create a lot of carbon and pollution. Others, like IT, finance, and specialized manufacturing, are much cleaner. New rules and tax policies need to clearly tell these two groups apart. We should give better rewards—like cheaper loans or tax breaks—to businesses that invest in clean activities. At the same time, we need to set very strict, non-negotiable rules and make it more expensive for high-polluting businesses to operate. Research shows that cleaner sectors are already sensitive to strict emissions rules. By making green investment more attractive and high-polluting investment more costly, governments can effectively push company money away from environmentally harmful activities. This also prevents us from getting stuck with long-lasting, high-emission infrastructure, both here and in other countries.

6.3 Enhancing Green OFDI

The third pillar of promoting beneficial Overseas Foreign Direct Investment (OFDI) focuses on active enablement through three coordinated strategies. Firstly, Regulatory Cooperation seeks to harmonize diverse environmental standards across host nations via bilateral and multilateral agreements, lowering administrative complexity for Multinational Enterprises (MNEs) and mitigating regulatory arbitrage, thus making green FDI more predictable and appealing. Secondly, Strengthening Absorptive Capacity is crucial to maximize the domestic benefits of reverse spillover, where MNEs repatriate knowledge of cutting-edge green technologies and practices; this requires the home country to invest in green infrastructure, dedicated human capital training, and local innovation systems to effectively integrate and diffuse the new knowledge across the economy (McGrath & Walker, 2023). Finally, the Integration of Green Finance mandates redesigning financial mechanisms, such as sustainability-linked loans and bonds, which tie favorable funding rates to verifiable environmental performance metrics, ensuring corporate accountability and significantly reducing the risk of greenwashing by requiring demonstrable progress.

6.4 Non State governance and accountability

The fourth approach is to give non-government groups more power. This involves strong standards set by industries, rules for supply chains, and strong monitoring by non-profit organizations. Making companies report publicly, consistently, and clearly on their Environmental, Social, and Governance (ESG) performance is key. This allows investors, customers, and society groups to properly judge and pressure multinational enterprises (MNEs). These non-government forces create a second level of responsibility, giving companies a "social license to operate" that requires them to maintain high standards even when local laws are weak. Therefore, pressure from stakeholders is vital for making sure companies follow the rules and act ethically.

6.5 Bilateral and multilateral Investment Treaties

Decades-old Bilateral and Multilateral Investment Treaties (BITs/MITs) focus mainly on protecting capital, not the environment. To close this gap, these treaties must be changed to prioritize sustainable development, give host countries room to create climate laws, and remove provisions that favor polluters. These fundamental agreements must be updated to align with modern climate agreements like the Paris Agreement, ensuring that the legal framework for international investment helps, rather than harms, the move to a global green economy.

Transforming OFDI into a powerful force for global sustainability requires a comprehensive and interconnected policy ecosystem operating across national, market, institutional, and global governance levels. This transition, particularly leveraging emerging economies' OFDI, is built upon five integrated pillars: first, embedding national sustainability and climate goals directly into OFDI policies through mandatory screening and targeted fiscal incentives; second, utilizing clear market signals via Green Taxonomies and climate risk disclosure mandates to channel private finance toward sustainable projects; third, strengthening supportive mechanisms like specialized Green Investment Promotion Agencies and fostering joint R&D ventures for technology transfer; fourth, formalizing non-state accountability through mandatory Human Rights and Environmental Due Diligence (HREDD) across global operations; and fifth, modernizing global legal frameworks, including International Investment Agreements, to prioritize climate action and support multilateral cooperation on issues like carbon pricing. The ultimate goal is not to halt international investment but to strategically redirect its flow to accelerate the world's urgent green transition.

7. DISCUSSION AND POLICY IMPLICATIONS

The findings highlight that OFDI from emerging economies can act as a strategic lever for decarbonizing transport systems, particularly when supported by AI-driven innovation, market-based incentives, and robust policy frameworks. This study substantiates the increasing recognition that the nexus between OFDI, AI, and transport decarbonization is both strategically vital and inherently intricate. These elements do not function as disparate determinants; rather, they interact through a robust transmission mechanism where OFDI facilitates the acquisition of cutting-edge technologies, AI optimizes efficiencies across the system, and transport networks constitute the operational sphere where tangible environmental benefits are actualized. OFDI fundamentally serves as a channel for cross-border technological diffusion, enabling enterprises, especially those originating from emerging economies, to internalize innovations developed in technologically sophisticated regions. This encompasses capital allocations directed toward electric mobility ecosystems, intelligent logistics platforms, and advanced infrastructure. Such investments transcend mere financial transactions; they integrate firms into international innovation networks, facilitating reverse knowledge transfer and technological enhancement. Consequently, OFDI functions not only as a driver of capital mobility but also as a critical mechanism for capability augmentation and the pursuit of green transformation. The incorporation of AI within this structure substantially augments the environmental ramifications of OFDI. AI-powered systems, including predictive logistics, intelligent traffic management, and autonomous transport solutions, enable the real-time optimization of transportation activities. These technologies yield a reduction in fuel consumption, minimize traffic congestion, and improve asset utilization, thereby contributing significantly to the curtailment of emissions. Crucially, when OFDI is channeled toward sectors with high AI intensity, it expedites the deployment of these data-driven solutions, effectively converting investment capital into demonstrable sustainability achievements.

However, the environmental consequences of this interrelationship are neither directly proportional nor uniformly beneficial. Empirical evidence indicates that emissions outcomes are contingent upon the quality of institutional frameworks, the efficacy of regulatory mechanisms, and the strategic direction of investments. In jurisdictions characterized by strong environmental governance, OFDI generally facilitates cleaner production methodologies and advanced transportation technologies. Moreover, the efficiency improvements generated by AI have the potential to trigger rebound effects, wherein the reduction in emissions per unit of output is negated by an expansion in the overall scale of operations. This interplay generates a series of critical trade-offs. While AI-enhanced transport systems foster improved efficiency, they also possess the potential to intensify digital and spatial inequalities, particularly within areas lacking adequate technological infrastructure. The increased automation in the transport and logistics sectors similarly presents a risk of employment displacement, particularly affecting low-skilled labour. From an investment standpoint, the substantial initial capital expenditure required for AI-enabled sustainable transport systems may discourage businesses, notwithstanding the prospective long-term economic and environmental advantages. These conflicting pressures emphasize the imperative to harmonize efficiency improvements with social inclusivity and enduring sustainability. The risks associated with the OFDI, AI and transport nexus further complicate this landscape. The absence of standardized metrics for Green FDI increases the likelihood of greenwashing, while dependence on foreign AI technologies may constrain domestic innovation capacity. Furthermore, the substantial data requirements of AI systems present complex challenges pertaining to data governance, cybersecurity, and privacy, factors that may erode confidence and impede widespread integration. These systemic limitations underscore that technological progress, in isolation, is inadequate; it necessitates the establishment of strong institutional and regulatory frameworks.

Despite these challenges, the convergence of OFDI and AI presents substantial opportunities for accelerating transport decarbonization. Strategic investments in AI-enabled mobility systems can facilitate the transition toward low-carbon, efficient, and integrated transport networks. Engagement in worldwide investment and innovation ecosystems permits enterprises to utilize international specialized knowledge, while scalable artificial intelligence solutions facilitate the replication of successful paradigms across diverse geographical areas. When synchronized with policy structures focused on climate objectives, OFDI has the potential to function as a significant catalyst for the attainment of sustainable development goals.

8. POLICY IMPLICATIONS

The analysis presents several significant policy implications for consideration by governments, international organizations, and industry stakeholders. A primary imperative involves the alignment of investment policies with environmental objectives. Governments ought to devise targeted incentives like tax concessions, green financing mechanisms, and carbon pricing instruments to attract and strategically channel OFDI towards sustainable transport and AI-driven innovations. Furthermore, the establishment of unambiguous standards and certification systems for Green FDI is essential to mitigate the risks associated with greenwashing and to enhance overall transparency. Furthermore, the reinforcement of institutional and regulatory frameworks is essential to ensure that OFDI generates favourable environmental outcomes. This necessitates the rigorous enforcement of environmental regulations, the promotion of accountability in cross-border investments, and the integration of comprehensive sustainability criteria into pertinent trade and investment agreements.

Policymakers need to invest in digital and physical infrastructure to enable AI adoption in transport, specifically by expanding data ecosystems, improving connectivity, and creating innovation hubs for public-private collaboration. This focus on domestic technological capabilities will also reduce reliance on foreign technologies and drive local innovation. Also, addressing the social dimensions inherent in technological transformation is paramount. Policy initiatives should prioritize the reskilling and upskilling of the workforce to effectively mitigate the potential adverse employment effects stemming from automation. Moreover, ensuring equitable access to AI-enabled transport solutions is crucial for bridging digital divides and fostering inclusive economic growth. Finally, a stronger emphasis is placed on international cooperation. Considering the global nature of both OFDI and climate challenges, coordinated efforts are essential to harmonize standards, disseminate best practices, and mobilize resources for sustainable transport initiatives. Multilateral frameworks are crucial in aligning investment flows with decarbonization objectives.

9. CONCLUSION

When companies from growing economies expand their businesses to other countries, their goal is no longer only to find new markets or earn higher profits. Their international presence is increasingly becoming a way through which better environmental practices and responsible ways of doing business spread across the world. When these companies set up operations in countries that have strict environmental rules, they are required to follow higher standards in order to operate successfully. These rules push them to improve the way they produce goods, use energy, and manage waste. As they adjust to these higher expectations, they begin using cleaner technologies, better monitoring systems, and more responsible business practices. What makes this process important is that the knowledge and experience they gain abroad do not remain limited to their overseas branches. When these companies return to their home countries or work with their domestic offices, they bring back what they have learned. This often leads to improvements in the way businesses operate at home, such as using energy more efficiently, reducing pollution, and managing resources more carefully. Over time, these changes can influence suppliers, partners, and other businesses around them, slowly raising environmental standards across the wider economy. However, this positive change does not happen automatically. For it to succeed, the home country must be able to understand and adopt the new ideas and practices being brought back. Businesses, research institutions, and government bodies must be open to learning and applying these improvements. At the same time, governments need to support this transition by encouraging investments in cleaner technologies and sustainable projects. When these conditions are in place, companies that invest abroad can become more than just profit-seeking businesses; they can play an important role in spreading responsible practices and contributing to a cleaner, more sustainable future for both their home countries and the world.

REFERENCES

Awate, S., Larsen, M. L., & Mudambi, R. (2015). Accessing vs sourcing knowledge: A comparative study of R&D internationalization between emerging and advanced economy firms. *Journal of International Business Studies*, *46*(1), 63–86. DOI: 10.1057/jibs.2014.46

Dunning, J. H. (1988). The Eclectic Paradigm of International Production: A Restatement and Some Possible Extensions. *Journal of International Business Studies*, *19*(1), 1–31. DOI: 10.1057/palgrave.jibs.8490372

Dunning, J. H. (2000). The Eclectic Paradigm as an Envelope for Theoretical and Context-specific Theories of MNE Activity. *Business History Review*.

Gereffi, G., & Fernandez-Stark, K. (2011). *Global Value Chain Analysis: A Primer*. Center on Globalization, Governance & Competitiveness.

IMF. (2024). *Climate Policy and Green FDI in Emerging Market and Developing Economies*. International Monetary Fund Staff Climate Note.

OECD. (2020). *International Regulatory Cooperation: Policy Brief*. Organisation for Economic Co-operation and Development.

Peng, M. W., Wang, D. Y., & Jiang, Y. (2008). An institution-based view of international business strategy: A focus on emerging economies. *Journal of International Business Studies*, *39*(5), 920–936. DOI: 10.1057/palgrave.jibs.8400377

Peng, M. W., Wang, J. C., Kathuria, N., Shen, J., & Welbourne Eleazar, M. J. (2023, June). Nishant Kathuria, Shen J., Eleazar M. J. W. (2023). Toward an institution-based paradigm. *Asia Pacific Journal of Management*, *40*(2), 353–382. Advance online publication. DOI: 10.1007/s10490-022-09861-6

Reserve Bank of India (RBI). (2025). *Census on Foreign Liabilities and Assets of Indian Direct Investment Entities*.

Sarker, T., & Serieux, J. (2022). The impact of reverse technology spillover on environmental performance in India. *Journal of Management Sciences*.

UNCTAD. (2025). *World Investment Report 2025*. United Nations.

UNESCAP. (n.d.). *Outward Foreign Direct Investment (OFDI) Toolkit: Know-how and technology*.

World Bank. (2024). *Global Economic Prospects: Strategic Frameworks for Development*.

ENDNOTES

[1] CSR - Corporate Social Responsibility (CSR) Initiatives

[2] SCM - Supply Chain Management

Chapter 4
From Emissions Targets to Market Behavior:
Evaluating Policy-Driven Decarbonization Pathways in Road and Freight Transport Systems

Shoyimkulov Asror
Termez University of Economics and Service, Termez, Uzbekistan

S. Aarthi
http://orcid.org/0009-0006-9064-2091
Marwadi University, Rajkot, India

R. N. Ravikumar
http://orcid.org/0009-0009-3705-1681
Marwadi University, Rajkot, India

Jabbarov Umarbek
Mamun University, Khiva, Uzbekistan

Kurbonov Jasurbek Pozilovich
Alfraganus University, Tashkent, Uzbekistan

ABSTRACT

The decarbonization of road and freight transport depends not only on emissions reduction targets, but on how these targets are translated into economic and regulatory signals that shape market behavior. This chapter examines policy-driven decarbonization pathways by analyzing the transmission of emissions targets into pricing instruments, standards, incentives, and procurement mechanisms, and the

DOI: 10.4018/979-8-3373-9003-1.ch004

resulting behavioral responses of transport and logistics actors. Using comparative case studies from advanced and emerging economies, the chapter demonstrates that strong, credible, and recurring policy signals induce more immediate operational and investment responses, while fragmented or constrained policy environments yield uneven outcomes. The analysis highlights the roles of institutional capacity, policy credibility, and actor heterogeneity in determining effectiveness. The chapter contributes a market-behavioral framework to support coherent, efficient, and resilient transport decarbonization policy design.

1. INTRODUCTION

One of the most complex problems of the contemporary climate policy is the decarbonization of the road and freight transport due to the fact that the industry is structurally defined by the fossil fuel and other systems, and long-lived capital products are organised in poorly coordinated markets. As the national and international ambition to reduce the target of emission increases, the emission related to the transport continues to peak across the regions due to the increased freight demands, urbanization, and the global supply chains. This continued lack of connection between climate ambition and actual outcomes has proven the need to go beyond the abstract ambitions of the policy to a new level where the effects of policy intervention with regard to real market behaviour can be realised (Lin & Bai, 2024). The road and freight transport systems do not respond to the policy intentions in that way, but based on the economic, regulatory and risk signals that are implicit in policy structures. The results of decarbonization are dependent on the influence of these signals on altering investment decisions, mode of operation, and technology uptake among heterogeneous actors. This chapter relates decarbonization of transport to market mediation, where the most important responses to behavioral change can be used to fill the gap between the stipulated emission targets and the measurable reductions of these emissions.

1.1 Decarbonization Challenges

Road and freight transport systems are characterized by unique decarbonization blinds due to the complexity of operations and cost sensitivity and technological limitations. Freight transport specially has very low profit margins and is dependent on long-lasting economic assets, including heavy-duty trucks, logistics centers, and fueling facilities. Those features decreased the rate of diffusion of low-carbon technologies despite the existence of policy incentives. Secondly, the industry is extremely fragmented with big logistics companies, small fleet companies, owner-drivers, and third-party service providers responding variously to regulatory and price cues. Geographic conditions also make the decarbonization process more challenging because the long-haul routes, rural connectivity, and cross-border traffic restrict the option of electrification and alternative fuels (Yao et al., 2022). The lack of standardized policies and application of policies inconsistently across jurisdictions may also undermine incentives and promote strategic conduct. In combination with additional structural factors, road and freight transport is especially endorsed to a slowing effect of emissions reduction despite increasing policy pressure.

1.2 From Emissions Targets to Market Responses

The targets of emissions are often expressed on national or sectoral levels but they need to be converted into real-life constraints and economic incentives encountered by market players. This chapter puts decarbonization in the context of behavioral and economic issues instead of technological or regulatory issues alone. The impact of policies is demonstrated in terms of costs structures, risk of compliance, and expectations of regulation in the future, which are used together to make the decision about the choice of vehicles, the routing, the design of logistics, and the investment in infrastructure. Poor or conflicting signals in the policy can result in little change in behavior, optimization through compliance, unwanted consequences including rebound demand and carbon leakage (Chen et al., 2020). On the other hand, properly balanced policy combinations may cause a lasting change in the market behaviour even when the technological maturity is not attained. The presented framing of the problem enables to interpret the issue of decarbonization as a dynamic process of policy creation and market adjustments, which indicate the role of credibility, timeliness, and coordination of instruments.

1.3 Scope and Contribution

The chapter takes a market-behavioral approach to discuss how the targets of emissions are implemented using policy instruments and then converted into the visible changes in the road and freight transport systems. It combines economic, regulatory and institutional aspects to determine the effectiveness of various policy combinations in determining investment pattern, operational practice and technology adoption among heterogeneous transport actors. The analysis specifically focuses on freight transportation, in which structural rigidities and coordination issues typically slow down the decarbonization process. The chapter is, in terms of methodology, a combination of comparative policy analysis and recent case evidence in order to determine the patterns in behavioral response and unintended effects. The analytical value is the fact that it goes beyond the current bodies of literature on decarbonization and follows the line of argumentation of how the policy objectives are translated into the market actions, instead of policy action being considered exogenous. Through this, the chapter offers a logical framework to consider the effectiveness of the policy, inform behaviorally sensitive policy development, and to assist in strategic decision-making in transport markets.

1.4 Research Gap and Contributions

Although a lot has been done in researching on transport decarbonization, there are still gaps in the knowledge of how the goals of the emission can be converted into tangible market action especially in the freight systems. The literature is mainly concerned with technological solutions or separated policy tools and not much has been done to understand the dynamic relationship between the design and behavioral reaction of heterogeneous transport actors. Moreover, the freight transport has not been researched as extensively as passenger mobility, even though it has an increasingly large proportion of emissions and is structurally complex. This chapter fills these gaps by formulating a policy-market analytical framework that is clear in its connection of the emissions targets, policy instruments, and behavioral outcomes. The study has a contribution of its own, by offering a freight perspective and making comparative information on various institutional and market settings. In this way, it is possible to have a more realistic and behaviorally based image of decarbonization routes in road and freight transport systems.

2. BACKGROUND TO THE STUDY

Policies of transport decarbonization have been developed in an expanded climate governance environment that is influenced by internationalisation, national legislations on climate, and sectoral approaches. Freight and road transport have slowly become fewer peripheral issues to be put at the core of national decarbonization strategies due to their significant contribution to greenhouse gas emissions. This development has been coupled with the formation of different policy tools that are directed at both affecting fuel consumption, automobile technologies, and operating efficiency (Kim et al., 2009). But the context of the background shows that there are long-standing conflicts between the ambitious climate commitments and the reality of transport markets. Such characteristics of the structure as fragmented ownership, varying operating conditions, and disproportional institutional capability have made it difficult to implement policy. This background is critical in explaining the perceived market reactions and why comparable policy objectives usually yield different results in various regions and groups of actors (Mathiesen

& Mæstad, 2004). The study background thus places the transport decarbonization in both its history, institutional and market context to form the foundation of the behavior-oriented analytical approach.

2.1 Evolution of Decarbonization Targets

The objectives of transport decarbonization have been growing larger in the past 20 years because of the international agreements on climate change and growing realization of the augmentation in transport emissions. The early commitments were concerned with increment of fuel efficiency and voluntary measures whilst the newer ones are direct cuts in emissions, periods within which internal combustion engines will be eliminated and carbon targets and budgets by industry. The transport of roads and freight is getting increasingly part of economy-wide net-zero plans, typically intermediate-targeted. In spite of this development, there is still no equal level of aspiration and enforceability of goals across jurisdictions (Zhu et al., 2023). The binding targets are adhered in certain areas where implementation avenues are bright and aspirational objectives are pursued in certain areas where accountability systems are few. It is a disproportional growth of the market expectations and investment confidence particularly on capital-thorough freight systems. Transport targets on decarbonization have therefore been an incremental, controversial change that places considerable focus on policy translation processes in the development of the real decarbonization results. Table 1 Summarization of the important milestones of the road and freight transport decarbonization targets and the policy tools employed in the selected jurisdictions.

Table 1. Evolution of Transport Decarbonization Targets

Phase	Policy Focus	Typical Targets	Dominant Instruments	Market Implication
Early phase	Efficiency improvement	Fuel economy targets	Fuel taxes, efficiency standards	Incremental operational optimization
Intermediate phase	Emissions reduction	Sectoral CO_2 targets	Emissions standards, subsidies	Technology differentiation begins
Transition phase	Structural change	ICE phase-out timelines	Carbon pricing, road user charges	Capital reallocation and fleet renewal
Net-zero phase	System transformation	Economy-wide net-zero	Integrated policy mixes	Market-wide behavioral realignment

2.2 Transport Policy Instruments

The policies used to ensure transport decarbonization have a broad spectrum, and they include: carbon pricing instruments, fuel taxes, vehicle emissions standards, road user charges, low-emission vehicle subsidies, and public procurement. These tools vary in the modes of influence, temporal orientation and distributional impacts. The price-based instruments are supposed to internalize the environmental costs whereas the regulatory standards are supposed to place direct restrictions on technology and operations. The policies that are infrastructure-based aim at minimizing adoption costs through charging networks and alternative fuel networks. The efficiency of individual instruments however is extremely situational and in most cases constrained when applied in solitude (Liu et al., 2015a). Using road and freight transport, the interaction of policies can enhance or weaken behavior responses based on the coherence and sequence. In addition, laxity in enforcing or reversal of the policy may harm the credibility and result in slow investment and strategic adherence. The functional role of each instrument is hence important in determining their overall contribution to the behavior of the market. Table 2 Categorization of pricing, regulatory, incentive based and infrastructure policies and elaborates how they majorly transmit behavior.

Table 2. Policy Instruments in Road and Freight Transport

Instrument Type	Examples	Primary Signal	Behavioral Channel
Price-based	Carbon pricing, fuel taxes	Cost increase	Demand moderation, routing efficiency
Regulatory	Emission standards, bans	Compliance constraint	Technology adoption
Incentive-based	Subsidies, tax credits	Risk reduction	Early investment
Infrastructure	Charging, fuel networks	Feasibility signal	Adoption acceleration
Procurement	Green public contracts	Demand certainty	Market scaling

2.3 Market Structure and Actor Heterogeneity

The road and freight transport markets can be considered very heterogeneous in the size of actors, scope of their operations, and risk tolerance. Big logistics companies usually have more financial power and data that allow them to react proactively to the policy signals by modernizing the fleet and optimizing operations. Small and medium-sized operators, on the contrary, tend to be credit constrained, they have less bargaining power and more sensitive to the cost volatility leading to more risk-averse or reactive reactions. The character of transported goods, the characteristics of roads, and the availability of infrastructure in the region also form the behavioral heterogeneity (Venkatesh & Raslavičius, 2024). It is possible that urban freight operators and long-haul carriers will react differently to congestion charges and access regulations depending on their jurisdictions. Such variations imply that standard policy tools are seldom used to yield standardized results. Rather, decarbonization routes can be seen to be the aggregate actions of various actors adjusting within their respective constraints. This heterogeneity is critical to the development of fair and powerful policy combinations that can have an impact on market behavior.

3. RESEARCH OBJECTIVES

The chapter is informed by a combination of research objectives that aim at explaining the way these transport decarbonization targets are converted into policy signals, which can be acted on, and how these actions influence market behavior within road and freight transport systems. The goals do not consider emissions cuts as a technical consequence, but as an economic incentive, regulatory design and behavioral reaction among a heterogeneous set of transport actors. It is focused on defining under which circumstances a decarbonization that is socially conducted by policy can be efficient, plausible, and sustainable over time, especially on the segment of the market that is freight-based and heavy capital-intensive.

- To examine how emissions reduction targets are operationalized through economic and regulatory instruments such as carbon pricing, fuel and vehicle taxation, emissions standards, road user charges, and investment incentives in road and freight transport systems.
- To analyze the transmission of policy signals to market behavior, focusing on how cost structures, compliance risks, and regulatory expectations influence investment, operational, and technology adoption decisions.
- To evaluate heterogeneous behavioral responses across road and freight transport actors, accounting for differences in fleet size, operational scale, geographic context, and technological readiness.
- To assess the effectiveness and limitations of different policy mixes in driving observable changes in vehicle choice, logistics organization, routing strategies, and infrastructure investment.
- To identify key policy design conditions including credibility, time consistency, coordination across governance levels, and institutional capacity—

that enable sustained and economically efficient decarbonization of road and freight transport markets.

4. CONCEPTUAL MODEL

The conceptual model that was generated in this chapter describes the idea of decarbonization as a dynamic process by which the emission goals are translated into policy instruments creating market indicators and triggering behavior change in road and freight transport systems. The model does not presuppose that regulation and emissions performance create a linear relationship, but instead, it focuses on the mediation using economic incentives, regulatory restrictions, and anticipations of how stringent the policy would be in the future. These signals are responded to by market actors depending on their cost structures, risks exposure, asset lifetimes and the flexibility of operations (Sahu et al., 2022). The model combines three essential elements that are the establishment of emissions targets and policy tools, the mechanisms of behavioral change among the actors of transport and logistics, and feedback of policy credibility to long-term investment and adaptation of the market. The framework is a heterogeneous and time-transient framework that includes both desired and unintended consequences of policy interventions. It is a conceptualization that offers the analytical gap between the policy design of climate and actual market dynamics, which can contribute to a more realistic assessment of decarbonization patterns in the road and freight transport systems. Figure 1. Demonstrates the effects of the behavioral change caused by emissions targets and policy instruments changing in response to market signals and feedback loops over time.

Figure 1. Dynamic Policy–Market Decarbonization Framework

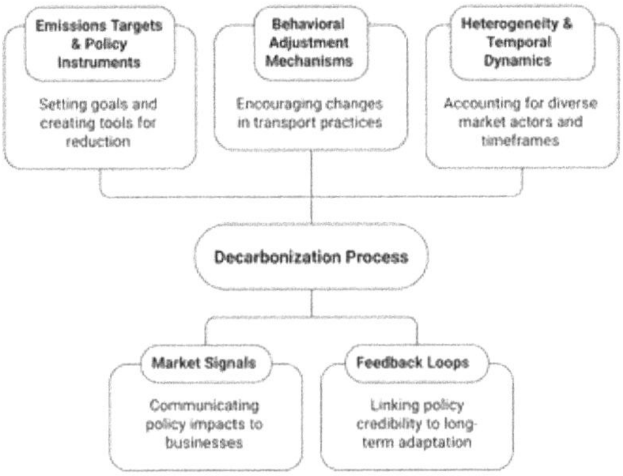

4.1 Targets, Instruments, and Signals

The policy tools that are used to make the emissions targets work impact the transport markets indirectly. All the transmission channels are carbon pricing, fuel taxes, vehicle taxes, emissions targets, road user taxes, subsidies and procurement regulations, which convert the abstract climate goals into a concrete cost, compliance and risk measures. These are established by the strength and clarity of the signals and these are established by the instrument design, coverage, enforcement and the consistency in time. Price based instrument also affects the marginal operating cost and the regulatory standards impose discrete technological or operating boundaries. The policies of subsidy and the infrastructure make the adoption easier as it minimizes the risk of initial investment (Islam et al., 2023). The transmission of market signals does not normally proceed smoothly even when transportation of freights is concerned as the operations across the borders and the jurisdictional fragmentation undermine incentives. When the policy signals are loose, uneven or ill coordinated then the market participants can slow down the adaptation or they might be having a small compliance policy. Being effective will therefore involve some policy combinations that will align short term incentives of operation with decarbonization goals that should be achieved in the long term.

4.2 Behavioral Adjustment Mechanisms

Policy signals impact the behaviour of transport and logistics actors in several ways, such as modifying vehicle acquisition, routing, logistics consolidation and the adoption of technologies. Companies weigh cost variations caused by policy and against cost and operational constraints, customer needs and competitive forces. Behavioral adjustment in freight transport can be typically incremental, which is associated with high capital intensity and long asset life. The benefit of operators first seeking efficiency through load optimization or route planning is that they can then make a commitment to low-carbon technologies. Risk perceptions, availability of finance and information also influence behavioral responses (Liu et al., 2015b). Small firms are inclined to be defensive in reaction to increased costs and large companies can take the initiative to decarbonize to advance regulatory risk and reputational risk. Such differentiated adjustment processes imply that the results of emissions policies are manifested by aggregated micro-level responses, as opposed to homogeneous reaction to the policy requirements.

4.3 Policy Credibility and Market Feedback

Time consistency and policy credibility is significant in the determination of long-term investment adaptation and market adjustment in the transport systems. The more the policy frameworks are perceived to be stable and durable the more the market actors will invest in low-carbon vehicles, infrastructure and digital optimization systems. On the other hand, the policy reversals or the lack of long-term signals become more frequent, which leads to uncertainty that discourages investments that cannot be reversed, and decarbonization is slower. The conceptual model also uses feedback loops in which the initial reactions in the market manipulate later policy improvement, development of infrastructures, and learning of technology. The higher the adoption, the lower the costs and the more feasible the operations which strengthen the behavioral change. Meanwhile, unexpected consequences like the rebound demand or carbon leakage can provoke the changes in the regulations (Liu & Mu, 2015). The above feedback mechanisms underscore the need to decarbonize as an adaptive process that needs a constant policy recalibration to ensure that individual incentives are kept within the overall climate goals. Table 3Altows the conceptual model between the emissions targets and policy instruments, behavioral adjustment mechanism and market outcome.

Table 3. Targets–Signals–Market Response Mapping

Emissions Target	Policy Instrument	Market Signal	Behavioral Response	Emissions Outcome
CO_2 reduction	Road user charges	Higher marginal cost	Route optimization	Reduced intensity
Fleet transition	Vehicle standards	Technology constraint	Fleet renewal	Structural reduction
Fuel substitution	Subsidies	Investment support	Alternative fuel uptake	Long-term abatement

5. RESEARCH METHODOLOGY

The study design is aimed at assessing the effects of decarbonization policies in the behavior of the market in road and freight transport systems based on the structured and comparative analysis. Since transport markets and policy environments are heterogeneous, the chapter embraces the approach of qualitative-comparative methodology which combines the policy analysis with behavioural and financial evaluation. The approach of the methodology focuses on how emissions targets can be converted into the policy instruments and the subsequent reactions of the transport actors under diverse institutional and market environments (Ashmore et al., 2018). The method gives priority to interpretive rigor, cross-case comparison and analytical generalization, instead of the causal estimation in a strict econometric sense. This allows recognizing of recurrent patterns, principles of designs, and limitations that influence the effectiveness of policies. The approach is especially appropriate to the capture of dynamic and context-specific responses, such as unintended effects and time-dependent adaptation. The approach will enable a subtle interpretation of policy-pursued decarbonization strategies in road and freight transport systems by integrating systematic policy analysis with specific evidence of the case.

5.1 Comparative Policy Analysis Framework

The chapter uses the comparative policy analysis framework to look at the effect of various constellations of decarbonization instruments on market behavior in road and freight transport. The framework evaluates designs of policies in different jurisdictions based on the type of instrument, scope, stringency, enforcement strategies, and temporal consistency. Emissions targets are perceived as upstream commitments whereas the policy instruments are examined as downstream way to convey incentives and limits to market participants (Association et al., 2023). The comparison is based on the effect of changes in policy mixes on cost structure, compliance requirements and expectations of investments. Institutional dimensions, such as governance capacity and transport, energy and climate authority coordination are also applied in the framework. The framework enables the systematic identification of convergent and divergent outcomes of other cases by organizing comparison on shared dimensions of analysis. This strategy justifies the analytical generalization by connecting observed market reactions to particular aspects of policy design as opposed to situational peculiarities per se.

5.2 Case Selection Criteria and Data Sources

The case studies are picked to determine the variation of policy ambition, institutional capacity as well as market structure in the road and freight transport systems. The criteria that are used in the selection are the availability of clear transport decarbonization goals, implementation of various policy tools, and market reactions during a specific time frame. The chapter puts emphasis on cases in recent times as a way of maintaining relevance on contemporary policy discussions and conditions of technology. The sources of data will be an official policy document, regulatory impact assessment, statistics of transport, industry reports, and secondary empirical studies. Available evidence of freight operators, logistics associations and providers of infrastructure is included to put behavioral responses into perspective (van Dijk et al., 2021). Triangulation and increased analytical validity are made possible by the use of various data sources. The cases are used to give a representation of the policy design as an illustrative example rather than offering exhaustive empirical coverage to explain comparative implications of the policy design to market behaviour under varying institutional and economic conditions.

5.3 Behavioral Outcome Assessment

The outcome of behavioral and market results is evaluated within the framework of a structured analytical approach that identifies links between policy tools and the visible transformations of the transport choice and market forces. The indicators analyzed include the vehicle technology option, the renewal frequency of the fleet, fleet routing, and scheduling, the consolidation of logistics, and investment in alternative fuels and infrastructure. Special emphasis is made on the variousiated responses of the groups of actors such as large logistics companies, small fleet operators, and cross-border carriers (Efstathiou et al., 2024). The method also looks into the unintended consequences, including the rebound effects, compliance strategy, and displacement of emissions between jurisdictions. Results are also interpreted qualitatively where the focus is to determine direction, magnitude and persistence of behavioral change as opposed to absolute quantification. The strategy of this analysis enables one to identify causal pathways and constraints under which policy effectiveness is determined and recognizes the complexity and adaptive nature of transport markets.

5.4 Analytical Framework

Decarbonization process is a gradual and interlinked process that is structured into a sequence of inputs (emissions target and policy environment), policy tools (pricing, regulation, incentives, infrastructure), market indications (cost, compliance and risk signals), and behavioral outputs (fleet decisions, routing and technology adoption). It is possible to decode the process of translating abstract climate objectives into market behavior logically with the help of this model. The heterogeneity of the transport systems, institutional diversity depending on context and policy effects make the implementation of a qualitative-comparative approach because of the constraints posed by the straight-forward econometric generalization. The cases are compared with the same indicators like the type of instrument, the degree of strength of the signal, the abilities of the institution, the organization of the market, and the reactions to the behavior that have been observed. The comparative design helps make an analytical generalisation of the policy design differences, in which the market behaviour differences are associated with policy design differences and the policy outcomes of decarbonization are different in different situations.

6. LITERATURE REVIEW

The decarbonization of transport has a multidimensional structure of the literature. It is expressed in economics, policy studies, behavioral science, and transport engineering because of the multidimensionality of road and freight system emissions reduction. The initial studies were mainly concerned with improvements in efficiency of technology and replacing fuels, and tend to assume that policy is an exogenous factor in emissions performance. Recent work has moved more in the direction of an assessment of policy instruments and their success in influencing market behavior and investment choices and long-term structural change (Xu et al., 2025). This literature indicates that the number of emissions that a policy will reduce is not a direct outcome of policy ambition but rather dependent on the interaction between policy instruments and market institutions with market behavior. Greater interest in freight transport is also demonstrated in the literature, in which the issue of decarbonization is compounded by operational complexity, capital intensity, and coordination needs across supply chains (Ravikumar & Aarthi, 2025b). Nevertheless, even with this increased sophistication, there is a still lack of understanding of how the targets of emission are converted into concrete market behavior and why the same policy intervention produces varied results across settings.

6.1 Economic vs Behavioral Perspectives

The transport decarbonization literature indicates that it is moving away to integrate behavioral views as opposed to the economic interpretation. Conventional economic strategies focus on market failures and recommend the use of tools like carbon pricing and fuel taxes to internalize the externalities and become more efficient (Falanga et al., 2025). Empirical evidence however points out that transport actors, especially in the freight systems, do not react the same to price signals because of limited rationality, contractual rigidities and risk aversion. The study of behavior underlines expectations, credibility of policies, and decision heuristics as the driving force behind investment and operation decisions. This deviation indicates that cost-based instruments might not be an effective way of decarbonization. Rather, the effectiveness of policy lies in the capacity to match economic incentives with behavioral realities especially in situations where the asset life and operational constraints restrict quick adapting (von Malmborg, 2025).

6.2 Single Instruments vs Policy Mixes

The literature illustrates that single policy tools are effective in theory but may not yield much or varied results when applied separately. Price instruments like carbon taxes have the capability to affect the efficiency of operations but can be counterbalanced by cost pass through in freight markets (Ige & Kabeya, 2025). Regulatory interventions, such as emission standards, assure compliance at the expense of flexibility and promote low compliance plans. Contrarily, the recent literature focuses on the effectiveness of the coherent policy blends that integrate pricing, regulation, incentives, and infrastructure facilitation. These combined strategies deal with several obstacles at the same time, such as cost, risk, and feasibility limitations. Although, there are contradictions on the ideal policy design, since poorly coordinated mixes may result in the conflicting signals. The success of decarbonization policies therefore does not just depend on the choice of the instruments but also their coherence, sequence and institutional compatibility (Aarthi et al., 2025). Table 4 presents a comparative synthesis of key studies in transport decarbonization, highlighting their focus areas, methods, major findings, and identified limitations.

Table 4. Comparison of Key Studies in Transport Decarbonization

Study	Focus Area	Method	Key Findings	Limitation
Xu et al.	Policy instruments & emissions reduction	Review / Policy analysis	Policy effectiveness depends on interaction with market behavior, not ambition alone	Limited micro-level behavioral analysis
Falanga et al.	Economic instruments (carbon pricing)	Policy review	Pricing mechanisms improve efficiency but uneven impact across sectors	Over-reliance on economic assumptions
von Malmborg	Behavioral and policy dynamics	Conceptual / qualitative	Policy credibility and expectations strongly influence decisions	Limited empirical validation
Ige & Kabeya	Cost and regulatory instruments	Analytical study	Cost pass-through reduces effectiveness in freight systems	Sector-specific (not transport-focused fully)
Aarthi et al.	Policy mix effectiveness	Conceptual / applied	Integrated policy mixes outperform single instruments	Limited comparative empirical cases
Namchimplee et al.	Freight transport systems	Case study	Freight systems face structural barriers to decarbonization	Narrow geographic scope
Picone et al.	Emission assessment models	Systematic review	Diverse models exist but lack behavioral integration	Weak linkage to policy-market mechanisms

6.3 Passenger vs Freight Focus

Historically, transport decarbonization literature has been concentrated on passenger mobility, and relatively little has been done to address the issue of freight systems, even though they contribute to emissions proportionately. Faster implementation of low-emission technologies is commonly reported in passenger transport studies because of shorter lifespan of assets, greater policy visibility and greater consumer demand (Namchimplee et al., 2025). Freight transport, on the contrary, is typified by capital intensity, low margins and complexity in operations limiting policy responsiveness. Empirical evidence indicates that the same policies that are effective in passenger transport may not necessarily be effective in freight situations resulting to mixed results. The lack of balance shows a severe gap in the literature, with the dynamics in freight, including logistics coordination, and cross-border activities being under-investigated. It is important to mitigate this gap to create viable and feasible decarbonization plans.

6.4 Developed vs Emerging Contexts

It has been shown that comparative literature shows that the decarbonization results of developed and emerging economies are mostly different as major issues are institutional capacity, infrastructure preparedness, and market maturity. The contexts developed are usually characterized by increased policy enforcement, consistent regulatory frameworks and easier access to low-carbon technologies, which allows more direct behavioral reactions. On the other hand, emerging economies have limitations that are associated with affordability, gaps in infrastructure, and heterogeneous market structures, which cause slower and uneven adoption. Although there are studies which point at the effectiveness of the strict cost-based tools in the developed economies, there are those which state that such tools can be ineffective in the emerging markets without the support systems to complement them (Picone et al., 2025). These conflicting results highlight the significance of the context-influenced policy formulation and disclose the shortcomings of the general prescriptions of the policy in accomplishing the transportation decarbonization.

7. CASE STUDIES

The case studies below contain policy-relevant evidence in the recent past on the way of how the targets of emissions are converted to tangible market indications and how road and freight participants react to various institutional and economic circumstances. The former case refers to a developed economy freight environment in which decarbonization is sought by means of a potent signal of cost, represented by road charges, to better understand fleet economics and logistics choices. The second instance is of an emerging-market setting, where ambitious decarbonization desire is limited by affordability and infrastructure preparation, along with a heterogeneous operator capacity, with the results of the policies expressed unevenly across the vehicle segments (Feng et al., 2025). The cases are combined to assess the interaction between instrument design (pricing, standards, incentives, procurement) and market structure (fleet composition, margins, asset lifetimes) in order to find out the rate of adoption, operational response, and unintended response. It is not an assertion of universal causality, but rather an attempt to elicit transferable policy mix information on the coherence of policy mixes, credibility, and behavior transmission on road and freight transport decarbonization pathways. Table 5 In comparing the two case studies, the researcher compares the two studies in the respect of policy mix, market structure, institutional capacity and observed behavioral responses.

Table 5. Comparative Case Study Overview

Dimension	Advanced Economy Case (Germany)	Emerging Market Case (India)
Core instrument	CO_2-based truck toll	Standards + incentives
Signal strength	High, recurring	Moderate, segmented
Freight focus	Long-haul heavy trucks	Mixed passenger–freight
Institutional capacity	Strong	Uneven
Behavioral response	Immediate cost adaptation	Gradual adoption

7.1 Case Study I: Advanced Economy Freight Case

A recent example of an application of road pricing translating the objectives of decarbonization into a direct, behavior shaping market signal to freight is the heavy goods vehicle (HGV) toll reform in Germany. The German toll system added the CO_2 emission classes as a tariff parameter since 1 December 2023, which associates the per-kilometre toll rates with performance of the emissions instead of considering freight movement as technology-neutral. This reform was implemented by the introduction of a CO_2 charge that is pegged at 200 per tonne of CO_2, which significantly added to the variable cost of trucking high-emission and enhanced fleet modernization and operational efficiency incentives (McLeod & Browne, 2023). Reporting by industry shows that the toll increase was dependent on the class of vehicle, but an average of approximately 83% with two illustrative rate changes of around €0.19/km to €0.348/km on typical €200 per tonne of CO_2 Class 1 configurations- which is an increase in conformity to the mentioned average. The anticipated behavioural channels consist of more intensive route optimization, more consideration on the load factors, and more rapidity in taking into account low-/zero-emission trucks where available, since repeated highway-kilometres are directly converted to an increase in marginal costs in the new structure. Figure 2 demonstrates the growth of the per-kilometre truck toll expenses prior to and following the reform (CO_2-related). Table 6 summarizes the key policy signals, behavioral responses, and market impacts observed in the Germany freight case.

Figure 2. Germany HGV Toll Increase

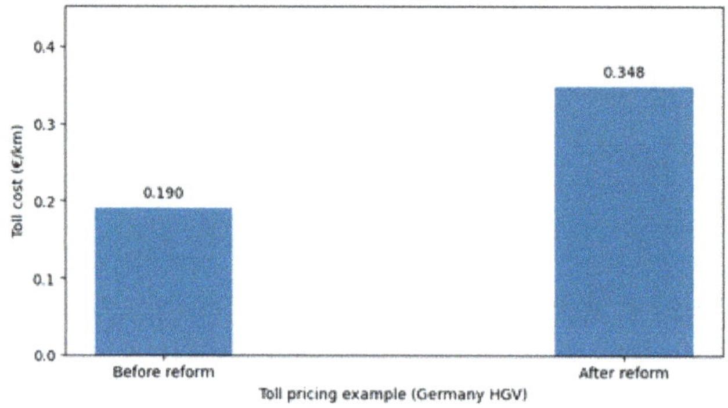

Table 6. Case Study I: Germany HGV Toll Reform – Key Insights

Dimension	Observation
Policy Instrument	CO_2-based road toll linked to emissions class
Signal Type	Strong, recurring cost signal
Behavioral Response	Route optimization, load consolidation, early fleet transition consideration
Market Impact	Immediate increase in operational costs (~83% toll rise)
Emissions Effect	Short-term intensity reduction, long-term structural shift potential
Limitation	Risk of rerouting and cross-border leakage

7.2 Case Study II: Emerging Market Road Transport Case

India represents a new decarbonization trajectory of the emerging market in which the reaction of the market is evident, but limited by the affordability, infrastructure and the heterogeneity of segments. The push in national policy has increased the pace of electrification, however, the penetration of EVs in many countries is lower than the global level: in India, in 2024, EV penetration was 7.66% compared to the world with 16.48% (resulting in slower diffusion rates despite an increase in sales volumes). Those constraints on implementation especially apply to heavier freight and long-haul operations, where the readiness of technologies and charging/fueling networks are considered limiting factors; the same evidence of the country states that longer-haul trucks removed a disproportionate portion of transport CO_2, but their share of the vehicle population is minimal, underlining the structural challenge of the rapid abatement in freight. At the policy level, India is increasing efficiency/emissions control by implementing new CAFE norms (targeted April 2027 31st March 2032) to lower average fleet emissions to 114 to 100g CO_2/km, with a targeted pathway to 76g CO_2/km in case EVs are sold in 11% of the car market by 2032 tightening the norms to achieve efficiency/emissions targets indicated to be annualized to 76g CO_2/km (Kotlars et al., 2025). Demand-support devices are also kept in focus: in the case of FAME-II, 6,862 e-buses were approved, and 5,135 were delivered by 28 Feb 2025, which means that about 74.8% will be delivered (5,135/6,862). This combination is an improvement, however, and it also points to delivery, infrastructure, and financing tensions that define the actual market action. Figure 3 Shows the selected policy and market percentages of India with regards to its advancement and limitations in decarbonizing the road transport. Table 7 presents the policy structure, market responses, and key limitations in the emerging-market transport decarbonization context.

Figure 3. India Road Transport Decarbonization Indicators

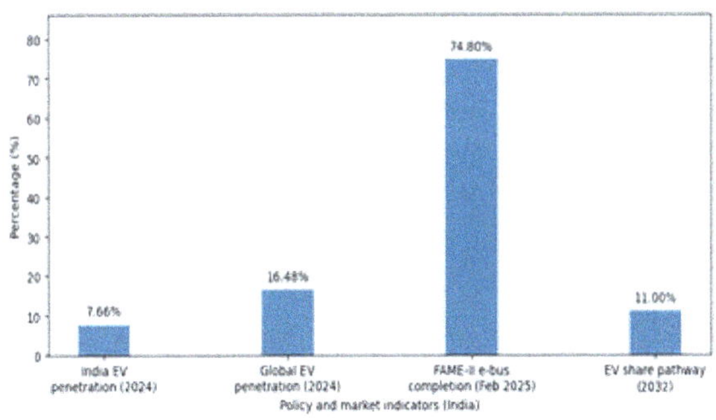

Table 7. Case Study II: India Road Transport – Key Insights

Dimension	Observation
Policy Instrument	Standards (CAFE), subsidies (FAME-II), incentives
Signal Type	Moderate, segmented policy signals
Behavioral Response	Gradual adoption, selective electrification
Market Impact	Slow EV penetration (7.66% vs global 16.48%)
Emissions Effect	Incremental and uneven reduction
Limitation	Infrastructure gaps, affordability constraints, delivery inefficiencies

7.3 Cross-Case Comparison

Strongness, credibility and reach of behavioural signal fundamentally forms the basis of policy effectiveness in the two instances. The toll reform in Germany popularizes the idea of decarbonization as a repetition of a kilometre charge that builds an immediate and permanent incentive program; the 83% average toll increase that is reported is an illustration of the strength of marginal-cost signals in responding to routing, pricing and strategic fleet decisions swiftly. Comparatively, the Indian path route is an amalgamation of purpose and tightening demand with motivations and purchases, yet the response of the market remains the segment-focused: a general 7.66% EV penetration (2024) demonstrates that the momentum is present, although it is hard to change rapidly since the freight technologies and infrastructure were not ready (Pinchasik et al., 2020). This comparison suggests that more developed economies can promote a faster shift in the behavior of freight with the assistance of the high-credibility cost instruments, and the countries of the emerging markets will require the coordinated packages that will facilitate the entry barriers and boost the capacity of delivery (e.g., the implementation of e-buss is reached at about 74.8% under FAME-II). Figure 4 Makes a comparison on the key signs of policy and market reaction signs between Germany and India.

Figure 4. Cross-Case Policy and Market Response Comparison

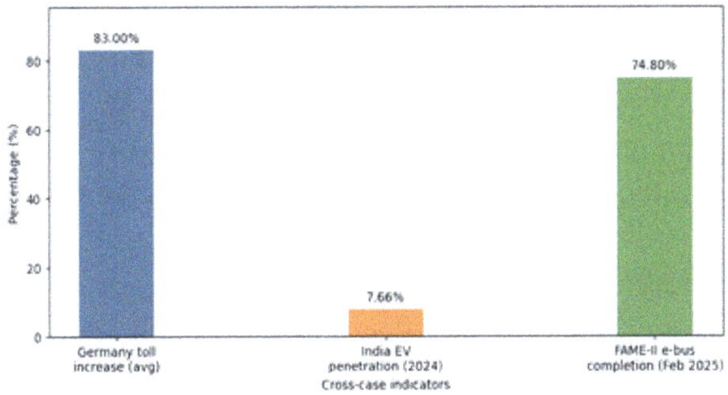

8. RESULTS AND DISCUSSION

As shown in the case studies, the results of decarbonization in the road and freight transport are mainly determined by the intensity, authority, and action range of the policy signals instead of the emissions objectives. Climate policies that convert climate objectives into periodic, economical relevant expenses or limits produce more immediate and precise market reactions than those which depend primarily on vision statements or start-up incentives. These outcomes indicate that transport actors react by making the mechanical changes in their operations first, and only then settle on capital-intensive changes in technology, especially in freight markets with long equipment payback and low profit margins. Simultaneously, the results indicate that decarbonization as a policy measure is hardly linear in most cases (Nonomura et al., 2023). Strategic adaptation, selective compliance, and spatial reallocation of activity are among the responses of behavior, potentially undermining the benefits of emissions provided it is not considered in the policy design. Institutional capacity and coordination turn out to be the key mediating variables as the credibility of the policy signals and the continuance of the behavioral change depends on them. In general, it is emphasized in the discussion that the process of decarbonization requires constant alignment between policy tools, market incentives, and the system of governance.

8.1 Policy Signals and Market Behavior

The comparative evidence suggests that powerful and repeated policy signals have a higher level of successful inducing behavior change than incentives that are one-time or far-off. Under the freight scenario of the developed economy, the introduction of CO_2 classes into the road tolls caused major changes in the marginal costs of operating the high-emission cars, which resulted in direct incentives of route optimization, a reduction in loads and reconsideration of the composition of the fleet. The documented 83% average toll increment demonstrates the ability of cost-related instruments to affect the daily operation decisions fast. By contrast, the case of the emerging-market indicates that the signals that are less strong or more indirect like the gradual tightening of standards, and partial subsidies produce slower and more dispersed responses to behavior (Agbede et al., 2021). As some of the segments advanced in terms of vehicle electrification, freight operators in situations where infrastructure was inadequate or financing limited reacted with hesitation. This indicates that policy signal strength, predictability and frequency are conclusive in determining future short-term operational behavior, as well as long-term investment planning.

8.2 Unintended Policy Effects

There are also some undesired behavioral consequences identified in the case studies that make decarbonization challenging. In developed economies, where strong prices are observed, it may be possible to stimulate compliance-based optimization, e.g. by shifting freight around and avoiding toll roads or presence across borders, resulting in leakage of emissions instead of absolute cuts. Equally, in some situations efficiency gains can reduce the costs per kilometre, leading to rebound consequences due to higher vehicle miles or ton-mile. The use of partial incentives and inconsistency in enforcement in an emerging-market environment can result into selective application with a cleaner technology being applied on a subsidized or visible basis with the rest of the population continuing with high-emission practices. Such trends explain why players in the market pursue cost-reduction policies to the best of their policy limits (Wu & Zhang, 2023). Such responses without coordination at the cross-jurisdictional level and complementary policies can diminish the environmental effectiveness of decarbonization policies. These unintended effects are therefore very important to anticipate and mitigate in order to translate policy ambition into longer-term emissions cut. Table 8 Compensates the main behavior changes including adjustment of fleet, optimization of routes, adoption of technology, and unintended effects among cases.

Table 8. Observed Market and Behavioral Outcomes

Outcome Dimension	Advanced Economy	Emerging Market
Fleet adjustment	Accelerated consideration of low-emission trucks	Selective electrification
Operational change	Routing and load consolidation	Limited operational change
Unintended effects	Cross-border rerouting	Segmental compliance
Emissions impact	Short-term intensity reduction	Gradual, uneven reduction

8.3 Institutional and Credibility Effects

Policy credibility and institutional capacity come out as key issues of market response in both cases. Transport actors in the contexts that are viewed to be stable in terms of the policy frameworks, well-enforced and coordinated across the governance levels show higher propensity to make irreversible investments in the low-carbon technologies and infrastructure. The case of the advanced economies indicates a fairly good administrative ability and enforcement and adds more confidence in the fact that increased operating costs associated with emissions will continue to exist in the long-term. Comparatively, in emerging markets, ineffective governance, and slow implementation as well as bottlenecks in the infrastructure undermine the policy credibility, which promotes short-term adjustment, as opposed to long-term change. There are also the coordination issues between transport, energy, and climate authorities that restrict market adaptation by creating doubt in future working conditions. These results show that the policies of decarbonization should be supported by strong institutions, long-term signals, and coordination of the agencies to ensure behavioral compliance with the emission goals and prevent policy fatigue and strategic inertia.

9. FUTURE RESEARCH DIRECTIONS

The future decarbonization in transport research must not stay in the position of the fixed assessment of the individual policy instruments but dynamic assessment that reflects long-term market readjustment, technological learning, and institutional change. As the evidence in the case indicates, market reactions take long time horizons to be affected and are influenced by the prospective policy stringency, availability of infrastructure as well as competitive forces. The nature of research agendas should then include the following; temporal dynamics, behavioral feedbacks and uncertainty in policy effectiveness assessment. It is also in increased demand to incorporate a data-driven and computational method to improve real time observation and interpretation of complex transport systems (Macharis & Nocera, 2019). Also, it is worth considering that as transport markets become more interdependent across jurisdiction, coordination, leakage and regulatory alignment issues become more critical. To solve these issues, interdisciplinary theories are necessary that would connect economics, data science, the science of governance and transport planning. The investigations conducted along these lines will help future studies to contribute to the development of adaptive, credible, and resilient decarbonization strategies in road and freight transportation systems.

9.1 Dynamic Policy and Market Change

The next research directions should concentrate on how the policies of decarbonization of transport change over time and how the market participants change their behaviour within the frames of the changing regulatory conditions. Longitudinal research designs are required in order to measure the delayed response to investment, path dependence, and lock-in effects that relate to long-lived transport assets. The focus of such work must be the impact of policy sequencing, escalation channels, and revisioning on expectations and risk management behavior amongst transport operators (Bagloee et al., 2016). Dynamical models can be used to estimate the influence of initial policy indicators in further adoption of technology and infrastructure development. The studies also should examine the mechanism by which firms learn and adjust as policy regimes get older, such as operational optimization to structural change. This is critical in understanding the dynamics that should be used when coming up with policies that will be sustainable in the long run and will not result into stagnation or unwanted reinforcement of high-emission practices.

9.2 Data-Driven Policy Evaluation

The proliferating amount of data on transport, logistics and emissions opens a fresh chance to assess decarbonization policies using data. To resolve the issues of the present study in the future, artificial intelligence and advanced analytics should be employed to trace the behavioral responses, detect new combinations, and evaluate the policy effects on a more time- and space-resilient level. Under alternative policy conditions, predictive analysis of the development of a fleet, routing behavior, and use of infrastructure can be supported by machine learning methods (Ravikumar & Aarthi, 2025a). The combination of real-time vehicle, charging network, and digital freight data will enhance the insights on the transformation of policy signals into the operational decisions. The methodological issues of data quality, interoperability and governance however are also still a problem. A study is required to come up with transparent, interpretable, and policy-relevant AI tools that complement existing methods of evaluation and that can increase the evidence base to adaptive transport policy design.

9.3 Cross-Border Governance

The transport markets are progressively running both across regional and national borders and thus cross-border coordination is a paramount field that will need future research. Research needs to examine the effect that variation in policy stringency, enforcement and timing on various jurisdictions in shaping routing decisions, investment location and emission leakage. A comparative analysis can be helpful in clarifying the circumstances in which harmonization or mutual recognition of standards can lead to the improvement of the effectiveness of policies. Meanwhile, the multi-level governance studies need to look into the interaction between national decarbonization policies and subnational ones, including congestion charges, access control, and urban logistics rules (Marisamy et al., 2025). Such interactions form an important understanding that would limit the conflict of policies and strengthens the consistency of market indication. The effectiveness of institutional coordination between transport, energy, and climate actors in the future should also be evaluated in a study to facilitate consistent and fair decarbonization trajectories.

10. MANAGERIAL IMPLICATIONS

The arguments presented in this chapter have significant implications to managers working in road and freight transport systems that are decarbonizing due to policy reasons. The policy frameworks are becoming more translations of the emissions targets into tangible cost, compliance and risk indicators that have a direct impact on operational feasibility and long-term competitiveness. The decarbonization policies are no longer to be seen as external boundary inflictions that managers must be able to receive without resistance but rather they must be incorporated into strategic planning and decision making (Naumov et al., 2023). The evidence suggests that companies that expect policy change and match their strategies with new regulatory movements are more equipped to cope with the risk of transition and extract efficiency benefits. The responses of managers should then be related to improving the flexibility, bettering data-driven decision-making, and boosting coordination between fleet, logistics, and investment functions. The active management of exposure to regulatory shocks, in addition to placing transport and logistics companies in the position to grow sustainably and resiliently in an increasingly carbon-constrained world, is possible by actively responding to policy signals.

10.1 Strategic Adaptation

Decarbonization policies should be perceived by the managers of transport and logistics companies as a kind of strategic signals instead of single regulatory demands. Powerful and consistent cost signals like road charges based on emissions require sustained adjustment in pricing and contracting strategies and service design. Strategic adaptation entails the incorporation of policy developments in the market forecasting, customer negotiating, and competitive positioning (Ravikumar & Aarthi, 2025c). Companies that operate diversified fleets with a high degree of flexibility in the routing are more likely to react to the varied cost structures in corridors and jurisdictions. Also, initial exposure to clean technologies and sustainability reporting may cause a decline in regulatory risks and development of reputational capital. Finding of the chapter implies that strategic responsiveness is especially important in the context of freight markets; when margins are being eroded and resilience is decreasing due to delayed adjustment. Managers able to match corporate strategy to policy courses can turn pressures of compliance to operational efficiency and long-term value creation opportunities.

10.2 Investment under Transition Risk

Planning of investments in transport markets is increasingly being done under uncertainty of regulations and transition risk. The policies of decarbonization impact the values of assets, lifecycle of technology and compatibility of infrastructure, complicating decisions related to capital allocation (Vleugel & Bal, 2018). Stranding of assets should be considered by the managers, especially in high-emission vehicles and infrastructure that depends on fossil fuels. Scenario planning and the use of staged investment approaches can serve to deal with uncertainty by keeping flexibility in its course preserving movement toward lower-emission operations. The implication of evidence shows that believable and stable policies stimulate firms to invest sooner, but volatile policies stimulate investment deferral. Managers are thus advised to observe policy signals at all the levels of governance and to include regulatory risk assessment in financial planning. A matching of investment and the anticipated policy course may minimize the risk of sudden changes in regulations and help to establish the transition paths.

10.3 Operations and Technology Strategy

One of the main short-term reactions to decarbonization policies is operational optimization, which is especially relevant to the freight transport industry where margins are low and capital rates turnover slow. Increased cost of emissions can be used by managers to utilize digital tools to enhance route planning, load consolidation, and energy efficiency. Fleet strategy must have a balance between incremental improvements of the efficiency and long-term changes toward the low and zero-emission technologies. Any fleet renewal should be based on decisions that require looking beyond the initial costs and take into account the changing regulatory demands and infrastructure accessibility (Liimatainen et al., 2015). The adoption of technology can best be embodied in larger operational and organizational changes as opposed to being implemented as an independent intervention. Findings in the chapter indicate that companies that integrate operational optimization and gradual adoption of technology would be in a better position to respond to decarbonization led by policies without compromising the reliability of services and cost competitiveness. Table 9 Summarises strategic, investment, and operational implications of firms and policy design lessons of regulators.

Table 9. Managerial and Policy Implications Summary

Stakeholder	Strategic Implication	Action Area
Transport firms	Anticipate cost signals	Fleet and pricing strategy
Logistics managers	Improve efficiency	Routing and consolidation
Policymakers	Ensure credibility	Long-term policy commitment
Regulators	Prevent leakage	Cross-border coordination

11. CONCLUSION

This chapter has discussed decarbonization of road and freight transport as market mediated process whereby the goal of emissions targets only affects the results to the extent that the goals are converted into credible and behaviorally effective policy signals. The evaluation shows that market transformation relies on policy ambitions rather than the aspirations of climate commitments and more so it depends on the construction, consistency and sustainability of the policy tools by which those commitments are enacted. Powerful and repeated cost-related signals, including road taxes in the form of emissions, prove to cause a more visible and immediate behavioral response than perceived or disjointed signals, especially in freight markets that feature long asset durations and small margins. Simultaneously, the results demonstrate that responses of markets are diverse and dynamic and depend on the firm size, nature of operation, the presence of infrastructure, and institutional capacity. Such dynamics highlight the need to have a balance between policy mixes that support pricing, regulation, and the ability to make investments to prevent an unintended effect of rebound demand, leakage, or optimization through compliance. In terms of policy design, the chapter brings into focus the key role of credibility, time consistency as well as coordination amongst the levels of governance to maintain investment confidence and to align the incentives of the individuals as well as the climate goals of the people. An economically efficient decarbonization is found when the costs of emissions are internalized and the flexibility left to the firms to find the least-cost adjustment pathways. Finally, the decarbonization of transport can and indeed should not be made resilient based on fixed regulatory requirements, but instead by dynamic policy frames that have the ability to adjust market behavior over time. These frameworks should combine the economic effectiveness, institutional resilience, and realism of behavior to make the shift towards low-carbon road and freight transport a process that is competitive, fair, and sustainable with the changing operational technological and market realities.

REFERENCES

Aarthi, S., Ravikumar, R. N., Sobirova, K., & Mamadiyarov, Z. (2025). Empowering a sustainable future through digital learning and the SDGs. In *Harnessing E-Learning to Create a Sustainable Future* (pp. 145–172). IGI Global Scientific Publishing., DOI: 10.4018/979-8-3373-0112-9.ch006

Agbede, O. O., Akhigbe, E. E., Ajayi, A. J., & Egbuhuzor, N. S. (2021). Assessing economic risks and returns of energy transitions with quantitative financial approaches. *International Journal of Multidisciplinary Research and Growth Evaluation*, *2*(1), 552–566. DOI: 10.54660/.IJMRGE.2021.2.1.552-566

Ashmore, D. P., Pojani, D., Thoreau, R., Christie, N., & Tyler, N. A. (2018). The symbolism of 'eco cars' across national cultures: Potential implications for policy formulation and transfer. *Transportation Research Part D, Transport and Environment*, *63*, 560–575. DOI: 10.1016/j.trd.2018.06.024

Association, T. K. L. R., Nan, M.-F., Cui, Y., & Zhang, M.-Z. (2023). A study on the optimization of reverse logistics network in China's automotive industry: Focusing on abandoned cars in China. *The Korean Logistics Research Association*, *33*(3), 5–21. DOI: 10.17825/klr.2023.33.3.5

Bagloee, S. A., Tavana, M., Asadi, M., & Oliver, T. (2016). Autonomous vehicles: Challenges, opportunities, and future implications for transportation policies. *Journal of Modern Transportation*, *24*(4), 284–303. DOI: 10.1007/s40534-016-0117-3

Chen, S., Wu, J., & Zong, Y. (2020). The impact of the freight transport modal shift policy on China's carbon emissions reduction. *Sustainability (Basel)*, *12*(2), 583. DOI: 10.3390/su12020583

Efstathiou, C. I., Arunachalam, S., Arter, C. A., & Buonocore, J. (2024). Assessing the tradeoffs in emissions, air quality and health benefits from excess power generation due to climate-related policies for the transportation sector. *Environmental Research Letters*, *19*(6), 064007. DOI: 10.1088/1748-9326/ad41f1

Falanga, A., Picone, M., Greco, F. M., & Cartenì, A. (2025). A roadmap to low-carbon freight transport: A review of EU directives and regulations. *WSEAS Transactions on Power Systems*, *20*(11), 114–132. DOI: 10.37394/232016.2025.20.11

Feng, F., Zheng, F., Zhang, Z., & Wang, L. (2025). A framework for low-carbon container multimodal transport route optimization under hybrid uncertainty: Model and case study. *Applied Sciences (Basel, Switzerland)*, *15*(12), 6894. DOI: 10.3390/app15126894

Ige, O. E., & Kabeya, M. (2025). Decarbonizing the cement industry: Technological, economic, and policy barriers to CO2 mitigation adoption. *Cleanroom Technology*, *7*(4), 85. DOI: 10.3390/cleantechnol7040085

Islam, M. S., Liu, G., Xu, D., Chen, Y., Li, H., & Chen, C. (2023). University-campus-based zero-carbon action plans for accelerating the zero-Carbon City transition. *Sustainability (Basel)*, *15*(18), 13504. DOI: 10.3390/su151813504

Kim, N. S., Janic, M., & van Wee, B. (2009). Trade-off between carbon dioxide emissions and logistics costs based on multiobjective optimization. *Transportation Research Record: Journal of the Transportation Research Board*, *2139*(1), 107–116. DOI: 10.3141/2139-13

Kotlars, A., Hudenko, J., Jurgelane-Kaldava, I., Stankevičienė, J., Gailis, M., Kukjans, I., & Batenko, A. (2025). Transitioning to hydrogen trucks in small economies: Policy, infrastructure, and innovation dynamics. *Sustainability (Basel)*, *17*(24), 11272. DOI: 10.3390/su172411272

Liimatainen, H., Hovi, I. B., Arvidsson, N., & Nykänen, L. (2015). Driving forces of road freight CO2 in 2030. *International Journal of Physical Distribution & Logistics Management*, *45*(3), 260–285. DOI: 10.1108/IJPDLM-10-2013-0255

Lin, P.-C., & Bai, H.-J. (2024). Emissions intensity comparisons and consumption-based CO2 accounting of transportation services. *Maritime Economics & Logistics*, *26*(1), 131–150. DOI: 10.1057/s41278-023-00259-9

Liu, L., Hwang, T., Lee, S., Ouyang, Y., Lee, B., Smith, S. J., Yan, F., Daenzer, K., & Bond, T. C. (2015a). Emission projections for long-haul freight trucks and rail in the United States through 2050. *Environmental Science & Technology*, *49*(19), 11569–11576. DOI: 10.1021/acs.est.5b01187 PMID: 26368392

Liu, L., Hwang, T., Lee, S., Ouyang, Y., Lee, B., Smith, S. J., Yan, F., Daenzer, K., & Bond, T. C. (2015b). Emission projections for long-haul freight trucks and rail in the United States through 2050. *Environmental Science & Technology*, *49*(19), 11569–11576. DOI: 10.1021/acs.est.5b01187 PMID: 26368392

Liu, P., & Mu, D. (2015). Evaluating sustainability of truck weight regulations: A system dynamics view. *Journal of Industrial Engineering and Management*, *8*(5). Advance online publication. DOI: 10.3926/jiem.1593

Macharis, C., & Nocera, S. (2019). The future of freight transport. *European Transport Research Review*, *11*(1), 21. Advance online publication. DOI: 10.1186/s12544-019-0359-3

Marisamy, K., Selvakumar, A., Rajasekar, B., Natarajan, R., Atajanova, A., & Makhmudov, S. (2025). Smart logistics integrating AI, IoT, blockchain, and Robotics for a sustainable Future. In *Emerging Trends in Smart Logistics Technologies* (pp. 73–104). IGI Global Scientific Publishing., DOI: 10.4018/979-8-3373-2434-0.ch003

Mathiesen, L., & Mæstad, O. (2004). Climate policy and the steel industry: Achieving global emission reductions by an incomplete climate agreement. *The Energy Journal (Cambridge, Mass.)*, *25*(4), 91–114. DOI: 10.5547/ISSN0195-6574-EJ-Vol25-No4-5

McLeod, S., & Browne, M. (2023). Planning for the sustainability of freight and logistics. *European Journal of Transport and Infrastructure Research*. https://doi .org/DOI: 10.18757/ejtir.2023.23.3.6145

Namchimplee, K., Inohae, T., & Saengsathien, A. (2025). Multimodal transport efficiency in agricultural supply chains: A case study of rail-road integration in Thailand's sugar logistics. *Acta Logistica*, *12*(4), 615–626. DOI: 10.22306/al.v12i4.696

Naumov, S., Keith, D. R., & Sterman, J. D. (2023). Accelerating vehicle fleet turnover to achieve sustainable mobility goals. *Journal of Operations Management*, *69*(1), 36–66. DOI: 10.1002/joom.1173

Nonomura, K., Hiekata, K., Nishino, N., & Nakashima, T. (2023). Evaluation of Feebate by multi-agent simulation for policy making in the complex international maritime transport. In *Advances in Transdisciplinary Engineering*. IOS Press., DOI: 10.3233/ATDE230653

Picone, M., Falanga, A., Henke, I., Greco, F. M., & Carteni, A. (2025). Decarbonizing road transport: A systematic review of methods and models for emission impact assessment. *WSEAS Transactions on Environment and Development*, *21*(56), 674–688. DOI: 10.37394/232015.2025.21.56

Pinchasik, D. R., Hovi, I. B., Mjøsund, C. S., Grønland, S. E., Fridell, E., & Jerksjö, M. (2020). Crossing borders and expanding modal shift measures: Effects on mode choice and emissions from freight transport in the Nordics. *Sustainability (Basel)*, *12*(3), 894. DOI: 10.3390/su12030894

Ravikumar, R. N., & Aarthi, S. (2025a). AI-driven digital twins and autonomous operations for sustainable logistics and procurement. In *Advances in Computational Intelligence and Robotics* (pp. 65–100). IGI Global Scientific Publishing. DOI: 10.4018/979-8-3373-7006-4.ch003

Ravikumar, R. N., & Aarthi, S. (2025b). Artificial Intelligence and IoT integration in supply chains. In *Leveraging Technology and Renewable Energy for Sustainable Supply Chains* (pp. 1–32). IGI Global Scientific Publishing., DOI: 10.4018/979-8-3373-3790-6.ch001

Ravikumar, R. N., & Aarthi, S. (2025c). Intelligent logistics. In *Advances in Computational Intelligence and Robotics* (pp. 217–248). IGI Global Scientific Publishing. DOI: 10.4018/979-8-3373-7006-4.ch008

Sahu, P. K., Pani, A., & Santos, G. (2022). Freight traffic impacts and logistics inefficiencies in India: Policy interventions and solution concepts for sustainable city logistics. *Transportation in Developing Economies*, *8*(2), 31. Advance online publication. DOI: 10.1007/s40890-022-00161-8

van Dijk, J., Farsi, M., & Weber, S. (2021). Travel mode choices in a greening market: The impact of electric vehicles and prior investments. *Transportation Research Record: Journal of the Transportation Research Board*, *2675*(11), 1205–1218. DOI: 10.1177/03611981211025279

Venkatesh, N. H., & Raslavičius, L. (2024). A National Innovation System concept-based analysis of autonomous vehicles' potential in reaching zero-emission fleets. *Technologies*, *12*(2), 26. DOI: 10.3390/technologies12020026

Vleugel, J. M., & Bal, F. (2018). Regional goods delivery: How to reduce its CO 2-, NO x- and PM 10- emissions? *International Journal of Energy Production and Management*, *3*(4), 338–347. DOI: 10.2495/EQ-V3-N4-338-347

von Malmborg, F. (2025). At the controls: Politics and policy entrepreneurs in EU policy to decarbonize maritime transport. *The Review of Policy Research*, *42*(5), 1243–1276. DOI: 10.1111/ropr.12609

Wu, Y., & Zhang, R. (2023). Evaluation model for a port hinterland intermodal freight network considering environmental impacts and capacity constraints. *Transportation Research Record: Journal of the Transportation Research Board*, *2677*(2), 462–478. DOI: 10.1177/03611981221107008

Xu, X., Kamboj, P., Almutairi, S., Gertin, T., Arora, A., Hejazi, M., & Center, K. A. P. S. and R. (2025). *Decarbonizing road freight transportation in Saudi Arabia*. King Abdullah Petroleum Studies and Research Center. DOI: 10.30573/KS--2025-DP10

Yao, Q., Zhu, S., & Li, Y. (2022). Green vehicle-routing problem of fresh agricultural products considering carbon emission. *International Journal of Environmental Research and Public Health*, *19*(14), 8675. DOI: 10.3390/ijerph19148675 PMID: 35886525

Zhu, L., Liu, Z., & Jian, W. (2023). Contribution assessment of carbon tax on the reduction of freight corridor carbon emissions through modal shift. *Transportation Research Record: Journal of the Transportation Research Board*, *2677*(10), 167–179. DOI: 10.1177/03611981231160538

KEY TERMS AND DEFINITIONS

Behavioral Response: Adjustments in operational, investment, or technology decisions made by transport actors in response to policy signals.

Carbon Leakage: The displacement of emissions to other regions or jurisdictions due to differences in policy stringency.

Carbon Pricing: A policy mechanism that assigns a monetary cost to carbon emissions to internalize environmental externalities.

Emissions Targets: Quantified goals set by governments to limit or reduce greenhouse gas emissions within a specified timeframe.

Fleet Electrification: The transition from internal combustion engine vehicles to electric or zero-emission vehicles.

Freight Transport: The movement of goods by road using light, medium, and heavy-duty vehicles across local, national, or international routes.

Institutional Capacity: The ability of public authorities to design, implement, monitor, and enforce decarbonization policies effectively.

Market Signals: Cost, risk, and compliance cues generated by policies that influence the decisions of transport and logistics actors.

Policy Credibility: The perceived stability and reliability of policy commitments over time.

Policy Instruments: Regulatory, economic, and institutional tools such as carbon pricing, standards, subsidies, and road charges used to implement emissions targets.

Policy Mix: A coordinated combination of multiple policy instruments designed to achieve decarbonization objectives.

Rebound Effect: An increase in transport activity that partially offsets emissions reductions gained from efficiency improvements.

Road User Charges: Fees imposed on vehicles based on distance traveled, vehicle type, or emissions performance.

Transition Risk: Financial and operational risks arising from regulatory changes, technological shifts, or market transformation during decarbonization.

Transport Decarbonization: The process of reducing greenhouse gas emissions from road and freight transport through policy, technology, and behavioral change.

Chapter 5

Decision Frameworks for Sustainable Urban Transport Systems

Sena Kumcu
http://orcid.org/0000-0002-9648-6281
Department of Industrial Engineering, Faculty of Engineering, Gazi University, Ankara, Turkey

Beste Desticioğlu Taşdemir
http://orcid.org/0000-0001-8321-4554
Department of Operations Research, Alparslan Defence Sciences and National Security Institute, National Defence University, Ankara, Turkey & Department of Econometrics, Erasmus School of Economics, Erasmus University Rotterdam, Rotterdam, The Netherlands

ABSTRACT

The rapid pace of urbanization, combined with mounting environmental concerns, has necessitated a strategic shift toward sustainable urban transport systems. Electric buses and high-speed rail (HSR) represent two of the most promising technologies in decarbonizing the transport sector. This chapter develops a structured selection criteria–based framework to support decision-making in evaluating these systems. Through this decision-making approach, the research seeks to fill a gap in comparative sustainability evaluations of urban transport technologies. Furthermore, the chapter highlights the relevance of applying multi-criteria decision-making (MCDM) models for robust planning under uncertainty. Drawing on performance indicators, the chapter provides a structured analysis to guide policymakers and stakeholders in prioritizing infrastructure investments with long-term climate and sustainability objectives.

DOI: 10.4018/979-8-3373-9003-1.ch005

1. INTRODUCTION

Global warming is one of the biggest problems facing the world today. According to a report published by the World Meteorological Organization (WMO) in 2022, the increase in greenhouse gas emissions in recent years has resulted in the highest average temperatures ever recorded over the past eight years. These high temperatures have caused droughts and devastating floods worldwide, affecting millions of people and causing billions of dollars in material losses (WMO, 2022). The biggest reason for this temperature increase is the recent rise in greenhouse gas emissions.

Accelerated urbanization coupled with rising population density has precipitated numerous issues in urban areas. Transportation represents one of the most pressing challenges concerning modern infrastructure. The increase of internal combustion vehicles causes traffic congestion and degrades air quality in urban regions. Elevated vehicular congestion in urban areas results in diminished travel velocity for inhabitants, thereby leading to substantial time loss in both productive and leisure activities. Simultaneously, traffic congestion jeopardizes access to destinations, particularly those located in the city center. Issues encompass road safety, increased air pollution, traffic noise, and climate change. All of these concerns negatively impact the quality of human life and the environment.

In recent decades, the need to transition from conventional transportation systems to low-carbon alternatives has become increasingly urgent. As the transport sector accounts for approximately one-quarter of global greenhouse gas (GHG) emissions, reducing its carbon footprint is critical to achieving climate targets. In response, policymakers have increasingly supported the adoption of clean and renewable energy solutions. Among these, electric vehicles have emerged as one of the most effective approaches to reducing transport-related emissions, with a growing number of models and technologies introduced in recent years (Biswas & Das, 2019). However, the development of sustainable and green cities requires more than the widespread adoption of individual electric vehicles. The integration of electric public transportation systems, particularly electric buses (EBs) and high-speed rail (HSR), plays a critical role in reducing congestion, improving system efficiency, and enabling large-scale low-emission mobility solutions.

Recent innovations show that digitalization and smart transportation systems are becoming important parts of low-carbon mobility, in addition to changes in technology. Digital technologies including sensors, communication networks, data analytics, and artificial intelligence make it possible to monitor, optimize, and regulate transportation systems in real time. These technologies help with battery management, smart charging, and route optimization in EBs. In HSR systems, they improve operational reliability, signaling efficiency, and infrastructure monitoring.

In conclusion, sustainable transportation should be perceived not merely as a technological transition, but as a comprehensive and interdisciplinary task encompassing environmental policy, urban management, technological progress, and data-driven decision-making processes. In this context, an organized and comprehensive strategy is needed to evaluate and select the right low-carbon transportation systems, taking into account environmental, technical, operational, and economic factors. This chapter contributes to the sustainable transportation literature in several ways:

- It addresses the sustainable transportation as a multi criteria decision problem involving environmental, technical, operational, and economic trade-offs.
- It organizes the dispersed literature into a practical and policy-relevant framework of evaluation criteria that can support municipalities, planners, investors, and transport authorities in decision-making process.
- It brings together the main low-carbon transportation modes within a broad decision support perspective and provides a conceptual basis for future transportation assessment studies.

This book chapter is structured as follows: Section 2 presents global transport emissions; Section 3 discusses sustainable urban transportation, with a focus on low-carbon mobility solutions specifically EBs and HSR by outlining key decision criteria for their effective selection and deployment. Section 4 examines the role of digitalization in low-carbon transportation. Finally, Section 5 concludes the chapter with a summary of the main insights.

2. GLOBAL TRANSPORT EMISSIONS

Every modern nation seeks higher living standards and economic opportunity. Trade and investments, that drive economic growth, depend on imports and exports. Globalization, or interconnection, is a major contributor of CO_2 emissions.

The transportation sector is a significant contributor to global emissions, despite global commitments to reduce emissions across all sectors following the Paris Agreement of 2015 (Liu et al.,2025). Achieving significant climate mitigation necessitates a considerable transition to low-carbon mobility options for both passenger and freight transportation. Transportation alone accounts for 51% of total oil consumption and thus represents a substantial share of global greenhouse gas (GHG) emissions (IRENA, 2018). This high proportion underscores the urgency for sectoral transformation.

In particular, analyses within the European Union (EU) reveal that between 2013 and 2023, most economic sectors managed to reduce their GHG emissions; however, emissions from the transportation and storage sectors increased by approximately 14% during the same period (EUROSTAT, 2024). As of 2010, the transport sector directly emitted around 7.0 gigatons (Gt) of CO_2 equivalent, accounting for nearly 23% of total energy-related emissions (IPCC, 2014). These data clearly show the scale of pressure that transportation activities exert on the global climate system.

As illustrated in Figure 1, greenhouse gas emissions from the European Union's transport sector have shown an upward trend since 1990, with projections extending to 2040. The transport sector is currently the largest source of GHG emissions in the EU and has made only limited progress in emission reduction over recent decades. Despite initiatives such as the growing adoption of electric vehicles and promotion of low-carbon fuels, transport-related emissions have only slightly decreased since 2005, with a temporary dip observed in 2020 due to the COVID-19 pandemic. Projections for 2024 estimate a modest increase of 0.7% in GHG emissions compared to 2023 levels. Member States anticipate that, under current conditions, domestic transport emissions will return to 1990 levels by 2030. However, emissions from international aviation and maritime transport are expected to rise further. With additional policy measures, emissions could be reduced to 13% below 1990 levels by 2030. Most planned strategies focus on promoting low-carbon fuels, encouraging the use of zero-emission technologies, and fostering modal shifts toward public transportation and active mobility solutions (EEA,2025).

Figure 1. Trends in greenhouse gas emissions from the european transport sector

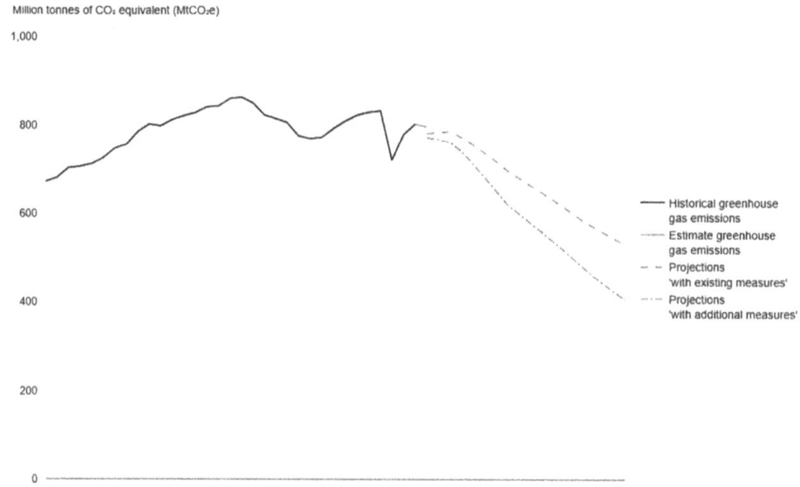

Among the various modes of transportation, namely road, air, maritime, and rail, road transport stands out as the predominant consumer of global energy resources

(OECD, 2002). Figure 2 illustrates the projected changes across different transportation modes worldwide between 2010 and 2070, based on sustainable development scenarios. According to the International Energy Agency (IEA), emissions from sectors including aviation, shipping, medium and heavy- trucks, light commercial vehicles, buses and minibuses, passenger cars, two/three-wheelers and rail are all expected to decline in the coming decades under aggressive decarbonization policies (IEA,2020).

Figure 2. Projected global CO_2 emissions by transport mode in the sustainable development scenario (2000–2070)

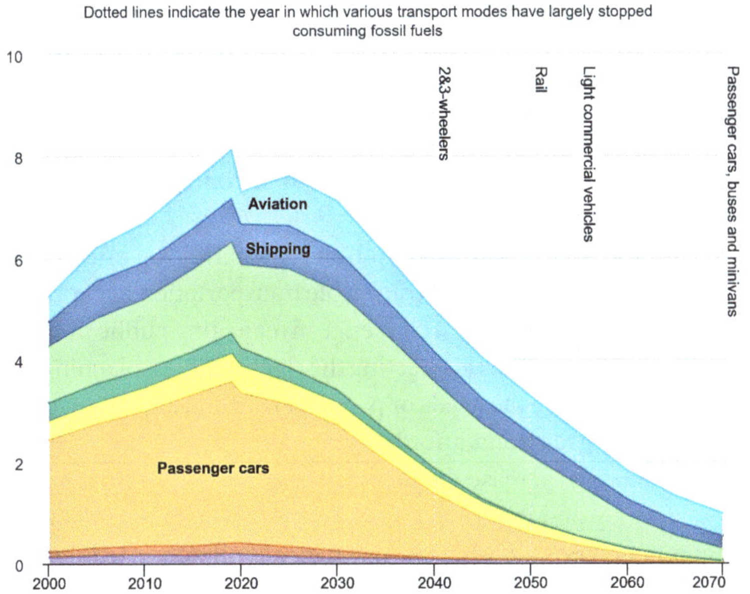

To reduce carbon dioxide emissions, industrialized nations ought to transition to renewable energy sources. Both wealthy and emerging nations must adopt creative energy efficiency strategies. Significantly, green transportation mitigates adverse environmental effects and fosters long-term sustainability. Hybrid and electric vehicles (EVs) significantly diminish CO_2 emissions, achieving long-term reductions of up to 45%. (Hussain et al., 2023).

The increase in CO_2 emissions worldwide due to transportation has been significantly reduced by the recent advances in the introduction of zero-emission vehicles (ZEVs), particularly battery electric cars (BEVs). Worldwide sales of EVs hit 17 million units in 2024, accounting for 22% of all vehicles sold; EV bus and truck markets expanded by 30% and 75%, respectively. One in ten automobiles in China are now electric, making these electrification improvements particularly noticeable there. But further decarbonization of power grids and further deployment in developing economies are prerequisites for ZEVs to fully decarbonize. To achieve the climate mitigation potential of electric transport in all regions, the report stresses the need of deeper policy alignment, technical collaboration, and investment in affordable access (IEA, 2025).

3. SUSTAINABLE URBAN TRANSPORTATION

Urbanization, propelled by population expansion, has engendered several issues in metropolitan regions. Transportation constitutes one of the most critical issues. The prevalent utilization of internal combustion engine cars results in heightened traffic congestion and deteriorates air quality in urban centers. Heightened traffic congestion in urban areas prolongs residents' travel times to their destinations. To mitigate these negative effects, planners need to encourage people to use public transportation within cities.

Efforts to improve public transportation in large cities are effective in solving traffic problems and creating a more sustainable transportation network by utilizing existing resources. Today, the biggest challenge in managing public transportation in large metropolitan municipalities is selecting the right vehicles, planning appropriate routes, and properly meeting the needs of passengers in that area. Due to factors such as higher passenger capacity and affordability, buses play a vital role in providing public transportation. To increase the use of public transportation in urban areas, it is necessary to develop and improve suitable transportation networks that can meet users' daily commute needs. Currently, the most commonly used mode of public transportation is undoubtedly buses. Therefore, buses are the best solution from an economic, environmental, and social perspective for ensuring balanced and sustainable urban transportation. Urban transportation undoubtedly needs to implement the concept of sustainability, which has gained worldwide importance in recent years. Sustainable transportation can be defined as safe, accessible transportation with low carbon emissions and efficient energy use, while minimizing economic, environmental, and social impacts.

In this context, electric buses and high speed railway that reduce carbon emissions have begun to be used to ensure sustainability in urban transportation.

3.1. Electric Buses

EVs play a significant role in reducing carbon emissions and ensuring urban sustainability. EVs are frequently preferred because they possess technology that reduces noise and environmental pollution. The transition to electric power in the transportation sector not only reduces carbon emissions and improves energy efficiency but also reduces exposure to sudden changes in oil and gas prices affected by global events (Guschinsky et al., 2021). Recently, the development of EV technologies, particularly the resolution of battery issues and the overcoming of range limitations, has encouraged the production and use of electric buses. The need for vehicles using clean energy for cleaner cities has also been a major contributing factor. Therefore, the use of electric buses in urban transportation has become increasingly widespread throughout the world recently.

Currently, three types of electric buses are used: battery electric buses, hybrid electric buses, and plug-in hybrid electric buses. Battery electric buses, or fully electric buses, lack an internal combustion engine and operate exclusively on an electric motor. Battery-powered EBs have additional advantages compared to the other two types, such as zero exhaust and noise emissions, and therefore have the potential to reduce the transportation sector's dependence on fossil fuels (Alamatsaz et al., 2022). Although the use of battery-powered buses dates back to the 2000s, their use has rapidly increased in recent years due to growing environmental awareness (Gong et al., 2020). Battery-powered EVs offer many advantages in urban transportation, such as low carbon emissions, quieter operation, and energy savings. Innovations in battery technology used in EVs are effective in extending the lifespan of vehicles, shortening battery charging times, and reducing energy consumption (Desticioglu Tasdemir and Asilogullari Ayan, 2025). To take advantage of the benefits offered by EVs in urban public transportation, EBs have begun to be used all over the world in recent years. Therefore, battery electric buses are examined in this study, and the buses referred to as EB are those with battery power.

Figure 3. Electric buses that are charging

In alignment with the European Union's climate policy and its objective of attaining zero emissions by 2050, the deployment of zero-emission buses has escalated, resulting in an increase of EBs in urban transport to 23% in recent years (Nix, 2022). Electric buses are currently the most preferred type of bus in the European Union. Finland, Denmark, and the Netherlands are among the leading countries in this regard (Mulholland & Rodríguez, 2022).

Advantages and Disadvantages of Electric Buses

Recently, EBs have become widely used worldwide to reduce carbon emissions in urban public transportation. While EBs offer advantages due to their low carbon emissions, they also have some disadvantages. This section examines both the advantages and disadvantages of EBs.

The advantages of EBs can be explained as follows:

1. Power supply via electricity: Electric buses use electricity as fuel instead of traditional buses powered by fossil fuels. This reduces the need for fossil fuels in buses used in public transportation, thus contributing to environmental sustainability (He, 2022). In addition, since the use of electrical energy is more cost-effective than fossil fuels, it also provides a cost advantage (Jagiełło et al., 2023).
2. Easy maintenance: EBs do not have complex transmissions or exhaust systems. EBs have a simple structure, four-wheel drive capability, and are easier to maintain (He, 2022).

3. Energy saving and environmental friendliness: Since EBs reduce harmful gas emissions (carbon, nitrogen, and sulfur gases) to zero, their use does not cause air pollution. Thanks to the energy conversion efficiency of the power plant and advanced pollution reduction and control equipment, EBs produce much less pollution than traditional buses. Furthermore, electric vehicles can reduce energy consumption in crowded city centers. On the other hand, the quieter operation of electric vehicles also helps reduce noise pollution (Jagiełło et al., 2023).

The disadvantages of EBs can be listed as follows:

1. Short distance range: EB buses have a range of approximately 300-400 km on a single charge. This range is lower than that of fossil fuel buses.
2. Higher cost compared to traditional buses: EB buses have higher sales prices than other traditional bus types. Furthermore, establishing the necessary charging infrastructure for EB buses also incurs significant costs (Jagiełło et al., 2023).
3. Long charging time: EBs fully charge in approximately 3-6 hours. For this reason, EBs are generally charged overnight or partially charged during the driver's rest periods (He,2022)
4. High after-sales maintenance costs: Although electric vehicles have a simpler structure, their power systems differ from those of traditional vehicles, making maintenance impossible for workers in traditional workshops. These vehicles require qualified personnel with specialized knowledge and experience. Therefore, EBs require more expensive after-sales service compared to traditional buses (He, 2022).

Different Types of Charging Technologies for Electric Buses

With the increasing environmental awareness worldwide in recent years, the creation of sustainable cities is becoming widespread. Reducing carbon emissions in public transportation is among the primary goals in sustainable cities. Electric buses are one of the most important public transportation options in reducing carbon emissions. Since electric buses have a shorter range, they need to be charged during the day. Therefore, the establishment of charging stations with appropriate features in suitable locations is of great importance to avoid disruptions in urban transportation. Charging strategies for electric buses include tank/overnight charging, battery swapping, fast charging, and wireless charging (Aamodt et al., 2021). This section discusses these charging strategies used in charging electric buses.

1. Depot/Overnight Charging: Depot/overnight charging refers to a charging infrastructure that charges electric buses with lower voltage over a longer period. This type of charging offers high efficiency and allows for multiple charging levels simultaneously. With depot charging, the configuration from the vehicle to the grid reduces power loss to the grid. This charging technology does not require an upgrade in battery life as is the case with fast charging. On the other hand, this charging technique has a more complex infrastructure and is directly affected by energy grid constraints. The cost of buses that can be charged with this technique is higher than those using other charging techniques. (Alamatsaz et al., 2022).
2. Fast Charging: Fast charging stations provide a high voltage in a short time, allowing buses to be charged quicklyThis charging method is the most effective means of rapidly charging electric buses. The bus charging duration ranges from 5 to 10 minutes. Electric buses using this charging technology have lower capacity, weight, and cost compared to buses that require battery replacement or use depot charging technology (Habib et al., 2018). The disadvantage of fast charging is that the installation of these charging stations is much more expensive than depot charging stations.
3. Battery Swapping: In battery swapping, the depleted batteries of electric buses are replaced with newly charged batteries. The rapid battery replacement is the most important advantage of this charging technique. This technology offers extended battery life due to slow charging and vehicle-to-grid configuration. On the other hand, the high initial investment costs and the need to rent large storage areas for storing spare batteries are the disadvantages of this technique (Tran and Choi, 2017).
4. Wireless Charging: In wireless charging, buses are charged while in motion. Wireless charging is a safe process, and the bus does not need to stop for the battery to be charged. However, wireless charging cannot provide a strong enough energy supply to the battery, and the power transmission range is much lower compared to other techniques. Furthermore, establishing such a charging infrastructure along bus routes requires significant investment (Zhang et al., 2018).

Selection Criteria for Electric Buses

With increasing environmental awareness recently, practices that reduce carbon emissions have become more important worldwide. Therefore, local governments have started to favor EBs for public transportation as a means to reduce carbon emissions in urban areas. Therefore, many bus companies in the global market have developed and launched EBs with different features and technologies. This section outlines the criteria for comparing electric buses across various brands and specifications.

1. Passenger Capacity: Determining passenger capacity is an important criterion for transportation planning. This criterion takes into account the total number of passengers, both seated and standing, that the bus can accommodate. When comparing alternatives, the higher the number of passengers carried in the bus, the more preferable the electric bus model becomes (Alamoodi et al., 2024).
2. Range: EBs have a shorter range compared to buses powered by diesel and compressed natural gas (CNG). Therefore, range is one of the most important criteria to consider when comparing electric buses. Range indicates the distance an electric bus can travel on a single charge (Alamoodi et al., 2024). “Range” refers to the distance a fully charged bus can travel on a single charge under ideal conditions, taking into account variables such as traffic, air temperature, and wind speed (He, 2022). The range of EBs varies depending on battery capacity, bus model, and operating conditions. Factors such as traffic density, use of air conditioning/heating systems, terrain, driver behavior, and the number of passengers carried on the bus all affect the bus's range (Petrović et al., 2025).
3. Maximum Speed: This criterion refers to the maximum speed an EB model can reach. Maximum speed criteria may vary depending on the model type and performance (Alamoodi et al., 2024). Since rapid transportation is a preferred option for residents, maximum speed is an important criterion when comparing alternative buses.
4. Battery Capacity: The battery capacity of EBs directly affects their range. The actual usage time of the batteries is also taken into account when comparing buses. The battery capacity, single-charge driving range, and charging and discharging efficiency influence the daily operation and management of electric buses. Battery capacity denotes the quantity of power supplied by the battery, influenced by factors such as temperature, termination voltage, and discharge rate (He, 2022).
5. Vehicle Comfort: This refers to the features added to make the EB usable and easy to use. The comfort of the vehicle increases its appeal and makes it easier to choose compared to other alternatives. For example, having a suitable width for comfort is a key factor in choosing that particular EB.
6. Charging Time: For EB services to continue without interruption, the buses need to be charged quickly or at night outside of operating hours. This criterion indicates the time required to charge the battery from its minimum capacity to its maximum capacity. Batteries are one of the most expensive components of EBs. Therefore, reducing battery costs and improving the performance of EBs are of great importance in determining the bus's desirability (Petrović et al.,

2025). Charging time is an important comparison criterion for EBs, because if the charging time is long, the buses' subsequent journeys may be disrupted (He, 2022).

7. Vehicle Design: This criterion evaluates design features such as the bus's dimensions, maximum load capacity, aesthetic appearance, and weight.
8. Maneuverability: This criterion compares the EBs's movement characteristics, such as maximum acceleration, turning ability, and minimum turning radius.
9. Gradeability: This criterion refers to the maximum height an EB can climb while maintaining its minimum speed (Alamoodi et al., 2024). As the climbing height increases, the bus's desirability compared to alternatives also increases.
10. International Standards: When determining which electric buses to choose, local governments take into account the standards and legal regulations established by their respective countries. Local governments compare alternative buses according to these standards and try to determine the most suitable brand and model (He, 2022).
11. Road Tests and Case Studies: Comparing the results of road tests and case studies conducted for electric buses with the data obtained from these tests, taking into account the characteristics of the region, is one of the criteria considered in determining the most suitable EB model (Gong et al., 2020). Test data obtained from road operation tests are more rational and more suitable for comparing buses (He, 2022).
12. Type of Battery Used in Electric Buses: Lithium nickel–cobalt-aluminum oxide batteries are the most produced, mainly in China, United States and Europe. Thus, it is necessary to make advances in battery technology to improve its capacity (kWh), cost control, security and reliability for greater energy storage without reducing payload. These barriers directly interfere with costs that require innovation and technological progress, including cost reductions due to scale effects. (Rodrigues and Seixas, 2022)
13. Economic Criteria: This criterion specifies the cost and financial sub-criteria examined for comparing EB models. Under this main criterion, cost items such as “Annual Energy Cost”, “Purchase Cost”, “Infrastructure Cost”, “Maintenance Cost”, “Purchase Cost per Passenger”, “Bus Charging Cost”, “Battery Cost”, “Emission Cost”, and “Noise Cost” are included. All of these criteria are considered as cost criteria. These costs are calculated on an annual basis and used in the comparison of buses by calculating them as total costs (Alamoodi et al., 2024).
14. Power Consumption per 100 km: This criterion considers the amount of electrical energy consumed by the vehicle for every 100 km of movement. This data allows for a comparison of how efficiently different types of buses use electricity per 100 km of movement (He, 2022). This criterion is calculated by

dividing power consumption by total driving distance and then multiplying the result by 100 (Gong et al., 2020).

15. Electric Bus Failure Rate: The frequency and severity of failures in EBs are important criteria for comparing buses. Different bus types can be compared by considering the total number of vehicles that fail or the number of failures per kilometer (He, 2022). This criterion is intimately connected to the vehicle's reliability. The criterion considers the failure frequency and severity of the electrical equipment. These components directly affect the maintenance costs and indirect operating costs of the EB (Gong et al., 2020).
16. Environmental Impact: This is an evaluation criterion aimed at minimizing negative environmental impacts such as noise and air pollution caused by vehicles. The environmental impact criterion considers factors that may negatively affect the environment in urban transportation and includes different elements for comparing EB models. Under the environmental impact criteria, the "Total Emissions" (including carbon, sulfur, and nitrogen component emissions) and "Noise Quantity Above Ambient Level" criteria are considered (Alamoodi et al., 2024).
17. Wheelchair Ramp: This criterion evaluates whether electric buses have wheelchair ramps in their equipment to support barrier-free transportation.

3.2. High-Speed Rail (HSR)

In the era of climate urgency, electric trains, especially HSR, are increasingly seen not only as a solution to transportation needs but also as a strategic pillar in global decarbonization efforts. Their low operating emissions, scalability, and compatibility with renewable electricity make them the cornerstone of sustainable urban and intercity transportation systems (Liu et al.,2025).

The International Union of Railways (UIC) defines HSR operations based on the integration of several key components. According to UIC standards, the minimum operating speed for newly constructed high-speed lines is 250 km/h, while for upgraded conventional lines the minimum threshold is set at 200 km/h (UIC,2018).

HSR is a substantial upgrade in transport technology, and it is an efficient, green, and environmentally friendly type of transportation (Li and Cheng, 2022). Moreover, HSR significantly contributes to mass transportation because to its reduced energy consumption and environmental pollution, larger capacity, and enhanced safety. As an increasing number of customers for sustainable travel, HSR is frequently characterized as the transportation modality of the future for various reasons. High-speed trains are crucial in fostering regional connectivity and promoting socio-economic equilibrium on a global scale (UIC, 2026).

HSR services were first introduced in Japan, followed by France and Germany. Although Japan is widely recognized as the pioneer of HSR, countries such as Spain, France, and China currently operate some of the most extensive and advanced high-speed rail networks in the world (Altan and Kızıltaş, 2020).

The historical development of high-speed rail worldwide is illustrated in Figure 4. As shown in the Figure 4, in 1830, George Stephenson invented the "Rocket" locomotive, which reached a speed of 50 km/h. In 1903, a Siemens-produced rail vehicle achieved 210 km/h. On October 1, 1964, the world's first modern high-speed rail system, the Shinkansen line, began operations in Japan at a speed of 210 km/h. In 1981, France introduced the TGV trains, marking Europe's first high-speed rail service at 260 km/h. In 1988, Italy's Pendolino and Germany's ICE trains commenced high-speed operations. By 1989, French TGV trains had reached speeds of 300 km/h. Spain entered the sector in 1992 with its AVE trains, followed by Belgium (1997), the United Kingdom (2003), South Korea (2004), and Taiwan (2007). China made a significant entry into the sector in 2008 with its CRH trains, supported by substantial investments, and subsequently emerged as a global leader in high-speed rail development. Türkiye and the Netherlands began high-speed operations in 2009, while Morocco and Saudi Arabia joined the sector in 2018 (UIC,2023).

Figure 4. Historical development of high-speed rail worldwide (UIC,2023)

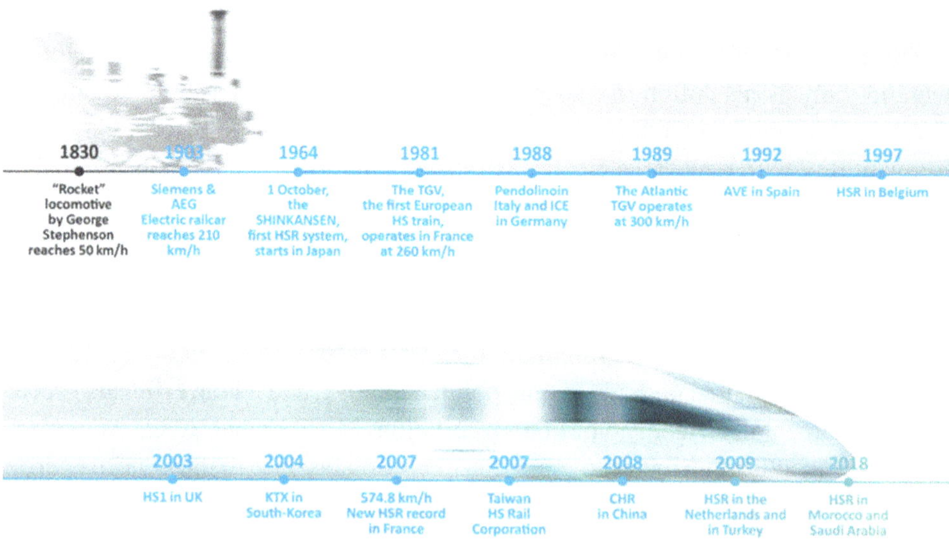

The widespread adoption of high-speed rail across diverse geographical regions suggests that HSR systems can be implemented under varying climatic, demographic, economic, political, and cultural conditions. Since their emergence in Europe, railways have undergone continuous development, particularly in terms of speed, comfort, and safety. During the Industrial Revolution, the speed of passenger trains was crucial for competitiveness initially not against other transport modes, but against rival railway operators. In later decades, however, the rapid advancement of air transport and road vehicles intensified intermodal competition, compelling the railway sector to further innovate and enhance its performance (UIC, 2023).

Urban transport systems, particularly HSR must be evaluated across a range of performance dimensions to ensure their alignment with sustainability, efficiency, and user expectations. To support decision-making in planning and investment, a structured set of selection criteria is essential. These criteria provides the most critical aspects of system design and operation, and they allow policymakers, engineers, and urban planners to compare options, monitor performance, and identify improvement areas.

In this context, six main criteria have emerged as the main criteria of HSR evaluation: environmental impact, operational efficiency, economic, mechanical performance, safety & control, and passenger experience. Each criteria encompasses that reflect the system's ability to deliver reliable, safe, low-carbon, and user-oriented mobility solutions. These criteria assist cities and governments in navigating complex trade-offs between environmental ambition, technical feasibility, public service obligations, and financial constraints. By applying structured evaluation frameworks, decision-makers can make informed, forward-looking choices that position HSR as a cornerstone of future-ready, low-carbon transportation systems. These main criteria and their corresponding measurement criteria are summarized in Figure 5.

Environmental Impact

The sustainability of HSR is measured by its CO_2 emissions per passenger-kilometer over its entire life cycle and its energy efficiency. Lower values in both indicate higher environmental performance, particularly when electricity is sourced from renewables.

- CO_2 Emissions per passenger-kilometre: This criterion calculated as the total CO_2 emissions from train operations divided by the passenger-kilometres traveled. It is typically expressed in grams of CO_2 per passenger-km (gCO_2/pkm). In practice, one sums the CO_2 from fuel or electricity use (and sometimes lifecycle infrastructure emissions) and divides by total passenger-kilometers. High-speed rail trains have very low values: for example, the French HSR Méditerranée line averages only ~11 gCO_2/pkm, versus ~152 g for cars and ~164 g for airplanes (UIC, 2011).

- Energy Efficiency: Electrified railways are one of the most energy-efficient modes of transportation. High-speed rail energy consumption relies on line geometry, operational tactics, and train technology. Train movement and ancillary systems require energy and tractive effort. Modernizing power systems, energy storage, rolling stock, and control and automation technologies can minimize railway energy use. Railway systems can save energy by using energy-efficient design principles. Train energy usage depends on line geometry. Energy consumption can be reduced by reducing longitudinal slopes and curvatures. Uphill trains use more energy than downhill trains, increasing running duration. Acceleration after braking uses more energy. The more frequent acceleration and braking will lead to higher energy consumption, but coasting will lead to energy saving (Watson et al.,2022).

Operational Efficiency

This criterion includes factors such as travel time, on-time performance, and number of stops reflect the system's ability to provide reliable, quick, and accessible service across regions.

- Travel Time: Typically measured as total journey time (hours) between key destinations (Farooq et al., 2019).
- On-time Performance: Ensuring the accuracy of on-board travel time (e.g., maintaining a 35-minute travel duration between stations) is a selection criteria for evaluating the reliability of high-speed rail operations. This metric reflects the effectiveness of system controller accuracy, pre-trip planning strategies, and real-time traffic control measures in minimizing delays and maintaining scheduled service (Annice & Lestari, 2023).
- Number of Stops: This evaluation criterion measures the degree of network connectivity in a high-speed rail (HSR) system by counting the number of intermediate stops along a route. While more stops can improve accessibility by linking more destinations, they may also increase overall travel time. Therefore, determining the optimal number of stops is crucial for balancing regional connectivity with travel efficiency (Farooq et al., 2019).

Economic

This criterion helps evaluate long-term affordability and return on investment; operating expenses and payback period determine the financial sustainability of HSR projects.

- Operating Costs: This evaluation criterion is important for the carrier. This costs include the costs for movement of the trains, for stop-braking and accelerating of the trains, for maintenance and repair of the rolling stock, for salaries for all personnel, for personnel at the stations on the route, and for infrastructure charges (Farooq et al., 2019).
- Payback Period: The payback period is among the most straightforward investment evaluation methods. It indicates the moment when the initial cash outlay of an investment is anticipated to be recouped from the cash inflows produced by the venture (Farooq et al., 2019).

Mechanical Performance

This criterion includes factors such as reliability of system, braking system performance, and traction efficiency reflect the train's robustness, safety, and maintenance needs.

- Reliability: This factor refers to the train system's ability to operate consistently without unexpected interruptions or breakdowns. It reflects the robustness of the vehicle and infrastructure in maintaining regular service over time, minimizing delays and maintenance disruptions. High reliability ensures passenger satisfaction, system safety, and cost-effective operations by reducing service failures and downtime (Annice & Lestari, 2023).
- Braking System Performance: This measures how effectively a train can slow and stop. In the high-speed train braking process, a constant and significant braking torque is consistently applied by a conventional braking controller to meet the demand for substantial braking capacity. Unexpected wheel locking transpires when the wheel–rail contact state deteriorates, resulting in a partial or complete loss of braking force or, perhaps, irreversible damage to both the wheels and rails. Consequently, active brake control systems have become essential in high-speed train operations to prevent wheel locking (Chen et al., 2021).
- Traction Drive System: Rail transit is vital to transportation. The traction drive system is a fundamental subsystem of rail transit trains, with its reliability directly influencing the safe operation of the train. The assessment of reliability for the traction drive system is crucial for the design, manufacturing, operation, and maintenance of rail transportation (Lin et al., 2018).

Safety & Control

The reliability of signaling and communication systems is crucial in preventing accidents and ensuring service continuity during high-speed operations.

- Signal and Control System: It is a crucial assurance for the safety and efficacy of trains. It primarily encompasses the train control system, the centralized dispatching system, and the station interlocking. The railway communication system facilitates specialized railway communication services. The existing high-speed railway communication system employs the GSM-R digital mobile communication system, which imposes stringent requirements on wireless field strength coverage, network service quality, and dependability (Chen et al., 2021).
- Construction Safety: It reflects the extent to which safety risks are identified, managed, and minimized during the construction phase. As highlighted by Lin et al. (2021), inadequate safety performance is directly linked to increased accident rates, project delays, and cost overruns. This criterion encompasses several measurable metrics, including the accident frequency rate (AFR), injury severity rate (ISR), safety inspection pass rate, and safety training coverage. Together, these criteria provide a structured approach to monitoring and improving construction site safety. Ensuring high construction safety not only protects workers but also contributes to the timely and cost-effective delivery of HSR infrastructure, enhancing long-term system reliability and public trust (Lin et al.,2018).

Passenger Experience

User-oriented criteria like comfort, noise levels, cleanliness, and staff service influence public perception and ridership, making them essential for system acceptance and success (Liu & Putro, 2024).

- Service Functions: It encompasses the accessibility of public transportation to and from the high-speed rail station, the ease of purchasing tickets, car parking availability, internal signage within the station, the punctuality of the high-speed train, the overall comprehensiveness and convenience of station and train facilities, the convenience and simplification of the transfer process, the arrangements of high-speed train carriages and seating, and the provision of drinking water.
- Service Environments: These criteria refer to the physical and ambient conditions that air quality, lighting, and temperature comfort on the high-speed

train, cleanliness of the high-speed rail station and train, and security order at the high-speed rail station and train.

- Personnel Quality: This includes the efficiency of entry procedures such as security checks and ticket verification, as well as the quality of assistance provided in waiting areas, during boarding, and onboard the train. Key aspects of personnel quality also involve the visibility and availability of staff members, their attitude toward passengers, and their ability to handle problems or emergencies in a timely and courteous manner. Additionally, special attention is given to services designed for vulnerable groups such as the elderly, people with disabilities, and pregnant passengers ensuring accessibility, dignity, and comfort for all users. Strong personnel performance enhances not only service efficiency but also passenger satisfaction and overall trust in the HSR system.
- Perceived Value: This includes satisfaction with cost-effectiveness (ticket price versus perceived benefits).

Figure 5. Assessment framework: selection criteria for HSR

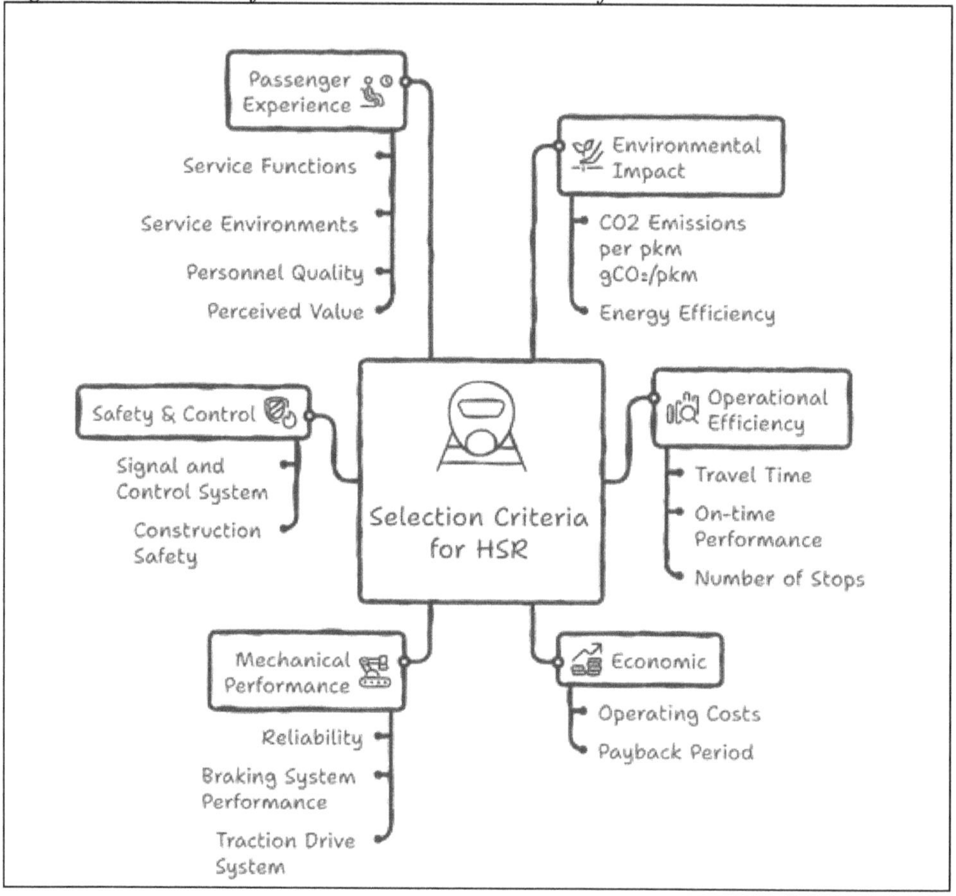

4. ROLE OF DIGITALIZATION IN LOW CARBON URBAN TRANSPORTATION

Digital technologies are playing an increasingly important role in the transition toward low-carbon transportation by enabling the collection, transmission, processing, and application of data within transportation systems. Digitalization in transportation is fundamentally supported by infrastructures such as sensors, communication technologies, and computing devices, along with mechanisms including the Internet of Things (IoT), cloud computing, blockchain, data trading, and digital twin technologies. In this context, these technologies are particularly important for the evaluation and operation of both electric buses and high-speed rail systems.

For electric buses, sensor-based and embedded systems are especially critical for monitoring vehicle conditions, battery performance, and energy storage status, while IoT- and cloud-based applications can improve traffic management, route optimization, charging coordination, and intelligent energy management. Similarly, for high-speed rail and broader transportation systems, digitalization contributes to traffic safety, efficiency, communication reliability, infrastructure monitoring, and control; all of which are directly related to criteria such as operational efficiency, reliability, braking performance, traction systems, and signaling and control systems. The development of artificial intelligence technologies has also had a profound impact on the capabilities of electric vehicles. In particular, this transition is further accelerated by recent advances in battery technologies, which are expected to make electric vehicles a cornerstone of electric transportation (Song et al., 2022).

Furthermore, artificial intelligence-based algorithms address critical challenges faced by electric vehicles, such as limited driving range and insufficient charging infrastructure. They have also enabled the development of more efficient vehicles with advanced autonomy and sustainability features. At the same time, artificial intelligence significantly contributes to overcoming many of the existing challenges associated with electric vehicles. The transportation sector has devoted considerable effort to the development of connected and autonomous vehicles, as well as AI- and control-based systems (Lee, 2020). This is particularly important for electric vehicles, as machine learning methods and deep learning algorithms enable them to achieve unprecedented levels of efficiency, safety, and autonomy.

Accordingly, digitalization should be regarded as a key enabler that strengthens the technical, operational, and control-related performance of low-carbon transportation systems. In this context, emerging technological developments should be closely monitored and, where appropriate, rapidly integrated into low-carbon transportation processes.

5. CONCLUSION

Achieving sustainable urban transportation necessitates strategic shifts towards technology that reduce emissions, enhance energy efficiency, and address both operational requirements and passenger expectations. This chapter has explored two leading low-carbon transportation options: electric buses and high-speed rail (HSR) through a structured, selection criteria–based evaluation framework.

Electric buses are being increasingly used in urban environments due to their low emission levels, quiet operation, and alignment with renewable energy goals. Their selection must include criteria including range, charge duration, passenger capacity, overall lifetime cost, and battery technology. High-speed rail systems, although designed for extended distances, have distinct benefits like reduced CO_2 emissions per passenger-kilometer, scalability, larger capacity and enhanced safety. The decision to invest in high-speed rail infrastructure must take into account main criteria such as environmental impact, operational efficiency, economic, mechanical performance, safety & control, and passenger experience.

This selection framework aims to aid policymakers, planners, and stakeholders in evaluating alternatives using various qualitative and quantitative criteria. The paradigm recognizes the multifaceted trade-offs inherent in transportation design, including the balance between affordability and performance, as well as environmental benefits and technological feasibility. Organizing these factors into cohesive categories facilitates transparent, systematic decision-making that aligns with environmental objectives.

Subsequent research ought to build upon this foundation by utilizing Multi-Criteria Decision-Making (MCDM) methodologies or hybrid fuzzy-based approaches. These methodologies facilitate the prioritizing of criteria within uncertainty and stakeholder contributions, hence augmenting the resilience and flexibility of decision results.

Furthermore, the inclusion of real-world case studies, stakeholder engagement, and dynamic simulation techniques will provide valuable insights into the long-term impacts and hazards associated with various transportation schemes. To ensure the resilience and future-proofing of transportation systems, continuous adjustments to selection criteria should be encouraged to align with technological advancements, regulatory changes, and evolving public expectations.

This study presents a framework for sustainable transportation planning that supports decisions aligned with environmental, economic, and social objectives, by applying an evaluation approach based on selection criteria.

REFERENCES

Aamodt, A., Cory, K. S., & Coney, K. (2021). *Electrifying transit: A guidebook for implementing battery electric buses (No. NREL/TP-7A40-76932)*. National Renewable Energy Laboratory. DOI: 10.2172/1779056

Alamatsaz, K., Hussain, S., Lai, C., & Eicker, U. (2022). Electric bus scheduling and timetabling, fast charging infrastructure planning, and their impact on the grid: A review. *Energies*, *15*(21), 7919. DOI: 10.3390/en15217919

Alamoodi, A. H., Albahri, O. S., Deveci, M., Albahri, A. S., Yussof, S., Dinçer, H., & Sharaf, I. M. (2024). Selection of electric bus models using 2-tuple linguistic T-spherical fuzzy-based decision-making model. *Expert Systems with Applications*, *249*, 123498. DOI: 10.1016/j.eswa.2024.123498

Altan, M. F., & Kızıltaş, M. Ç. (2020). Ulusal, bölgesel ve uluslararası bazda yüksek hızlı demiryollarının gelişimi, mevcut durumu ve yatırım planlarına dair bir derleme. *Dicle Üniversitesi Mühendislik Fakültesi Mühendislik Dergisi*, *11*(2), 715–722. DOI: 10.24012/dumf.450985

Annice, F., & Lestari, Y. D. (2023). Proposed Design of Service Quality Performance Management System for Indonesian HSR.

Biswas, T. K., & Das, M. C. (2019). Selection of commercially available electric vehicle using fuzzy AHP-MABAC. *Journal of The Institution of Engineers (India): Series C, 100*(3), 531-537.

Chen, B., Huang, Z., Zhang, R., Jiang, F., Liu, W., Li, H., Wang, J., & Peng, J. (2021). Adaptive slip ratio estimation for active braking control of high-speed trains. *ISA Transactions*, *112*, 302–314. DOI: 10.1016/j.isatra.2020.11.027 PMID: 33293045

European Environment Agency (EEA). (2025). Greenhouse gas emissions from transport in Europe. [Internet]. Available from: https://www.eea.europa.eu/en/analysis/indicators/greenhouse-gas-emissions-from-transport?activeAccordion=546a7c35-9188-4d23-94ee-005d97c26f2b

EUROSTAT. (2024). Greenhouse gas emission accounts. [Internet]. Available from: https://ec.europa.eu/eurostat/statistics-explained/index.php?title=Greenhouse_gas_emission_accounts

Farooq, A., Xie, M., Stoilova, S., & Ahmad, F. (2019). Multicriteria Evaluation of Transport Plan for High-Speed Rail: An Application to Beijing-Xiongan. *Mathematical Problems in Engineering*, *2019*(1), 8319432. DOI: 10.1155/2019/8319432

Gong, J., He, J., Cheng, C., King, M., Yan, X., He, Z., & Zhang, H. (2020). Road test-based electric bus selection: A case study of the Nanjing bus company. *Energies, 13*(5), 1253. DOI: 10.3390/en13051253

Guschinsky, N., Kovalyov, M. Y., Rozin, B., & Brauner, N. (2021). Fleet and charging infrastructure decisions for fast-charging city electric bus service. *Computers & Operations Research, 135*, 105449. DOI: 10.1016/j.cor.2021.105449

Habib, S., Khan, M. M., Abbas, F., Sang, L., Shahid, M. U., & Tang, H. (2018). A comprehensive study of implemented international standards, technical challenges, impacts and prospects for electric vehicles. *IEEE Access : Practical Innovations, Open Solutions, 6*, 13866–13890. DOI: 10.1109/ACCESS.2018.2812303

He, Z. (2022). Battery electric bus selection based on entropy weight method and road operation test: Using nanjing bus company as an example. *Mathematical Problems in Engineering, 2022*(1), 1696578. DOI: 10.1155/2022/1696578

Hussain, Z., Kaleem Khan, M., & Xia, Z. (2023). Investigating the role of green transport, environmental taxes and expenditures in mitigating the transport CO2 emissions. *Transportation Letters, 15*(5), 439–449. DOI: 10.1080/19427867.2022.2065592

International Energy Agency (IEA). (2020). Global CO2 emissions in transport by mode in the Sustainable Development Scenario, 2000-2070. [Internet]. Available from: https://www.iea.org/data-and-statistics/charts/global-co2-emissions-in-transport-by-mode-in-the-sustainable-development-scenario-2000-2070

International Energy Agency (IEA). (2025). The Breakthrough Agenda Report 2025. [Internet]. Available from: https://www.iea.org/reports/breakthrough-agenda-report-2025

International Union of Railways (UIC). (2011). Wider Benefits Of High-Speed Rail Confirmed In New Studies. [Internet]. Available from: https://www.uic.org/com/IMG/pdf/111208_high_speed_rail_study.pdf

International Union of Railways (UIC). (2018). The definition of High Speed Rail. [Internet]. Available from: https://uic.org/com/enews/nr/596-high-speed/article/the-definition-of-high-speed-rail

International Union of Railways (UIC). (2023). High-speed rail history. [Internet]. Available from: https://uic.org/passenger/highspeed/article/high-speed-rail-history

International Union of Railways (UIC). (2026). Intercity and High-Speed. [Internet]. Available from: https://uic.org/passenger/highspeed/

IPCC. (2014). Transport. In *Climate Change 2014: Mitigation of Climate Change. Contribution of Working Group III to the Fifth Assessment Report of the Intergovernmental Panel on Climate Change*. Cambridge University Press.

IRENA. (2018). *Biogas for road vehicles: Technology brief.* International Renewable Energy Agency.

Jagiełło, A., Wołek, M., & Bizon, W. (2023). Comparison of tender criteria for electric and diesel buses in Poland—Has the ongoing revolution in urban transport been overlooked? *Energies*, *16*(11), 4280. DOI: 10.3390/en16114280

Lee, M. (2020). An analysis of the effects of artificial intelligence on electric vehicle technology innovation using patent data. *World Patent Information*, *63*, 102002. DOI: 10.1016/j.wpi.2020.102002

Li, X., & Cheng, Z. (2022). Does high-speed rail improve urban carbon emission efficiency in China? *Socio-Economic Planning Sciences*, *84*, 101308. DOI: 10.1016/j.seps.2022.101308

Lin, S., Fang, X., Lin, F., Yang, Z., & Wang, X. (2018). Reliability of rail transit traction drive system-A review. *Microelectronics and Reliability*, *88*, 1281–1285. DOI: 10.1016/j.microrel.2018.07.037

Liu, D., Wang, J., Xu, L., Zhang, H., & Tan, X. (2025). Comparison of energy consumption and carbon emissions of high-speed rail with other transportation modes from life cycle perspective: A case of Beijing-Shanghai. *Research in Transportation Business & Management*, *59*, 101278. DOI: 10.1016/j.rtbm.2024.101278

Liu, S., & Putro, U. S. (2024). Passenger service satisfaction evaluation of Jakarta-Bandung high-speed railway. *European Journal of Business and Management Research*, *9*(4), 115–126. DOI: 10.24018/ejbmr.2024.9.4.2432

Mulholland, E., & Rodríguez, F. (2022). *The rapid deployment of zero-emission buses in Europe*. International Council on Clean Transportation.

Nix, J. (2022). Cities Are Buying More Electric Buses, But an EU Deadline Is Needed. [Internet]. Available from: https://www.transportenvironment.org/discover/cities-are-buying-more-electric-buses-but-an-eu-deadline-is-needed

OECD. (2002). Strategies to reduce greenhouse gas emissions from road transport: Analytical methods, organization for economic co-operation and development. https://www.itf-oecd.org/sites/default/files/docs/02greenhousee.pdf

Petrović, N., Jovanović, V., Marković, S., Marinković, D., & Nikolić, B. (2025). Multi-criteria decision-making approach for choising e-Bus for urban public transport in the city of Niš. *Acta Technica Jaurinensis*, *18*(1), 1–8. DOI: 10.14513/actatechjaur.00758

Rodrigues, A. L., & Seixas, S. R. (2022). Battery-electric buses and their implementation barriers: Analysis and prospects for sustainability. *Sustainable Energy Technologies and Assessments*, *51*, 101896. DOI: 10.1016/j.seta.2021.101896

Song, J., He, G., Wang, J., & Zhang, P. (2022). Shaping future low-carbon energy and transportation systems: Digital technologies and applications. *IEnergy*, *1*(3), 285–305. DOI: 10.23919/IEN.2022.0040

Tasdemir, B. D., & Ayan, M. A. (2025). Driving to Future Integrating Digital Transformation to Sustainable Transportation. In *Developing Dynamic and Sustainable Supply Chains to Achieve Sustainable Development Goals* (pp. 91–120). IGI Global Scientific Publishing. DOI: 10.4018/979-8-3693-6284-6.ch004

Tran, D. H., & Choi, W. (2017). Design of a high-efficiency wireless power transfer system with intermediate coils for the on-board chargers of electric vehicles. *IEEE Transactions on Power Electronics*, *33*(1), 175–187. DOI: 10.1109/TPEL.2017.2662067

Watson, I., Ali, A., & Bayyati, A. (2022). Energy efficiency of high-speed railways. *Advances in Environmental and Engineering Research*, *3*(4), 1–22. DOI: 10.21926/aeer.2204055

World Meteorological Organization (WMO). (2022). Provisional state of the global climate 2022. [Internet]. Available from: https://wmo.int/publication-series/provisional-state-of-global-climate-2022

Zhang, T., Chen, X., Yu, Z., Zhu, X., & Shi, D. (2018). A Monte Carlo simulation approach to evaluate service capacities of EV charging and battery swapping stations. *IEEE Transactions on Industrial Informatics*, *14*(9), 3914–3923. DOI: 10.1109/TII.2018.2796498

Chapter 6
Digital Twins and Data-Driven Infrastructure Management

Atul Kumar
http://orcid.org/0000-0003-3859-0686
Dnyaan Prasad Global University, India

Muzaffar Shojonov
http://orcid.org/0009-0000-2061-2555
Urgench State University, Urgench, Uzbekistan

Shaturaev Jakhongir
Termez University of Economics and Service, Termez, Uzbekistan

Allambergenova Mukhabbat Khasanbaevna
Nukus State Pedagogical Institute, Uzbekistan

Jabbarov Umarbek
Mamun University, Khiva, Uzbekistan

Abdullayev Abdulla Fayzulla Ugli
Tashkent State University of Economy, Tashkent, Uzbekistan

ABSTRACT

Digital twins represent transformative technology for decarbonized transport infrastructure management, integrating real-time data analytics, artificial intelligence, and predictive modeling. This chapter examines the convergence of digital twin technology and data-driven decision-making in sustainable transportation systems, exploring economic implications, market mechanisms, and policy innovations driving decarbonization. Through comprehensive analysis of current applications, technological frameworks, and implementation strategies, this work demonstrates how digital twins enable optimized infrastructure performance, reduced carbon emissions, and enhanced operational efficiency. Key findings reveal that integrating

DOI: 10.4018/979-8-3373-9003-1.ch006

AI-powered digital twins with IoT sensors, machine learning algorithms, and cloud computing platforms creates intelligent transportation systems capable of real-time monitoring, predictive maintenance, and adaptive control.

1. INTRODUCTION

The global transportation sector accounts for approximately 24% of direct CO2 emissions from fossil fuel combustion, presenting one of the most significant challenges in climate change mitigation (Rapson & Muehlegger, 2023a). As nations commit to net-zero emissions targets, transforming transportation infrastructure through digital innovation has emerged as a critical pathway toward decarbonization. Digital twin technology—virtual replicas of physical assets, processes, and systems synchronized through real-time data—offers unprecedented capabilities for optimizing infrastructure performance, reducing environmental impacts, and enabling intelligent decision-making (Wu et al., 2025).

1.1 Background and Context

1.1.1 The Decarbonization Imperative

Transportation decarbonization requires fundamental transformations across vehicle technologies, energy systems, infrastructure design, and mobility patterns. Traditional infrastructure management approaches, characterized by reactive maintenance, limited monitoring capabilities, and siloed data systems, prove inadequate for achieving ambitious climate targets. The transition to sustainable transport necessitates integrated solutions combining electrification, alternative fuels, modal shifts, and intelligent infrastructure management (Horesh & Quinn, 2024).

1.1.2 Digital Transformation in Transportation

Digital twin technology represents the confluence of several technological advancements: Internet of Things (IoT) sensor networks, artificial intelligence and machine learning algorithms, cloud computing infrastructure, big data analytics, and 5G communications. These technologies collectively enable the creation of dynamic virtual representations that mirror physical transportation assets with high fidelity, supporting predictive analytics, scenario simulation, and autonomous decision-making (Yan et al., 2023).

1.1.3 Economic and Policy Dimensions

The economics of transportation decarbonization involve complex trade-offs between upfront investments, operational savings, environmental benefits, and societal costs. Digital twins enhance economic efficiency by optimizing asset utilization, reducing maintenance costs, extending infrastructure lifespans, and enabling evidence-based policy interventions. Market mechanisms such as carbon pricing, subsidies for clean technologies, and performance-based contracts create economic incentives aligned with decarbonization objectives (Pretis, 2022).

1.2 Research Objectives and Scope

This chapter pursues four primary objectives:

1. **Technological Analysis:** Examine digital twin architectures, enabling technologies, and implementation frameworks specific to transportation infrastructure management
2. **Economic Evaluation:** Assess cost-benefit relationships, market mechanisms, and financial models supporting digital infrastructure investments for decarbonization
3. **Policy Investigation:** Analyze regulatory frameworks, governance models, and policy innovations facilitating digital twin adoption in sustainable transport
4. **Integration Synthesis:** Explore synergies between digital twins, data-driven decision-making, and decarbonization strategies across diverse transportation modes

1.3 Chapter Organization

Following this introduction, Section 2 establishes the theoretical and conceptual foundations of digital twins in transportation infrastructure. Section 3 examines enabling technologies and technical architectures. Section 4 explores applications across different transportation modes and infrastructure types. Section 5 analyzes economic dimensions and market mechanisms. Section 6 investigates policy frameworks and governance models. Section 7 addresses implementation challenges and proposes solutions. Section 8 presents case studies demonstrating successful deployments. Section 9 discusses future directions and emerging trends. Section 10 provides conclusions and recommendations.

2. CONCEPTUAL FOUNDATIONS OF DIGITAL TWINS IN TRANSPORTATION

2.1 Defining Digital Twins for Transport Infrastructure

2.1.1 Core Concepts and Characteristics

Digital twins in transportation infrastructure represent comprehensive virtual models that continuously evolve through bidirectional data exchange with physical counterparts. Unlike static simulations or standalone models, digital twins exhibit four defining characteristics: real-time synchronization with physical assets through sensor data streams, predictive and prescriptive analytics capabilities enabling future state projections, multiscale integration spanning individual components to entire transportation networks, and autonomous decision-making support through AI-powered algorithms (Ge & Qin, 2024).

2.1.2 Taxonomy of Digital Twin Applications

Transportation digital twins manifest across multiple scales and purposes. Component-level twins monitor individual infrastructure elements such as bridge sensors, railway tracks, or pavement conditions. Asset-level twins integrate multiple components into cohesive representations of complete structures like bridges, tunnels, or stations. System-level twins model entire transportation networks including highways, rail systems, or urban mobility ecosystems. Process twins focus on operational workflows such as traffic management, maintenance scheduling, or logistics optimization (Yan et al., 2023).

2.1.3 Theoretical Frameworks

Several theoretical frameworks underpin digital twin development. The Five-Dimension Model conceptualizes digital twins through physical entities, virtual models, services, data, and connections. The Capability Maturity Model defines progressive sophistication levels from descriptive visualization through diagnostic analysis, predictive forecasting, prescriptive optimization, to autonomous operation. The Lifecycle Integration Framework emphasizes continuity across design, construction, operation, maintenance, and decommissioning phases (Yan et al., 2023).

2.2 Data-Driven Infrastructure Management Paradigm

2.2.1 From Reactive to Predictive Management

Traditional infrastructure management relies on scheduled inspections, reactive repairs, and experience-based decisions. Data-driven approaches leverage continuous monitoring, statistical analysis, and machine learning to predict failures, optimize interventions, and allocate resources efficiently. This paradigm shift reduces unexpected failures by 40-50%, extends asset lifespans by 20-30%, and decreases maintenance costs by 15-25% according to empirical studies (Mahmoodian et al., 2022).

2.2.2 Decision-Making Under Uncertainty

Transportation infrastructure operates in environments characterized by uncertainty: variable traffic patterns, unpredictable weather conditions, evolving regulatory requirements, and stochastic deterioration processes. Data-driven approaches employ probabilistic models, risk assessment frameworks, and adaptive algorithms to support robust decision-making. Digital twins enable scenario analysis, sensitivity testing, and Monte Carlo simulations that quantify uncertainties and evaluate intervention strategies (Hu et al., 2023).

2.2.3 Integration with Decarbonization Objectives

Data-driven management directly supports decarbonization through multiple mechanisms. Energy consumption optimization algorithms reduce operational emissions by 10-20% through intelligent traffic flow management and modal coordination. Predictive maintenance minimizes emergency repairs requiring carbon-intensive mobilization. Asset lifecycle extension defers embodied carbon from replacement infrastructure. Real-time monitoring enables verification and validation of emission reduction claims for carbon accounting and trading schemes (Winkler et al., 2023).

2.3 Convergence with Sustainable Transportation

2.3.1 Electric Vehicle Infrastructure Integration

Digital twins play crucial roles in electric vehicle (EV) charging infrastructure management. Predictive algorithms optimize charging station placement based on traffic patterns, grid capacity, and user demand. Real-time monitoring balances electrical loads, coordinates vehicle-to-grid services, and minimizes renewable energy curtailment. System-level twins integrate EV fleets with transportation networks and power grids, enabling coordinated charging strategies that reduce peak demand and maximize clean energy utilization (Forsythe et al., 2023).

2.3.2 Multimodal Transportation Systems

Decarbonization requires modal shifts toward public transportation, cycling, and walking. Digital twins support multimodal integration by modeling transfer points, synchronizing schedules, optimizing route networks, and providing real-time information to travelers. Network-level twins simulate impacts of infrastructure investments on modal splits, accessibility, and emissions, informing evidence-based planning decisions (Lefèvre et al., 2021).

2.3.3 Circular Economy and Material Flows

Sustainable infrastructure management incorporates circular economy principles: material reuse, component refurbishment, and waste minimization. Digital twins track material inventories, monitor component conditions, and identify reuse opportunities. Lifecycle assessments integrated into digital twin platforms quantify environmental impacts across infrastructure lifecycles, supporting decisions that minimize embodied carbon and resource consumption (Kaewunruen et al., 2023).

3. ENABLING TECHNOLOGIES AND TECHNICAL ARCHITECTURES

3.1 Sensor Networks and IoT Integration

3.1.1 Sensor Technologies for Infrastructure Monitoring

Modern transportation infrastructure employs diverse sensor types. Structural health monitoring utilizes accelerometers, strain gauges, displacement sensors, and fiber optic systems to detect deformations, vibrations, and material degradation. Environmental sensors measure temperature, humidity, precipitation, and air quality affecting infrastructure performance and user safety. Traffic sensors including inductive loops, cameras, radar, and LiDAR capture vehicle flows, speeds, classifications, and trajectories. Energy sensors monitor consumption patterns in electrified transportation systems (Kaewunruen et al., 2023).

Figure 1. Digital Twin Architecture for Transportation Infrastructure Management

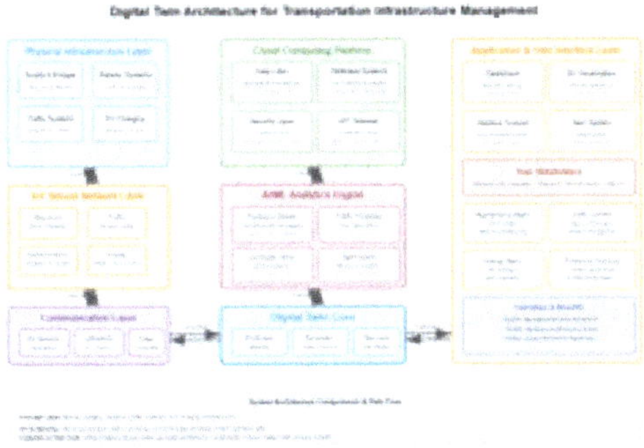

This diagram illustrates the comprehensive architecture integrating IoT sensor networks, cloud computing platforms, AI/ML analytics engines, and visualization interfaces that constitute modern digital twin systems for transportation infrastructure.

3.1.2 Communication Protocols and Data Transmission

Reliable data transmission requires robust communication infrastructure. 5G networks enable high-bandwidth, low-latency connectivity supporting real-time control applications. LoRaWAN and NB-IoT provide energy-efficient long-range communications for battery-powered sensors. Edge computing architectures process data locally, reducing bandwidth requirements and enabling faster response times for time-critical applications. Standardized protocols such as MQTT, CoAP, and OPC UA ensure interoperability across heterogeneous systems (Wu et al., 2025).

3.1.3 Data Quality and Calibration

Sensor data quality fundamentally determines digital twin accuracy. Calibration protocols maintain measurement precision through periodic reference comparisons and automated drift detection. Data validation algorithms identify outliers, instrument failures, and transmission errors through statistical analysis and physical consistency checks. Redundancy strategies employ multiple sensors for critical measurements, enabling fault detection and graceful degradation (Dan et al., 2022).

3.2 Artificial Intelligence and Machine Learning

3.2.1 Predictive Maintenance Algorithms

Machine learning models predict infrastructure deterioration and failure probabilities based on historical data, current conditions, and environmental factors. Random forests, gradient boosting machines, and neural networks achieve prediction accuracies exceeding 85% for pavement conditions, bridge components, and railway track geometry. Reinforcement learning optimizes maintenance scheduling by balancing performance requirements, budget constraints, and disruption minimization (Sresakoolchai & Kaewunruen, 2023).

3.2.2 Traffic Flow Prediction and Management

Deep learning architectures including convolutional neural networks (CNNs), recurrent neural networks (RNNs), and graph neural networks (GNNs) model complex spatiotemporal traffic patterns. CNN-based models extract spatial features from traffic network topologies. LSTM and GRU networks capture temporal dependencies in traffic time series. Attention mechanisms identify influential factors and relationships. State-of-the-art models achieve 15-minute ahead prediction accuracies of 92-95% for urban arterials and highways (Sroczyński & Czyżewski, 2023).

3.2.3 Computer Vision for Infrastructure Inspection

Computer vision algorithms automate infrastructure condition assessment through image and video analysis. Object detection models identify cracks, spalls, corrosion, and defects in bridges, tunnels, and pavements. Semantic segmentation classifies damage severity and extent. Instance segmentation distinguishes individual defects for quantitative analysis. Vision-based systems reduce inspection costs by 40-60% while increasing coverage and consistency compared to manual inspections (Li & Zhang, 2023).

3.3 Cloud Computing and Data Management

3.3.1 Cloud Platforms for Digital Twins

Cloud computing provides scalable computational resources, storage capacity, and managed services essential for digital twin implementations. Platform-as-a-Service (PaaS) offerings such as Microsoft Azure Digital Twins, AWS IoT TwinMaker, and Google Cloud IoT Core accelerate development through pre-built components for data ingestion, modeling, and visualization. Infrastructure-as-a-Service (IaaS) enables custom architectures for specialized requirements (Ge & Qin, 2024).

3.3.2 Data Lakes and Analytics Pipelines

Transportation digital twins generate massive data volumes—terabytes daily for large metropolitan networks. Data lakes provide flexible storage for structured, semi-structured, and unstructured data including sensor streams, images, videos, and documents. Apache Kafka, Apache Flink, and Apache Spark enable real-time stream processing. ETL (Extract, Transform, Load) pipelines clean, integrate, and structure data for analytics and machine learning workflows (Hu et al., 2023).

3.3.3 Cybersecurity and Data Privacy

Digital twin systems present cybersecurity challenges including unauthorized access, data manipulation, denial-of-service attacks, and privacy violations. Defense strategies employ multiple layers: network segmentation isolates critical systems, encryption protects data in transit and at rest, authentication and authorization control access, intrusion detection identifies suspicious activities, and blockchain technologies ensure data integrity and auditability. Privacy-preserving techniques such as differential privacy and federated learning enable analytics while protecting sensitive information (Lv et al., 2022).

3.4 Visualization and User Interfaces

3.4.1 3D Modeling and Virtual Reality

Three-dimensional visualization enables intuitive understanding of complex infrastructure systems. Building Information Modeling (BIM) and Geographic Information Systems (GIS) provide geometric foundations. Augmented Reality (AR) overlays digital information onto physical environments for field inspections and maintenance. Virtual Reality (VR) enables immersive exploration for planning, design review, and training applications (Yan et al., 2023).

3.4.2 Dashboards and Decision Support

Interactive dashboards synthesize diverse data streams into actionable insights. Key Performance Indicators (KPIs) track metrics including asset condition, traffic performance, energy consumption, and emissions. Time-series visualizations reveal trends and anomalies. Geospatial maps display network-wide conditions and incidents. Alert systems notify operators of critical events requiring immediate attention (Wu et al., 2025).

3.4.3 Scenario Simulation and What-If Analysis

Digital twins enable experimentation without physical risks or costs. Traffic simulation models evaluate impacts of infrastructure changes, signal timing adjustments, or incident management strategies. Structural analysis simulates responses to extreme events such as earthquakes or floods. Energy models assess effects of electrification scenarios on grid demands and emissions. Monte Carlo methods quantify uncertainties and risk distributions (Kušić et al., 2023).

4. APPLICATIONS ACROSS TRANSPORTATION MODES

4.1 Highway and Road Networks

4.1.1 Pavement Management Systems

Digital twins for pavement infrastructure integrate condition data from automated surveys using ground-penetrating radar, laser profilers, and imaging systems. Deterioration models predict International Roughness Index (IRI), rutting, and cracking evolution under traffic loads and environmental stresses. Optimization algorithms determine cost-effective maintenance and rehabilitation strategies over multi-year planning horizons. Implementation studies demonstrate 20-30% reductions in life-cycle costs compared to traditional approaches (Mahmoodian et al., 2022).

4.1.2 Bridge Health Monitoring

Bridge digital twins employ structural health monitoring systems combining accelerometers, strain gauges, displacement sensors, and environmental monitors. Modal analysis identifies natural frequencies, mode shapes, and damping characteristics. Finite element models, calibrated through measured responses, assess structural capacity and safety margins. Early warning systems detect abnormal behaviors potentially indicating damage or overload conditions. Case studies show 35% reductions in inspection costs and 50% improvements in damage detection rates (Kaewunruen et al., 2023).

4.1.3 Traffic Management and Optimization

Real-time traffic digital twins fuse data from loop detectors, cameras, probe vehicles, and mobile apps. Short-term forecasting models predict congestion 15-60 minutes ahead with 90%+ accuracy. Adaptive signal control algorithms optimize timing plans based on current and predicted conditions, reducing delays by 10-25% and emissions by 8-15%. Incident detection systems identify accidents within 2-3 minutes, enabling rapid response (Li & Zhang, 2023).

Figure 2. AI-Powered Traffic Flow Prediction and Management System

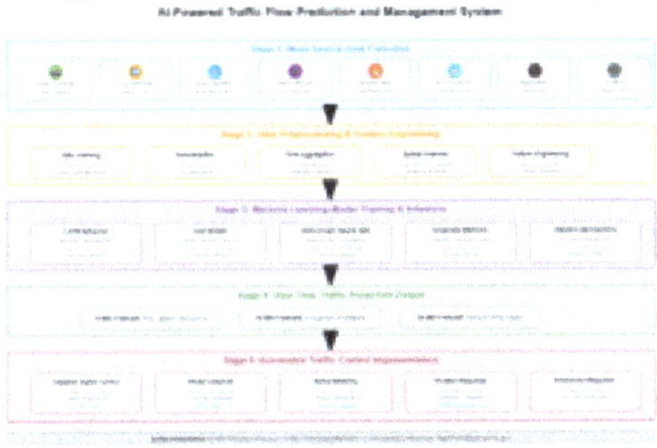

This flowchart demonstrates the complete process of data collection from multiple sensors, preprocessing, machine learning model training and inference, real-time prediction generation, and automated traffic control implementation in intelligent transportation systems.

4.2 Railway Systems

4.2.1 Track Geometry and Maintenance

Railway digital twins monitor track geometry parameters including alignment, cross-level, gauge, and surface irregularities through track recording vehicles and wayside sensors. Degradation models predict geometry evolution accounting for tonnage, speed, curvature, and maintenance history. Tamping and grinding interventions are optimized to maintain ride quality while minimizing costs and service disruptions. Deep reinforcement learning approaches achieve 15-20% improvements in maintenance efficiency over rule-based systems (Sresakoolchai & Kaewunruen, 2023).

4.2.2 Rolling Stock Condition Monitoring

Train-borne sensors monitor wheel-rail forces, bearing temperatures, brake conditions, and suspension performance. Vibration analysis detects bearing defects, wheel flats, and component looseness. Thermal imaging identifies overheating brakes and bearings. Predictive models forecast remaining useful life, enabling condition-based maintenance that reduces unexpected failures by 40-50% compared to scheduled maintenance regimes (Kaewunruen et al., 2023).

4.2.3 Energy-Efficient Operations

Railway digital twins optimize traction energy consumption through eco-driving algorithms that determine speed profiles minimizing energy while meeting schedule constraints. Regenerative braking coordination maximizes energy recovery. Network-level twins coordinate train movements to balance electrical loads and utilize regenerated energy. Studies demonstrate 10-20% energy savings through optimized operations, directly reducing carbon emissions from electrified railways (Yan et al., 2023).

4.3 Urban Transportation and Smart Cities

4.3.1 Integrated Multimodal Systems

City-scale digital twins integrate highways, transit, cycling, and pedestrian networks. Agent-based models simulate individual travel behaviors under alternative policies or infrastructure scenarios. Accessibility analyses evaluate equity dimensions of transportation provision. Air quality models couple with traffic simulations to assess health impacts. Urban planners employ digital twins to evaluate impacts of congestion pricing, parking policies, transit investments, and land use changes (Ge & Qin, 2024).

4.3.2 Public Transit Optimization

Transit digital twins monitor vehicle positions, passenger counts, fare transactions, and schedule adherence. Real-time predictions inform passengers of arrival times via mobile apps and station displays. Dynamic route adjustments respond to disruptions and demand variations. Long-term planning models optimize route networks, frequencies, and vehicle assignments based on observed ridership patterns and future growth projections (Wu et al., 2025).

4.3.3 Electric Vehicle Charging Infrastructure

EV charging network digital twins model charging station utilization, queue lengths, and power demands. Predictive models forecast charging needs based on EV adoption trends, travel patterns, and user preferences. Optimization algorithms determine locations for new charging stations maximizing accessibility while considering grid constraints and construction costs. Smart charging algorithms coordinate vehicle charging to flatten load curves and maximize renewable energy utilization (Forsythe et al., 2023).

4.4 Freight and Logistics

4.4.1 Port and Intermodal Terminals

Logistics digital twins model container flows, equipment movements, and vessel operations in ports and intermodal facilities. Discrete-event simulations optimize berth allocations, crane assignments, and storage yard operations. Predictive models forecast vessel arrivals and cargo volumes enabling proactive resource planning. Integration with inland transportation networks optimizes drayage operations and reduces empty container repositioning (Yan et al., 2023).

4.4.2 Last-Mile Delivery Optimization

Urban freight digital twins address last-mile delivery challenges through vehicle routing optimization, delivery time windows, and consolidation opportunities. Electric cargo bike and drone delivery scenarios evaluate emissions reductions and operational feasibility. Geofencing and access restrictions in urban centers are simulated to assess impacts on delivery costs and emissions (Wu et al., 2025).

4.4.3 Supply Chain Resilience

Network-level digital twins model supply chain vulnerabilities to disruptions including infrastructure failures, natural disasters, and demand shocks. Scenario analysis identifies critical nodes and links. Redundancy and diversification strategies are evaluated for cost-effectiveness. Real-time tracking enables rapid response and rerouting during disruptions (Ge & Qin, 2024).

5. ECONOMIC DIMENSIONS AND MARKET MECHANISMS

5.1 Cost-Benefit Analysis of Digital Twin Implementation

5.1.1 Investment Requirements

Digital twin implementation requires substantial upfront investments across several categories. Sensor networks and monitoring systems typically cost $50,000-$500,000 per kilometer for highways, $100,000-$1,000,000 per bridge for structural health monitoring, and $200,000-$2,000,000 per station for railway systems. Software platforms including data management, analytics, and visualization tools range from $100,000 for small deployments to $10,000,000+ for comprehensive metropolitan systems. Personnel costs for data scientists, software engineers, and domain experts represent 40-60% of ongoing operational expenses (Mahmoodian et al., 2022).

Table 1. Cost-Benefit Analysis of Digital Twin Implementation Across Transportation Modes

Transportation Mode	Initial Investment ($/ km or $/unit)	Annual Operating Cost (% of Initial)	Maintenance Cost Reduction (%)	Asset Life Extension (years)	ROI Period (years)
Highway/Road Network	$50,000 - $500,000	8 - 12%	15 - 25%	3 - 5	4 - 7
Bridge Infrastructure	$100,000 - $1,000,000/ bridge	6 - 10%	20 - 35%	5 - 10	5 - 8
Railway Track System	$75,000 - $600,000	7 - 11%	18 - 28%	4 - 7	4 - 6
Urban Transit (per vehicle)	$15,000 - $80,000	10 - 15%	12 - 22%	2 - 4	5 - 9
Smart Traffic Management	$200,000 - $2,000,000/ intersection	12 - 18%	10 - 20%	3 - 5	3 - 6
EV Charging Network	$25,000 - $150,000/ station	15 - 20%	8 - 18%	2 - 4	4 - 7

Note: Costs vary significantly based on infrastructure scale, technology maturity, and regional factors. ROI calculations include maintenance savings, operational efficiencies, and extended asset lifecycles.

5.1.2 Operational Benefits and Savings

Quantified benefits manifest across multiple dimensions. Maintenance cost reductions of 15-35% result from optimized intervention timing, reduced emergency repairs, and extended asset lifecycles. Operational efficiency improvements including traffic flow optimization, energy consumption reduction, and capacity utilization yield 10-25% cost savings. Safety improvements reduce accident-related costs by 20-40% through better monitoring, rapid incident detection, and predictive risk management. Environmental benefits include 8-20% emissions reductions through optimized operations (Wu et al., 2025).

5.1.3 Return on Investment Analysis

ROI analysis for digital twin implementations typically shows payback periods of 3-8 years depending on scale and application. Highway management systems demonstrate 4-7 year paybacks through maintenance optimization. Bridge monitoring systems achieve 5-8 year returns via reduced inspection costs and extended structural lifespans. Railway applications show 4-6 year paybacks through maintenance efficiency and energy savings. Urban traffic management systems often achieve 3-6 year returns through congestion reduction and emissions savings (Hu et al., 2023).

5.2 Market Mechanisms for Decarbonization

5.2.1 Carbon Pricing and Transportation

Carbon pricing mechanisms including carbon taxes and cap-and-trade systems create economic incentives for emissions reductions. British Columbia's carbon tax, increasing from $30 CAD/tonne in 2012 to $50 CAD/tonne in 2021, reduced transportation fuel consumption by 7-15% according to econometric analyses. Digital twins enhance carbon pricing effectiveness by enabling accurate emissions monitoring, verification of reduction claims, and optimization of low-carbon alternatives. Real-time emissions accounting integrated into digital twin platforms supports carbon trading and offset markets (Pretis, 2022).

5.2.2 Performance-Based Contracting

Performance-based contracts shift risk from asset owners to service providers, incentivizing efficient management. Availability-based contracts specify penalties for inadequate service levels, motivating proactive maintenance. Digital twins enable transparent performance monitoring, automated compliance verification, and data-driven dispute resolution. Case studies in highway and railway concessions demonstrate 10-20% efficiency improvements under performance-based arrangements supported by digital monitoring (Mahmoodian et al., 2022).

5.2.3 Public-Private Partnerships

Public-Private Partnerships (PPPs) leverage private sector expertise and capital for infrastructure development and operation. Digital twin platforms facilitate PPP implementation through enhanced transparency, risk allocation, and performance monitoring. Shared digital infrastructure reduces information asymmetries between public and private partners. Performance metrics tracked through digital twins inform revenue-sharing arrangements and regulatory oversight (Yan et al., 2023).

5.3 Economic Modeling of EV Adoption and Infrastructure

5.3.1 Total Cost of Ownership Analysis

Electric vehicle total cost of ownership (TCO) reflects purchase prices, fuel costs, maintenance expenses, insurance, and residual values. TCO parity with internal combustion vehicles varies by vehicle class, electricity prices, and utilization patterns. Digital twin-based fleet management systems optimize charging strategies, reduce electricity costs through demand response, and extend battery lifespans through controlled charging profiles. Simulation studies demonstrate 15-25% TCO reductions through optimized operations (Forsythe et al., 2023).

Figure 3. EV Total Cost of Ownership vs. ICE Vehicles (2021-2030)

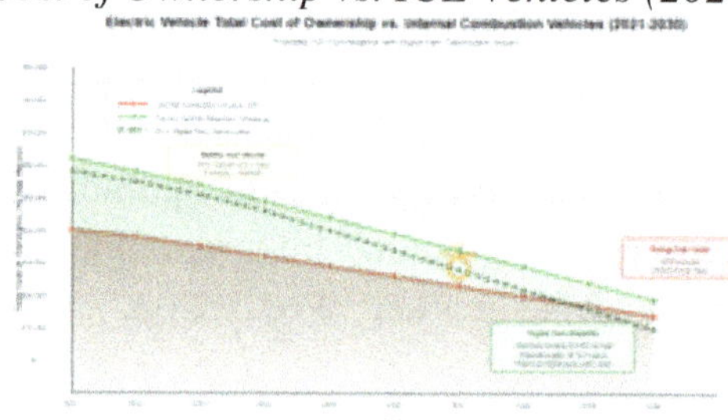

This line graph illustrates the convergence of EV and ICE vehicle costs over time, showing how declining battery prices, increasing fuel costs, and optimized charging through digital twin systems drive EV economic competitiveness.

5.3.2 Charging Infrastructure Economics

Charging station profitability depends on utilization rates, electricity prices, installation costs, and revenue models. Fast-charging stations require high utilization

(>20% daily) for profitability while Level 2 chargers serve destination charging with lower capital costs. Digital twins optimize charging station placement based on traffic patterns, existing coverage gaps, and predicted demand growth. Dynamic pricing algorithms maximize revenue while managing grid impacts (Archsmith et al., 2022).

5.3.3 Grid Integration and Value Streams

Vehicle-to-grid (V2G) services enable EVs to provide grid balancing, frequency regulation, and renewable energy integration. Digital twins coordinate EV charging and discharging to maximize value from multiple revenue streams: energy arbitrage, ancillary services, capacity credits, and demand response payments. Simulation studies indicate potential annual revenues of $200-$800 per vehicle from optimized grid services (Rapson & Muehlegger, 2023b).

5.4 Financing Mechanisms and Investment Models

5.4.1 Green Bonds and Climate Finance

Green bonds finance environmentally beneficial projects including sustainable transportation infrastructure. Global green bond issuance for transportation reached $42 billion in 2023. Digital twins enhance green bond attractiveness through transparent impact measurement, automated reporting, and third-party verification of environmental benefits. Blockchain-based digital twins enable fractional ownership and decentralized finance applications (Wu et al., 2025).

5.4.2 Infrastructure Investment Funds

Institutional investors including pension funds and sovereign wealth funds increasingly target infrastructure assets offering stable, long-term returns. Digital twin platforms enhance asset attractiveness through improved risk management, optimized operations, and data-driven performance improvement. Infrastructure funds allocating to digitally-enabled assets report 12-18% higher risk-adjusted returns compared to traditional infrastructure investments (Yan et al., 2023).

5.4.3 Innovative Funding Mechanisms

Value capture mechanisms including tax increment financing, special assessment districts, and development fees fund transportation improvements through beneficiary contributions. Digital twins quantify accessibility improvements, property value increases, and economic development impacts supporting value capture calculations. Mobility-as-a-Service platforms generate revenue streams supplementing public funding. Usage-based pricing enabled by digital monitoring creates sustainable funding sources (Ge & Qin, 2024).

6. POLICY FRAMEWORKS AND GOVERNANCE MODELS

6.1 Regulatory Frameworks for Digital Infrastructure

6.1.1 Data Governance and Standards

Effective digital twin deployment requires comprehensive data governance addressing ownership, access rights, quality standards, and interoperability. European Union's Data Governance Act establishes frameworks for data sharing across public and private entities. ISO standards including ISO 23247 (Digital Twin Framework for Manufacturing) provide technical specifications adaptable to transportation contexts. National transportation agencies develop domain-specific standards for data formats, APIs, and metadata (Yan et al., 2023).

6.1.2 Privacy and Ethical Considerations

Transportation data includes personally identifiable information raising privacy concerns. General Data Protection Regulation (GDPR) in Europe and similar legislation globally mandate consent mechanisms, data minimization, and individual rights. Anonymization and aggregation techniques balance analytics needs with privacy protection. Ethical frameworks address algorithmic bias, fairness in infrastructure allocation, and equity impacts of automated decision-making (Wu et al., 2025).

6.1.3 Cybersecurity Regulations

Transportation infrastructure constitutes critical infrastructure requiring robust cybersecurity. U.S. Cybersecurity and Infrastructure Security Agency (CISA) guidelines, EU Network and Information Security Directive, and sector-specific standards mandate security measures, incident reporting, and resilience testing. Digital twin operators implement security frameworks complying with ISO 27001, NIST Cybersecurity Framework, and industry-specific requirements (Lv et al., 2022).

6.2 Policy Instruments for Decarbonization

6.2.1 Emissions Standards and Regulations

Vehicle emissions standards including Corporate Average Fuel Economy (CAFE) in the United States, Euro emissions standards in Europe, and China's New Energy Vehicle mandate drive technology adoption. Zero-emission vehicle (ZEV) mandates require manufacturers to sell minimum percentages of electric vehicles. Digital twins support compliance monitoring, emissions testing, and real-world performance verification (Horesh & Quinn, 2024).

6.2.2 Infrastructure Investment Policies

Government infrastructure programs increasingly prioritize climate objectives. U.S. Infrastructure Investment and Jobs Act allocates $7.5 billion for EV charging infrastructure. European Union's Trans-European Transport Network (TEN-T) integrates sustainability requirements. Digital twin capabilities inform investment prioritization, project evaluation, and impact assessment (Briand et al., 2023).

6.2.3 Carbon Reduction Targets and Pathways

National climate commitments under Paris Agreement establish transportation emissions reduction targets. Deep decarbonization pathways for transportation typically involve: electrification of light-duty vehicles by 2030-2040, heavy-duty vehicle transitions to hydrogen or electric by 2040-2050, sustainable aviation fuels reaching 50%+ by 2050, and modal shifts toward public transit, rail, and active transportation. Digital twins enable pathway modeling, progress tracking, and adaptive policy adjustments (Harry-Villain et al., 2025).

6.3 International Cooperation and Knowledge Transfer

6.3.1 Technology Transfer Mechanisms

Technology diffusion from developed to developing economies accelerates global decarbonization. International partnerships, development assistance programs, and technology licensing facilitate knowledge transfer. Digital twin platforms developed in advanced economies require adaptation to local contexts including data availability, technical capacity, and institutional frameworks. South-South cooperation among emerging economies shares experiences and solutions (Briand et al., 2023).

6.3.2 Harmonization of Standards

International standards harmonization reduces costs and enhances interoperability. Organizations including International Organization for Standardization (ISO), International Electrotechnical Commission (IEC), and International Telecommunication Union (ITU) develop global standards. Regional harmonization initiatives such as European Union directives create larger markets supporting economies of scale (Yan et al., 2023).

6.3.3 Capacity Building Programs

Successful digital twin adoption requires technical skills, institutional capacity, and organizational change management. Capacity building programs provide training, technical assistance, and knowledge exchange. International organizations, bilateral aid programs, and academic partnerships support capacity development particularly in emerging economies (Lefèvre et al., 2021).

6.4 Governance Models and Institutional Arrangements

6.4.1 Public Sector Leadership

Government agencies often lead digital twin initiatives given public ownership of much transportation infrastructure. Centralized models concentrate expertise and resources enabling comprehensive deployments. Challenges include bureaucratic inertia, funding constraints, and procurement complexity. Successful public sector implementations establish dedicated digital transformation units, secure sustained funding, and adopt agile development methodologies (Wu et al., 2025).

6.4.2 Public-Private Collaboration

Hybrid governance models leverage public sector mandates with private sector innovation and efficiency. Concession agreements, build-operate-transfer arrangements, and joint ventures structure collaboration. Digital twin platforms facilitate transparent information sharing, performance monitoring, and accountability. Regulatory frameworks define roles, responsibilities, and risk allocation (Mahmoodian et al., 2022).

6.4.3 Multi-Stakeholder Platforms

Transportation digital twins affect diverse stakeholders: government agencies, infrastructure operators, technology providers, users, and communities. Multi-stakeholder governance platforms facilitate participation, align interests, and build consensus. Advisory boards, user committees, and public consultation processes enhance legitimacy and responsiveness. Open data initiatives and API access enable third-party innovation (Ge & Qin, 2024).

7. IMPLEMENTATION CHALLENGES AND SOLUTIONS

7.1 Technical Challenges

7.1.1 Data Integration and Interoperability

Transportation systems involve heterogeneous data sources: sensors with varying protocols, legacy systems with proprietary formats, and external data from weather services, map providers, and social media. Interoperability challenges impede seamless integration. Solutions include: adopting open standards (OGC, GTFS, DATEX II), implementing data translation layers and middleware, establishing master data management frameworks, and developing ontologies defining semantic relationships (Yan et al., 2023).

7.1.2 Scalability and Performance

City-scale and national-scale digital twins generate massive data volumes—petabytes annually for large metropolitan regions. Computational demands for real-time analytics, machine learning model training, and high-fidelity simulations exceed conventional infrastructure capabilities. Solutions involve: cloud-native architectures with elastic scalability, edge computing for distributed processing, data reduction techniques including compression and aggregation, and hierarchical modeling approaches balancing fidelity with computational efficiency (Wu et al., 2025).

7.1.3 Model Validation and Calibration

Digital twin accuracy depends on model validity and calibration. Validation challenges include: limited ground truth data for rare events, nonlinear system behaviors difficult to model, emergent properties in complex networks, and evolving conditions invalidating static models. Solutions encompass: systematic calibration using optimization algorithms, continuous validation against measured data, ensemble modeling combining multiple approaches, and adaptive models updating through machine learning (Kušić et al., 2023).

7.2 Organizational and Institutional Challenges

7.2.1 Skills Gaps and Workforce Development

Digital twin implementation requires multidisciplinary expertise spanning civil engineering, data science, software development, and domain knowledge. Skills shortages particularly in data analytics and AI/ML represent significant constraints. Solutions include: workforce training and reskilling programs, university partnerships for talent pipelines, consulting and managed service arrangements, and user-friendly tools reducing specialized expertise requirements (Wu et al., 2025).

7.2.2 Organizational Change Management

Digital transformation requires cultural shifts from traditional engineering practices to data-driven decision-making. Resistance to change, unclear roles and responsibilities, and misaligned incentives impede adoption. Change management strategies involve: executive leadership and vision communication, stakeholder engagement and participatory design, phased implementation demonstrating quick wins, and performance metrics aligning individual and organizational objectives (Hu et al., 2023).

7.2.3 Procurement and Contracting

Traditional procurement processes emphasizing lowest cost and detailed specifications suit conventional infrastructure but constrain digital innovation requiring flexibility and iteration. Solutions include: performance-based specifications defining outcomes rather than methods, agile contracting with iterative delivery, innovation partnerships enabling co-development, and pre-commercial procurement supporting early-stage technologies (Mahmoodian et al., 2022).

7.3 Financial and Economic Challenges

7.3.1 Funding Constraints

Public sector budget limitations and competing priorities constrain digital twin investments. High upfront costs and uncertain returns deter adoption despite long-term benefits. Solutions involve: phased implementation spreading costs over time, public-private partnerships leveraging private capital, demonstrating ROI through pilot projects, and accessing climate finance through green bonds and development assistance (Yan et al., 2023).

7.3.2 Business Model Uncertainty

Sustainable business models for digital twin platforms remain uncertain. Revenue sources including user fees, data monetization, and service provision face challenges around willingness-to-pay, data privacy concerns, and competitive dynamics. Successful models typically combine: core public funding for basic infrastructure, value-added services generating revenues, ecosystem approaches enabling third-party innovation, and data marketplaces facilitating controlled data sharing (Wu et al., 2025).

7.3.3 Cost Allocation and Benefit Sharing

Digital twin benefits accrue unevenly across stakeholders raising cost allocation and benefit sharing challenges. Network effects and public good characteristics complicate pricing. Solutions encompass: cost-benefit analyses quantifying stakeholder impacts, negotiated agreements among beneficiaries, regulatory frameworks mandating contributions, and subsidy mechanisms compensating underserved populations (Ge & Qin, 2024).

7.4 Social and Ethical Challenges

7.4.1 Equity and Access

Digital infrastructure investments risk exacerbating inequalities if benefits concentrate in affluent areas while underserved communities lack access. Algorithmic decision-making may perpetuate historical biases in infrastructure allocation. Equity-oriented approaches include: explicit equity objectives in digital twin design, community participation in requirement definition, accessibility standards ensuring universal usability, and impact assessments identifying distributional effects (Winkler et al., 2023).

7.4.2 Privacy and Surveillance Concerns

Ubiquitous sensing and tracking raise legitimate privacy and surveillance concerns. Public resistance to monitoring threatens social license for digital twin deployments.

Privacy-protective measures encompass: privacy-by-design principles embedding protection throughout system lifecycle, transparency regarding data collection and usage, consent mechanisms for optional data sharing, and oversight mechanisms including data protection officers and ethics committees (Yan et al., 2023).

7.4.3 Algorithmic Accountability

Automated decision-making through AI/ML algorithms raises accountability questions when errors occur or outcomes prove unfair. Black-box models provide limited explainability. Accountability frameworks include: explainable AI techniques enhancing interpretability, human-in-the-loop approaches maintaining human oversight, audit trails documenting decisions and rationales, and liability frameworks assigning responsibility (Ajayi et al., 2025).

8. CASE STUDIES AND BEST PRACTICES

8.1 Singapore Intelligent Transportation System

8.1.1 System Overview

Singapore's Land Transport Authority developed a comprehensive digital twin of the island nation's multimodal transportation network. The system integrates real-time data from 10,000+ sensors, cameras, and connected vehicles covering highways, rail transit, bus systems, and cycling infrastructure. Cloud-based analytics platforms process 50+ terabytes of data monthly. Advanced visualization interfaces provide operators, planners, and researchers with unified views of network performance (Ge & Qin, 2024).

8.1.2 Key Features and Capabilities

The Singapore digital twin demonstrates several advanced capabilities. Traffic prediction models achieve 95% accuracy for 30-minute forecasts enabling proactive congestion management. Incident detection systems identify accidents within 90 seconds with 97% accuracy. Public transit optimization reduced average waiting times by 18% while improving on-time performance from 84% to 92%. Integrated multimodal journey planning considers real-time conditions across all modes (Wu et al., 2025).

8.1.3 Outcomes and Lessons Learned

Quantified outcomes include: 15% reduction in average travel times, 12% decrease in traffic-related emissions, 25% improvement in incident response times, and 30% increase in public transit ridership. Success factors encompassed: strong government leadership and sustained funding, comprehensive data governance frameworks, extensive stakeholder engagement, and phased implementation starting with high-impact corridors. Challenges included: initial resistance from transport operators, data quality issues requiring extensive cleansing, and integration complexity across legacy systems (Yan et al., 2023).

8.2 Netherlands Railway Infrastructure Management

8.2.1 Implementation Approach

ProRail, the Dutch railway infrastructure manager, developed digital twins for the 7,000+ kilometer rail network. The system integrates track geometry measurements, bridge and tunnel monitoring, signaling system data, and weather information. Predictive maintenance models forecast track degradation, switch failures, and overhead line wear. Reinforcement learning algorithms optimize maintenance schedules balancing performance, costs, and service disruptions (Sresakoolchai & Kaewunruen, 2023).

8.2.2 Operational Improvements

Digital twin deployment achieved: 22% reduction in maintenance costs through optimized intervention timing, 35% decrease in unplanned service disruptions via early failure detection, 18% improvement in track availability through efficient work planning, and 12% energy savings via optimized train operations. Additional benefits included enhanced safety through proactive risk management and improved customer satisfaction from reduced delays (Kaewunruen et al., 2023).

8.2.3 Scaling and Expansion

Following initial success on priority corridors, ProRail expanded digital twin coverage network-wide. Modular architecture enabled incremental deployment. Standardized data models and APIs facilitated integration with rolling stock operators, traffic controllers, and maintenance contractors. Open innovation platforms encouraged third-party application development. International knowledge sharing through EU projects disseminated best practices (Yan et al., 2023).

8.3 Los Angeles Smart Intersection Program

8.3.1 Program Design

Los Angeles Department of Transportation deployed AI-powered digital twins at 150 signalized intersections across high-congestion corridors. Each intersection features video analytics, connected vehicle interfaces, and edge computing processors. Machine learning models predict traffic volumes, pedestrian crossings, and transit arrivals. Adaptive signal control optimizes green time allocations in real-time (Wu et al., 2025).

8.3.2 Environmental Benefits

The program prioritized emissions reductions and air quality improvements in environmental justice communities. Results demonstrated: 14% decrease in corridor travel times, 11% reduction in fuel consumption and CO2 emissions, 8% improvement in air quality (PM2.5 and NOx), and 20% reduction in pedestrian wait times. Environmental benefits proved most significant during peak congestion periods when traditional signal timing performed poorly (Horesh & Quinn, 2024).

8.3.3 Replication Strategy

Success factors enabling replication included: open-source software stack reducing costs, modular hardware architecture supporting phased deployment, comprehensive evaluation demonstrating clear benefits, and extensive stakeholder engagement building support. Los Angeles shared technical specifications, implementation guides, and lessons learned with other cities. Federal funding programs subsequently supported similar deployments in 40+ U.S. cities (Ge & Qin, 2024).

8.4 Norway Electric Vehicle Charging Network

8.4.1 Network Development

Norway achieved world-leading 94% EV market share in 2024 supported by comprehensive charging infrastructure. Digital twin platforms optimize charging station placement, capacity planning, and grid integration. Predictive models forecast charging demand based on EV adoption trends, travel patterns, and seasonal variations. Real-time monitoring tracks station utilization, queue lengths, and equipment status (Forsythe et al., 2023).

8.4.2 Grid Integration Strategies

Smart charging algorithms coordinate vehicle charging with renewable energy availability and grid constraints. Vehicle-to-grid pilots enable EVs to provide frequency regulation and peak shaving services. Aggregated flexibility from 500,000+ EVs provides 1,000+ MW of controllable load supporting grid stability. Economic modeling demonstrates 18% reduction in total charging costs through optimized timing and 25% increase in renewable energy utilization (Archsmith et al., 2022).

8.4.3 Policy Enablers

Success resulted from integrated policies: generous purchase incentives making EVs cost-competitive, extensive charging infrastructure funded through petroleum taxes, preferential access to bus lanes and toll exemptions, and regulatory frameworks supporting grid integration. Digital twin platforms enabled evidence-based policy refinement as market matured. International knowledge sharing supported EV transitions globally (Rapson & Muehlegger, 2023b).

9. FUTURE DIRECTIONS AND EMERGING TRENDS

9.1 Autonomous Vehicle Integration

9.1.1 Connected and Automated Vehicles

Autonomous vehicles rely on digital infrastructure for safe and efficient operation. High-definition maps, V2X communications, and edge computing support perception, planning, and control. Digital twins simulate mixed traffic flows including conventional and autonomous vehicles, evaluate infrastructure readiness, and optimize dedicated lanes or zones. Transition pathways model gradual automation adoption and infrastructure adaptation requirements (Wu et al., 2025).

9.1.2 Shared Autonomous Fleets

Mobility-as-a-Service platforms combining autonomous vehicles with public transit, micromobility, and walking promise emissions reductions through higher vehicle utilization and modal shifts. Digital twins optimize fleet sizing, vehicle routing, and station placement. Scenario analyses evaluate impacts on congestion, emissions, equity, and urban form. Governance frameworks address liability, safety standards, and service requirements (Ge & Qin, 2024).

9.1.3 Freight Automation

Autonomous trucks, delivery robots, and drones transform freight logistics. Digital twins optimize warehouse locations, route networks, and modal integration. Platooning algorithms coordinate truck convoys reducing fuel consumption by 10-15%. Last-mile automation uses sidewalks, bike lanes, and airspace requiring infrastructure adaptations and regulatory frameworks (Yan et al., 2023).

9.2 Advanced Materials and Sensing Technologies

9.2.1 Self-Sensing Infrastructure

Next-generation materials with embedded sensing capabilities enable continuous structural health monitoring without external sensors. Concrete with piezoelectric aggregates detects stress changes. Asphalt with conductive additives monitors traffic loads and pavement conditions. Fiber-reinforced composites provide distributed strain sensing. Self-sensing materials reduce installation costs while improving coverage and reliability (Kaewunruen et al., 2023).

9.2.2 Nanomaterials and Smart Materials

Nanomaterial-enhanced asphalt exhibits self-healing properties repairing micro-cracks automatically. Phase-change materials regulate pavement temperatures reducing heat island effects and improving durability. Photocatalytic coatings decompose air pollutants improving air quality. Digital twins optimize material selection and lifecycle management incorporating advanced material properties (Mahmoodian et al., 2022).

9.2.3 Energy Harvesting Infrastructure

Transportation infrastructure integrated with energy harvesting technologies generates renewable power. Piezoelectric pavements convert vehicle-induced vibrations to electricity. Solar roadways and bike paths generate power for lighting and charging. Wind turbines along highways capture vehicle-induced airflows. Digital twins optimize energy harvesting system placement, sizing, and grid integration (Wu et al., 2025).

9.3 Quantum Computing and Advanced Analytics

9.3.1 Quantum Optimization Algorithms

Quantum computers promise exponential speedups for combinatorial optimization problems including traffic routing, maintenance scheduling, and network design. Quantum annealing solves large-scale vehicle routing problems intractable for classical computers. Variational quantum eigensolvers optimize charging station placement considering grid constraints. Near-term quantum advantage applications target specific digital twin optimization problems (Ge & Qin, 2024).

9.3.2 Quantum Machine Learning

Quantum machine learning algorithms potentially enhance prediction accuracy and training efficiency. Quantum neural networks model complex traffic dynamics. Quantum support vector machines classify infrastructure defects from imagery. Hybrid classical-quantum approaches combine conventional deep learning with quantum subroutines for specific tasks (Yan et al., 2023).

9.3.3 Practical Implementation Timeline

Quantum computing for transportation digital twins remains largely experimental with practical applications projected for 2030s. Current research focuses on algorithm development, benchmark comparisons with classical methods, and identifying suitable problem structures. Infrastructure managers should monitor developments while continuing classical computing investments (Wu et al., 2025).

9.4 Circular Economy and Sustainability

9.4.1 Material Passport Systems

Digital twins incorporating material passports track infrastructure components throughout lifecycles enabling circular economy practices. Blockchain-based systems record material compositions, treatment histories, and environmental impacts. End-of-life planning identifies reuse and recycling opportunities maximizing resource efficiency and minimizing waste (Kaewunruen et al., 2023).

9.4.2 Lifecycle Environmental Assessment

Integrated lifecycle assessment tools within digital twin platforms quantify environmental impacts across infrastructure lifecycles: raw material extraction, manufacturing, construction, operation, maintenance, and end-of-life. Optimizations balance operational carbon (emissions during use) with embodied carbon (emissions from materials and construction) identifying truly sustainable solutions (Winkler et al., 2023).

9.4.3 Biodiversity and Ecosystem Integration

Transportation infrastructure affects ecosystems through habitat fragmentation, pollution, and disturbance. Digital twins incorporating ecological models assess biodiversity impacts, optimize wildlife crossing locations, and monitor habitat conditions. Nature-based solutions including green infrastructure and ecological corridors are evaluated for cost-effectiveness and environmental benefits (Yan et al., 2023).

9.5 Social Equity and Inclusive Design

9.5.1 Equity-Oriented Digital Twins

Future digital twins explicitly incorporate equity objectives: accessibility for disabled persons, affordability for low-income populations, and service coverage for disadvantaged communities. Equity metrics track spatial distributions of benefits and burdens. Participatory design processes engage affected communities ensuring responsive solutions (Wu et al., 2025).

9.5.2 Digital Inclusion

Ensuring equitable access to digital twin benefits requires addressing digital divides. User-friendly interfaces accommodate varying technical literacy. Multilingual support serves diverse populations. Offline access modes serve areas with limited connectivity. Community computing centers provide shared access (Ge & Qin, 2024).

9.5.3 Just Transitions

Transportation decarbonization transitions affect workers in fossil fuel industries, automotive manufacturing, and related sectors. Digital twin-based transition planning models workforce impacts, identifies retraining needs, and evaluates policy interventions. Just transition frameworks ensure workers and communities share decarbonization benefits (Briand et al., 2023).

10. CONCLUSIONS AND RECOMMENDATIONS

10.1 Summary of Key Findings

This chapter has comprehensively examined digital twins and data-driven infrastructure management in the context of decarbonized transport systems. Several key findings emerge:

Technological Maturity: Digital twin technology has advanced from conceptual frameworks to operational deployments demonstrating measurable benefits. Integration of IoT sensors, AI/ML analytics, cloud computing, and visualization platforms creates comprehensive systems supporting predictive maintenance, traffic optimization, and emissions reduction. Mature implementations in Singapore, Netherlands, and Norway demonstrate 10-35% improvements across performance metrics including travel times, maintenance costs, and emissions.

Economic Viability: Cost-benefit analyses demonstrate positive returns on digital twin investments with payback periods of 3-8 years across different transportation modes. Benefits arise from maintenance optimization (15-35% cost reductions), operational efficiency (10-25% improvements), enhanced safety (20-40% accident cost reductions), and environmental improvements (8-20% emissions reductions). Financing mechanisms including green bonds, public-private partnerships, and infrastructure funds increasingly support digital infrastructure investments.

Policy Integration: Effective digital twin deployment requires supportive policy frameworks addressing data governance, privacy protection, cybersecurity, and interoperability standards. Decarbonization policies including carbon pricing, emissions standards, infrastructure investments, and climate targets create contexts where digital twins generate maximum value. International cooperation on standards harmonization, technology transfer, and capacity building accelerates global adoption.

Implementation Challenges: Despite demonstrated benefits, adoption faces significant barriers including data integration complexity, scalability constraints, workforce skills gaps, organizational resistance, funding limitations, and social equity concerns. Successful implementations address these challenges through comprehensive change management, phased deployment strategies, stakeholder engagement, and continuous learning.

Future Potential: Emerging trends including autonomous vehicles, advanced materials, quantum computing, circular economy integration, and equity-focused design promise enhanced capabilities and broader impacts. Realizing this potential requires sustained research and development, supportive policies, and collaborative governance models.

10.2 Strategic Recommendations

Based on the analysis presented, several strategic recommendations emerge for different stakeholder groups:

10.2.1 For Policymakers and Government Agencies

Establish Comprehensive Data Governance Frameworks: Develop clear policies on data ownership, access rights, privacy protection, and interoperability standards. Balance innovation incentives with privacy safeguards and cybersecurity requirements.

Invest in Digital Infrastructure: Allocate sustained funding for sensor networks, computing platforms, and technical capacity. Prioritize high-impact applications demonstrating clear benefits while building long-term capabilities.

Integrate Digital Twins with Climate Policies: Explicitly incorporate digital twin capabilities into climate action plans, transportation decarbonization strategies, and infrastructure investment programs. Use digital twins for emissions monitoring, policy evaluation, and adaptive management.

Support Workforce Development: Fund training programs, university partnerships, and professional development initiatives building multidisciplinary expertise in data science, AI/ML, and transportation engineering.

Enable Public-Private Collaboration: Create regulatory frameworks, contractual mechanisms, and financial instruments facilitating public-private partnerships. Share data appropriately while protecting commercial interests and public values.

10.2.2 For Infrastructure Owners and Operators

Start with High-Impact Pilots: Begin digital twin deployment on high-priority assets or corridors demonstrating clear value propositions. Use successful pilots to build organizational support and secure additional resources.

Invest in Data Quality: Prioritize sensor calibration, data validation, and integration infrastructure. High-quality data fundamentally determines digital twin value.

Develop Internal Capabilities: Build internal expertise through hiring, training, and organizational restructuring. Balance external consultants providing specialized skills with internal teams owning long-term operations.

Embrace Agile Methodologies: Adopt iterative development approaches allowing rapid prototyping, user feedback incorporation, and continuous improvement. Avoid waterfall approaches expecting complete specifications upfront.

Measure and Communicate Benefits: Establish clear performance metrics, conduct rigorous evaluations, and communicate results to stakeholders. Demonstrated value justifies continued investment and expansion.

10.2.3 For Technology Providers and Researchers

Focus on Interoperability: Develop systems using open standards, well-documented APIs, and modular architectures. Avoid proprietary lock-in constraining customer flexibility.

Prioritize User Experience: Design interfaces for domain experts, not just data scientists. Intuitive visualization, automated insights, and decision support enhance adoption and impact.

Address Scalability Proactively: Architect systems for growth from initial deployments to network-wide coverage. Cloud-native designs, edge computing, and hierarchical modeling support scalability.

Incorporate Equity Objectives: Engage diverse communities in design processes. Ensure accessibility, affordability, and responsiveness to varied user needs.

Pursue Interdisciplinary Research: Advance digital twin capabilities through research integrating civil engineering, computer science, economics, and social sciences. Address remaining technical challenges while exploring broader societal implications.

10.3 Research Gaps and Future Directions

Despite significant progress, several research gaps warrant attention:

Standardization and Interoperability: Further work on data models, ontologies, APIs, and reference architectures supporting seamless integration across vendors, jurisdictions, and domains.

Economic Valuation Methodologies: Refined approaches for quantifying intangible benefits including resilience, flexibility, and option value. Better methods for assessing distributional impacts and equity outcomes.

Organizational Change Management: Understanding effective strategies for digital transformation in public sector transportation agencies. Identifying critical success factors and common failure modes.

Long-Term Sustainability: Investigating business models, governance structures, and technical architectures ensuring digital twin longevity beyond initial deployments.

Social and Ethical Dimensions: Deeper exploration of privacy protection, algorithmic accountability, equity impacts, and public acceptance. Development of frameworks balancing efficiency with social values.

Integration with Emerging Technologies: Research on digital twin synergies with autonomous vehicles, quantum computing, advanced materials, and other emerging innovations.

10.4 Final Remarks

Digital twins represent transformative opportunities for transportation infrastructure management and decarbonization. The technology has matured from conceptual frameworks to operational systems demonstrating measurable benefits across efficiency, safety, and sustainability dimensions. However, realizing full potential requires addressing persistent challenges around data integration, organizational capacity, equitable access, and sustainable business models.

The convergence of digital twins with decarbonization imperatives creates particularly compelling opportunities. Real-time monitoring, predictive analytics, and optimized operations directly reduce emissions while improving service quality. Economic analysis demonstrates favorable returns on investment, particularly when environmental and social benefits are valued appropriately. Policy integration through carbon pricing, performance standards, and infrastructure investments enhances value creation.

Success requires coordinated action across multiple stakeholder groups: policymakers establishing supportive frameworks, infrastructure operators implementing systems, technology providers developing solutions, researchers advancing capabilities, and communities engaging in inclusive design. International cooperation on standards, knowledge sharing, and capacity building accelerates global progress.

As transportation systems undergo fundamental transformations toward sustainability, digital twins will play increasingly central roles. The path forward demands sustained commitment, adaptive learning, and inclusive collaboration. By embracing digital innovation while maintaining focus on equity, sustainability, and resilience, the transportation sector can achieve ambitious decarbonization targets while enhancing mobility for all.

DISCLOSURE OF AI-ASSISTED TOOLS

In the preparation of this manuscript, AI-assisted writing tools (including large language model-based assistants) were used to support literature synthesis, structural drafting, and language editing. All content, arguments, and scholarly interpretations were critically reviewed, verified, and revised by the authors, who take full responsibility for the accuracy, integrity, and originality of the work. The use of AI tools in this manuscript is disclosed in accordance with the publisher's policies on generative AI in academic publishing.

REFERENCES

Ajayi, O. O., Kurien, A., Djouani, K., & Dieng, L. (2025). Artificial intelligence for infrastructure resilience: Transportation systems as a strategic case for policy and practice. *Sustainability (Basel), 17*(20), 8992. Advance online publication. DOI: 10.3390/su17208992

Archsmith, J., Muehlegger, E., & Rapson, D. S. (2022). Future paths of electric vehicle adoption in the United States: Predictable determinants, obstacles, and opportunities. *Environmental and Energy Policy and the Economy, 3*, 71–110. DOI: 10.1086/717219

Briand, Y., Pye, S., D'Agosto, M. de A., Goes, G. V., Schmitz-Gonçalves, D. N., Garg, A., Gupta, D., Vishwanathan, S. S., Siagian, U. W. R., Ahjum, F., & Trollip, H. (2023). Passenger transport decarbonization in emerging economies: Policy lessons from modelling long-term deep decarbonization pathways. *Climate Policy, 23*(10), 1–21. DOI: 10.1080/14693062.2023.2194859

Dan, D., Ying, Y., & Ge, L. (2022). Digital twin system of bridges group based on machine vision fusion monitoring of bridge traffic load. *IEEE Transactions on Intelligent Transportation Systems, 23*(11), 22190–22205. DOI: 10.1109/TITS.2021.3130025

Forsythe, C. R., Gillingham, K. T., Michalek, J. J., & Whitefoot, K. S. (2023). Technology advancement is driving electric vehicle adoption. *Proceedings of the National Academy of Sciences of the United States of America, 120*(23), e2219396120. Advance online publication. DOI: 10.1073/pnas.2219396120 PMID: 37252977

Ge, C., & Qin, S. (2024). Digital twin intelligent transportation system (DT-ITS)—A systematic review. *IET Intelligent Transport Systems, 18*(7), 1165–1192. DOI: 10.1049/itr2.12539

Harry-Villain, L., Briand, Y., Waisman, H., Rudolph, F., Hall, C., van Asselt, H., Gjerek, M., Merkert, R., D'Agosto, M. de A., & Goes, G. V. (2025). Analyzing sectoral policies for deep decarbonization: The case of national freight transportation. *Climate Policy, 25*(1), 1–14. DOI: 10.1080/14693062.2025.2485192

Horesh, N., & Quinn, J. C. (2024). Fuel shifts reduce most of the greenhouse gas emissions from transportation in the United States. *Communications Earth & Environment, 5*(1), 781. Advance online publication. DOI: 10.1038/s43247-024-01924-4

Hu, G., Liu, Y., Liu, K., & Yang, X. (2023). Research on data-driven dynamic decision-making mechanism of mega infrastructure project construction. *Sustainability (Basel), 15*(12), 9219. Advance online publication. DOI: 10.3390/su15129219

Kaewunruen, S., AbdelHadi, M., Kongpuang, M., Pansuk, W., & Remennikov, A. M. (2023). Digital twins for managing railway bridge maintenance, resilience, and climate change adaptation. *Sensors (Basel), 23*(1), 252. Advance online publication. DOI: 10.3390/s23010252 PMID: 36616851

Kušić, K., Schumann, R., & Ivanjko, E. (2023). A digital twin in transportation: Real-time synergy of traffic data streams and simulation for virtualizing motorway dynamics. *Advanced Engineering Informatics, 55*, 101858. Advance online publication. DOI: 10.1016/j.aei.2022.101858

Lefèvre, J., Briand, Y., Pye, S., Tovilla, J., Li, F., Oshiro, K., Waisman, H., Cayla, J.-M., & Zhang, R. (2021). A pathway design framework for sectoral deep decarbonization: The case of passenger transportation. *Climate Policy, 21*(1), 93–106. DOI: 10.1080/14693062.2020.1804817

Li, Y., & Zhang, W. (2023). Traffic flow digital twin generation for highway scenario based on radar-camera paired fusion. *Scientific Reports, 13*(1), 642. Advance online publication. DOI: 10.1038/s41598-023-27696-z PMID: 36635372

Lv, Z., Li, Y., Feng, H., & Lv, H. (2022). Deep learning for security in digital twins of cooperative intelligent transportation systems. *IEEE Transactions on Intelligent Transportation Systems, 23*(9), 16666–16675. DOI: 10.1109/TITS.2021.3113779

Mahmoodian, M., Shahrivar, F., Setunge, S., & Mazaheri, S. (2022). Development of digital twin for intelligent maintenance of civil infrastructure. *Sustainability (Basel), 14*(14), 8664. Advance online publication. DOI: 10.3390/su14148664

Pretis, F. (2022). Does a carbon tax reduce CO2 emissions? Evidence from British Columbia. *Environmental and Resource Economics, 83*(1), 115–144. DOI: 10.1007/s10640-022-00679-w

Rapson, D. S., & Muehlegger, E. (2023a). Global transportation decarbonization. *The Journal of Economic Perspectives, 37*(3), 163–188. DOI: 10.1257/jep.37.3.163

Rapson, D. S., & Muehlegger, E. (2023b). The economics of electric vehicles. *Review of Environmental Economics and Policy, 17*(2), 274–294. DOI: 10.1086/725484

Sresakoolchai, J., & Kaewunruen, S. (2023). Railway infrastructure maintenance efficiency improvement using deep reinforcement learning integrated with digital twin based on track geometry and component defects. *Scientific Reports, 13*(1), 2439. Advance online publication. DOI: 10.1038/s41598-023-29526-8 PMID: 36765166

Sroczyński, A., & Czyżewski, A. (2023). Road traffic can be predicted by machine learning equally effectively as by complex microscopic model. *Scientific Reports*, *13*(1), 14523. Advance online publication. DOI: 10.1038/s41598-023-41902-y PMID: 37666950

Winkler, L., Pearce, D., Nelson, J., & Babacan, O. (2023). The effect of sustainable mobility transition policies on cumulative urban transport emissions and energy demand. *Nature Communications*, *14*(1), 2357. Advance online publication. DOI: 10.1038/s41467-023-37728-x PMID: 37095105

Wu, D., Zheng, A., Yu, W., Cao, H., Ling, Q., Liu, J., & Zhou, D. (2025). Digital twin technology in transportation infrastructure: A comprehensive survey of current applications, challenges, and future directions. *Applied Sciences (Basel, Switzerland)*, *15*(4), 1911. Advance online publication. DOI: 10.3390/app15041911

Yan, B., Yang, F., Qiu, S., Wang, J., Cai, B., Wang, S., Zaheer, Q., Wang, W., Chen, Y., & Hu, W. (2023). Digital twin in transportation infrastructure management: A systematic review. *Intelligent Transportation Infrastructure*, *2*, liad024. Advance online publication. DOI: 10.1093/iti/liad024

KEY TERMS AND DEFINITIONS

Data-Driven Infrastructure Management: An approach to infrastructure operation and maintenance that relies on continuous monitoring, statistical analysis, and machine learning algorithms to optimize decisions, predict failures, and allocate resources efficiently.

Decarbonization: The process of reducing carbon dioxide emissions associated with transportation activities through vehicle electrification, alternative fuels, operational efficiency improvements, and modal shifts toward low-carbon modes.

Digital Twin: A virtual representation of a physical asset, process, or system that is continuously updated through real-time data exchange, enabling monitoring, analysis, prediction, and optimization throughout the asset lifecycle.

Internet of Things (IoT): A network of physical devices embedded with sensors, software, and connectivity that enables data collection, exchange, and remote monitoring and control of infrastructure assets.

Machine Learning: A subset of artificial intelligence focused on algorithms that learn patterns from data and make predictions or decisions without being explicitly programmed for specific tasks.

Predictive Maintenance: A maintenance strategy that uses data analytics and machine learning to predict when equipment failures are likely to occur, enabling timely interventions that prevent breakdowns while minimizing unnecessary maintenance.

Smart Infrastructure: Transportation infrastructure enhanced with digital technologies including sensors, communications, analytics, and automation to improve performance, efficiency, safety, and sustainability.

Chapter 7
Economic Signals and Artificial Intelligence for Sustainable Transport and Low-Carbon Logistics Systems

Turdiev Abdullo Sagdullaevich
Alfraganus University, Tashkent, Uzbekistan

S. Aarthi
http://orcid.org/0009-0006-9064-2091
Marwadi University, Rajkot, India

R. N. Ravikumar
http://orcid.org/0009-0009-3705-1681
Marwadi University, Rajkot, India

Shoyimkulov Asror
Termez University of Economics and Service, Termez, Uzbekistan

Jabbarov Umarbek
Mamun University, Khiva, Uzbekistan

ABSTRACT

Supply chains involve transport and logistics systems that are significant sources of global carbon emission and thus their decarbonization is a key sustainability issue. This chapter discusses how economic indicators and Artificial Intelligence (AI)

DOI: 10.4018/979-8-3373-9003-1.ch007

may be combined to promote low-carbon transport and logistic systems. It takes a conceptual and analytical approach based on recent case studies on urban transport and freight logistics. The paper shows that the optimization through AI, when accompanied by the emissions-based pricing and incentives, could be an effective way of enhancing the efficiency of the supply chain and minimizing logistics-related emissions. The chapter makes a contribution because it suggests a single framework that interconnects economic indicators, AI-based decision-making, and regulatory policies. The results indicate that efficient transport decarbonization involves collaborative signal planning to provide sustainable, efficient and scalable mobility and logistics networks.

1. INTRODUCTION

The issue of transport decarbonization is multidimensional and complicated and requires the application of not only technological innovation but also of economic, behavioral, and institutional aspects. The transport and logistics have been key in the creation of emissions in the supply chains with freight movement, last-mile delivery, and network coordination adding to the activities associated with carbon emissions. Although low-carbon technologies and intelligent transport systems have been developed, the reduction of the emissions is still inadequate because of the inappropriate economic incentives and inconsistency in the policy development. Artificial Intelligence (AI) is more and more involved in transportation and logistics decision-making (routing, pricing, and scheduling algorithms), but its ability to affect sustainability can be determined by the development of design and consistency of economic indicators (Woody et al., 2024). Without the adequate agreement, AI systems can support the inefficient and carbon-intensive trends. Thus, the key to the coordination of the transport and logistics systems toward the low-carbon, efficient, and sustainable supply chain results that will guarantee not only the improvement of environmental performance but operational efficiency is to incorporate economic signal design in the context of AI-enabled optimization.

1.1 Transport Coordination Challenge

The issue of transport decarbonization has more than one actor, the decisions of which are interrelated, both spatially, on a temporal level, and institutionally. People, logistics, fleet owners, and digital solutions make decisions depending on individual costs, convenience, and service quality, whereas climate mitigation needs joint reduction of emissions that are not directly reflected in the market prices. This lack of coordination leads to a breakdown in coordination, as individual rationality keeps producing carbon intensive outcomes. Jamming on the roads, over-utilization of freight miles, and slow uptake of the electrification of the fleet are examples of how externalities can cause distortion in system-level performance (Abduljabbar et al., 2019). The lack of economic coordination also becomes aggravated by the difficulty of fragmented governance at local, national, and international governance making the policy signals to overlap or contradict. The key to successful decarbonization is as such the coordination of individual incentives with social goals via the well-crafted economic signals. The coordination tools which are pricing mechanisms, taxes, and subsidies assist in changing environmental objectives into operational decision variables. In a world devoid of this kind of alignment, even high-tech digital and AI-enabled transport systems can be run in an incentive environment that structurally encourages high-mobility-emission patterns.

1.2 Technology Limits

Technologies-based solutions to decarbonization of transport can tend to believe that efficiency in the transport system and cleaner technologies would automatically lead to a drop in emissions. Nonetheless, there is empirical evidence that technological improvements in themselves often have rebound effects, induced demand, as well as uneven uptake by income groups and regions. New technologies like electric cars, smart navigation, smart logistics, etc. can help decrease the number of emissions per trip, but overall emission levels may still increase when the number of trips grows or when other carbon-intensive transportation methods are not taxed (Ravikumar & Aarthi, 2025d). Additionally, current economic incentives, investment in infrastructure, and regulation frameworks influence technology implementation and could be out "of step" with technology. In cases where the fuel taxes, congestion charges, or emission prices are weak or erratic, AI-based optimization tools will reduce individual expenses instead of the environmental effects. This drawback underscores the inadequacy of the treatment of AI and digitalization as a neutral solution. Devoid of complementary economic signal design, technology will be optimizing within distorted incentive structures, and thus limiting the decarbonization potential, and solidifying systemic inefficiencies.

1.3 Economic Signals & AI

The power of economic signals is closely related to the determination of the contribution of AI mediated mobility systems to transport behavior and emissions outcomes. Prices, taxes, tolls and subsidies are informational inputs, which inform an algorithmic decision-making in routing, scheduling and pricing platforms. With economic indicators, which capture externalities of environmental impact, AI systems can internalize the costs of carbon and make decisions in line with the objectives of reducing emissions. On the other hand, scale-increasing carbon-intensive trends in AI systems are promoted by mispriced energy, subsidies were under-priced, or subsidies did not focus on the right areas (Kidokoro, 2010). New possibilities also emerge with dynamic and adaptive signal design and AI can be used to make changes to the price in real time depending on congestion, emissions intensity, or the state of the network. This interaction converts the economic signals which are represented by fixed policy instruments into constantly revised coordination mechanisms (Isalkar, 2024). To the extent that AI-mediated mobility systems are successful hinges on their computational sophistication, however, and more on the form and coherence of the economic signals that they are operationalizing.

1.4 Research Gap and Contributions

Although there is an increasing literature on the topic of Artificial Intelligence in transport and the design of economic signals, the available research mostly considers them in isolation. The existing literature is either on AI-based optimization as the means of efficiency or pricing as the means of emissions reduction, and there is not much of a combination between these two points of view. Moreover, the contribution of transport and logistics systems to supply chains is a subject that is not thoroughly researched in decarbonization models. This chapter fills these gaps through the creation of a cohesive conceptual framework that would incorporate the economic signals, AI-driven decision-making, and logistics systems into the supply chains. The main contributions are: (i) the conceptualization of economic signals as the input to AI-based transport optimization, (ii) the connection between transport decarbonization and supply chain efficiency, and (iii) the offer of design principles of scalable and sustainable low-carbon transport and logistics systems.

2. BACKGROUND TO THE STUDY

The use of economic instruments to affect mobility behavior has long been a part of transport policy, but its success has been widely inconsistent across situations and time. Conventional pricing arrangements like fuel taxes, vehicle registration and tax, and toll were planned to be used to raise revenue and fund infrastructure development and environmental goals are often secondary. Later on, the policy on climate has proposed emissions-based policies, such as carbon pricing and different vehicle taxation, to internalize the externalities of the environment (Candia Riquelme, 2025). At the same time, the development of Artificial Intelligence has also changed the processes of the design, operation and pricing of transport systems, introducing new interfaces between policy tools and operational choices. Although these changes have taken place, most transport systems have still not corrected their incentives to promote carbon-intensive modes and practices. Knowledge of the historical development of pricing tools, the advent of Artificial Intelligence-based systems, and the inability to reconcile signal distortions are key information on orchestrating combined decarbonization policies with an interlinking of technologies and economics.

2.1 Pricing Evolution

The transport policy instrument of pricing and incentive has been changing and is no longer a simple cost-recovery instrument, but an instrument to change behavior and environmental performance. The initial policies focused on fuel tax and infrastructure toll funding road construction and maintenance, and small regard was given to the congestion or road emission externalities. In the long run, congestion pricing, efficiency levels and differentiated registration fees were introduced to deal with traffic control and local pollution (Sahoo, 2025). Climate issues also broadened the policy repertoire to cover carbon taxes, carbon trading schemes and performance-based subsidies on low-emission cars. Nevertheless, these tools have been employed separately and thus, they have created mixed and conflicting signals. The decision has been undermined by political constraints, equity issues and institutional inertia with regard to the strength and consistency of pricing actions (Song et al., 2025). Due to this, the pricing systems of transportation are often not very effective in bringing about decarbonization since the actual social cost of emissions is not being adequately recognized. Table 1 Summarizes major pricing and incentive tools (fuel taxes, congestion charges, carbon pricing) and its major policy goals in the long term.

Table 1. Pricing Instruments Overview

Economic Signal Instrument	Primary Objective	Policy Focus Period	Key Limitation
Fuel taxation	Revenue generation	Early–mid transport policy	Weak linkage to emissions
Vehicle registration fees	Ownership regulation	Pre-climate policy era	Limited behavioral impact
Congestion pricing	Traffic management	Urban policy expansion	Public acceptance challenges

continued on following page

Table 1. Continued

Economic Signal Instrument	Primary Objective	Policy Focus Period	Key Limitation
Emissions-based taxation	Carbon internalization	Climate policy phase	Fragmented implementation
Carbon pricing mechanisms	System-level decarbonization	Recent policy frameworks	Coordination complexity

2.2 AI Transport Platforms

Transport decision systems based on AI are currently becoming important intermediaries in mobility systems, and influence the decisions of routing, scheduling, pricing, and fleet management. Machine learning models are progressively used to predict traffic, demand forecast, as well as optimize logistics and respond to the dynamic state of network in real-time. Digital platforms integrate massive data sets of vehicles, infrastructure and users in a way that such data sets can be synchronized at scale never before through algorithms (Marisamy et al., 2025). The systems restructure the transmission and response of economic signals when automated decisions process inject prices and incentives into the systems. However, AI platforms are mostly optimized in terms of cost, speed or performance of services, rather than environmental performance, except when specified otherwise. They augment the impacts of the existing pricing frameworks and hence indicate design becomes more consequential to them. The phenomenon of AI, therefore, creates the need of constant economic paradigms that would guide the algorithm optimization of low-carbon outcomes. Such AI-based systems are also becoming integrated into logistics and supply chain systems, which facilitate freight movement, warehouse coordination, and optimization of the last mile. Consequently, transport decisions are not isolated anymore but rather embedded in overall end-to-end supply chain activities, in which the increase of efficiency positively affects the cost of logistics and emissions. The integration shows the need to align AI-based transport systems with logistics sustainability in the logistics systems. Table 2 Swimming AI solutions (machine learning, optimization, predictive analytics) to transport operations such as routing, pricing and demand management.

Table 2. AI in Transport Decisions

AI Capability	Transport Application	Decision Variable Influenced	Environmental Relevance
Machine learning	Traffic and demand forecasting	Travel timing and volume	Emissions intensity
Optimization algorithms	Routing and scheduling	Distance and congestion	Fuel and energy use
Predictive analytics	Pricing and toll design	Cost responsiveness	Modal shift
Platform algorithms	Logistics coordination	Load consolidation	Freight emissions
Real-time analytics	Network management	Capacity utilization	System efficiency

2.3 Signal Misalignment

Although the tools of policy and digital technologies have developed, there is still a fixed signal misalignment of carbon-intensive mobility systems. Subsidies on fuel and under-pricing of the use of the roads and poor pricing of the emission is still prevalent, especially in the road transport and freight sectors. Such distortions promote overuse of vehicles, inefficient logistic trends and slow uptake of low-carbon technologies (Ravikumar & Aarthi, 2025a). Fragmented governance is another factor that contributes to misalignment, inadequate policies of local congestion, national tax systems and regional carbon markets are functioning separately. The engagement of AI based systems with these distorted signals will optimize carbon-intensive behavior in a more efficient manner and aggravates instead of correcting the environmental performance. The equity issue also makes reforming difficult, since trying to have uniform pricing instruments can create unequal burden on the vulnerable groups unless it is well planned. To tackle the endemic malalignment then, there is a need to consider integrated signal design between the economic incentives, technology potential, and governance arrangements to enable socially acceptable decarbonization pathways.

3. RESEARCH OBJECTIVES

The goal of the chapter is to formulate a consistent analytical insight into how the economic signals could be strategized and operationalized in the AI-enabled transport systems in order to assist the low-carbon mobility shifts. Instead of considering pricing, incentives, and Artificial Intelligence as distinct policy or technological aspects, the chapter presents them in a coordinated fashion, as two or three mechanisms that mutually affect transport behavior, investment decisions and the results of the system at the system level. The research aims are designed in a way that they shed light on the conceptual role of economic signals, analyze how they interact with AI-based decision platforms and estimate the policy and governance conditions that are necessary to implement them in a well-functioning and equitable way.

- To conceptualize economic signals as behavioral information carriers that translate environmental externalities into decision-relevant inputs shaping individual, organizational, and platform-mediated transport choices.
- To analyze how AI capabilities interact with pricing and incentive instruments, enabling dynamic, data-driven, and adaptive signal design across transport networks.
- To evaluate the effectiveness of AI-enabled economic signals in influencing modal choice, routing, fleet composition, and logistics organization toward low-carbon outcomes.
- To examine policy and governance implications of signal design, with particular attention to data governance, transparency, accountability, and public acceptance in AI-mediated pricing systems.
- To identify design principles for coherent and inclusive economic signal architectures that align local, national, and regional transport policies while addressing distributional and equity concerns.

4. CONCEPTUAL MODEL

The developed conceptual framework of this chapter represents transport decarbonization as a product of interaction in the system of Artificial Intelligence, economic indicators, and multi-level governance. Instead of considering AI a stand-alone optimization solution, the model places the technology at the center of bridging that in between, that augments and perceives pricing and incentive signals through transport networks (Oteri et al., 2023). Economic tools like carbon pricing, congestion charges, performance-based subsidies are considered as carriers of information and they affect algorithm-based decision-making, behavioral reactions, and system equilibria. The model is a combination of behavioral, network, and system-level dynamics to describe how individual decisions combine together into group outcomes mediated by AI. At the heart of the framework lies the fact that signal effectiveness is pegged on adaptivity, coherence, and institutional credibility. Feedback systems can enable constant re-calibration of prices and incentives based on the observed results, and the dynamic harmonization of climate goals and transport functions is possible (Arun Chakravarthy et al., 2025). This combined viewpoint offers a framework of the way in which AI-assisted economically significant signal designs may guide transport systems to both effective, scalable, and socially agreeable low-carbon solutions. The figure demonstrates the impact of economic signals, which AI systems understand and amplify in multi-level governance systems, on behavioral, network, and system dynamics in feedback mechanisms to decarbonize transportation.

Figure 1. AI–Signal Framework

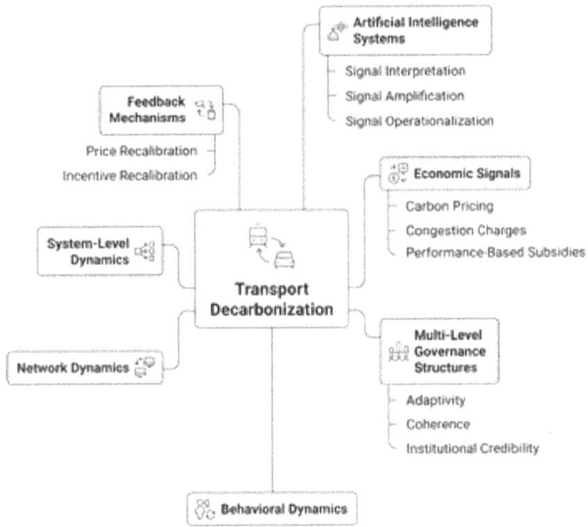

4.1 AI–Signal Framework

The framework of AI-Economic Signals Interaction The idea of Artificial Intelligence as a processing layer that transforms economic signals into operation decisions in transport systems is known as the AI-Economic Signals Interaction Framework. The AI-enabled platforms receive structured inputs in the form of prices, taxes, tolls, and subsidies which impact routing, scheduling, fleet allocation and demand management. These signals are calculated by machine learning and optimization algorithms along with real-time data of traffic conditions, energy consumption, and load on the service (Vezyroglou & Siokis, 2025). Carbon costs are internalized by the AI systems when the economic signals are true to environmental externalities, and the systems are optimised towards low-emission. On the other hand, the distortion or inconsistency of signals makes algorithms to legitimize carbon-intensive behaviors on the scale. The framework points out that AI is not producing policy goals on its own but only operationalising those in signal structures. In this regard, the ecological performance of AI-enabled transport choices depends on how the design, consistency and reliability of the economic signals derived by the policy frameworks are designed. Table 3 Offers the conceptual structure that connects the economic indicators, AI mediation, behavior patterns, and system outcomes.

Table 3. Signal–AI Interaction Mapping

Economic Signal Type	AI Mediation Layer	Behavioral Response	System-Level Outcome
Congestion charges	Dynamic routing algorithms	Trip rescheduling	Reduced congestion
Emissions-based tolls	Fleet optimization tools	Vehicle choice	Lower emissions
Dynamic pricing	Demand prediction models	Mode switching	Network efficiency
Performance subsidies	Investment analytics	Technology adoption	Fleet decarbonization
Carbon pricing	Cost optimization engines	Cost minimization	Emissions internalization

4.2 Response Pathways

The conceptual model identifies three related chains of responses by which economic indicators and AI-mediated choices can affect the results of transport decarbonization. On the behavioral level, customers and operators are reacting to changes in price by changing their travel frequency, mode choice, routing preference, and investment decisions. Combined behavioral reactions at the network level transform traffic patterns, congestion patterns, and logistics efficiency, which is becoming increasingly operated by AI coordination platforms. At the system level, the long-run changes due to signals include the alterations in fleet make-up, use of infrastructure and long-term emission trends (Sutikno & Purnama, 2025). These are reinforcing loops because local behavior changes are spread out to form networks that create system-wide responses. These interactions are accelerated through AI which quickly adjusts demand and supply according to the changes in signals. The model emphasizes that a lack of alignment at any of the paths can be counterproductive to the decarbonization objectives, which explains the necessity of combined signal design that would predict behavior change, network effects, and long-run systems dynamics.

4.3 Feedback & Adaptivity

The other important feature of the conceptual model is the design of the feedback loops that enable the flexibility and dynamism of design of economic signals. It is possible to provide real-time analysis of the policy effectiveness since AI systems generate data about the actuality of travel behavior, the intensity of emission, and congestion and system performance on a regular basis. Such data flows allow the pricing and incentive tools to be re-tuned according to the perceived outcomes and not pre-established policy settings (Pithale, 2025). Dynamic optimization can be used to make the signals such as congestion charges or emissions-based tolls vary with time and space to improve the allocative efficiency as well as reduce the unintentional consequences. Feedback loops wherein policy changes are informed by reactions to the empirical system are also used to reinforce learning processes. The institutional capacity, transparency and the trust of the people is the success of adaptivity, however. Without the proper governmental frameworks, dynamic signal adjustment can even be considered inhumane or unjust (Jorgenson et al., 2018). This model therefore embraces both the technical adaptivity and the requirements of governance so as to be legitimate and long term effective. The figure 2 shows that the successful efforts to have efficiency in transport with proper design of economic signals are reached by the successful combination of feedback loops, adaptivity, optimization, institutional capacity, transparency and public trust.

Figure 2. Signal Design Pathways

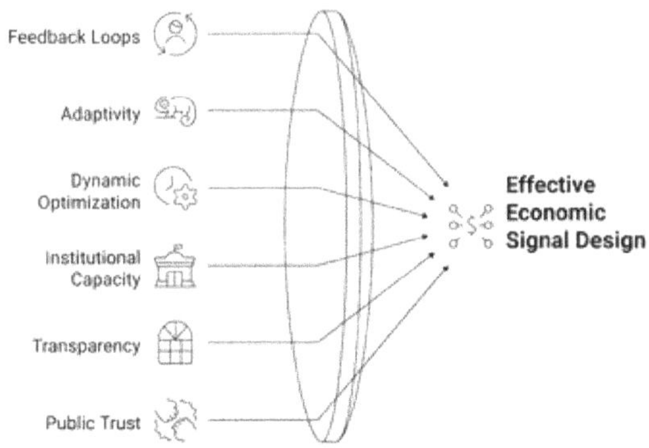

5. RESEARCH METHODOLOGY

The chapter takes a qualitative and analytical research approach that is aimed at synthesizing the economic theory, the analysis of AI systems, and the research of transport policy. Since the research objectives are conceptual in nature the methodology is oriented on synthesis as opposed to empirical estimation. Several literature strands are considered systematically to find patterns, complementarities, and conflicts between the design of economic signals and the use of AI to make transport decisions (Gosipathala, 2025). Comparison is done on policy instruments and technological applications in order to determine how they relate to the decarbonization goals. Illustrative Case studies provide a ground on conceptual arguments based on real world implementation in recent past, but do not purport to causal generalization. The approach to the methodology allows exploring the interaction of pricing, incentives, and AI in various governance contexts in a systematic way (Ravikumar & Aarthi, 2025b). The focus is put on the interpretive coherence, analytical rigor, as well as policy relevance, so that the end product is a practically oriented framework that is theoretically based at the same time.

5.1 Conceptual Synthesis

In this study, the synthesis approach used is conceptual and analytical in order to combine the findings of welfare economics, behavioral economics, market design, and Artificial Intelligence. Instead of studying these areas separately, the analysis determines the general assumptions, complementarities, and points of tension applicable to transport decarbonization. It is through the prism of AI mediation that the current pricing and incentive practices are reevaluated in terms of the way algorithm-based decision-making alters the conventional policy tools (Mohsen & Mohsen, 2025). Synthesis is conceptual in nature, and aims at eliciting generalizable design principles, as opposed to testing empirical hypotheses. It is especially appropriate to the developing policy areas where empirical evidence is insufficient and dynamic. The chapter offers a coherent foundation upon which economic indicators and AI can be collaboratively developed to facilitate low-carbon transport and logistics systems under different institutional and operational settings by integrating various fragments of literature into a single analysis framework.

5.2 Policy Mapping

The framework to apply this systematic analysis is policy instrument mapping, which analyzes the major pricing and incentive instruments implemented in the decarbonization of transport such as carbon pricing, congestion charge, dynamic tolling, fuel tax, and performance-based subsidies. A case is made to examine each tool regarding its aims, operation design, and connection with AI-enabled decision platforms. A comparative logic is used to determine the performance of various instruments in different institutional and technological settings. The comparison brings out sources of signal coherence and conflict between levels of policy, and how AI may serve to improve or decrease the effectiveness of policy. This type of mapping of instruments can be used to determine the structural gaps, overlaps, and misalignments that define the transport behavior. The practice promotes the creation of combined signal design measures as opposed to policy interventions in isolation. Table 4 Comparisons key pricing instruments based on signal strength, adaptivity, enforcement mechanism and anticipated behavioral impact.

Table 4. Policy Signal Comparison

Policy Instrument	Signal Strength	Adaptivity	Enforcement Mode	Expected Behavioral Effect
Static fuel tax	Low–moderate	Low	Fiscal	Gradual demand reduction
Congestion pricing	High	Medium	Digital tolling	Immediate demand shift
Dynamic tolling	High	High	Algorithmic	Temporal reallocation
Emissions-based truck toll	High	Low–medium	Distance-based	Fleet modernization
Performance incentives	Targeted	Medium	Contractual	Technology adoption

5.3 Case Analysis

Recent case studies are used in the chapter as interpretive examples of the application of AI-enabled economic signal design. These examples are chosen to represent various transport situations, especially road transport in cities and the freight transport system, where the pressure to reduce emissions is the greatest. Instead of the cases being empirical validation, the cases are applied to frame conceptual arguments and expose practical issues pertaining to implementation, governance, and equity. The discussion is about the structure of pricing and incentive cues and the mediation of reactions by AI systems and the results of reduction of emissions, efficiency, and acceptance among the population (Oyewale & Bassey, 2024). Lessons and design principles are commonly extracted using cross-case interpretation. This practical application of the conceptual framework contributes to the increased practical applicability of the method, without sacrificing analytical generality.

5.4 Framework Development Approach

This sub-section describes how the idea of the conceptual framework was developed by incorporating economic signals, Artificial Intelligence, and transport and logistics systems into the supply chains. It presents a logical approach that implies identifying the key variables, visualization of their relationships, and organization of relationships among pricing mechanisms, AI-informed decision-making, and transport outcomes. The framework dwells on the linkage of environmental goals with both operational and strategic choices within transport and logistics operations. The combination of the analysis of the economic theory and AI-based optimization, as well as the aspects of transport policy, provides the approach with both analytical and practical consistency. It also takes into consideration the dynamic properties of transport systems wherein real time data and adaptive algorithms affect behavioral and network level responses. The framework offers a solid analytical framework upon which to explore the connection among coordinated economic signals, AI capabilities, to promote low-carbon, efficient, and sustainable supply chain operations under a wide range of institutional and operational settings.

5.5 Validation through Case Evidence

The subsection will describe the support of the given conceptual framework by the help of the latest real-life case studies. Instead of being used as empirical validation, the cases are used to show the applicability and relevance of the framework to transport situations in a variety of contexts, such as urban mobility and freight logistics systems. This analysis evaluates the impact of economic signals on decision-making under the mediation of AI-driven platforms, which are factors like pricing mechanisms and incentives. Special concerns are paid to the effects of these interactions on behavioral response, operational performance, and emissions. The case-based method allows identifying the trends and lessons that can be used to outline the practical aspects of the implementation of economic clues and AI in transport systems. In addition, it also points to the impact of context-specific variables, such as governance structures and policy design, on the outcomes of implementation. Altogether, the applicability of the framework to the practical setting is reinforced by the use of case evidence, which does not undermine the conceptual generalizability of the framework in different institutional, geographic, and operational contexts.

6. LITERATURE REVIEW

The transport decarbonization literature is coming to the realization that the result of the transport emissions is not only determined by technological change but also due to the economic signals that inform behavior and investment. It has been found in research in transport economics, energy systems and policy studies that there will always be coordination failures due to mispriced externalities, fragmented incentives, and institutional constraints. Artificial Intelligence and intelligent transport systems have been shown to work parallelly to show the increasing presence of algorithmic decision-making in routing, pricing and demand management (Biswas, 2025). The above bodies of literature, however, are often ana conceptualized and little is done to understand the joint effects of economic signals and AI systems on transport outcomes. This review brings together the findings of three interconnected strands, namely, economic signal design, AI-enabled transport applications, and socio-institutional constraints, and aligns the findings with this chapter objective.

6.1 Signal Design in Transport and Energy Systems

Research on economic signal design has focused on evaluating pricing and incentive schemes as the key instruments to internalize environmental externality in the transport and energy system. Taxes on fuel, congestion payment, vehicle taxation based on emissions and carbon charge are commonly discussed as having the potential to impact travel demand, modal choice and fleet structure. The literature demonstrates that appropriately defined price signals are able to lower emissions and congestion and enhance allocative efficiency (Kopytsia & Kvyetnyy, 2025). Nevertheless, there is evidence that can point to the large amount of variance in effectiveness caused by political constraints, institutional fragmentation, and resistance of people. Dynamic pricing and market-based instruments have also proved to be more responsive to the conditions of the demand and supply in energy systems and can offer transport policy lessons (Feng et al., 2025). There is a common theme that fixed and loosely coupled signals restrict behavioral change, which implies that adaptive and combined signal architectures need to be able to react to real-time situations.

6.2 Artificial Intelligence Applications

The relevant literature on the application of AI in transport is devoted to optimization, prediction, and real-time coordination. Traffic prediction, dynamic routing, optimization of logistics, and demand management with the help of machine learning models have become common and can result in efficiency improvements over transport networks. Recent papers focus on the use of AI in dynamic pricing, such as congestion tolling, ride-hailing prices, and freight rate optimization. These systems enable the price to be adjusted to the network conditions, demand, and service constraints. Nonetheless, much of this literature is silent concerning pricing parameters as an exogenous input as opposed to policy variables that are subject to environmental objectives. Consequently, AI-based optimization can usually tend to focus on cost minimization and service performance without internalizing the effects of emissions. New research indicates that making environmental cues an aspect of algorithmic goals can dramatically change results, which is why the need to design AI to align with the structure of economic signals is important.

6.3 Equity & Constraints

There exists a plethora of literature regarding social and institutional issues surrounding such issue as economic signal design in transport decarbonization. However, the effect of pricing instruments may be regressive unless it is supported by the complementary actions, and this is where the issues of affordability and accessibility emerge. There are also studies that report rebound effects, i.e., cost reductions and a new wave of travel as a result of efficiency improvements can offset the scarcity of the gains of the reduction of emissions. Implementation is also hindered by institutional constraints such as fragmented governance, low levels of data transparency and poor regulatory capacity (Sun et al., 2025). The general acceptance by the public is a key factor of policy sustainability, especially in dynamic and AI-driven pricing schemes that are viewed as non-transparent or non-equitable. The need to have complementary policies like revenue recycling, specific subsidies, and clear structures of governance, are emphasized in the literature. These two points of knowledge indicate that the ineffective decarbonization process cannot be successful without both technically efficient signals and socially and institutionally inclusive design strategies.

7. CASE STUDIES

To provide an example of how the economic signals can be operationalized, using the technology-mediated decision environments to affect the outcome of low-carbon mobility, the two recent cases are presented below. The cases are chosen to be representative of two high-emission areas discussed in the chapter (urban road transport and road freight): where pricing and incentives are directly involved in behavior, routing, and investment decisions. Both cases illustrate the effects of signal design create significant outcomes (traffic, emissions, safety, or cost) when carried out at scale and expressed in automated systems. The former looks at the example of the Central Business District Tolling Program in New York City, where time- and vehicle-based charges are implemented via a digital tolling architecture and have already achieved measured improvements in the traffic, pollution, and system performance (Boriboonsomsin et al., 2024). The second example is the CO 2-differentiated truck toll reform in Germany that introduces the emissions intensity in the freight prices and makes price changes across the vehicle classes relative to each other. The cases combined allow cross-cases to be learned about effectiveness, equity, governance, and popular acceptance.

7.1 Urban Pricing Case

The case is an example of freight logistics decarbonization in supply chains whereby the price of emissions determines the efficiency of logistics and the choice of fleets. New York City rolled out its Central Business District Tolling Program (CBDTP) on January 5, 2025, which levies a digital toll on vehicles entering the Manhattan Congestion Relief Zone (below 60th Street) by using a digital tolling and enforcement system to operationalize differentiated prices based on vehicle type and time of the day. During the first year of official program reporting, significant changes in the system were noted large-scale: 27 million vehicles less were on the cover of the zone, which is 11% less traffic. Performance measurements revealed significant network improvements, as well, with crossing rates going up by as much as 51%, indicating that there was significant congestion relief and not redistribution of delay. The environmental and safety performance were also reported in addition to mobility performance: pollution was reduced by 22% in the area and the region as a whole, crashes were down by 7% and traffic injuries by 8% lower. Responses to transit systems were also recorded such as 7% increase in transit ridership which is in line with the mode-shift effects that should be anticipated with properly calibrated road-use pricing (Master & Islam, 2025). Figure 3 represents a percentage change in traffic, speed, pollution, safety, and transit usages after AI-congestion pricing in New York City.

Figure 3. Congestion Pricing Outcomes

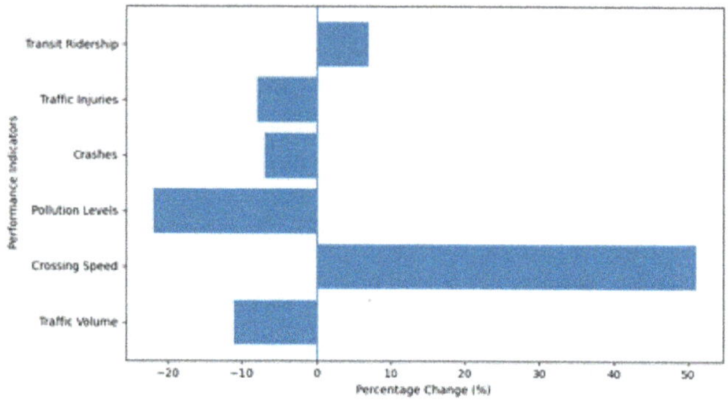

7.2 Freight Logistics Decarbonization

The truck toll reform in Germany added a charge for CO_2 element that takes effect on December 1, 2023, imposing the intensity of emission on the per-kilometre freight price and varying the toll on the vehicles according to their emissions category. The reform also involved a CO_2 charge of €200 per tonne of CO_2 on heavy duty vehicles which was in line with the EU requirements of distinguishing road user charges based on the performance in CO_2. Industry and logistics reporting has noted that the new structure created sharp price movements: at typical heavy mixes, the tolls would rise by approximately 83%, and illustrative examples show increases from about €0.19/km to ~€0.35/km depending on vehicle class (Biswas, 2022). The change revealed an increase in marginal cost of high-emission freight movements and enhanced the business case of modernizing the fleets, consolidating the routes, reallocating the mode, and improving operational efficiency (Sang et al., 2025). The reform exists within the wider national climate targets, such as a 65% (as against 1990) reduction in greenhouse gas emissions by 2030 (which supports the signal to the policy that carbon-intensive freight operations will become increasingly more expensive). Figure 4 presents percentage movements in freight toll expenditure and climate targets caused by the emissions-based truck toll reform of Germany.

Figure 4. Freight Pricing Impacts

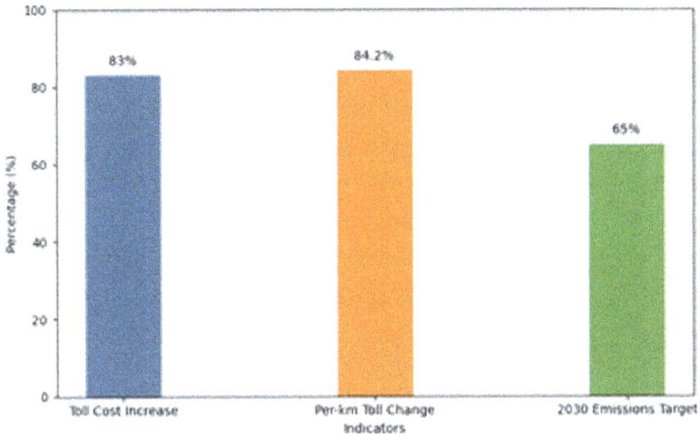

7.3 Cross-Case Insights

In both instances, results are determined by the strength of the price signal, its credibility and the operationality of the price signal in day-to-day decisions. New York City is responsive to demand-side changes: Traffic is reduced by 11%, pollution is reduced by 22%, gains in safety indicators by 7 and 8%, and transit increases by up to 50% crossing and 7% increasing transit ridership, suggesting that the behavior in large-scale settings can be shifted with a well-designed congestion pricing program. In Germany, supply-side and investment signaling is observed: a toll with the amount depending on emissions generated formed a substantial cost difference (83% toll-related costs are typically high in practice), and reinforced the motives of smaller-emission fleets and more efficient freight. It is a sum of the two lessons that the signal is multiplied by AI/digital mediation accordingly, thus governance (transparency, equity provisions, and revenue recycling) should be structured in parallel with the algorithmic and pricing structure (Orlov, 2017). Table 5 Summarizes the results of the two case studies in terms of emissions, traffic, efficiency and behavioral change (percentage).

Table 5. Case Study Outcomes

Case Study Context	Key Economic Signal	Measured Outcome	Percentage Change
Urban road transport	Congestion pricing	Traffic volume	−11%
Urban road transport	Congestion pricing	Pollution levels	−22%
Urban road transport	Congestion pricing	Transit ridership	+7%
Freight transport	Emissions-based toll	Toll cost increase	+83%
Freight transport	**Emissions-based toll**	**Incentive for low-emission fleets**	**Qualitative increase**

8. RESULTS AND DISCUSSION

As illustrated in the case studies, economic signal design implemented on the basis of digital and AI-mediated systems may lead to quantifiable results in reducing emissions, improving the efficiency of the system, and modifying behavior. Pricing and incentive schemes in both the urban passenger transport and freight logistics had effects on the decision-making at scale by changing the relative costs and instilling an environmental factor into the standard operational decision-making. The findings show that the efficiency of AI-based transport systems is highly dependent on the quality of compatibility between objectives of algorithmic optimization and the economic indications of the policy frameworks (Ballis & Dimitriou, 2020). In environments with clear signals, differentiation and credible enforcement of these signals, behavioral responses would be measurable in short periods which would translate to network-level performance benefits and emission cuts. On the other hand, it is also pointed out in the discussion that strong signals have the potential of creating unintended distributional or spatial consequences unless well-crafted. The results support the premise that AI reinforces the incentive structure that it is provided with, and economic signal coherence is a decisive element of successful sustainable and socially acceptable mobility transitions to low-carbon levels (Aarthi et al., 2025). The results indicate the enhancement of supply chain effectiveness and logistics-related emission.

8.1 Emissions Outcomes

The results of the two cases indicate some stable correlation between economic signal strength and decarbonization performance. In the urban congestion pricing example, the traffic volumes reduced, the average traveling speed was higher, and the polluting indicators have dropped significantly, which means that users were able to respond to the price indicators by changing the timing of travel, changing mode selection, and altering the necessity to travel. Such changes in behavior were converted to network level efficiency gains such as less network congestion and better safety outcomes. With the drastic rise in emissions-differentiated tolls in the freight pricing example, the structure of costs in terms of vehicle classes shifted with the increase in incentives to optimize routes, consolidate loads, and modernize the fleet (Bharti et al., 2024). Even though the behavioral changes in freight systems are slower compared to passenger traffic, the reform in pricing established a clear indication of investment preference in low-emitting vehicles and efficiency in operations. Combined, the findings indicate that with a high level of differentiation of economic signals and their consistent application, the AI-powered platforms can be used to achieve a quick behavior change and reduce the number of emissions.

8.2 Signal Risks

The findings also highlight the dangers of misplacing or lack of completeness of the economic signal in the transport systems mediated by AI. Precise pricing instruments may cause unwanted spatial redirection, cost trickle-down impacts or equity issues in the absence of complimentary actions. In the congestion pricing settings, traffic can either move away to the nearby places when there is a bad design of boundary conditions, as compared to the freight systems where increase in toll will simply be passed down to consumers without a reduction in emission when there are no other alternatives. The AI systems increase such risks by maximizing an action at scale, switching demand or routing decisions in a way that increases local effects. The issues of signal design are therefore amplified by algorithmic amplification, as are its successes (Rozkrut et al., 2025). These discoveries underscore the fact that AI does not fix the flaws in the polices; rather, it hastens down the consequences. To implement effective decarbonization, it is therefore necessary to predict the design of signals that takes into consideration the behavioral adaptation, network spillovers and distributional effects prior to implementation.

8.3 Design Conditions

The argument singles out some of the conditions required to have scalable and consistent signal design in AI-enabled transport systems. To start with, the signals should be credible, predictable and the difference between them should be increased enough in order to influence behavior without causing excessive volatility. Second, the consistency of congestion pricing measures at local, national, and international levels is necessary to avoid contradictory incentives between local and national congestion pricing and regional or international carbon regime. Third, it should have adaptive capacity integrated into it by having transparent feedback loops which will enable the adjustment of signals according to observed emissions and efficiency results. Fourth, the governance structures should assure transparency of data, accountable algorithms and legitimacy of the populace especially in cases of dynamic pricing when it comes to the day-to-day mobility costs (Cadet et al., 2024). Lastly, the distributional effects should be mitigated by revenue recycling, compensation focussing, or differentiated pricing to enable it to be socially acceptable. The examples indicate that in case of meeting these conditions, AI-based economic indicators can be scaled beyond pilot settings and implemented into long-term low-carbon mobility policies. Table 6 Summarizes governance, technical, and social circumstances needed to support effective and inclusive signal design.

Table 6. Signal Design Conditions

Design Dimension	Required Condition	Purpose
Signal coherence	Cross-policy alignment	Avoid conflicting incentives
Adaptivity	Data-driven adjustment	Improve efficiency
Transparency	Explainable pricing logic	Build public trust
Equity safeguards	Revenue recycling	Maintain inclusiveness
Governance capacity	Institutional oversight	Ensure accountability

9. FUTURE RESEARCH DIRECTIONS

Future studies in the area of transport decarbonization should shift away at models that evaluate prices at their field-value to models that engage the interaction between Artificial Intelligence, economic signals and institutional design. Since AI is increasingly involved in making transport decisions, the existing policy evaluation models might not be capable of evaluating the long-term effects of emissions, behavioral readjustments, and system resilience. Studies are required to know how adaptive pricing processes can change over the years, how the policy coherence may be preserved across the jurisdictions and how the governance systems may be designed to be transparent and accountable in the world of algorithms (Ravikumar & Aarthi, 2025c). Moreover, the growth of AI-powered pricing also poses critical questions of data ownership, equity, and legitimacy that have not been studied properly. These gaps will be important in designing the scalable and socially acceptable low-carbon mobility transitions (Mandala et al., 2024). The recommendations outlined below identify the most important areas that conceptual, methodological, and policy-oriented studies can contribute to the enhancement of knowledge and inform future decarbonization policies in the transport industry.

9.1 Adaptive Pricing

The research on adaptive and learning-based pricing architectures is a potential future direction of transport decarbonization. Future research should also analyze how reinforcement learning, predictive analytics and real-time optimization can be implemented in dynamically adjusting congestion charges, emissions-based tolls and incentives to behavioral and network outcomes that are observed. This needs research to determine the stability, efficiency and fairness of such adaptive systems over long time horizons (Alawad et al., 2020). The algorithmic approaches to achieving a balance between short-term efficiency benefits and long-term emissions targets should be given special consideration, as well as the ways of integrating policy constraints into algorithmic goals. The empirical studies would be able to investigate the circumstances in which adaptive pricing minimizes rebound effects instead of increasing them. Theory is also needed to establish governance principles that do not allow too much volatility to occur and make learning-based systems interpretable, predictable, and consistent with the aims of the public policy. Figure 5 depicts a layered architecture of the use of core AI technologies to support dynamic pricing, system analysis, integration of policies, and governance in the study of adaptive transport pricing.

Figure 5. Adaptive Pricing Architecture

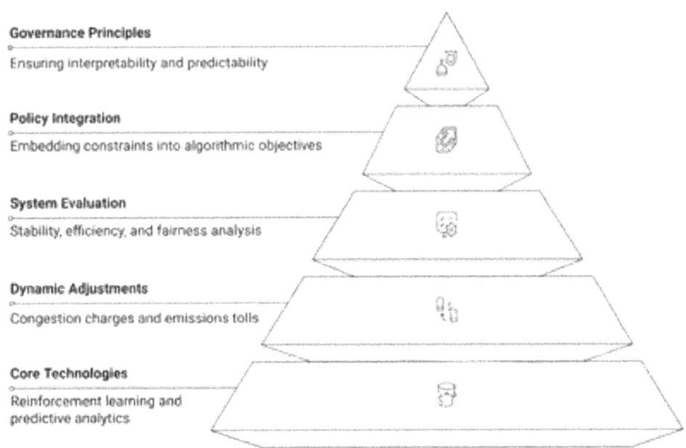

9.2 Policy Coordination

Cross-border and multilevel policy coordination is an important though under-researched issue in the future. Transport systems are run between the municipal, national and the regional boundaries, but the pricing and incentive tools are usually created in isolation. Economic indicators using AI should be studied on how to be aligned across borders to avoid carbon leakage, regulatory arbitrage and routing behavior distortions. Local congestion pricing could be compared to other policy options, such as national fuel taxation and local or international carbon markets. The ways of modeling can be created to estimate the cumulative impacts of layered signals on behavior and emissions (Kaneti et al., 2025). Also, the institutional research must study governance structures that can coordinate information sharing, implementation, and revenue distribution at various policy levels. Enhancing the multilevel coherence is critical towards the establishment of economic signals that will serve to strengthen instead of weaken decarbonization goals through transport networks that are interconnected.

9.3 Data Governance

The spread of AI-based pricing and incentives schemes brings some very basic concerns regarding the policy of data management and the responsibility of algorithms. The frameworks of controlling access, ownership, and privacy of data in transport mechanisms where pricing is based on the continuous data gathering should be examined in the future. The transparency of the algorithmic decision-making process is especially relevant to ensuring the social confidence of people and making them subject to control. Research is required to determine the feasibility of operationalizing the explainability, auditability and fairness constraints in AI-based pricing models (Adabara et al., 2025). The mechanisms to enable the participation of the population and institutional checks that enable stakeholders to challenge or review the results of the algorithms should also be examined in research. In the absence of strong governance mechanisms adaptive pricing mechanisms can easily be viewed as opaque or unfair, and lack legitimacy and acceptance (Ravikumar & Aarthi, 2025b). Further research work in this field will prove important to reconcile technological innovation to democratic accountability and ethical transport policy formulation.

10. MANAGERIAL IMPLICATIONS

The research results of this chapter hold significant implications to managers who work in a transport system that is more mediated by AI. The pricing and incentive mechanisms determine the behaviour of the user towards the product or service, operational efficiency, investment decision and strategic positioning in the long term. The transport operators, infrastructure managers and platform providers should acknowledge that economic signals are not extrinsic limitations but fundamental variables of system design that determine algorithmic optimization and performance results (Puzio et al., 2025). Proper decarbonization agendas engagement thus demands a combination of pricing logic, AI capabilities as well as sustainability aims in the managerial decision-making process. The case studies reveal that aligned economic signals can enhance efficiency in the system besides enabling reduction in emissions, but on the other hand, the misaligned signals expose risks and lack of efficiency in operations. Managers are essential in decoding the policy signals into running strategies and making sure that systems based on AI can produce commercial and environmental value.

10.1 Strategic Pricing

Due to the increasing pressures of adjusting the pricing strategies to the emissions-based charges, congestion pricing and the dynamic tolling regimes, the transport operators are under pressure to adjust their pricing mechanisms. Managers have to predict the influence of these signals on the demand trends, cost structures, and competition position. Strategic pricing design entails integrating the environmental costs in planning route, differentiation of services and the investments of the fleet (Knights et al., 2024). The AI-based analytics will be able to assist in scenario analysis and enable operators to compare the cost and emission outcomes of different pricing conditions. Economic signals Proactive response to economic signals lessens regulatory risk and increases resilience to operations. Operators who match pricing policies with decarbonization goals have a greater opportunity to be in a better position to benefit performance-based incentives and avoid punishments related to high-carbon performance. The task of the manager is to strike the right balance between short-term cost pressures and long-term sustainability and positioning in the market.

10.2 AI-Driven Decision Support

AI-based decision support systems are increasingly used by infrastructure managers to handle the congestion and maintenance management as well as capacity utilization. The indicators of economics like tolls and access charges determine the way these systems distribute capacity and make investment priorities. Managers have to make sure that AI-related tools are tailored to show policy goals associated with emissions reduction and performance of the systems. It is possible to test alternate pricing options, test network reactions, and learn unforeseen consequences before implementation using decision support systems (Amirah, 2024). The use of environmental performance metrics in AI dashboards will improve strategic control and responsibility. Another important role played by infrastructure managers is in spreading the pricing rationales to the masses thus making them acceptable and legitimate. The proper deployment of AI-based decision support enhances the alignment of operational management and decarbonization (long-term).

10.3 Incentive Alignment

To match commercial incentives and climate goals, it is critical to redefine the approach to value creation and measure value in transport organizations. Managers should encompass the emissions performance in the key performance indicators, investment appraisal and in the contractual arrangements. Such economic indicators like emissions-based pricing and subsidies change the relative profitability of the transport activity and promote the transition toward the use of low-carbon services. Monitoring systems, based on AI can offer more granular information that may be used to support incentive plans and performance-based contracts based on climate objectives (Chen, 2025). Nevertheless, alignment also needs organizational commitment and coordination among the different departments including finance, operations, and technology. Having climate goals embedded into the decision structures of their commercial operations, organizations will be able to turn regulatory compliance into competitive edge. The findings presented in the chapter indicate that alignment is best achieved when economic signals, AI capabilities and managerial incentives are collectively developed and not done in isolation.

11. CONCLUSION

It is shown in this chapter that economically efficient and socially acceptable transitions to low-carbon mobility requires not only the implementation of Artificial Intelligence technology, but also crucially, the design and consistency of the economic signals all transport behavior, investment, and system development. Through the combination of the insights provided by transport economics, AI-enabled decision-making, and the latest policy practices, the chapter demonstrates the co-evolution of AI and economic signals, as the underlying structures, strength, and plausibility of pricing and incentives systems are amplified by means of algorithmic optimization. As evident in the case studies, the ability of congestion charges and emissions-based tolls to create quantifiable changes in traffic volumes, emissions, and inefficiencies as well as to stimulate changes in the modes and operations toward cleaner methods is achieved when these charges and tolls are distinctively differentiated, digitally implemented, and credibly instituted. Meanwhile, the discussion also notes that signals that are misaligned or mismanaged may have unintended distributional impacts, spatial distraction, and promote inequality through algorithms. Policy and market design The chapter provides a coherent conceptual system that combines the behavioral responses with network effects and system-level dynamics and provides an indication of how the pricing instruments, AI platforms, and governance structures can be co-designed. The results highlight the significance of adaptive pricing, coordination of the multilevel policy, governmental transparent data, and recycling of the revenue to ensure legitimacy and inclusiveness. Finally, the chapter states that the transition to low-carbon mobility will not succeed based on an individual approach either with technology or with pricing but rather with the strategic form of economic signaling that mobilizes AI potential to transform transport systems according to long-term climate goals and protect efficiency, equality, and social trust.

REFERENCES

Aarthi, S., Ravikumar, R. N., Sobirova, K., & Mamadiyarov, Z. (2025). Empowering a sustainable future through digital learning and the SDGs. In *Harnessing E-Learning to Create a Sustainable Future* (pp. 145–172). IGI Global Scientific Publishing., DOI: 10.4018/979-8-3373-0112-9.ch006

Abduljabbar, R., Dia, H., Liyanage, S., & Bagloee, S. A. (2019). Applications of Artificial Intelligence in transport: An overview. *Sustainability (Basel), 11*(1), 189. DOI: 10.3390/su11010189

Adabara, I., Olaniyi Sadiq, B., & Shuaibu, N. A., Ibrahim Danjuma, Y., & Maninti, V. (2025). Trustworthy agentic AI systems: a cross-layer review of architectures, threat models, and governance strategies for real-world deployment. *F1000Research, 14*, 905. DOI: 10.12688/f1000research.169927.1

Alawad, H., An, M., & Kaewunruen, S. (2020). Utilizing an adaptive neuro-fuzzy inference system (ANFIS) for overcrowding level risk assessment in railway stations. *Applied Sciences (Basel, Switzerland), 10*(15), 5156. DOI: 10.3390/app10155156

Amirah. (2024). Editorial: Smart Parking Management System using Artificial Intelligence. *Journal of Computer Science Application and Engineering (JOSAPEN), 2*(1), 20–23. DOI: 10.70356/josapen.v2i1.25

Arun Chakravarthy, R., Sureshkumar, C., Arun, M., & Ranjani Shree, R. S. (2025). Advancements in intelligent traffic monitoring system design for smart urban infrastructure. In *Building a Green Future Through Essential Decision-Making Competencies* (pp. 27–62). IGI Global., DOI: 10.4018/979-8-3373-0189-1.ch002

Ballis, H., & Dimitriou, L. (2020). Evaluation of Reinforcement Learning traffic signalling strategies for alternative objectives: Implementation in the network of Nicosia, Cyprus. *Transport and Telecommunication Journal, 21*(4), 295–302. DOI: 10.2478/ttj-2020-0024

Bharti, M., Baswaraju, S., Nijhawan, G., Sharma, N., Kumar, A., Saleh Mashkour, M., & Nalli, N. (2024). Reduction of green house gases emission: Towards a sustainable future. *E3S Web of Conferences, 552*, 01116. DOI: 10.1051/e3sconf/202455201116

Biswas, I. (2025). Relational accountability in AI-driven pharmaceutical practices: An ethics approach to bias, inequity and structural harm. *Journal of Medical Ethics*, jme-2025-110913. Advance online publication. DOI: 10.1136/jme-2025-110913 PMID: 40930712

Biswas, P. (2022). Flight price prediction: A case study. *International Journal for Research in Applied Science and Engineering Technology, 10*(6), 89–94. DOI: 10.22214/ijraset.2022.43666

Boriboonsomsin, K., Tanvir, S., & Barth, M. (2024). Modeling the impacts of low emission zone on route diversion and emissions of heavy-duty trucks: A Southern California case study. *Transportation Research Record: Journal of the Transportation Research Board, 2678*(1), 794–805. DOI: 10.1177/03611981231172747

Cadet, E., Babatunde, L. A., Ajayi, J. O., Erigh, E. D., Obuse, E., Essien, I. A., & Ayanbode, N. (2024). Developing scalable compliance architectures for cross-industry regulatory alignment. *International Journal of Scientific Research in Humanities and Social Sciences, 1*(2), 494–524. DOI: 10.32628/IJSRSSH242556

Candia Riquelme, D. A. (2025). *Assessing innovative transport technologies and policies*. DOI: 10.5463/thesis.1257

Chen, Y. (2025). A study on the allocation of funds within the global climate governance framework: Based on the interaction between green bonds and carbon markets. *International Journal of Global Economics and Management, 8*(1), 208–214. DOI: 10.62051/ijgem.v8n1.23

Feng, F., Zheng, F., Zhang, Z., & Wang, L. (2025). A framework for low-carbon container multimodal transport route optimization under hybrid uncertainty: Model and case study. *Applied Sciences (Basel, Switzerland), 15*(12), 6894. DOI: 10.3390/app15126894

Gosipathala, S. B. (2025). Cognitive AI-powered predictive analytics for dynamic toll pricing optimization in smart transportation networks. *International Journal For Multidisciplinary Research, 7*(2), 57206. Advance online publication. DOI: 10.36948/ijfmr.2025.v07i02.57206

Islam, M.Master of Engineering in Civil Engineering Lamar University TX USA. (2025). Analysis of Ai-enabled Adaptive Traffic Control Systems for urban mobility optimization through intelligent road network management. *Review of Applied Science and Technology, 04*(02), 207–232. DOI: 10.63125/358pgg63

Jorgenson, D. W., Goettle, R. J., Ho, M. S., & Wilcoxen, P. J. (2018). The welfare consequences of taxing carbon. *Climate Change Economics (Singapore), 09*(01), 1840013. DOI: 10.1142/S2010007818400134

Kaneti, V. R., Yamini, B., Nagarajan, S., Adaikkammai, A., Anto Gracious, L. A., Siva Subramanian, R., & Girija, P. (2025). Smart transportation systems and sustainable urban mobility. In *Revolutionizing Urban Development and Governance With Emerging Technologies* (pp. 261–288). IGI Global., DOI: 10.4018/979-8-3373-1375-7.ch009

Kidokoro, Y. (2010). Revenue recycling within transport networks. *Journal of Urban Economics*, *68*(1), 46–55. DOI: 10.1016/j.jue.2010.02.001

Knights, V., Petrovska, O., & Prchkovska, M. (2024). Enhancing smart parking management through machine learning and AI integration in IoT environments. In *Navigating the Internet of Things in the 22nd Century - Concepts, Applications, and Innovations [Working Title]*. IntechOpen. DOI: 10.5772/intechopen.1006490

Kopytsia, V. O., & Kvyetnyy, R. N. (2025). Analysis of approaches to improving intelligent parking management technologies. *Optoelectronic Information-Power Technologies*, *49*(1), 157–167. DOI: 10.31649/1681-7893-2025-49-1-157-167

Mandala, V., Surabhi, S. N. R. D., Kommisetty, P. D. N. K., Kuppala, B. M. S. R., & Ingole, R. (2024). *Towards carbon-free automotive futures: Leveraging AI and ML for sustainable transformation*. Educational Administration Theory and Practices., DOI: 10.53555/kuey.v30i5.3474

Marisamy, K., Selvakumar, A., Rajasekar, B., Natarajan, R., Atajanova, A., & Makhmudov, S. (2025). Smart logistics integrating AI, IoT, blockchain, and Robotics for a sustainable Future. In *Emerging Trends in Smart Logistics Technologies* (pp. 73–104). IGI Global Scientific Publishing., DOI: 10.4018/979-8-3373-2434-0.ch003

Mohsen, B. M., & Mohsen, M. (2025). Reducing emissions through AI-driven multimodal transport optimization in IoT-connected environments. *International Journal of Energy Research, 2025*(1). DOI: 10.1155/er/2399288

Orlov, A. (2017). Distributional effects of higher natural gas prices in Russia. *Energy Policy*, *109*, 590–600. DOI: 10.1016/j.enpol.2017.07.047

Oteri, O. J., Onukwulu, E. C., Igwe, A. N., Ewim, C. P.-M., Ibeh, A. I., & Sobowale, A. (2023). Artificial Intelligence in product pricing and revenue optimization: Leveraging data-driven decision-making. *International Journal of Multidisciplinary Research and Growth Evaluation*, *4*(1), 842–851. DOI: 10.54660/.IJMRGE.2023.4.1-842-851

Oyewale, K., & Bassey, K. E. (2024). Climate action and social equity: Mitigation strategies and carbon credits. *World Journal of Advanced Research and Reviews*, *24*(2), 187–201. DOI: 10.30574/wjarr.2024.24.2.3325

Pithale, R. K.Rohit Kashinath Pithale. (2025). The economics of public transport in Mumbai: A critical analysis of inefficiencies and policy failures. *International Journal For Multidisciplinary Research*, *7*(1), 37881. Advance online publication. DOI: 10.36948/ijfmr.2025.v07i01.37881

Puzio, E., Drożdż, W., & Kolon, M. (2025). The role of intelligent transport systems and smart technologies in urban traffic management in Polish smart cities. *Energies*, *18*(10), 2580. DOI: 10.3390/en18102580

Ravikumar, R. N., & Aarthi, S. (2025). AI-driven governance. In *Advances in Computational Intelligence and Robotics* (pp. 343–372). IGI Global Scientific Publishing., DOI: 10.4018/979-8-3373-3760-9.ch012

Ravikumar, R. N., & Aarthi, S. (2025a). AI-driven digital twins and autonomous operations for sustainable logistics and procurement. In *Advances in Computational Intelligence and Robotics* (pp. 65–100). IGI Global Scientific Publishing. DOI: 10.4018/979-8-3373-7006-4.ch003

Ravikumar, R. N., & Aarthi, S. (2025b). Human-AI synergy for organizational resilience. In *Advances in Computational Intelligence and Robotics* (pp. 287–322). IGI Global Scientific Publishing. https://doi.org/DOI: 10.4018/979-8-3373-7416-1.ch011

Ravikumar, R. N., & Aarthi, S. (2025c). Intelligent logistics. In *Advances in Computational Intelligence and Robotics* (pp. 217–248). IGI Global Scientific Publishing. DOI: 10.4018/979-8-3373-7006-4.ch008

Isalkar, M. A. S., & Sambhe, R. U. (2024). Artificial Intelligence in Transportation: A Review. *International Journal of Scientific Research in Science, Engineering and Technology*, *11*(2), 142–146. DOI: 10.32628/IJSRSET2411212

Rozkrut, M., Kucharski, A., Nermend, K., & Waśniewski, J. (2025). The governmental hand in the algorithmic age: Policy levers, challenges, and implications in shaping artificial intelligence skills. In *Intelligent Management and Artificial Intelligence: Trends, Challenges, and Opportunities, Vol.1* (pp. 557–582). Wydawnictwo Naukowe Uniwersytetu Szczecińskiego. DOI: 10.18276/978-83-8419-028-9-38

Sahoo, A. P. (2025). Revolutionizing eCommerce: AI-powered dynamic pricing strategies. *World Journal of Advanced Research and Reviews*, *26*(2), 4194–4201. DOI: 10.30574/wjarr.2025.26.2.2070

Sang, L. T., Ravikumar, R. N., Aarthi, S., & Ben, T. L. (2025). Optimizing sales and inventory performance using AI and business intelligence in POS environments. In *Advances in Computational Intelligence and Robotics* (pp. 259–290). IGI Global Scientific Publishing. DOI: 10.4018/979-8-3373-4392-1.ch011

Song, L., Chen, C., & Lin, F. (2025). AI algorithmic pricing for online platforms: A literature review. *Advances in Economics. Management and Political Sciences, 196*(1), 125–139. DOI: 10.54254/2754-1169/2025.BJ24935

Sun, T. Q., Liu, Y., Fu, X., & Rogers, J. (2025). Global innovation cooperation and governance: Evidence from China. *Science & Public Policy, 52*(3), 436–437. DOI: 10.1093/scipol/scae089

Sutikno, T., & Purnama, H. S. (2025). The smart e-bike ecosystem integrates internet of things and artificial intelligence. *Computer Science and Information Technology, 6*(3), 307–314. DOI: 10.11591/csit.v6i3.p307-314

Vezyroglou, K., & Siokis, F. (2025). Pricing in the sharing economy—A hybrid approach leveraging econometrics, machine learning, and artificial intelligence. *Information (Basel), 16*(6), 450. DOI: 10.3390/info16060450

Woody, M., Stolper, S., Vaishnav, P., & Keoleian, G. A. (2024). Vehicle scrappage policies for transportation decarbonization. *Environmental Research: Energy, 1*(3), 033002. DOI: 10.1088/2753-3751/ad63aa

KEY TERMS AND DEFINITIONS

Algorithmic Accountability: Mechanisms that ensure AI systems are transparent, explainable, auditable, and aligned with policy and ethical standards.

Algorithmic Decision-Making: Automated decision processes in which AI systems determine actions such as routing, pricing, or scheduling based on predefined objectives and data inputs.

Artificial Intelligence (AI) in Transport: The use of machine learning, optimization algorithms, and data-driven systems to support routing, pricing, scheduling, and demand management in mobility and logistics networks.

Behavioral Response: Changes in travel or logistics decisions made by individuals or organizations in reaction to economic signals such as price increases or incentives.

Congestion Pricing: A road-use charging mechanism that varies prices based on location, time, or traffic conditions to reduce congestion and associated emissions.

Data Governance: The rules, standards, and institutional arrangements governing the collection, use, sharing, and protection of data in transport systems.

Dynamic Pricing: A pricing approach in which charges are adjusted in real time or periodically in response to demand, congestion, or environmental conditions.

Economic Signals: Prices, taxes, tolls, and incentives that communicate costs, benefits, and policy priorities to transport users and operators, influencing their behavior and decisions.

Emissions-Based Pricing: Pricing instruments that differentiate charges according to the carbon intensity or emissions performance of vehicles or transport activities.

Low-Carbon Mobility: Transport systems and practices designed to minimize greenhouse gas emissions while maintaining accessibility, efficiency, and economic viability.

Policy Coherence: Alignment and consistency across transport policies at local, national, and international levels to avoid conflicting economic signals.

Rebound Effect: A phenomenon where efficiency improvements reduce costs and unintentionally increase demand, partially offsetting emissions reductions.

Revenue Recycling: The practice of redistributing revenues from pricing instruments, such as congestion charges or carbon taxes, to support equity, public transport, or targeted subsidies.

System-Level Outcomes: Aggregate effects of individual and network-level decisions, including emissions trends, congestion levels, and overall transport efficiency.

Chapter 8
Cost-Benefit Analysis of Low-Carbon Mobility Solutions

Deepak Gupta
http://orcid.org/0000-0003-3929-1362
Institute of Technology and Management, Gwalior, India

Ergashev Nuriddin Gayratovich
http://orcid.org/0000-0002-8274-6193
Karshi State Technical University. Karshi, Uzbekistan

Mirzaev Abdullaevich
Tashkent State University of Economy, Uzbekistan

Davlatova Toshpulatovna
Termiz State University of Engineering and Agrotechnology, Termiz, Uzbekistan

Yarmatov Sharofiddin
Termez University of Economics and Service, Termez, Uzbekistan

Begimov Uktam
Alfraganus University, Tashkent, Uzbekistan

ABSTRACT

Transport is responsible for approximately 24% of global CO2 emissions, making it a critical sector for decarbonization. This chapter presents a comprehensive cost-benefit analysis (CBA) of low-carbon mobility solutions, including battery electric vehicles (BEVs), hydrogen fuel cell vehicles (FCEVs), public transit systems, and active transport modes such as cycling and walking. Drawing on life-cycle assessment (LCA) methodologies, total cost of ownership (TCO) models, and estimates of the social cost of carbon (SCC), the analysis quantifies both the private and social returns to low-carbon investment. Evidence suggests that BEVs and public transit deliver benefit-cost ratios significantly above unity when externalities are monetized, while active transport yields some of the highest co-benefits through reduced congestion, improved public health, and lower infrastructure costs.

DOI: 10.4018/979-8-3373-9003-1.ch008

1. INTRODUCTION

The transport industry is experiencing extenuating circumstances in the process of the low-carbon economy in the world. Transport contributes almost a quarter of all carbon dioxide (CO2) emissions to the atmosphere per year directly proportional to the use of energy, hence, it is a contributor of economic efficiency, social connectivity and environmental degradation as well. The comprehensive nature of deep decarbonization has generated an interest in alternative car technology, remodelled transit systems, and behavioural change towards less-emission methods that has never been seen before. Nevertheless, the decision on the paths to follow and even the magnitude of these paths cannot be reached without a stern economic examination that goes well beyond the market prices to incorporate health, climatic and equity effects.

Cost-benefit analysis (CBA) provides a systematic way of comparing the social value of competing transport investments and policies in totality. When considered properly, with the inclusion of externalities, e.g., air pollution damage, greenhouse emission, and traffic jams, CBA can show that so-called expensive low-carbon solutions can be very cost-effective (Rennert et al., 2022). Conversely, a pure market-price solution has the systematic impact of subsidizing the social costs of the mobility pegged on fossil fuel and sending incorrect signals to investment, which strengthens a structural bias in transport analysis that has in the past encouraged the growth of road capacity at the cost of modal diversification. The chapter brings together a comprehensive model of CBA into the spectrum of the available transport choices with low carbon and locates all these within the current evidence base in the cost, emissions and policy lever.

A number of methodological developments encourage a review of the transport CBA at this point. To start with, the peer-reviewed literature on the lifecycle emissions of electric and hydrogen vehicle has been growing substantially over the past few years, and that is why the benefits of climate effects could be estimated with greater accuracy and hence were differentiated by geography. Second, the social cost of carbon is now quite substantially updated to be more substantial after the enhancement of the integrated assessment modelling, equity weighting, and probabilistic climate sensitivity distributions (Rennert et al., 2022). Third, the health co-benefits of modal shift to active and public transport have reached maturity that allows monetization. All these developments combined fundamentally alter the benefit-cost calculus of the majority of the large categories of low-carbon transport investments.

The chapter is a wide-ranging one incorporating both supply side (clean vehicle technologies and fuels) and demand side (transit systems, land use policy and active travel infrastructure). This integrated perspective is informed by the realization that the transport sector cuts of emissions as mandated by the temperature limits in the

Paris Agreement are only achievable through changing the whole vehicle fleet, the energy system, and the urban form. No tools or technologies or policy tools will be enough; the complementary interventions with their interaction will play a primary role in deep decarbonization economics.

The next step of the chapter is the following. The theoretical basic of CBA in practice with respect to transport externalities is stated in section 2. Section 3, the authors take into account battery electric vehicles and lifecycle emissions. Section 4 is focused on hydrogen fuel cell cars. Part 5 is concerned with the active transport and the public transport. In section 6 it is compared on similar benefit-cost basis. Section 7 is related to policy instruments and Section 8 is related to integration and dynamic issues. Section 9 will end with the instructions to the research in the future.

2. THEORETICAL FOUNDATIONS: CBA AND TRANSPORT EXTERNALITIES

2.1 The Social Cost of Carbon and Transport CBA

The social cost of carbon (SCC)- the monetary value of the aggregated damages of the release of one additional metric ton of CO2 into the atmosphere at present value are one of the fundamental parameters of any CBA of low-carbon mobility. The new systematic evidence places the SCC approximately four times larger than the estimates of the previous regulation, with the central values in the USD 185 per metric ton (2020 dollars) interval, which reflect amendments of climate damages functions, weighting of equity, and the discount rate (Rennert et al., 2022). The cost benefit calculus is basically reinvigorated by the application of an increased SCC: projects in transport that appear marginally beneficial in low carbon terms become highly positive-NPV when SCC is appropriately taken into account.

The transport appraisal implication is far-reaching. An increase in the external carbon cost of USD 280 per 10,000 km of a car which emits 200 grams of CO 2 per kilometer of driving against a car which emits 60 grams of CO 2 per kilometer of driving, is like, or greater, than the annual fuel cost difference. Conventional transport CBA models that exclude or underestimate the SCC therefore generate systematically biased investment advice in favor of fossil fuel incumbents as compared to alternatives that are cleaner. This methodological implication suggests that any transport appraisal involving the adoption of the atmospheric commons as a free disposal resource is implicitly subsidizing economically material carbon-intensive decisions.

The estimate by Rennert et al. (2022) is also particularly important as it uses a probabilistic ensemble of climate damages models, includes damages caused by human health, loss of agricultural productivity and ecosystem degradation, and uses equity weighting to value climate damages to lower income populations and future generations. This methodological breadth is as compared to the past government estimates that had fewer models and low discount rate on future damages. The practical implication to transport CBA practitioners is to embrace the sensitivity analysis of a variety of SCC values, between the lower-end regulatory floor estimates and the upper and more central but uncertain academic estimates, such that decision-makers may see how BCRs are sensitive to this important but uncertain parameter.

2.2 Externality Typology in Low-Carbon Transport CBA

Transport externalities have many dimensions and carbon is only one of them. The current externalities in air quality like PM2.5 and NOx produced by internal combustion engines come with high health costs, reduced labor productivity, reduced mortality and reduced ecosystems services. This finding has been supported by the air quality and recreation behavior study where the results have shown that pollution damages have greater welfare impacts, and the visitor activity in national parks has been significantly reduced through air pollution incidents (Keiser et al., 2018). These damages are quantifiable methodologically but analytically required, and must then be added to streams of benefits of cleaner transportation methods. Exclusion of the benefit of air systematically underestimates the social benefits of transport electrification, particularly in urban areas, where the levels of combustion-related pollution are large.

The less commonly popular, yet more commonly recognized feature of transport CBA is physical activity externality. Active forms of transportation such as walking and cycling have a positive health externality in that they generate the appropriate amount of physical activity, reduce cardiovascular disease, diabetes, and obesity. Van den Bijgaart et al. (2023) demonstrates that the optimal fuel taxation should internalize the carbon damages as well as health benefits of the induced physical activity that will follow the change in travelers to active methods as a result of the increase of fuel costs. This framing of two-sided externality significantly increases optimal price of carbon and benefits-cost ratios of cycling infrastructure, and offers a major complement of climate policy and public health policy, which is typically overlooked in sector-specific analysis.

Noise externalities are yet another type of transport-based harm, which, although not addressed in the climate context directly, is economically relevant and is disproportionately represented by the communities with low income living near major road and railways. The noise pollution in urban areas caused by the electric vehicles is lower when compared to ICE vehicles and is especially less in low-speed areas where tire and aerodynamic noises dominate over the engine noise. This advantage cannot be quantified accurately although it is reflected in hedonic property prices research and quality-of-life surveys. Noise benefits should be part of a comprehensive CBA framework of urban transport electrification along with the more frequently measured air quality and carbon benefits.

Externalities of congestion make the analysis even more complicated. The transition of mode to and through public transport and active transport leads to a decrease in congestion in the road network, creating time savings and productivity gains to other users in the road network. These spillover advantages are extremely context-sensitive: more in dense urbanized corridors, less in rural or low-traffic settings, but the leading category of benefits in the congested metropolitan settings. A full CBA system should thus incorporate congestion, health, climate and noise externality as well as the direct benefits and costs incurred by individual travelers.

2.3 Discount Rates and Intergenerational Equity

Discount rate specifically implies heavily on transport CBA because much of the greatest gains of decarbonization like avoiding climate damages, improved health outcomes will be paid over the long period of time that is decades or centuries into the future. The conventional social discount rates used in government appraisals (usually 37 percent) quickly dilute future benefits in comparison to current expenditures. This time lag systematically underestimates the long-run investments in infrastructure and is underestimating the value of technologies that reduce a long-run or cumulative environmental burden. Rennert et al. (2022) have a well-articulated argument: equity-weighted discount rates instead of constant exponential discounting values result in the estimation of the SCC that is more than three times higher, which, in turn, fundamentally alters what transport investments go through the social benefit-cost threshold.

The methodological approach to the choice of the discount rate to be used in transport CBA is not merely a technical parameter, but also an ethical statement on the relative significance attached to the current and future welfare. A decrease in the rate of discount means that people are more concerned about the future generations; an increase shows that people are more concerned about the present. Because the benefits of low-carbon transport investment will be experienced in the future (as money saved by not damaging the environment); and many of the benefits will be experienced in the future (as money saved by not damaging the environment); the discount rate option will have a disproportionate effect on the apparent cost-effectiveness of the transition. It is in turn required of the practitioners to not only supply BCRs at a single central estimate, but rather to supply BCRs at more than one discount rate scenario, and that they should be transparent at least with respect to the ethical assumptions which their chosen rate entails.

3. ELECTRIC VEHICLES: LIFECYCLE COSTS AND BENEFITS

3.1 Life Cycle Assessment Methodology for EVs

The empirical basis of the rating of net environmental performance of battery electric vehicles in comparison to internal combustion engine (ICE) counterparts lies in life cycle assessment (LCA). The entire LCA will comprise the extraction of the raw materials, the production process, the energy used in the usage and the disposal of the end-of- life. The amount of emissions emitted by BEVs in the use phase is entirely dependent on the carbon content of the electricity grid in which they operate and thus, time and place of analysis is of primary concern. Das et al. (2024) summarise the current literature on EV LCA and establish the fact that even on current and future global electricity grids, at current and future levels of carbon intensity, BEVs produce quantitatively lower lifecycle GHG emissions than similar vehicles powered by ICEs- on average, BEVs emit 40-70 percent the emissions per kilometer of similar ICEs.

Zhang et al. (23) bring this discussion to a worldwide and regional comparative system and claim that lifecycle emissions of BEVs range between approximately 60 and 95 gCO2eq/km in regions with moderately decarbonized grids and it reduces to less than 30 gCO2eq/km in regions where renewable electricity is the main electricity source. This is desirable to lifecycle emissions of 180240 gCO2eq/km of conventional gasoline powered vehicles and which accrue to a high net GHG benefit in an average 150000km vehicle life. In a case study of Hong Kong, Shafique et al. (2022) establish that BEVs have significantly lower global warming potential in all of the scenarios under consideration, and manufacturing-phase emissions are compensated after two to four years of operation. Also, Gao et al. (2023) provide an overview of lifecycle carbon reduction pathways and refer to the following three levers as the most efficient in improving the environmental performance of EVs: battery manufacturing, grid decarbonization, and end-of-life recycling.

Battery manufacturing emissions treatment is another critical methodological concern of EV LCA because this is the only single-largest contributor to BEV lifecycle GHG in most regions. The manufacturing of batteries is energy-consuming and the GHG intensity of the production stage is highly dependent on the energy mix of the country and plant where the battery was manufactured. As the battery manufacturing industry is slowly moving to locations where the grid is cleaner (both through policy and through corporate sustainability commitments), the average manufacturing-phase kilowatt-hour of battery capacity is declining. The LCA studies which fail to capture this trajectory will inadvertently exaggerate the lifecycle emissions disadvantage of EVs compared to those generated in succeeding years, which provides another reason in favor of dynamic instead of static appraisal techniques.

3.2 Total Cost of Ownership Analysis

The total cost of ownership (TCO) is one method of paying a financial comparison in kilometers or years, which combines the purchase price, fuel and energy and maintenance, insurance and residual value of the car plus service life. With the case of BEVs, the cost of the electric battery is the most likely to influence the costs of the battery on the price of the battery, the cost of electricity and the availability of a charging system. In their study, Hasan et al. (2021) examine New Zealand and find out that under the market setting where large-scale EV incentive initiatives are non-existent, the TCO of BEVs is competitive or even less than that of petrol vehicles when full lifetime operating expenses are considered, in particular, as battery prices continue to drop at a fast rate.

The Norwegian case discussed by Bjerkan et al. (2016) is a great illustration of how policy incentives can reduce the effective TCO of BEVs by a significant factor and initiate a mass adoption. Norway obtained some of the highest market shares of BEVs in the world through purchase tax exemptions, low annual registration, free, or subsidized parking, toll road exemptions and access to bus lanes. This TCO equality with policy improvement that takes the form of direct commercialization of policy gains proves that even in the markets where EVs continue to be sold at a high relative price compared to ICE options, it is the public investment and pricing reform that ultimately fills the viability gap. Nehiba (2024) also presents another aspect, the elasticity of EV driving to the prices of electricity, which proves to be positively correlated with low electricity prices, partly, due to the influence of energy policy, and, therefore, the increased use of the vehicles in larger quantities and, accordingly, the overall reduction in the quantity of carbon in the air.

The cost of maintenance is an item that can be singled out in terms of EV TCO analysis as it is a structurally cheaper feature of ongoing costs of BEVs compared to ICE vehicles. Battery electric drives are less prone to moving parts, do not need any oil changes and less wear on the brakes since they have regen brakes. Empirical evidence provided by fleet operators in several nations confirms that savings in maintenance cost of BEVs during an average vehicle life are USD 0.0205 per kilometer of savings relative to the ICE equivalents, which is significant to TCO parity. By adding these savings in maintenance to the savings in fuel costs, the overall operating cost benefit of BEVs is significant even in non-purchase subsidy markets, as long as charging infrastructure is available and reliable.

3.3 Carbon Reduction Pathways and Grid Decarbonization

The entire climate advantage of electromobility can only be achieved when the electricity supply is decarbonized. Hu et al. (2023) present empirical data on China that shows that EV adoption has already resulted in quantifiable CO2 concentration reductions in urban areas, yet that this reduction is significantly larger in provinces with less polluted electricity mixes. With renewable energy prices having dropped sharply, now being the cheapest source of new electricity generation in most of the world, Bogdanov et al. (2021) anticipate that cheap renewable electricity will be the enabler of the global energy and transport transition. Their simulation supports that conditions that attain high EV adoption and high grid decarbonization can provide transport sector emissions cuts of 85-95% by mid-century. Sun et al. (2023) support these results in five leading economies and state that EV penetration is linked to statistically significant improvements in environmental pollution indices, with the effect sizes increasing with renewable energy goals that are set in ambitious economies. Shafique and Luo (2022) take a deductive LCA approach, evaluating the effect of enhancing grid mixes in the future on the relative environmental performance of BEVs. Their results indicate a bettering environmental performance of BEVs as grid strength decreases across the vehicle lifetime, which claims that LCA analyses pegged on the current electricity mix underestimate the overall climate advantage of EVs used in the present time. Zhao et al. (2022) contextualize this as a part of the overall carbon neutrality strategy in China, with electrification of transport and renewable energy growth being the most cost-effective way of meeting the 2060 carbon neutrality goal. This interplay between transport and energy policy highlights the need of cross-sector coordination in transport CBA frameworks that go beyond the transport sector to reflect the co-evolution of clean vehicle implementation and electricity system decarbonization.

3.4 Supply Chain Risks and Critical Minerals

The high rate at which BEVs are being scaled has raised questions on the availability of the supply chains of the key minerals, especially lithium, cobalt, nickel, and manganese, which are utilized in the production of batteries. The supply chain risks, as a CBA perspective, are contingent cost, which lowers the expected net present value of aggressive EV deployment plans that are highly dependent on a few concentrated mineral sources.

In the CBA viewpoint, the supply chain risk can be included as a real-options cost: option value of technological diversity and supply redundancy decreases the likelihood of expensive production failures that would result in lost emission mitigations and social welfare benefits. Supply chain resilience must be, instead of being an implicit element of cost-benefit appraisal of EV support programs by policymakers, an explicit dimension of such programs.

Figure 1. Lifecycle GHG Emissions Comparison Across Mobility Solutions

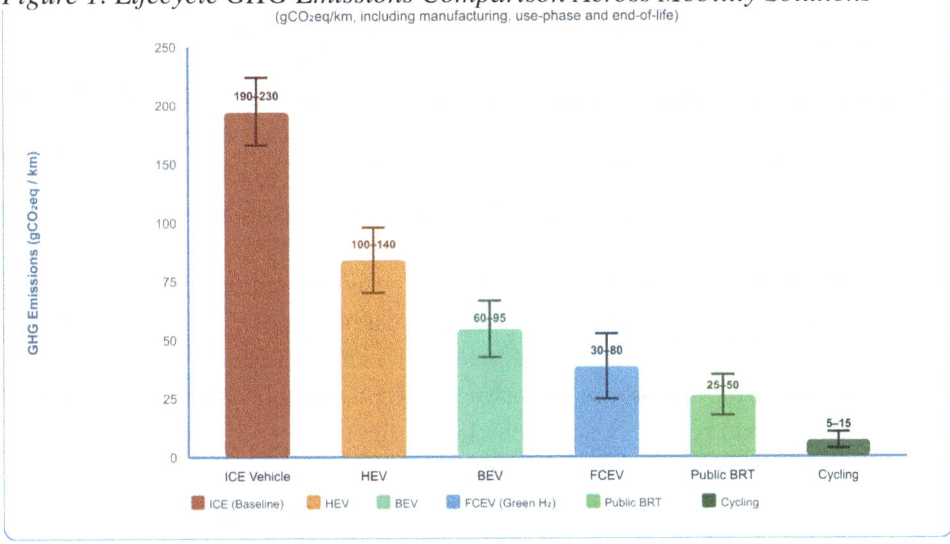

Figure 1 illustrates the Bar chart comparing lifecycle GHG emissions across six transport modes with uncertainty ranges. From lowest to highest: Cycling (5–15), Public BRT (25–50), FCEV (30–80), BEV (60–95), HEV (100–140), ICE Vehicle (190–230 gCO2eq/km). Error bands reflect grid carbon intensity variation across regions and scenarios.

4. HYDROGEN FUEL CELL VEHICLES: OPPORTUNITIES AND CBA IMPLICATIONS

4.1 Hydrogen Technology Overview and Environmental Performance

Hydrogen fuel cell electric vehicles (FCEVs) represent a distinct pathway for transport decarbonization, particularly relevant for applications where battery energy density and recharging time impose constraints—notably in heavy-duty freight, long-distance passenger transport, maritime shipping, and aviation. Hassan et al (2023) provide a comprehensive review of FCEV opportunities and challenges, highlighting that FCEVs emit only water vapor at the point of use and can be refueled in minutes, offering an operational profile closer to that of conventional vehicles than battery EVs. However, the environmental performance of FCEVs is fundamentally contingent on whether the hydrogen used is produced via electrolysis powered by renewable electricity (green hydrogen) or via steam methane reforming of natural gas (grey hydrogen), which actually carries a higher lifecycle emission profile than some ICE vehicles when methane leakage is accounted for.

The TCO of FCEVs currently exceeds that of both BEVs and ICE vehicles in most applications, reflecting high capital costs for fuel cell stacks, limited refueling infrastructure, and the premium cost of green hydrogen. Rout et al. (2022) conduct a comparative TCO analysis for heavy-duty vehicles powered by hydrogen, electricity, and diesel, finding that hydrogen powertrains carry a TCO premium of 20–40% over battery electric alternatives at current cost levels, but project significant convergence as hydrogen production scales and electrolyzer costs decline. From a CBA standpoint, the key question is whether the specific-use advantages of hydrogen—range, refueling speed, payload capacity—generate sufficient operational benefits to justify the cost premium, particularly in sectors where BEV limitations are most binding. For heavy-duty road freight, where vehicles routinely travel 500–800 km per day and require rapid refueling to maintain productive asset utilization, the operational case for hydrogen FCEVs is materially stronger than for passenger vehicles.

4.2 The Green Hydrogen Premium and Policy Implications

The difference in the cost of production of green and grey hydrogen is the focus of the economic issues of FCEV decarbonization. Green hydrogen generated through renewable electrolysis is already USD 3- USD 8 /kg, which is in contrast to USD 1- USD 2 /kg of grey hydrogen generated through natural gas reforming. To seal this gap, a continuation of renewable electricity price cuts, as simulated by Bogdanov et al. (2021), and the introduction of a price on carbon are needed to reflect the entire social cost of grey hydrogen generation. The effective cost of the carbon of grey hydrogen increases significantly at an SCC of USD 185/tonne (Rennert et al., 2022) and including the upstream methane emissions of natural gas supply chains, closing the economic difference with green alternatives.

Hydrogen production tax credits, contracts for difference, and renewable portfolio standards of hydrogen facility can also be used as policy instruments to speed up the shift to green hydrogen. The hydrogen strategy of the European Union, with an aim of 10 million tonnes per year of domestic production of renewable hydrogen, is the most ambitious such commitment in the world, and serves as an example to other jurisdictions. CBA-wise, the realization of scale economies in the electrolysis and distribution of hydrogen should also be considered to justify the government spending on green hydrogen infrastructure not only on the direct transport decarbonization advantages but also on the resulting spill-over industrial advantages of clean hydrogen to steel, chemicals, and other hard-to-abate industries. This broader social pay-off significantly enhances the BCR of hydrogen infrastructure investment compared to the appraisal that only takes into account the benefits of transport, and reinforces the importance of cross-sector planning frameworks that embodies these economy-wide complementarities.

5. PUBLIC TRANSIT AND ACTIVE TRANSPORT: SYSTEMIC BENEFITS AND CBA

5.1 Public Transit: Collective Efficiency and Emission Reduction

Public transport (buses, rail, bus rapid transit (BRT), and metro) represents a radically different solution to decarbonization of transportation compared to electrification of vehicles. Instead of replacing clean technologies with current travel patterns, the public transit transforms the mobility demand by focusing on the movement of people, decreasing the number of vehicle-kilometers travelled, and by introducing denser land use patterns that further decreases the necessity of motorized travel. Millard-Ball and Schipper (2011) record indicators of peak travel in a number of high-income nations, indicating that urbanization and transit investment can be a structural factor to reduce the growth of per-capita travel demand, with implications of great importance to long-run carbon paths.

The public transit investment CBA is complicated and strongly contextualized. Khong et al. (2023) examine the public transportation in Can Tho City, Vietnam, and determine the cost-benefit and mode preference analysis of the well-designed BRT schemes and the benefit-cost ratio is in the range of 2.0-3.5 when all the mentioned factors agglomeration economies, road congestion reduction, air quality factors, and avoided vehicle costs are monetized. These BCRs are ridership sensitive but strong in a variety of situations when externalities are added. Santos et al. (2013) discuss the determinants of modal split in European cities and identify frequency, reliability, and transit service integration as the main determinants of mode choice, which is why the quality of the services offered is crucial to investing in the physical infrastructure. Their discussion identifies the fallacy of investing in transit infrastructure without also raising the quality of service- a misallocation that has created ineffective public transit systems in many cities that constructed the hardware without creating the software of efficient, enticing service.

Winkler et al. (2023) simulate the overall impact of policies to transition to sustainable mobility, such as transit investment, congestion charging, and parking reform, on urban transport emissions in a large sample of cities. According to their findings, the integrated policy packages are significantly more efficient than the use of the single-instrument approaches, and the cumulative emission cuts of 40-60 percent can be realized by 2050 in urban areas that implement the complete approach to sustainable mobility. Briand et al. (2023) apply this analysis to emerging economies, finding that investment in public transit is the only policy lever that is most cost-effective to decarbonize transport in the rapidly urbanizing settings where the infrastructure lock-in of car-centric development can still be avoided. The timeframe of seizing this cheap decarbonization prospect via transit-based development and modal balanced infrastructure capital is shrinking fast as urbanization increases and car ownership proliferates throughout the Global South.

5.2 Active Transport: Health Co-Benefits and Infrastructure CBA

Active transport - mainly cycling and walking - is among the most desirable cost-benefit ratios of any transport intervention, when health externalities are completely monetized. Bland et al. (2024) meta-analyses the findings of economic analyses of large-scale cycling and walking infrastructure, with the overall BCRs of 3-10 dependent on the location and density of urban areas, indicating the benefits of reducing carbon emissions, increasing health benefits, decreasing healthcare system expenditures, and alleviating congestion. Significantly, the health benefits on their own, which result as a consequence of higher degrees of physical activity, often dominate the benefit stream, so active transport infrastructure is one of the very few policy investments that have environmental and health co-benefits, which are mutually reinforcing and not in conflict.

The analysis of break-even of cycling infrastructure investment by Candio and Frew (2023) calculates the extent of behavioral change needed to justify the costs of infrastructure on social welfare grounds. Their findings prove that even small changes in mode share such as cycling substituting at least 2-5 per cent of short car travel can result in the creation of a positive net present value of typical cycling-infrastructure packages. Such a low break-even suggests that cycling investment can be strong even with conservative behavioral conditions, and much less than observed mode shift in cities with high-quality and connected cycling networks built. Van den Bijgaart et al. (2023) support this finding by showing that fuel taxation intended to internalize carbon externalities also produces health benefits due to induced active transport, which is why carbon pricing is an appropriate supplementary tool to active infrastructure investment.

Special attention should be paid to the distributional aspect of active transport investment. In contrast to vehicle electrification subsidies, which are skewed towards middle- and upper-income households who own vehicles and can afford high-quality technology, cycling and walking infrastructure enhancements are more likely to have broad-based welfare benefits that spill into lower-income groups who are least mobile and most susceptible to air pollution associated with traffic. Infrastructure

CBA analyses including distributional weighting of benefits going to lower-income populations have regularly found active transport investments to be doing even better than unweighted analyses would indicate, giving them the argument that they deserve a priority in urban transport investment programmes.

6. COMPARATIVE COST-BENEFIT ANALYSIS

6.1 Framework and Assumptions

The comparative CBA in this section has a consistent methodological framework implemented throughout the key low-carbon mobility pathways outlined above. The analysis uses the social discount rate of 3.5 percent, which is the suggestion of Rennert et al. (2022) on the use of inter-generational equity in weighting climate-relevant appraisals. The carbon damages monetization includes an SCC of USD 185/ metric ton CO2-equivalent. The health externalities associated with air pollution are estimated on the basis of WHO mortality concentration-response functions at regional backgrounds of exposure. The local labor market wage rates are used to estimate congestion costs as a proxy of time value. The cost of infrastructure and vehicles is based on the latest comparative literature.

The analysis of that is done on a representative 15-year appraisal period according to normal vehicle or infrastructure asset life cycles. All the monetary values are given in constant 2023 USD. The SCC (range USD 50300/tonne), grid carbon intensity (current vs. 2030 projected) and discount rate (2- 7 percent) are sensitized to ascertain the strength of BCR rankings. The following limitations of this cross-modal comparison should be pointed out: both technologies are utilized under varied conditions of operation with varied options of baseline, and the BCRs may be more considered as the estimative orders of magnitude and directional comparisons than the point estimate. Table 1 and Graph 1 display the results respectively.

6.2 Results and Interpretation

Table 1 summarizes the important parameters and indicator BCRs of each mobility solution. The results indicate a uniform trend: the solutions that will remove tailpipe emissions and create health and congestion co-benefits have the largest social BCRs. Active transport (cycling) tops the BCR metric with health externalities added- a result that is strong across a broad spectrum of sensitivity conditions. The next is the BCR of the Public BRT since it is effective in transporting high volumes of people with minimal per-passenger-kilometer emissions, as long as the ridership objectives are achieved. The BEVs exhibit BCRs that are well above unity throughout the central case, which is mainly reflected by carbon and air pollution damages avoided compared to the ICE base.

FCEVs have the lowest BCRs in the current period because the cost premium of green hydrogen production is very high, but sensitivity analysis indicates that BCRs will increase to above 1.5 with projected 2030 hydrogen cost paths and a carbon price pathway that would give 2030 temperature goals of the Paris Agreement. The HEV shows a performance marginally above the viability threshold with central assumptions, including some fuel efficiency and emissions performance benefits relative to the pure ICE baseline, but with much worse performance relative to BEVs, due to the continued reliance on fossil fuels in the use phase. The ICE vehicles which act as the counterfactual benchmark produce BCRs less than 1.0 when central SCC assumptions are taken, which confirms the assumption of continued use of conventional motorized transport being a negative-NPV proposition to society when all externalities are considered. Direct implications of this finding to the policies of vehicle fleets are as follows: any subsidy or taxation policy that keeps ICE vehicles competitive with their actual social cost is an economically unreasonable gift to the society by individual motorists.

6.3 Sensitivity Analysis and Robustness

A significant policy test is how sensitive the BCR rankings are to the significant change of assumptions. Three of the sensitive dimensions of special interest in the present analysis are the SCC level, the carbon intensity of the grid, and the social discount rate. Increasing SCC to the higher end of the realistic near-term range of USD 185/tonne to USD 300/tonne (maximum of the realistic range of near-term SCCs according to Rennert et al., 2022) increases BCRs of all the low-carbon choices, and, simultaneously, reduces ICE BCR This is because, at that point, the absolute increases of

The grid carbon intensity is the most important element in the establishment of the BEV BCR change across geographies. BEV lifecycle emissions can be nearly the same as efficient HEVs in coal-heavy electricity markets, which substantially decreases the carbon benefit aspect of the BCR. In near-zero-carbon electricity markets, like Norway, Iceland, or what is estimated by the early 2030s in a range of European and East Asian economies, BEV BCRs increase to the range of 3.0-4.0 under central SCC assumptions, as a result of an almost total removal of transport-related climate harm compared to the ICE baseline. This prospective element of this sensitivity is crucial: any BEV purchased in a relatively high-carbon grid today will operate under a more decarbonized grid environment over the lifetime of the vehicle, which is 15 years, so the carbon intensity that will be relevant to it is the time-weighted average current carbon intensity during the lifetime of the vehicle.

The study based on current-year grid intensity, held constant, is a systematic understatement of the predicted BCR of current BEV investments, according to Shafique and Luo (2022).

The interaction of discount rate sensitivity of modes of transport is asymmetrical. BCRs are greatly enhanced with lower discount rates in capital-intensive public transit and cycling infrastructure, where initial costs are high and returns over the long-run are gained. With the vehicle investments with shorter payback periods, the sensitivity to discount rate is not as high. This asymmetry suggests that transit and active infrastructure are best benefited in comparison with vehicle-based solutions when appraisal uses the lower discount rates that are needed to support intergenerational equity weighting, which supports the argument of methodological consistency in applying such discount rates to all types of transport investment and not only to the climate damage component of the SCC. Together the sensitivity results suggest that the claim that the investment in low-carbon transport is robust in a wide range of plausible parameter values and that the central estimates of the BCR values presented below should be taken as a low estimate of the social benefits that the transition is likely to obtain.

Table 1. Comparative Cost-Benefit Analysis of Low-Carbon Mobility Solutions

Mobility Solution	Lifecycle GHG (gCO2eq/km)	TCO (USD/km)	BCR (Approx.)	Key Benefit	Key Risk
Battery Electric Vehicle (BEV)	~60–95	~0.28–0.35	1.8–2.4	Zero tailpipe emissions	Battery supply chain constraints
Hydrogen Fuel Cell (FCEV)	~30–80	~0.38–0.55	1.2–1.6	Fast refuelling, long range	Green hydrogen cost & availability
Public Transit (Bus Rapid Transit)	~25–50 (per pkm)	~0.12–0.22	2.0–3.5	High ridership efficiency	High upfront capital cost
Active Transport (Cycling)	~5–15	~0.03–0.08	3.5–6.0	Health co-benefits	Infrastructure investment needed
ICE Vehicle (Baseline)	~190–230	~0.35–0.50	0.6–0.9	Established infrastructure	High carbon & health costs
Hybrid Electric Vehicle (HEV)	~100–140	~0.30–0.42	1.1–1.5	Bridge technology	Still relies on fossil fuel

Note: Lifecycle GHG and TCO values are indicative ranges derived from the reviewed literature. BCRs are calculated under the central scenario (SCC = USD 185/t, discount rate = 3.5%, grid carbon intensity = current average). BCR = Benefit-Cost Ratio; pkm = passenger-kilometer. Sources: Das et al. (2024); Zhang et al. (2023); Rout et al. (2022); Khong et al. (2023); Bland et al. (2024); Hasan et al. (2021).

Figure 2. Comparative Benefit-Cost Ratios Under Central and High-SCC Scenarios

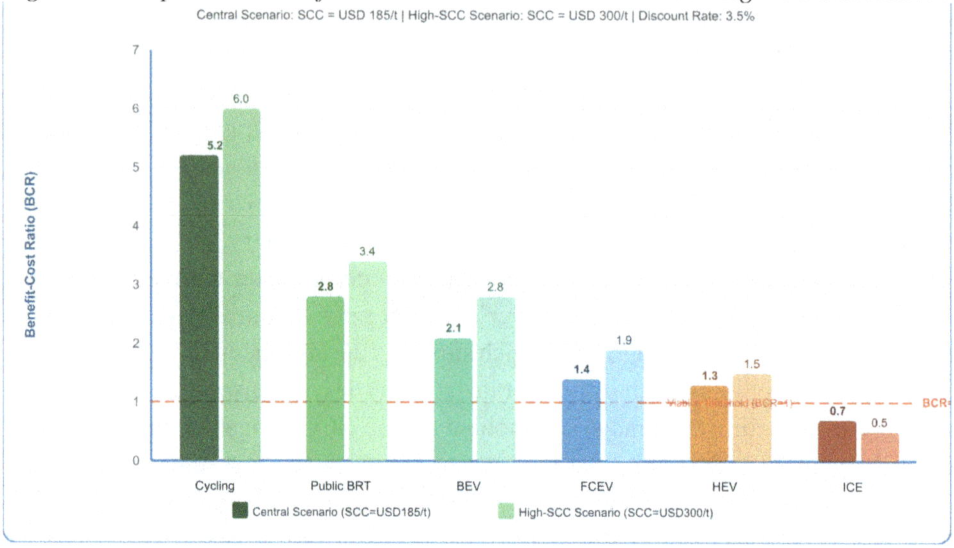

Figure 2 illustrates the bar chart comparing BCRs across six transport modes under two scenarios. Central Scenario (SCC=USD185/t): Cycling 5.2, BRT 2.8, BEV 2.1, FCEV 1.4, HEV 1.3, ICE 0.7. High-SCC Scenario (SCC=USD300/t): Cycling 6.0, BRT 3.4, BEV 2.8, FCEV 1.9, HEV 1.5, ICE 0.5. Dashed red line marks viability threshold at BCR=1.0.

7. POLICY INSTRUMENTS FOR CLOSING THE VIABILITY GAP

7.1 Carbon Pricing and Emissions Trading

The most economically efficient tool that is generally considered to internalize the social cost of transport emissions is carbon pricing either as a carbon tax or an emissions trading scheme (ETS). Carbon pricing legitimately rightly addresses the market failure at the core of the transport decarbonization issue by raising the operating cost of fossil fuel cars and improving the relative price competitiveness of low-carbon substitutes. Bai and Ru (2024) provide rigorous international data that carbon emission trading programs are associated with statistically significant reductions in industrial and transport emissions, and the size of effects increases over time, as market participants adjust long-run capitals allocation. Their cross-national debate concludes that the confidence and permanence of commitment to carbon pricing is a decisive element of investment response, and thus the value of sustainable legislative systems to ETS design.

Integration of the transport industry into carbon pricing systems has traditionally been partial with road transport often taken care of by fuel excise taxes and not by direct carbon markets. The significant question of design relative to CBA is whether the amount of price of carbon is sufficient to completely internalize the SCC. Even with existing ETS prices, with most jurisdictions setting prices at USD 25-90/tonne, the carbon price is still significantly lower than the central SCC estimate of USD 185/tonne by Rennert et al. (2022), which means that there is still a long-standing subsidy of low-carbon mobility. A major policy agenda and a possible important contributor to social welfare benefits is to seal this price difference. Carbon pricing can too be reused to aid active transport infrastructure, transit subsidies or direct household transfer, which can offset retrogressive impacts, and constitute a self-reinforcing policy package, which can boost efficiency and equity in the transport system.

The carbon pricing mechanism, be it a carbon tax or an emissions trading scheme (ETS) has been generally seen as a most economically efficient tool to internalize the social cost of transport emissions. Carbon pricing is an approach to the market failure in the centre of the transport decarbonization problem, which raises the operating cost of fossil fuel vehicles, and improves the relative price competitiveness of low-carbon substitutes. In a study by Bai and Ru (2024), there is rigorous evidence regarding the relationship between carbon emissions trading schemes and statistically significant reductions in industrial and transport emissions and an accelerating effect size over time as market participants reallocate capital over the long run. Their cross-national research confirms that the reasonability and sustainability of carbon-pricing commitments play a vital role in determining investment responses, and the value of long-term legislative frameworks to ETS design.

Introduction of transport into carbon pricing systems has long been an incomplete process with road transport normally reflected by fuel excise taxes instead of actual carbon markets. The main CBA question is, should the price level of carbon be high enough to internalize the SCC? The carbon price at existing ETS prices in most jurisdictions, generally USD 25-90/tonne, is far short of the central estimate of the SCC of USD 185/tonne in Rennert et al. (2022), suggesting that it continues to represent a subsidy similar to low-carbon mobility. Sealing this price gap constitutes a significant policy agenda and a possible huge amount of social welfare payoff. The re-investment of carbon pricing can also be in active transport infrastructure, transit subsidies, or direct household transfers, which offsets regressive impacts, and the policy package is self-reinforcing, enhancing efficiency as well as equity in the transport system.

7.2 Vehicle Standards, Feebates, and Purchase Incentives

In settings where political factors restrict the extent of price that can be imposed on carbon, alternative regulatory and fiscal policies can hasten the uptake of low-carbon cars. Fuel economy and emission standards set a performance lower limit on the new vehicles sales, which phase out the fleet structure to cleaner technologies. Feebate schemes, which impose charges on high-emission cars and subsidies on low-emission cars, can do the same at a lower fiscal cost than blanket purchase subsidies, by creating a self-financing cycle where the transport externality is charged at the point of sale, rather than the point of operation.

The case of Norway described by Bjerkan et al. (2016) illustrates how effective incentive packages can impact the market in an extraordinary way. Norway was able to drive BEV market share of more than 70 percent of new vehicle sales by the early 2020s through a system of fiscal privileges and operational advantages, an economic revolution unparalleled in the entire world. The implicit subsidy-per-tonne of avoided CO2 in the Norwegian scheme, though large in absolute terms, is attractive compared to the SCC when the air quality, congestion and health co-benefits are fully monetized and in addition to the carbon benefit. The finding demonstrates that high-intensity incentive programs may be able to survive a CBA test in cases where the accounting of the benefits is done in full, and teaches a valuable lesson to other governments in contemplating designing EV support programs.

7.3 Public Investment in Infrastructure and Transit

Publicly investing in charging infrastructure, transit systems and active travel networks should maximize the social value of low-carbon vehicle technologies, to create the necessary changes of behavior. Winkler et al. (2023) in a simulation of the interactions between an infrastructure investment and a pricing reform discover that policies that embody either both infrastructure bottlenecks on the supply side or price signals on the demand side can provoke synergistic emission reductions that are greater than the sum of the parts. The same interaction effect is observed as the more extensive body of transport demand literature, which highlights the mode choice as a product of relative cost, time of travel, reliability, comfort which might be coordinated by coordinated public investment.

With public transit, in particular, Briand et al. (2023) note that there is a critical mass: transit networks must reach a certain degree of network density and frequency of service before they can generate the ridership and modal shift necessary to generate positive social returns. The value below which the underutilized transit infrastructure leads to the BCRs under 1.0 and over 1.0, the network externality of transit leads to social returns that grow very quickly. This nonlinearity has consequences on transit benefits which are applicable to sequencing public investment: new services should be anchored to existing desire lines of travel, and the network coverage should be extended to other destinations. The lesson of the transport planner is that the order of transit investment is as important as the size and that CBA models should reflect the dynamic change in ridership and network effects compared to using the first year traffic assumption.

7.4 Distributional Considerations and Just Transition

The distributional impacts, who pays and who benefits of the transition should be fully managed by a complete CBA of transport decarbonization. Unless properly designed, carbon pricing, fuel tax and vehicle standards might have retrogressive impacts on the poor and middle-income households in that most of the households in the low-income bracket spend a higher percentage of their income on transport and are usually unable to afford the capital to purchase low emissions cars or houses near transport. Active transportation and public transit investments, in their turn, will be more likely to disproportionately benefit the lower-income population relying on low-cost mobility options and at risk of experiencing a greater air pollution burden because of traffic.

The ranking of policy tools can change dramatically when viewed through the prism of CBA; distributional weighting, in which more weight is given to welfare change accrued by the lower-income groups can change it. Distributional CBA is able to give higher scores to investments that yield broad-based access benefit, reduce household spending on transportation by low-income consumers, and externalize air quality costs on disadvantaged communities than in unweighted analysis. The just transition imperative thus accommodates and does not conflict with cost-effectiveness in the majority of cases of transport policy. The decarbonization policies created by policymakers must both include efficiency-enhancing policies and be explicitly protective of equity, with low-income EV subsidies, transit passes, and focused investment in active transportation in low-income communities to make sure that the costs of the transition are not concentrated among the most vulnerable.

8. DISCUSSION: INTEGRATION, UNCERTAINTY, AND THE DYNAMIC CBA CHALLENGE

8.1 The Case for Integrated Appraisal

The evidence discussed in this chapter provides a good argument that piecemeal CBA, which considers one technology or policy tool separately, is a systematic underestimation of the costs and benefits of transport decarbonization. The social value of an investment in cycling infrastructure is that complementary road pricing creates the incentive to switch to modal; the BCR of BEV charging infrastructure will depend on the rate of grid decarbonization; the net benefit of implementing hydrogen fuel cells to freight will depend on the trend of the cost of green hydrogen production, which will depend on renewable electricity policy. These dependencies require a system level approach to transport CBA that reflects the dynamics between technology, infrastructure, pricing and behavior.

Some system-level modeling methods, including energy system models, transport demand models, and integrated assessment models can be viewed as the interactions but introduce a lot of additional uncertainty. The tools that are needed to communicate the set of plausible outcomes to the decision-makers are sensitivity analysis and scenario-based appraisal. The cost of the risk of inaction of policy in the event of uncertainty is a judgment on its own part, and is in general systematically underweighted in the customary practice of appraisal. The value of early action as an option, to maintain the capacity to meet high-ambitious climate targets and the lock-in of high-carbon infrastructure, should be included as a benefit of the CBA of transformative transport investments. One of the most severe of the carbon lock-in issues is transport where 10-20 year vehicle life, 30-50 year road/transit infrastructure and urban land use patterns embedded by present development options have the potential to last a century or more.

The AI-aided transport planning tools point to the avenues of potentially effective methodological solutions to how integrated CBA can be operationalized in practice. Machine learning techniques can be used to improve the accuracy of deep uncertainty travel demand forecasting, and optimization algorithms can be used to identify transport investment portfolios that are optimal in terms of social net present value, with a large solution space. The integration of real-time data streams, which are associated with linked vehicles, transit sensors, and city mobility platforms, into the ongoing appraisal and performance monitoring systems offers an opportunity to adapt transport investment to adaptable cost and emission trends, rather than invest in decisions made based on point-in-time estimations.

8.2 Dynamic Cost Trajectories and Technology Learning

The other peculiar feature of the current decarbonization scenario in the transport sector is the breathtaking pace of cost reduction in key key enabling technologies, lithium-ion batteries, solar photovoltaical and wind power. Based on the existing cost structures, Static CBA creates systematically pessimistic estimates of the social returns to low-carbon investment in transport by ignoring the dynamics of learning-by-doing that will result in cost reduction in the future. Viable CBA models that use technology learning curves and endogenous costs paths show much greater BCRs to early investment in a scaling low-carbon transport technologies, since the benefits of a single unit of early deployment spread through to all future units that enjoy the benefit of lower costs of manufacture.

Bogdanov et al. (2021) describe this process by introducing their model of a global energy system, which proves that in the past, the initial investment in renewable electricity generation has caused a cost decrease, and the present state of affairs is that clean power nowadays is the cheapest source of new electricity in most markets. The same learning dynamics apply to BEV batteries, fuel cell systems, and cycling infrastructure, in which it can be assumed that BCR estimates based on existing cost estimates lack the systematic underestimation of the social value of investment. These dynamic benefits can be internalised within policy frameworks, and justify them on good CBA grounds despite the ambiguous outcomes which would be achieved by a static analysis.

Market scale, policy support and technology learning generate great path dependencies in the transport decarbonization transition. Early and prolonged policy backing of technologies can attain adequate scale to create cost savings that in the long term can make them self-sustaining in the market, despite withdrawal of subsidies. Not well supported technologies in the initial stages can find themselves in a high cost, low volume equilibrium that causes such technologies not to ever attain the scale of competitiveness in cost. These tipping-point dynamics need to be observed by the practitioners of CBA and the social returns to transport policy should not be determined by them on the basis of the immediate net present value but on the basis of how likely they are to initiate the path of beneficial technologies with a large long-run social value.

9. CONCLUSION

In the chapter, a comprehensive cost-benefit framework of evaluation of low-carbon mobility solutions has been constructed using a comprehensive and rapidly growing collection of empirical studies of lifecycle emissions, total cost of ownership as well as the social value of transport externalities. The overall conclusion is clear: monetizing the entire set of climate, health, and congestion externalities using best-practice SCC estimates, virtually all low-carbon transport solutions, such as BEVs, hydrogen FCEVs, public transit, and active transport, would yield social BCRs that are much higher than those of the fossil-fuel baseline, most exceeding 2.0 under central conditions and going higher

Active transport and public transport are particularly high-value investments where there are also health co-benefits because only these types of transport can achieve a reduction in carbon, and more physical health outcomes and a reduction in the long-run cost of mobility by all income groups. It is known that BEV adoption is cost-effective in a wide range of contexts and BCRs are sensitive to carbon intensity in the grid and the cost of battery supply chains and resistant to moderate grid carbon intensity and changes in battery supply chains. Hydrogen FCEVs have by far the most difficult near-term economics, but are a valuable avenue to decarbonize the applications where battery limitations are binding, and their BCRs rise with the production of green hydrogen and a rise in carbon price to SCC-consistency levels.

The implications of the policies are clear. By combining a combination of carbon prices at or close to SCC, vehicle standards and purchase incentives, and incorporating public investment in charging, transit, and active travel infrastructure, the viability gap between market prices and social costs can be narrowed. The element of distribution must be included to appraisal systems so that to make the transition favorable and efficient. Carbon pricing and feebates should be reinvested into initiatives that help to support lower-income households, such as subsidized transit access, active transit infrastructure in underserved areas, and income-based EV purchase subsidies.

CBA frameworks should be designed to capture the dynamic cost paths, interaction of technology and systemic co-benefits that are systematically discounted by the traditional analysis that relies on partial equilibrium. CBA methods will also be essential to incorporate technology learning, supply chain risks, distributional weighting, and cross-sectoral spillovers, particularly interdependency between transport electrification and electricity system decarbonization in providing credible advice regarding investments in the rapidly changing world of transport decarbonization. Future research must consider how to design integrated modeling frameworks, which can optimize concurrently the technology of vehicles, transit investment, land use, and pricing policy, and can be scaled to the data environments and institutional environments of both high-income and fast urbanizing developing countries.

Well defined economics of decarbonization of transport give a good argument that extensive and rapid action in each of the avenues investigated in this chapter makes sense. Combined with the electric cars, electrified transit and active transport infrastructure, and purpose-built carbon pricing, the concerted action of these measures will not only be an environmental necessity, but a high-payoff social investment. The challenge confronting researchers, policymakers and practitioners is to design and adopt appraisal frameworks that can reflect this economic reality and they must also be capable of presenting the results in a manner that can pass through a political process and inform the large-scale capital allocation choices on which the transport decarbonization transition depends.

Figure 3. Integrated CBA Framework for Low-Carbon Mobility Solutions

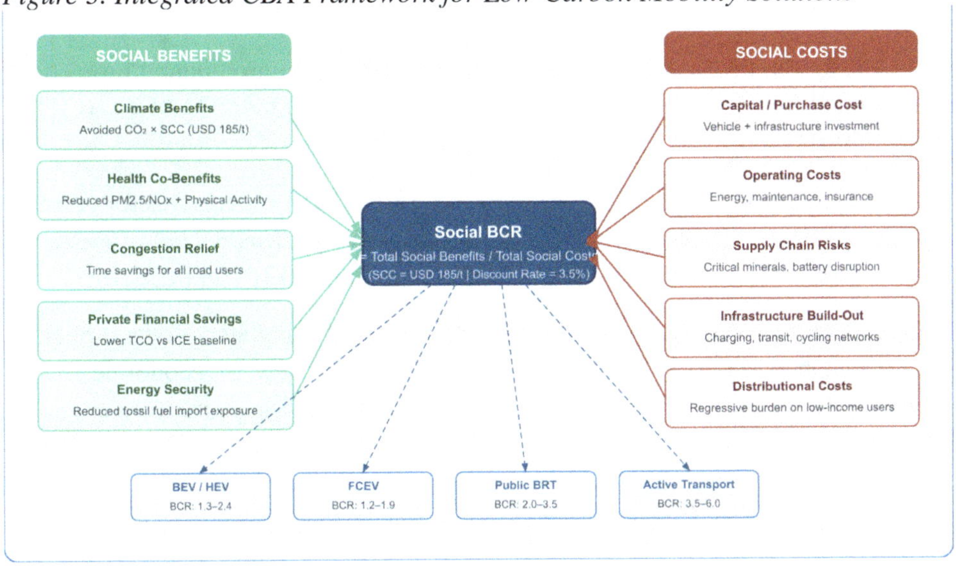

Figure 3 illustrates the flow from Social Benefits (Climate Benefits, Health Co-Benefits, Congestion Relief, Financial Savings, Energy Security) and Social Costs (Capital Costs, Operating Costs, Supply Chain Risks, Infrastructure, Distributional Costs) into the central Social BCR calculation, which then outputs indicative BCRs for each technology pathway: BEV/HEV (1.3–2.4), FCEV (1.2–1.9), Public BRT (2.0–3.5), Active Transport (3.5–6.0).

REFERENCES

Bai, J., & Ru, H. (2024). Carbon emissions trading and environmental protection: International evidence. *Management Science*, *70*(7), 4593–4603. DOI: 10.1287/mnsc.2023.03143

Bjerkan, K. Y., Nørbech, T. E., & Nordtømme, M. E. (2016). Incentives for promoting battery electric vehicle (BEV) adoption in Norway. *Transportation Research Part D, Transport and Environment*, *43*, 169–180. DOI: 10.1016/j.trd.2015.12.002

Bland, M., Burke, M. I., & Bertolaccini, K. (2024). Taking steps toward healthy and sustainable transport investment: A systematic review of economic evaluations in the academic literature on large-scale active transport infrastructure. *International Journal of Sustainable Transportation*, *18*(3), 201–220. DOI: 10.1080/15568318.2023.2296952

Bogdanov, D., Ram, M., Aghahosseini, A., Gulagi, A., Oyewo, A. S., Child, M., Caldera, U., Sadovskaia, K., Farfan, J., Barbosa, L. S. N. S., Fasihi, M., Khalili, S., Traber, T., & Breyer, C. (2021). Low-cost renewable electricity as the key driver of the global energy transition towards sustainability. *Energy*, *227*, 120467. DOI: 10.1016/j.energy.2021.120467

Briand, Y., Pye, S., D'Agosto, M. de A., Goes, G. V., Neves Schmitz-Gonçalves, D., Garg, A., Gupta, D., Vishwanathan, S. S., Siagian, U. W. R., Ahjum, F., & Trollip, H. (2023). Passenger transport decarbonization in emerging economies: Policy lessons from modelling long-term deep decarbonization pathways. *Climate Policy*, *23*(7), 882–897. DOI: 10.1080/14693062.2023.2194859

Candio, P., & Frew, E. (2023). How much behaviour change is required for the investment in cycling infrastructure to be sustainable? A break-even analysis. *PLoS One*, *18*(4), e0284634. DOI: 10.1371/journal.pone.0284634 PMID: 37075055

Das, P. K., Bhat, M. Y., & Sajith, S. (2024). Life cycle assessment of electric vehicles: A systematic review of literature. *Environmental Science and Pollution Research International*, *31*(1), 73–89. DOI: 10.1007/s11356-023-30999-3 PMID: 38038907

Gao, Z., Xu, Y., Liu, X., Zhang, L., Liu, Y., & Chen, S. (2023). Electric vehicle lifecycle carbon emission reduction: A review. *Carbon Neutralization*, *2*(5), 528–550. DOI: 10.1002/cnl2.81

Hasan, M. A., Frame, D. J., Chapman, R., & Archie, K. M. (2021). Costs and emissions: Comparing electric and petrol-powered cars in New Zealand. *Transportation Research Part D, Transport and Environment*, *90*, 102671. DOI: 10.1016/j.trd.2020.102671

Hassan, Q., Itimad, D. J. A., Sameen, A. Z., & Salman, M. H. (2023). Hydrogen fuel cell vehicles: Opportunities and challenges. *Sustainability (Basel), 15*(15), 11501. DOI: 10.3390/su151511501

Hu, H., Yuan, H., Hu, H., Xiong, S., Wang, Z., Wang, Z., & Zhou, X. (2023). How does adoption of electric vehicles reduce carbon emissions? Evidence from China. *Heliyon, 9*(9), e20296. DOI: 10.1016/j.heliyon.2023.e20296 PMID: 37809651

Keiser, D., Lade, G. E., & Rudik, I. (2018). Air pollution and visitation at US national parks. Science Advances, 4(7), eaat1613. DOI: 10.1126/sciadv.aat1613

Khong, T. D., Tong, Y. D., & Bui, L. T. H. (2023). Cost-benefit analysis and model preference of public transportation in Can Tho City, Vietnam. *Sustainability (Basel), 15*(9), 7247. DOI: 10.3390/su15097247

Millard-Ball, A., & Schipper, L. (2011). Are we reaching peak travel? Trends in passenger transport in eight industrialized countries. *Transport Reviews, 31*(3), 357–378. DOI: 10.1080/01441647.2010.518291

Nehiba, C. (2024). Electric vehicle usage, pollution damages, and the electricity price elasticity of driving. *Journal of Environmental Economics and Management, 124*, 102915. DOI: 10.1016/j.jeem.2023.102915 PMID: 39022448

Rennert, K., Errickson, F., Prest, B. C., Rennels, L., Newell, R. G., Pizer, W., Kingdon, C., Wingenroth, J., Cooke, R., Parthum, B., Smith, D., Cromar, K., Diaz, D., Moore, F. C., Müller, U. K., Plevin, R. J., Raftery, A. E., Ševčíková, H., Sheets, H., & Anthoff, D. (2022). Comprehensive evidence implies a higher social cost of CO2. *Nature, 610*(7933), 687–692. DOI: 10.1038/s41586-022-05224-9 PMID: 36049503

Rout, C., Li, H., Dupont, V., & Wadud, Z. (2022). A comparative total cost of ownership analysis of heavy duty on-road and off-road vehicles powered by hydrogen, electricity, and diesel. *Heliyon, 8*(12), e12417. DOI: 10.1016/j.heliyon.2022.e12417 PMID: 36593823

Santos, G., Maoh, H., Potoglou, D., & von Brunn, T. (2013). Factors influencing modal split of commuting journeys in medium-size European cities. *Journal of Transport Geography, 30*, 127–137. DOI: 10.1016/j.jtrangeo.2013.04.005

Shafique, M., Azam, A., Rafiq, M., & Luo, X. (2022). Life cycle assessment of electric vehicles and internal combustion engine vehicles: A case study of Hong Kong. *Research in Transportation Economics, 91*, 101112. DOI: 10.1016/j.retrec.2021.101112

Shafique, M., & Luo, X. (2022). Environmental life cycle assessment of battery electric vehicles from the current and future energy mix perspective. *Journal of Environmental Management*, *303*, 114050. DOI: 10.1016/j.jenvman.2021.114050 PMID: 34872799

Sun, D., Sampene, A. K., & Asante, D. (2023). An investigation on the role of electric vehicles in alleviating environmental pollution: Evidence from five leading economies. *Environmental Science and Pollution Research International*, *30*(7), 18244–18259. DOI: 10.1007/s11356-022-23386-x PMID: 36208376

van den Bijgaart, I., Gerlagh, R., & Mattauch, L. (2023). Healthy climate, healthy bodies: Optimal fuel taxation and physical activity. *Economica*, *90*(360), 1233–1261. DOI: 10.1111/ecca.12497

Winkler, L., Nelson, J., & Babacan, O. (2023). The effect of sustainable mobility transition policies on cumulative urban transport emissions and energy demand. *Nature Communications*, *14*(1), 2357. DOI: 10.1038/s41467-023-37728-x PMID: 37095105

Zhang, H., Xue, B., Li, S., Yu, Y., Li, X., Chang, Z., Wu, H., Hu, Y., Huang, K., Liu, L., Chen, L., & Su, Y. (2023). Life cycle environmental impact assessment for battery-powered electric vehicles at the global and regional levels. *Scientific Reports*, *13*(1), 7952. DOI: 10.1038/s41598-023-35150-3 PMID: 37193809

Zhao, X., Ma, X., Chen, B., Shang, Y., & Song, M. (2022). Challenges toward carbon neutrality in China: Strategies and countermeasures. *Resources, Conservation and Recycling*, *176*, 105959. DOI: 10.1016/j.resconrec.2021.105959

KEY TERMS AND DEFINITIONS

Cost-Benefit Analysis: A methodical evaluation of the monetary and non-monetary costs and benefits of a project, policy or investment at a certain time. It helps decision-makers to comprehend whether the benefits will outweigh the costs and it helps to allocate resources properly.

Life-Cycle Assessment: Methodology A technique to evaluate the environmental impact of a product, process or service throughout its life cycle - beginning with the extraction and production of raw materials and continuing through its use, disposal or recycling.

Low-Carbon Mobility: Mobility systems and practices that are supposed to lower the emission of greenhouse gases. It comprises of public transportation, bicycle riding, walking, and carpooling as well as adopting cleaner technologies to decrease reliance on fossil fuels and the effects of climate changes.

Social Cost of Carbon: This is a form of economic measure that approximates the financial loss that is incurred as a result of one additional ton of carbon dioxide being released into the atmosphere. It takes into consideration health, agricultural, property, and ecosystem effects of climate.

Total Cost of Ownership: This is the total direct and indirect expenses that will be incurred by buying the asset and using it over its useful life, purchase, maintenance, fuel/energy, insurance, and disposal costs.

Chapter 9
Green Finance, AI-Enabled Investment Strategies, and Renewable Energy for Decarbonizing Transport Infrastructure in Emerging Economies

Aarohi Kumari
http://orcid.org/0009-0000-1762-8783
Vivekananda Global University, India

Gautam Jha
http://orcid.org/0009-0008-5874-2628
Vivekananda Global University, India

Vikas Rana
http://orcid.org/0000-0003-2538-9641
Vivekananda Global University, India

Pratishtha Singh
http://orcid.org/0009-0000-4972-5932
Vivekananda Global University, India

Pratyush Sinha
http://orcid.org/0009-0005-6155-9347
Vivekananda Global University, India

DOI: 10.4018/979-8-3373-9003-1.ch009

ABSTRACT

Due to urbanization, the increase in income, and the expanding infrastructure within cities are all contributing to an increase in CO_2 emissions from transportation. This research looks at 23 years of data on the emission levels of 143 developing countries for the purpose of assessing whether renewable energy sources and green financing can reduce transportation emissions. The results of our analysis indicate that renewable energy does have a positive impact on reducing emissions, but an increase in income will cause an increase in the number of vehicles being used. Pollution is expected to follow an inverted-U pattern, and infrastructure 'locked' into the emission-producing behavior of vehicles will continue to produce emissions, indicating that sustainable transportation investment must be made for the long-term.

1. INTRODUCTION

The transportation industry is recognized by developing nations as the biggest and fastest-growing source of carbon dioxide (CO2) emissions. With urbanization, higher incomes, and logistics growing alongside an increasing number of vehicles, emission issues in transportation have become a common challenge. Emissions in transportation will grow due to economic expansion that leads to more fuel usage. There are strong connections between the emissions produced in the transportations sector and infrastructure, which can last for a long time, like roads, logistics, and fleets, making the decarbonization process much more complicated and time-consuming compared to others (Timilsina & Shrestha, 2009; International Energy Agency, 2023).

The decarbonizing of the transportation systems will bring about a radical structural transformation that will involve the use of electric vehicles, movement using energy generated by renewable sources, and the improvement of logistics services. However, switching to the above-mentioned transport systems can turn out to be quite expensive for developing nations since they lack the necessary capital resources needed to implement such a transformation. Huge amounts of capital must be invested to establish an electric car fleet, convert the rail network to use electricity, construct new cargo lines, and develop a renewable energy source to power such transportation systems and electricity generation (Organization for Economic Co-operation and Development, 2021; McKinnon, 2018).

It goes without saying that many countries belonging to the group of less economically developed nations cannot afford such large investments due to poor budget conditions, high-interest rates, and the underdevelopment of their capital markets. It follows that the creation of green financing tools has become one of the most crucial ways of providing sustainable transportation networks with funds (Organization for Economic Co-operation and Development, 2021; International Transport Forum, 2023).

Options such as green bonds, climate finance, blended finance, and public private partnership (PPP) have emerged as key methods for financing low carbon transport projects. Financing in this manner provides a means through which financing projects such as electric mobility, transportation networks that use renewable energy sources, intelligent logistics and energy efficient transport networks is possible. Through reducing the risks involved in such ventures and enhancing availability of finance for them, green financing enables low carbon strategies to be implemented in the transport sector. The incorporation of renewable energy in transport networks ensures less reliance on fossil fuels and the development of electrified transport networks (McKinnon, 2018; Apergis & Payne, 2010).

New decarbonization measures for transport are emerging in tandem with the deployment of AI and other technological advances. With the help of AI and IoT technologies, one may achieve improved operation efficiencies for all processes within a supply chain, from traffic signal optimization and congestion-free roads to the development of transit plans based on predictive modeling and the utilization of intelligent transport systems. AI-driven optimization systems will decrease fuel consumption of transportation while improving load management by decreasing the time when a transport unit is not operating under full efficiency. Smart mobility for cities will combine all the three key aspects—public transport, electric mobility, and renewable energy—to form a unified low-emissions transportation network. In addition, other technologies, including green finance and renewable energy, may be useful for enhancing the performance of transport networks and achieving faster decarbonization.

Nevertheless, empirical investigations regarding the association among renewables, green financial flows, and transport-related emissions are relatively scarce. In addition, almost all past empirical analyses have mainly focused on analyzing the associations among renewables, transport emissions and green financing using aggregates or totals of emissions or energy consumption, rather than looking specifically at the relationship associated with transport emissions only. Most of the empirical literature employs a static modeling strategy that fails to capture the persistence of transport emissions since these emissions tend to be sticky in nature due to infrastructure lock-in effects (Timilsina & Shrestha, 2009; Saboori et al., 2014).

The present chapter is motivated by the above gaps and examines CO_2 emissions arising from the transport sector in 143 emerging economies over 23 years. Econometric techniques employed in this chapter include Fixed Effects Models, "Environmental Kuznets Curve (EKC)" interactions, dynamic Fixed Effects Estimation, Threshold Regression, and various robustness tests such as sensitivity to model specifications and outliers. Such models allow examining linear relationships, nonlinear relationships associated with the income effect, persistence of emissions, and regime-dependent effects of renewables on transport emissions.

This chapter makes four key contributions. Firstly, the chapter provides evidence on the influence of renewable energy use on reducing emissions in developing countries' transportation sectors. Secondly, the chapter considers dynamics and persistence in terms of infrastructure lock-in effects on the transportation system. Thirdly, the chapter addresses threshold effects on the relationship between renewable energy and emissions considering different income levels at which the effect differs depending on the development stage. Finally, the chapter addresses green finance, sustainable transportation infrastructure, and AI-enabled mobility system policies.

The following structure has been chosen for further discussion. Section 2 highlights the study objectives. Section 3 provides an overview of the relevant literature concerning transport emissions, renewable energy, green finance, and AI-based transport systems. Section 4 discusses the data and variables used for the analysis. Section 5 highlights econometric methodologies applied in the study. Section 6 provides empirical results. Section 7 discusses visualizations based on the data obtained. Section 8 highlights the policy implications for the decarbonization of transport. Section 9 discusses AI and digitalization aspects around sustainable transport. Section 10 offers a conclusion to the current chapter.

2. OBJECTIVES OF THE STUDY

In this chapter, the objective is to examine the contribution that renewable energy uptake and green finance can make towards mitigating carbon dioxide emissions from the transport sector in developing countries. The chapter intends to explore the connections between economic development, renewable energy consumption, and transport sector emissions in the domain of sustainable transport and transport infrastructure development.

The specific objectives of the study are as follows:

The purpose of our study is to examine the effects of renewable energy on CO2 emissions from transportation within developing countries. Our objective is to find out if increased reliance on renewable energy will enable us to achieve decarbonization and create sustainable transportation emissions within developing nations.

- To assess the pattern through which transportation emissions rise and eventually fall in response to increasing economic development.

- To validate the theory of the Environmental Kuznets Curve (EKC) that suggests transportation emissions increase during economic growth and start falling once the economy has reached a threshold of activity.
- To understand the persistence and the influence of past emissions on the present level of emissions due to the durable characteristics of transportation infrastructure and capital stock.
- To examine whether the effects of renewable energy depend on income levels and demonstrate that the application of green financing can be beneficial for implementing sustainable transportation emissions decarbonization policies.

3. LITERATURE REVIEW

3.1 Transport Emissions and Economic Growth

There are plenty of studies showing how economic growth causes a rise in the emissions produced by the transport sector. Higher income causes more vehicles to be purchased, higher freight transport, and higher requirements for mobility, all leading to more energy use and emissions from transport. Urban sprawling, increased commuting distances, and logistics arise due to economic growth, which consequently causes more emissions from the transport sector. Unlike emissions produced by the industrial sector, emissions from the transport sector depend on certain behavioral and structural factors like urban design and the infrastructure associated with transport (Timilsina & Shrestha, 2009; Sadorsky, 2009) (Timilsina & Shrestha, 2009; Sadorsky, 2009).

As has been shown in previous research, when income increases in developing countries, the need for mobility also increases, and this need is at its highest when the developing country is in the initial phase of its industrialization journey. With development, there is an increasing share of emissions due to freight transportation in the total emissions in the transport sector of the developing country. In fact, road transport is the primary mode of freight transportation, for instance, trucks. Consequently, road transport accounts for the majority of greenhouse gas emissions from the transport sector. The reality that transport includes road transport leads to the structural lock-in of emissions for several decades due to the long life of transport infrastructure (roads) and road-based vehicles (McKinnon, 2018; International Energy Agency, 2023).

3.2 Environmental Kuznets Curve (EKC) Hypothesis in the Transport Sector

According to the Environmental Kuznets Curve, developed by an economist named Simon Kuznets in the 1950s, the connection between pollution and income involves the inverted-U shape. This implies that there is a situation in which increased pollution arises due to increased levels of emission resulting from economic growth until the income level is reached, and after this, there is a fall in emissions. Various empirical works have been carried out regarding the use of Environmental Kuznets Curve in several sectors based on their levels of emissions. The sector that applies through Environmental Kuznets Curve is transport, where there is an increase in GDP, more cars are bought, and thus increased pollution arises (Grossman & Krueger, 1995; Dinda, 2004) (Stern, 2004; Saboori et al., 2014).

The findings from research conducted on the transport sector of the EKC hypothesis indicate inconclusive evidence. Some researchers highlight the existence of some form of evidence for the presence of the inverted U-shape pattern, while others point out that there exists a positive correlation between transport emissions and income levels. Several developing countries possess a low level of income where transport emissions continue to rise because of economic growth. The existence of several structural factors such as inefficient mass transportation, dependency on non-renewable energy sources, and urbanization explains the delay in turning points. It is imperative to emphasize that reducing transport emissions by focusing solely on income growth alone will be insufficient; therefore, renewable energy should be prioritized (Saboori et al., 2014; Timilsina & Shrestha, 2009).

3.3 Renewable Energy and Transport Emissions Reduction

Renewable energy should be employed to cut down the emissions since renewable energy will be replacing conventional energy sources that have been relied on up until now for energy production. Renewable energy can play an active role in cutting emissions from the transportation sector, using biofuels, and electrification of means of transport. Electrifying the transport sector by powering them with renewable energy sources will make it possible for our dependence on petroleum energy sources to become less. This will make it possible for the carbon footprint of the transport sector to be cut down significantly (Apergis & Payne, 2010; Dong et al., 2018).

The application of renewable energy sources can help reduce the emission level, but the problem is that there is a lack of evidence about the impact of the process on transport only. Research studies have emphasized the issue of the creation of energy sources rather than the means of transporting energy. Recent research shows that there is the importance of using renewable energy sources in the infrastructure of transport. The impact of reduction in transport emissions through the application of renewable energy is dependent upon three aspects: type of energy sources for generating power, level of electrification, and current state of transport infrastructure. It will not be easy for developing countries to enhance renewable fuel usage in the transport sector due to unavailability of green finance and infrastructure (Sadorsky, 2009; Apergis & Payne, 2014).

3.4 Green Finance and Sustainable Transport Infrastructure

Green Finance has emerged as an essential source of funds for sustainable infrastructure-based projects and other financial strategies that promote the shift to a low-carbon world. Green Bonds, Climate Finance, Blended Finance, and Public-Private Partnerships have been identified as potential sources of finance for environmentally sustainable projects. Green Finance has also been adopted by the Transportation Sector to provide funding for the move towards electric mobility (i.e., electric cars) and rail electrification (McKinnon, 2018; Organisation for Economic Co-operation and Development, 2021; International Transport Forum, 2023).

There are many limitations that are encountered while making decisions regarding the decarbonization of the transport industry in developing countries, and one of the primary limitations is the expensive costs of electric transport and rail development, as well as improvements in logistics. In addition, these costs demand a huge amount of money, especially at the early stages. The concept of green finance can help make these projects profitable and at the same time create a safe environment for private entities to venture into such enterprises. Many financing companies worldwide have directed their efforts towards decarbonization of transport since it is one of the main strategies to mitigate climate change. Nevertheless, although there is great interest in decarbonization of the transport industry, limited information is available on the relationship between green finance and greenhouse gas emission mitigation in developing countries (Sadorsky, 2009; Dong et al., 2018).

3.5 Dynamic Persistence and Infrastructure Lock-In

The transport activities generate persistent emissions because of the high durability of transportation infrastructures and the capital expenditure made for the construction of such infrastructures. The capital expenditures in several infrastructural assets (such as roads, vehicles, logistics facilities, etc.) generate persistent emission patterns that depend mainly on the carbon footprint of roads built, vehicle type, or logistics facilities used and their useful lives; hence, how quickly they shift to low-carbon support systems will determine this.

In literature on dynamic panel data models, it is argued that emissions from sectors like transport have a very high degree of persistence. There is a kind of lock-in problem concerning this kind of infrastructure. Hence, the interventions that will be undertaken to make the situation better should focus more on structural changes. For us to ensure sustainable development in this sector, we must start shifting our focus from infrastructure that uses fossil fuel sources to those that use renewable sources (Hansen, 1999; Apergis & Payne, 2014) (McKinnon, 2018; Organisation for Economic Co-operation and Development, 2021).

3.6 Threshold Effects and Heterogeneity in Emerging Economies

There will be different ways for different countries to put into action the transport policy regarding renewable energy. There are three basic things that affect the installation, including economic conditions, physical infrastructure, and the application of technology. It becomes easier to find out the specific relations that exist between the implementation of the two policies using threshold regression models. The implementation stages of the two different policies affect their implementation. The low-income countries will greatly benefit from the use of renewable energy since there are less developed infrastructures that lead to emissions. The high-income countries cannot benefit from the use of renewable energy infrastructures since there is a system in place for the use of energy from non-renewables (Hansen, 1999; Zhang et al., 2021).

Emerging economies are not alike in their transport network systems, urbanization systems, and energy consumption systems. The extent of emissions increase, and climate policy effectiveness will depend on the contributing factors at the national level that determine these elements. In comprehending the stage at which the implementation of a sustainable transport policy should start and how such implementations will be different depending on your current state, you can efficiently establish investment approaches towards sustainable transport alternatives. Such approaches are extremely useful in establishing environmental financing approaches in different developmental stages (Zhang et al., 2021; Sadorsky, 2009).

3.7 AI and Digitalization in Transport Decarbonization

The reduction in carbon emissions by the transport industry could be attributed to artificial intelligence and digitalization. Transportation networks using the application of AI would facilitate the development of a sustainable operation system through smart routing, traffic management, logistics prediction, and mobility solutions. The techniques in the utilization of AI technology would contribute towards the reduction of fuel consumption, congestion, and inefficiency within the transport industry. Furthermore, with smart logistics, the transportation of goods would be facilitated in an optimal manner, whereby there would be minimal instances of vehicles with no cargo and maximizing productivity.

Also, the usage of artificial intelligence in the transport industry is significant in creating mobility through effective electric transport optimization, energy consumption estimation, and implementation of alternative ways of production of electrical power. This one uses natural sources of energy while ITS uses current traffic data to manage and plan the routes to minimize pollution caused during transport of both cargo and passengers. Digital technologies have created multimodal transport systems that have made it possible to increase accessibility to public transport without having to use private cars (International Energy Agency, 2023; International Transport Forum, 2023).

3.8 Research Gap and Contribution

Even though there has been a growing number of literatures on renewable energies and emissions, there has been little work done on the topic of transport decarbonization in developing countries. Most of the literature available usually employs emission data while ignoring dynamism, threshold effects, and lock-in effects. Moreover, most of the literature on transportation emissions has failed to look at the issues of green finance and artificial intelligence (Apergis & Payne, 2010; Dong et al., 2018; Timilsina & Shrestha, 2009).

This chapter aims at filling the gap through empirical evidence based on transportation utilizing the panel dataset of 143 developing nations. The study has been conducted under the framework of examining all three components together - renewables, economic growth, and infrastructure, keeping dynamic persistence and threshold in mind. In addition to that, green finance and artificial intelligence (AI)-driven transportation infrastructure have also been explored in this chapter.

4. DATA AND VARIABLES

4.1 Data Sources and Panel Structure

The current study utilizes panel data for 143 developing nations spanning over 23 years. The dataset used in this analysis was derived from World Bank's World Development Indicators and Our World in Data, which have been employed to investigate the relationship among renewable energy, economic growth, and CO2 emissions within the transport industry (World Bank, 2024b; World Bank, 2024c; World Bank, 2024d; World Bank, 2024e; Our World in Data, 2024).

In the analysis, CO2 emissions from transportation would be the dependent variable, representing carbon emissions arising from transportation systems and logistics systems. Key independent variables include consumption of renewable energy compared to total energy consumption. Economic growth measured by GDP growth rate, energy intensity, and percentage of urbanization would be among the control variables in this analysis.

Table 1. Variable Definitions and Data Sources

Variable	Description	Unit	Source
ln_CO2	Log of transport-sector CO_2 emissions	metric tons	Our World in Data
Renewable_ Energy	Renewable energy share of total energy consumption	percent	World Bank
ln_GDP	Log of GDP (constant USD)	USD	World Bank
Energy_Intensity	Energy use per unit of GDP	MJ per USD	World Bank
Urban_Population	Urban population share	percent	World Bank
ln_CO2_L1	Lagged transport CO_2 emissions	metric tons	Calculated

Note. All variables are annual. Logarithmic transformations are applied where indicated. Subscripts i and t represent the country and year, respectively.

4.2 Descriptive Statistics

As per the descriptive statistics, one can get an idea about how the variables used in this study are distributed and varying. As per the results of descriptive statistics, it is clear that the emerging markets differ greatly in emission level, per capita income, and sources of renewable energy. In addition, it has also been seen that transport emissions differ a lot from country to country.

The disparity in the valuation of the shares of renewable energy demonstrates that the levels of transition to energy are not the same among different economies. There are disparities in energy intensity due to variations in energy efficiency and modes of transport used. The valuation of urban populations' shares is not the same among different economies, showing different levels of urbanization.

Table 2. Descriptive Statistics

Descriptive Statistics										
Variable	**count**	**mean**	**std**	**min**	**25%**	**median**	**75%**	**max**	**skewness**	**kurtosis**
Total_CO2	3822	160.6287488	787.5308766	0.007	2.034	9.901	59.37325	11284.401	9.468218638	100.5447182
GDP_WB	3822	3.61883E+11	1.57907E+12	13964732.3	5434683532	22028687446	1.43485E+11	2.56048E+13	9.243005365	101.1301788
Urban_ Population	3822	57.96088335	22.99746478	8.0438145	39.62120298	59.84183637	76.35749147	100	-0.12283491	-0.9358054
Renewable_ Energy	3770	32.85090186	29.56467474	0	7.3	23.9	54.6	96	0.666469456	-0.89456514
Energy_ Intensity	3822	5.488178964	3.601614207	0.9	3.26	4.38	6.44	30.44	2.30022056	6.904698125

4.3 Correlation Analysis

A correlation test is undertaken between the important independent variables to establish whether there is any kind of relation between them and to examine problems of multicollinearity. From the correlation matrix, it is evident that there is a strong positive correlation between GDP and transport emission due to scale effects. There is a negative correlation between renewable energy and transport emissions.

The relation between urban population and renewable energy is not very high, as far as the structure of these two factors is concerned in various nations. There is only a weak relationship between energy intensity and emissions, which indicates that efficiency may indirectly affect emissions. Overall, as per the correlation analysis, the issue of multicollinearity does not exist.

Table 3. Correlation Matrix

Correlation Matrix (Pairwise Pearson Correlations)					
	Total_CO2	**GDP_WB**	**Urban_ Population**	**Renewable_ Energy**	**Energy_ Intensity**
Total_CO2	1	**0.819550626**	0.075542075	-0.124132722	0.025876249
GDP_WB	**0.819550626**	1	0.164808177	-0.141445711	-0.047680304
Urban_Population	0.075542075	0.164808177	1	**-0.594121617**	-0.136507076
Renewable_ Energy	-0.124132722	-0.141445711	**-0.594121617**	1	0.188957506
Energy_Intensity	0.025876249	-0.047680304	-0.136507076	0.188957506	1

Note. Correlation values are calculated using the panel dataset. Values close to ±1 indicate strong relationships.

The outcome of the descriptive statistics analysis shows heterogeneity amongst emerging economies and calls for the application of panel econometric modeling. The data set forms the foundation of the empirical analysis to assess the adoption of renewable energy, economic development, and transport of greenhouse gases.

5. METHODOLOGY

This study employs a multi-model panel econometric framework to examine the determinants of transport-sector carbon emissions in emerging economies. The methodology integrates fixed effects estimation, nonlinear income modeling, interaction effects, dynamic persistence analysis, robustness testing, and threshold regression. This approach allows the analysis to capture linear, nonlinear, dynamic, and regime-dependent relationships within a unified framework.

5.1 Baseline Fixed Effects Model

The baseline specification controls unobserved country-specific heterogeneity and timespecific global shocks.

Equation (1)

$$lnCO_{2,it} = \alpha_i + \lambda_t + \beta_1 Renewable_{it} + \beta_2 lnGDP_{it} + \beta_3 EnergyIntensity_{it} + \beta_4 Urban_{it} + \varepsilon_{it}$$

Where:

- α_i= country fixed effects
- λ_t= time fixed effects
- $Renewable_{it}$= renewable energy share
- GDP_{it}= economic growth
- $EnergyIntensity_{it}$= energy intensity
- $Urban_{it}$= urban population share

5.2 Environmental Kuznets Curve (EKC) Model

To test nonlinear income effects, the EKC model includes a squared income term.

Equation (2)

$$lnCO_{2,it} = \alpha + \beta_1 lnGDP_{it} + \beta_2 \left(lnGDP_{it}\right)^2 + \beta_3 RE_{it} + \mu_i + \lambda_t + \varepsilon_{it}$$

EKC condition:

$\beta_1 > 0 and \beta_2 < 0$

Turning point income:

$$GDP^* = exp\left(\frac{\beta_1}{2\beta_2}\right)$$

5.3 Dynamic Fixed Effects Model

Transport emissions exhibit persistence due to infrastructure lock-in and long-lived capital stock. The dynamic specification includes a lagged dependent variable.

Equation (3)

$$lnCO_{2,it} = \delta lnCO_{2,it-1} + \beta_1 Renewable_{it} + \beta_2 lnGDP_{it} + \beta_3 EnergyIntensity_{it} + \beta_4 Urban_{it} + \alpha_i + \lambda_t + \varepsilon_{it}$$

Where:

- $lnCO_{2,it-1}$= lagged emissions
- δ= persistence coefficient

$0 < \delta < 1$

A higher value of δindicates stronger persistence in transport emissions.

Long-run renewable effect:

$$Long - run\ effect = \frac{\beta_1}{1 - \delta}$$

5.4 Threshold Regression Model

To examine regime-dependent effects, a threshold regression model is estimated.

Equation (4)

$$lnCO_{2,it} = \{\beta_1 Renewable_{it} + \theta X_{it} + \alpha_i + \lambda_t + \varepsilon_{it}, if\ lnGDP_{it} \le \gamma\ \beta_2 Renewable_{it} + \theta X_{it} + \alpha_i + \lambda_t + \varepsilon_{it}, if\ lnGDP_{it} > \gamma$$

Where:

- γ= estimated income threshold
- X_{it}= control variables

5.5 Robustness Checks

To ensure the stability of results, robustness tests are conducted using:

- Lagged renewable energy
- Alternative fixed effects
- Per-capita emissions
- Reduced control models

These checks confirm that the relationship between renewable energy and transport emissions remains consistent across specifications.

6. EMPIRICAL RESULTS

The Findings from a range of studies are presented in this section (Renewable Energy, GDP and Transport Emissions) using panel econometric models. The model types include fixed-effects estimation (short-run effects) Environmental Kuznets Curve (medium-run effects), as well as dynamic fixed-effects, threshold regression, and robustness testing models. The results of all these analyses show evidence of structural, non-linear, and dynamic influences in transportation emissions.

6.1 Baseline Fixed Effects Results

The study uses a fixed effects regression model based on the pre-treatment data in order to measure the impact of renewable energy on transport emissions, taking into account other factors such as economic growth, energy consumption relative to GDP, and the number of people living in urban areas.

Table 4. Fixed Effects Panel Regression (Model 1: FE)

Fixed Effects Panel Regression (Model 1: FE)				
Variable	**Coefficient**	**Std. Error**	**CI Lower**	**CI Upper**
Renewable Energy	-0.029***	-0.003	-0.035	-0.023
Energy Intensity	0.022	-0.02	-0.008	0.053
Urban Population	0.007	-0.005	-0.003	0.018
ln GDP	0.297***	-0.063	0.174	0.42
constant	-3.914**	-1.68	-7.198	-0.629

As per the results, the generation of energy from renewable sources leads to a decrease in CO2e emissions from the transportation industry. The negative and significant effect of the utilization of renewable energy (1% level) shows that an increase in the amount of renewable energy will lower total CO2e emissions generated from transportation systems. It therefore follows that utilizing renewable energy systems in the transportation system may help in decarbonizing them.

The coefficient of the economic growth index is positive and statistically significant, which means that as the income rises, the volume of transport emissions rises as well. The rise in transport emissions is because of the scale effect, which means that when there is an increase in income, there is a corresponding increase in the need for movement. This is evidenced by the increase in the number of vehicles and the volume of freight transportation caused by an increase in the movement.

Urban population index coefficient has a positive mean that urban population causes the demand for higher transportation resources & at the same time urbanization cannot be shown statistically to create increased transportation emissions.

As energy demand increases, CO2 emissions will also rise because of an increase in the amount of CO2 produced from the inefficient use of energy, according to the energy efficiency coefficient indices. Conversely, there is no evidence supporting claims that urbanization has caused a decrease in energy efficiency (for example, through an increase in CO2 emissions).

6.2 Environmental Kuznets Curve (EKC) Results

To examine nonlinear income effects, the EKC model includes squared GDP and interaction terms. This specification tests whether transport emissions follow an inverted U-shaped relationship with economic growth.

Table 5. Environmental Kuznets Curve (EKC) Model – Model 2

Environmental Kuznets Curve (EKC) Model – Model 2				
Variable	**Coefficient**	**Std. Error**	**CI Lower**	**CI Upper**
Renewable Energy	-0.061***	-0.017	-0.095	-0.027
ln GDP	0.807**	-0.372	0.078	1.537
ln GDP sq	-0.011	-0.007	-0.025	0.003
Renew x lnGDP	0.001*	-0.001	0	0.003
Energy Intensity	0.024*	-0.014	-0.004	0.052
Urban Population	0.007	-0.005	-0.003	0.017
constant	-9.579*	-5.082	-19.54	0.382

The Environmental Kuznets Curve (EKC) suggests that the economic development-transport emissions correlation isn't a straightforward one, based on the results of the research. The positive GDP coefficient along with the negative squared GDP coefficient indicate that the relationship is in the form of an inverted U-shape, which is consistent with the EKC hypothesis as applied to transport emissions and therefore supports the EKC hypothesis.

Renewable energy coefficients remain negative and significant. This means that as renewable energy increases, the emissions of CO2 decrease. Renewable energy has also been noted to have an impact on GDP specified that income levels affect its impacts. The study shows that the influence of renewable energy on carbon emissions in transport systems grows with economic growth.

6.3 Dynamic Fixed Effects Results

Long-lived infrastructure, fleets of vehicles, and logistics systems contribute to the persistence of transport emissions. The embedded lagged emissions in dynamic fixed effects model indicates that past emissions have a strong influence on current emissions, which show strong persistence in transport emissions. The coefficient for the lagged emissions variable is very high and statistically significant, indicating that infrastructure lock-in effects may occur in transport systems because of past emissions.

Table 6. Dynamic Fixed Effects Model – Model 4

Dynamic Fixed Effects Model – Model 4				
Variable	**Coefficient**	**Std. Error**	**CI Lower**	**CI Upper**
Renewable Energy	-0.008***	-0.001	-0.01	-0.006
ln GDP	0.076***	-0.016	0.046	0.107
Energy Intensity	0.009**	-0.004	0.002	0.017
Urban Population	0	-0.002	-0.003	0.004
constant	-1.073**	-0.422	-1.9	-0.246

Renewable energy will continue to reduce emissions; however, in the short term, the magnitude of the reduction will be lower than it was previously. Transport emissions are still positively related to economic growth. Energy use has a positive and statistically significant energy intensity coefficient, indicating an increase in emissions due to the use of inefficient energy sources. The urban population does not show a statistically significant relationship to transport emissions.

These findings demonstrate that transport decarbonization will require a longer-term structural transformation because of the strong persistence of emissions from transport.

6.4 Threshold Regression Results

The threshold regression model evaluates whether renewable energy has different impacts across income regimes.

Table 7. Threshold Model – Renewable Energy Regimes

Threshold Model – Renewable Energy Regimes				
Variable	**Coefficient**	**Std. Error**	**CI Lower**	**CI Upper**
Renew Low	-0.030***	-0.003	-0.036	-0.024
Renew High	-0.027***	-0.003	-0.033	-0.021
ln GDP	0.278***	-0.06	0.161	0.396
Energy Intensity	0.023*	-0.013	-0.002	0.049
Urban Population	0.006	-0.005	-0.003	0.015
constant	-3.399**	-1.582	-6.499	-0.299

Based on the findings of the threshold regression analysis, there was a positive relationship between renewable energy and transport emissions at both high and low-income levels; however, in the lower-income countries, there was a much larger coefficient associated with renewable energy, indicating that they had the most potential to reduce CO2 emissions associated with transportation through using renewable energy. Thus, the investment in RE technology when it is first available will provide a large benefit by reducing CO2 emissions produced from transportation.

The results of this study show that there is a positive correlation between transportation emissions and economic growth in addition to energy intensity and urban population level having positive coefficients that are statistically insignificant but still show a strong correlation to one another. Therefore, the conclusion can be made that all levels of economic development support the fact that introducing environmentally friendly sources of energy will decrease the total amount of transportation emissions caused from the burning of fossil fuels.

6.5 Robustness Results

Robustness checks are conducted using lagged renewable energy to confirm the stability of results.

Table 8. Robustness Check – Lagged Renewable Energy (L1)

Robustness Check – Lagged Renewable Energy (L1)				
Variable	**Coefficient**	**Std. Error**	**CI Lower**	**CI Upper**
ln GDP	0.253***	-0.06	0.136	0.37
Energy Intensity	0.02	-0.014	-0.009	0.048
Urban Population	0.005	-0.007	-0.009	0.019
constant	-18.984***	-1.633	-22.185	-15.783

This study has confirmed that renewable energy's contribution towards decreasing transport emissions is durable; thus, the impact of the adoption of renewable energy has a long-term or permanent effect on reducing levels of emissions. However, the association between an increase in economic growth and an increase in emissions continues to be statistically significant while the variables tested here were found to not have any statistical significance with respect to reducing emissions.

Overall, the results from the various analyses performed in this study lend further support to the credibility of the empirical analyses within this study; overall, the consistent conclusion across all studies indicates that the adoption of renewable energy has a statistically meaningful, and therefore, significant impact on decreasing CO_2 emissions from the transportation sector in developing countries.

7. GRAPHICAL ANALYSIS

The charts below provide substantial visual representation to back up empirical evidence from data collected via Econometrics. This includes visualization of the relationships between Renewable Energy, Economic Growth, Energy Consumption, and CO2 GHG Emissions from the Transport Sector in Emerging Economic Countries based upon the use of the Panel Dataset. Furthermore, these graphical representations help to support regression results by identifying trends, persistence, heterogeneity, and threshold-based effects across all related variables.

7.1 Renewable Energy and Transport Emissions

The relationship between renewable energy adoption and CO_2 emissions is illustrated in Figure 1. The scatter plot shows a negative association between renewable energy share and transport emissions across countries. Higher renewable energy adoption corresponds to lower emission levels.

Figure 1. CO_2 Emissions vs Renewable Energy Share

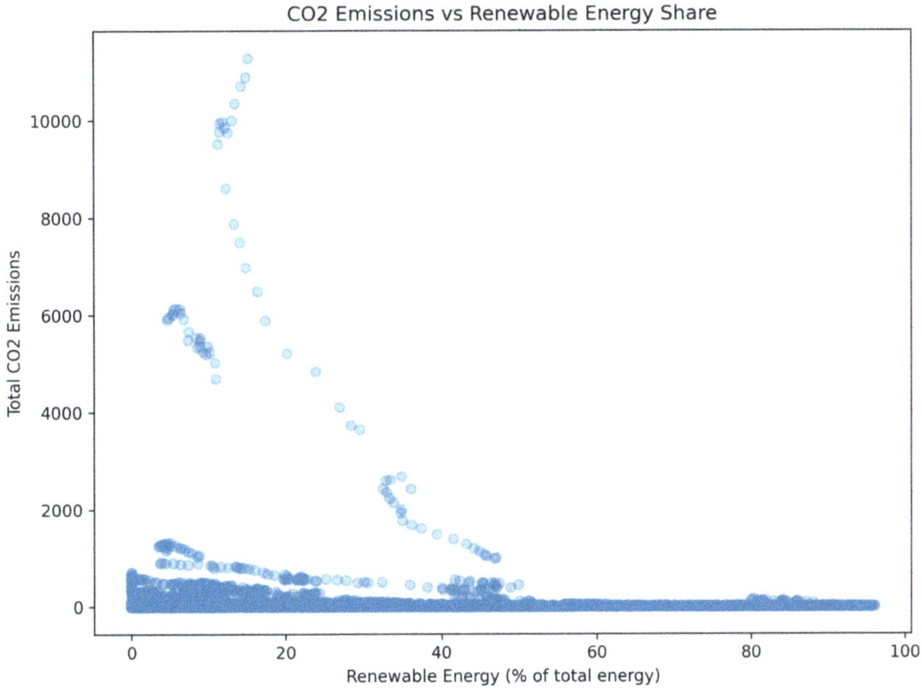

As shown in Figure 1, there is a clear link between the amount of renewable energy being used and the corresponding reduction in CO_2 emitted by several different countries. For example, as countries increase their use of renewable energy sources (indicated by the increasing % of total energy coming from renewables), their transportation-based CO_2 emissions tend to decrease because of this relationship. Similarly, if we consider the negative slope or negative relationship that's observed, we can see that by increasing the overall % of energy that's generated from renewable sources, the total amount of CO_2 produced by running transportation also tends to decrease as well.

7.2 Transport Emissions Trends in Emerging Economies

Figure 2 presents trends in transport CO_2 emissions across selected emerging economies. The figure shows increasing emissions over time, reflecting rising mobility demand and economic expansion.

Figure 2. Transport CO_2 Emissions in Emerging Economies (2010–2023)

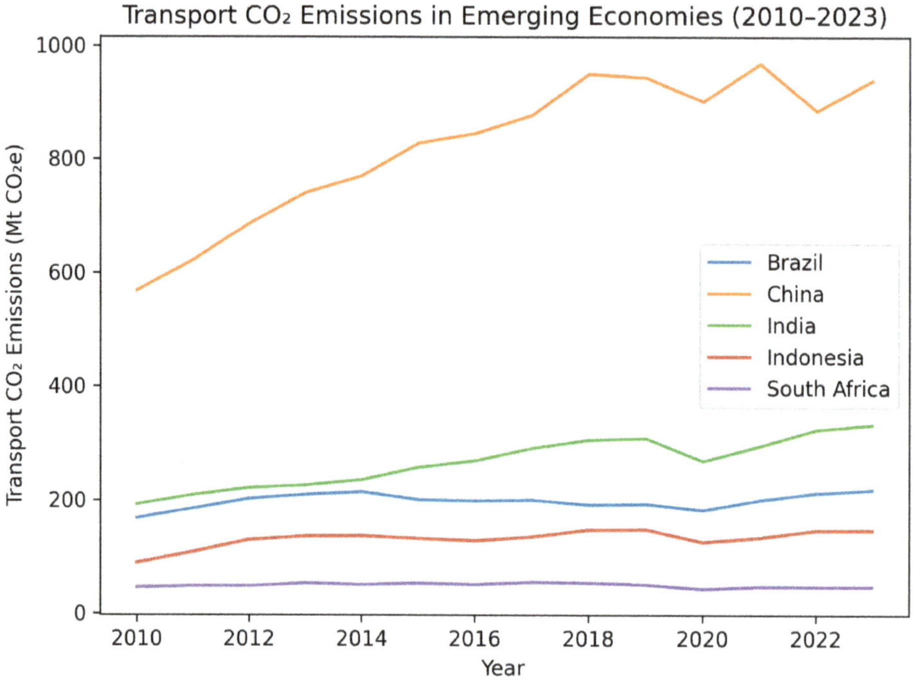

Transport emissions growth looks to be consistent on the rise across many different countries - particularly those that are emerging from lower levels of development. The relationship between economic production and transport emissions demonstrated through the regression analysis can be seen as a positive correlation. The other key result shown in this graph relates to differences in trends of transport emissions between countries worldwide.

7.3 Energy Use and Population Density

The analysis of the relationship between energy consumption and population density in developing economies as depicted in Figure 3 illustrates significant differences structurally (in terms of energy consumption) between countries in each of these areas will have similar levels of consumption and population.

Figure 3. Energy Use and Population Density in Emerging Economies

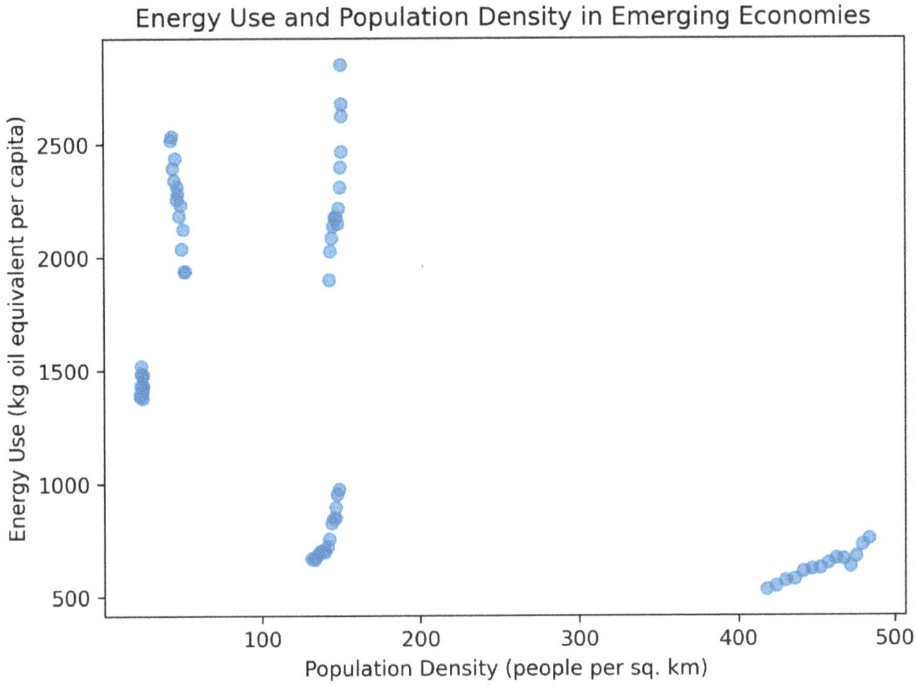

The relationship between energy consumption and population density for those countries will demonstrate that there are many countries in the world where there are large populations; however, there are less amounts of energy utilized than would typically be expected based on the population size of the most populous cities/towns in those countries. Moreover, although a large portion of those same high-density economies still have some areas that are consuming a great deal of electricity because those areas do not have good public transit systems, they also have many areas that are not providing these public transit services. For that reason, energy consumption can have a very significant effect on transportation emissions.

7.4 Threshold Effect of Population Density

Figure 4 illustrates the threshold relationship between population density and transport emissions. The vertical line indicates the estimated threshold of separating regimes.

Figure 4. Threshold Effect of Population Density on Transport Emissions

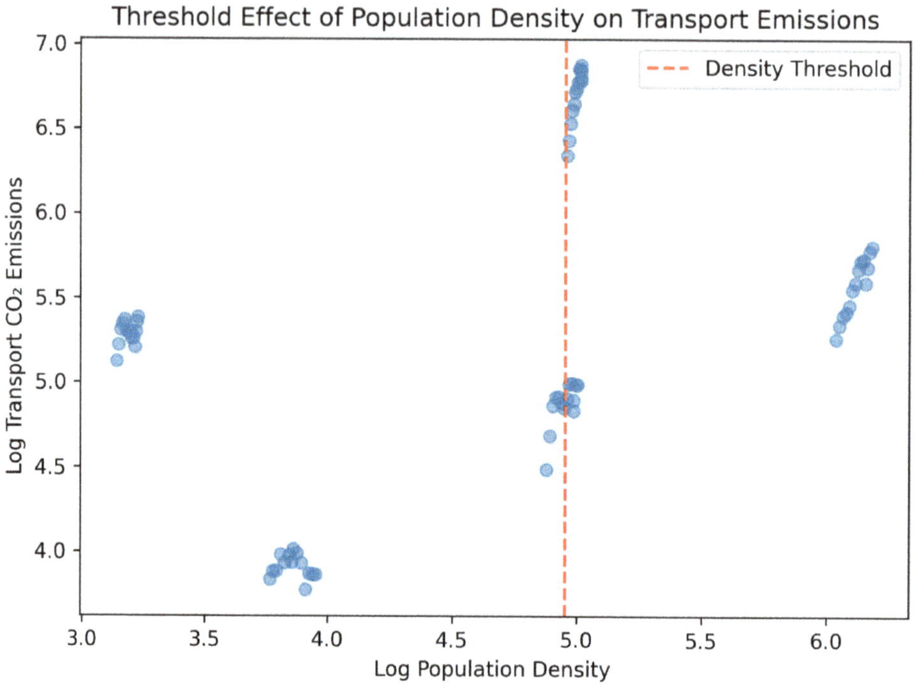

Different density regimes result in different patterns of emissions as shown in the figure; for example, among high density economies there will be one set of patterns whereas there will be another set of patterns among low density economies. The results of threshold regressions presented earlier support this finding.

7.5 Distribution of Transport Emissions Across Countries

Figure 5 presents boxplots showing the distribution of transport emissions across selected emerging economies.

Figure 5. Distribution of Transport CO_2 Emissions by Country

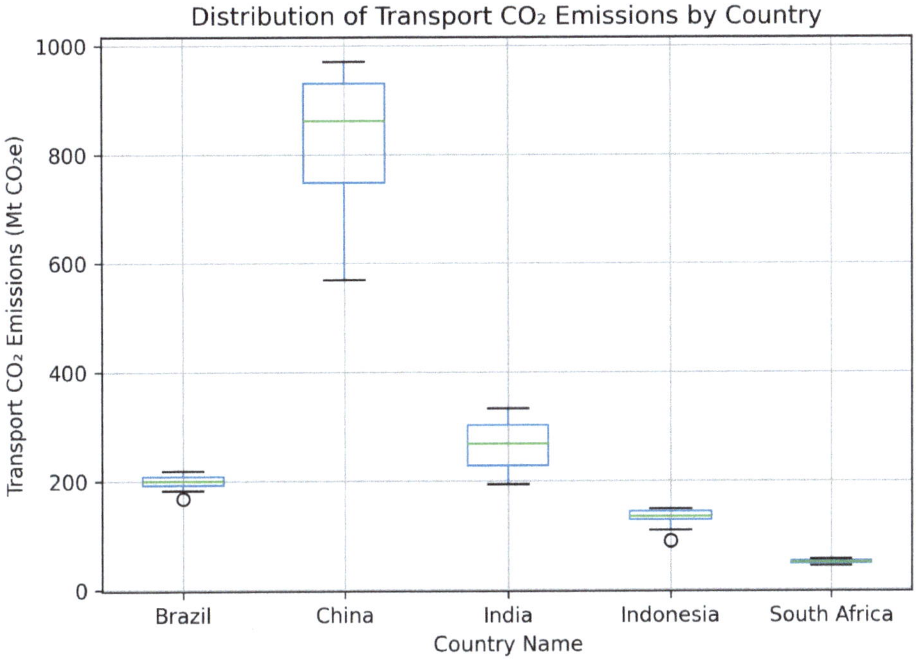

The figure highlights substantial heterogeneity across countries. Some economies exhibit significantly higher emissions, while others maintain relatively lower emission levels. This variation justifies the use of panel fixed effects models.

7.6 Economic Growth and Transport Emissions

According to Figure 6, transport emissions are positively related to Gross Domestic Product (GDP) and have a positive correlation to GDP through a scatterplot.

Figure 6. Economic Scale and Transport Emissions

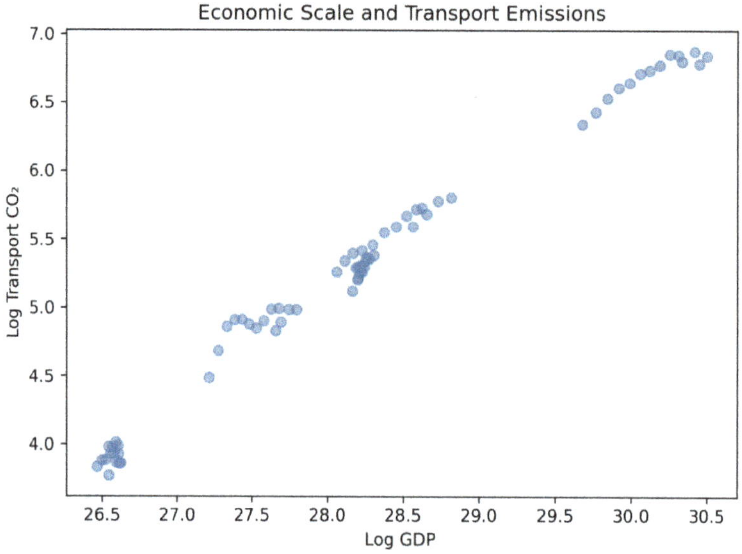

As economic activity increases, transport emissions increase (i.e., positive correlation/relationship).

These positive transport emissions with GDP values also support the positive coefficient (positive effect) for GDP discovered through a regression analysis with the original data set used in this study.

7.7 Persistence in Transport Emissions

Figure 7 shows the relationship between lagged emissions and current emissions.

Figure 7. Persistence in Transport CO_2 Emissions

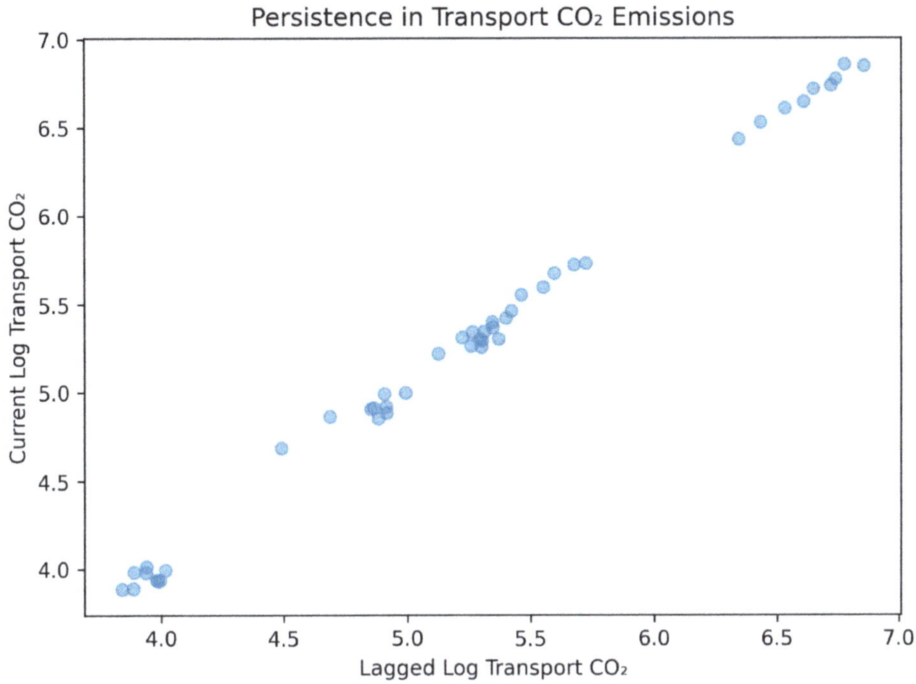

The strong positive relationship indicates high persistence in transport emissions. This supports the dynamic fixed effects model, which finds strong infrastructure lock-in effects.

7.8 Energy Use and Transport Emissions

Figure 8 presents the relationship between energy use and transport emissions.

Figure 8. Energy Use and Transport Emissions

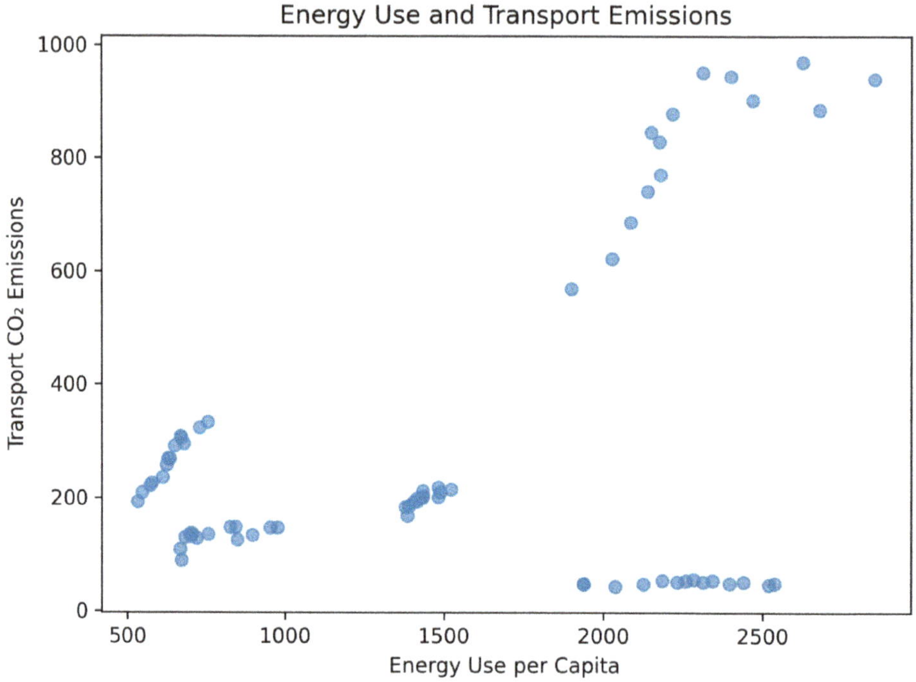

The figure shows that higher energy consumption is associated with higher transport emissions. This supports the positive coefficient on energy intensity in regression models.

7.9 Transport Emissions by Density Regime

Figure 9 presents average transport emissions across density regimes.

Figure 9. Transport Emissions by Density Regime

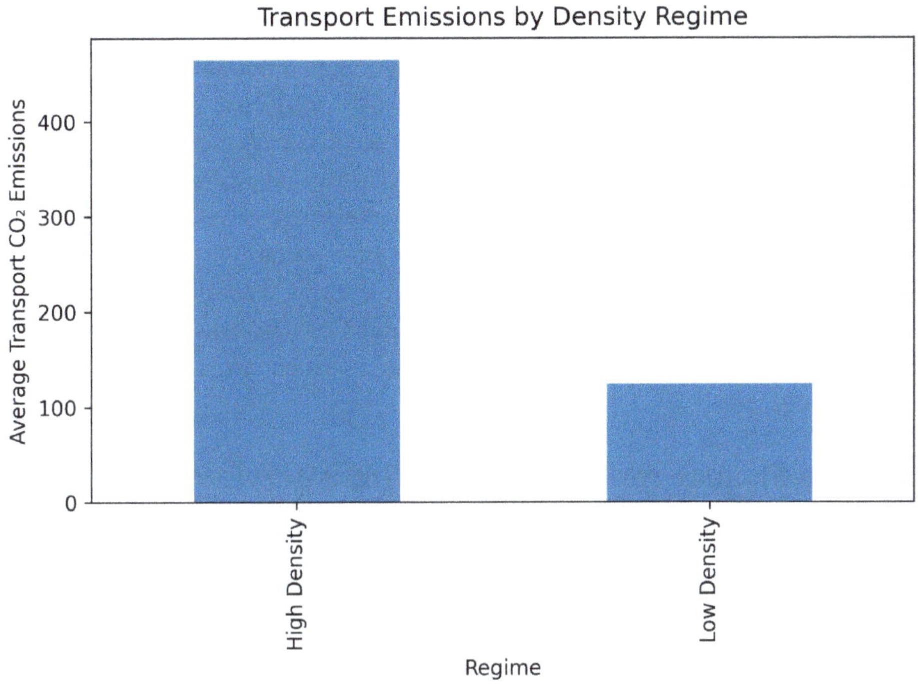

This indicates that there are observable differences in terms of emissions depending on whether someone lives within a dense or not-dense economy, which further supports the threshold regressions that were conducted earlier. The variance in emissions of densities between high-density economies and low-density economies demonstrates the presence of structural differences.

8. POLICY IMPLICATIONS

This research's findings are pertinent to policymakers aiming to decarbonize transport networks, especially in developing countries. More use of renewable energy will lead to fewer emissions from transportation. But there is another story: emissions go up when the economy grows because people are doing more.

So, we shouldn't encourage economic growth. Instead, a careful balance must be found. Developing countries need strong transport policies that help their economies grow in a way that lasts by:

Helping with green finance Making infrastructure better.

8.1 Integrating Renewable Energy Into Transportation Systems

The negative and statistically significant coefficient of renewable energy in all model parameters shows how important it is to include renewable energy in transportation networks. Using renewable energy to power electric cars can cut down on carbon emissions a lot. Policies should help electric cars, public transport that runs on renewable energy, and goods systems that run on electricity. Investing in charging stations powered by renewable energy, electric buses, and electrifying railroads can speed up the switch to low-carbon transportation.

Emerging economies need to put renewable energy at the top of their list of things to do when it comes to transportation logistics networks. Using solar and wind energy in transport systems over time cuts down on emissions and the need for fossil fuels.

8.2 Green Finance for Long-Lasting Transport Infrastructure

The results show that green finance is needed to make transport less harmful to the environment. Building long-lasting transport infrastructure costs a lot of money, and it can be hard to get into countries that aren't very developed. Green finance tools that encourage investment in low-carbon transport projects include green bonds, climate funds, blended financing, and public-private partnerships.

Green financing can help pay for things like environmentally friendly freight corridors, transportation systems powered by renewable energy, and infrastructure for electric mobility. International banks and climate funds can give a lot of money to help decarbonize transportation. Governments should also make rules that encourage green investments in transport and logistics infrastructure.

8.3 Managing Lock-In in Infrastructure

The dynamic fixed effects model shows that transport releases stay high for a long time, which is a result of infrastructure lock-in. Once carbon-heavy transport infrastructure is built, greenhouse gases stay high for a long time. This result shows that it is important to invest in environmentally friendly transport infrastructure early on.

Policy changes should focus on long-term structural changes like integrated transport planning, energy-efficient logistics systems, and electrified mobility. Investing in fossil fuel-based transportation infrastructure now could lead to future emissions lock-in. Policies for urban planning should support multimodal mobility systems, more public transportation, and cities that are easy to get around in.

8.4 Strategies for Decreasing Carbon Emissions in Transport Based on Income

The threshold regression results show that renewable energy lowers transport emissions in both high and low-income economies, with bigger benefits in low-income economies. This means that building renewable energy infrastructure early on will lead to bigger cuts in emissions. Before emissions become a reality, policy makers in developing countries should make investments in renewable transport as their top priority.

Low-income countries should focus on building public transport systems, sustainable mobility infrastructure, and energy efficient networks that run on renewable energy. In emerging economies with higher incomes, smart mobility systems and the electrification of transport should be sped up.

8.5 Rules for Moving Around Cities in a Sustainable Way

Urbanization has a big effect on transportation emissions because more people need to move around. Sustainable urban mobility policies can help lower emissions by promoting public transportation, non-motorized transportation, and integrated mobility systems. Investing in shared mobility platforms, electric buses, and metro systems can help people use fewer private cars.

Urban transportation design should include smart transportation systems and renewable energy. Compact urban design makes transportation more efficient and shorter travel times. Also, smart traffic management and congestion pricing can help cities cut down on pollution.

8.6 Getting rid of Carbon in Logistics and Freight

In developing countries, freight transportation is a major source of transportation emissions. Achieving climate targets requires decarbonizing logistics networks. Rail-based logistics, energy-efficient supply chains, and electric freight transportation should all be promoted by policy. Adding renewable energy to ports and logistical hubs can help cut down on emissions even more.

Digital logistics solutions can make loads more efficient, cut down on empty vehicle trips, and find the best routes. Both pollution and fuel consumption are decreased by these actions. Transportation decarbonization can be greatly aided by renewable energy-powered sustainable freight corridors.

8.7 Role of Policy Coordination

Transport decarbonization requires energy policy to align with transport policy and financial regulation. The first needs deployment of renewables to be done in concert with strategies for electrification of transport. Green finance regimes need to be designed to support long-term infrastructure investments. The coordination of necessary policies ensures that investments in renewable energy are associated with reductions in transport emissions.

This requires permanent policies for decarbonizing transport, integrating renewable energy uptake with green financing, and sustainable smart transport systems. Policies like these, when closely coordinated, can accelerate the transition to sustainable mobility in developing economies.

9. DIGITALIZATION AND AI IN THE TRANSPORTATION INDUSTRY - THE DECARBONATION PROCESS OF TRANSPORTATION SYSTEMS

Transportation Systems Are Transforming and Being Reshaped with Digitalization and Artificial Intelligence That Are Creating New Methods for Reducing Carbon Emissions Associated with Transportation Systems. By Using AI-Driven Optimization, Smart Mobility Systems and Digital Logistics Platforms in Combination, Energy Use and Overall Efficiency Oo Transportation Can Be Drastically Reduced, Therefore Reducing Transportation Emissions Significantly. As A Result, Developing Countries Who Have A Rapidly Growing Demand For Transportation Can Utilize AI-Powered Solutions to Distinguish Between the Growth of Mobility and the Growth Of Emission.

9.1 Traffic Optimization Driven by AI

Alright, so you are aware that you are sitting at a red light in your car. And You're just waiting when there's absolutely no one else around? Burning gasoline for nothing at all? It irritates me. AI traffic systems are attempting to address precisely that kind of foolish inefficiency.

It's actually very cool how it operates. These systems collect data from throughout the globe. signals, traffic cameras, road sensors, and everything else they can obtain. Additionally, traffic lights react to current events rather than endlessly cycling through red, yellow, and green on a schedule that a city planner established decades ago.

9.2 Intelligent Freight and Logistics Management

Freight transport is one of the fastest-growing sources of transport emissions, particularly in developing economies where road-based logistics dominates. Heavy-duty trucks alone account for over 35% of direct CO_2 emissions from road transport, despite representing a small share of vehicles. Freight logistics overall contributes about 7–8% of global greenhouse-gas emissions, making efficiency improvements in this segment critical for decarbonization.

A major inefficiency in freight systems is poor load utilization and fragmented routing. Studies show that 15–20% of truck miles are driven empty, leading to wasted fuel, congestion, and avoidable emissions. AI-based logistics platforms address this issue using real-time data, predictive analytics, and automated load matching. These systems optimize delivery schedules, route planning, and vehicle allocation to reduce empty trips and maximize cargo utilization. AI-enabled route optimization alone can reduce fuel use and emissions by 15–30% in some scenarios, while broader AI logistics adoption can cut sector emissions by around 10–15% through improved capacity management and operational efficiency.

AI also improves operational decision-making across freight networks. Machine-learning models analyze traffic, weather, demand forecasts, and warehouse availability to dynamically assign loads and minimize travel distance. In real-world deployments, AI freight-matching platforms have reduced empty miles by 10–15%, while improving truck utilization and delivery efficiency. Additionally, predictive maintenance and driver-behavior analytics further reduce fuel consumption and idle time, improving both economic and environmental performance.

Another critical dimension is AI-enabled multimodal logistics, which shifts freight from high-emission road transport to lower-carbon modes such as rail, inland waterways, and coastal shipping. Road freight typically produces significantly higher emissions per tonne-kilometre than rail or waterways, making modal optimization essential for decarbonization. Intelligent logistics platforms evaluate cost, time, and carbon intensity simultaneously, selecting the most efficient combination of truck-rail-ship transport. Research shows that coordinated multimodal freight systems can dramatically reduce fossil-fuel use and carbon emissions compared with road-dominant logistics structures.

Overall, AI-driven intelligent freight management reduces emissions through three main mechanisms:

- improved capacity utilization (fewer empty trucks),
- optimized routing and scheduling (shorter distances and lower fuel use), and
- modal shifts to low-carbon transport options.

These digital freight ecosystems not only lower emissions but also reduce logistics costs, improve delivery reliability, and increase supply-chain transparency—making them a central pillar in the decarbonization of transportation systems, particularly in emerging economies where logistics inefficiencies remain high.

9.3 Combining AI with Electric Vehicles

AI is improving electric mobility in many significant ways. These AI algorithms, for instance, assist in determining when devices should be charged. Additionally, they are more effective at reducing peak demand periods when everyone is using it at once and integrating renewable energy sources. That appears to have an impact.

By ensuring that our energy use aligns with nearby renewable energy sources, smart charging networks do comparable tasks. That likely reduces the amount of carbon released into the atmosphere. Although I'm not entirely certain of the precise figures, this seems like a reasonable sum. AI in battery management systems is another example.

9.4 Planning for Urban Mobility Based on Data

By using real-time data to organize transportation, digitization gives us to make decisions that truly take into understanding people's movements and current needs. To create smarter, more effective networks, AI systems it analyze travel patterns, identify changes based on people's demand, and determine the capacity of our infrastructure. This strategy gives a variety of different modes of transportation, including bikes, car sharing, buses and trains. And, digitization primarily helps us to invest in infrastructure where it matters the most. AI can do predictive research to identify the pathways where people most require renewable energy sources or electric charging.

9.5 Mobility Planning Through Digitization

Mobile mobility platforms help to combine different forms of transport, including buses, trains, car-shares and bicycles, to make it simple for consumers to select the option that has the least impact on the environment. This, coupled with a wide range of available features such as integrated ticketing and real-time tracking, enables consumers to more easily use public transport rather than drive their own cars.

The switch from gas-guzzling automobiles to more eco-friendly options with less harmful effects on the atmosphere will reduce carbon emissions, so this digital platform provides significant benefits; ease of operation requires interoperability among multiple systems. In addition to improving air quality, improved public transportation will advance urban modernization in developing economies through environmentally responsible alternatives.

9.6 AI and Emissions Monitoring

Artificial Intelligence is transforming the way that we monitor transportation-related pollution sources. Satellite surveillance, ground-level sensors, and computer-based tracking systems allow us to see in real time how much pollution from vehicles and transportation networks the world is producing. With access to accurate real-time data, politicians will be able to make good laws and determine what really works, thus expediting change in their policies. With the combination of artificial intelligence (AI), digital technology, renewable energy, and green financing, there is now a powerful approach for mitigating transportation emissions. Smarter infrastructure, enhancements in logistics and intelligent transportation, when utilized together, enable the reductions of pollutants from our planet and promote economic growth. Countries with fast-growing transportation networks will find these solutions to be helpful; however, they will also likely be essential for some nations as they develop their transportation networks.

10. CONCLUSION

This chapter analyzed how deploying renewable energy and using green finance strategies can reduce carbon emissions from the transport sector in emerging economies. This analysis involved the use of a broad econometric method based on the use of a panel data method with fixed effects, EKC interaction, dynamic fixed effects, robustness checks, and threshold regression to capture the linear/non-linear/dynamic/regime-dependent relationships that are key to achieving decarbonization in transport

There are several important conclusions from the analysis; firstly, the use of renewable energy generally has a negative effect on transport emissions across all models considered, thereby confirming that renewable energy is a key pathway to mitigating transport emissions. Secondly, income growth will have a positive effect on transport emissions as it is a scale effect, whilst only partial support for the EKC has been found, indicating that economic growth does not guarantee decarbonization for emerging economies. Thirdly, the dynamic model found a very high persistence of emissions, indicating that the infrastructure is "locked in" and that progress will take time, thus indicating that short-run policy interventions will need to be supported by longrun investments. Fourthly, the threshold regression analysis indicates that renewable energy is effective in all income groups; however, the abatement benefit will be higher in lower-income contexts and highlight the importance of intervening early.

The findings from the EKC model have provided insufficient evidence for the existence of a nonlinear association between income and emissions from transport. First, there is a positive association between emissions and income; however, the incorporation of renewable energy plays a vital role in altering this trend. There is a significant link between renewable energy and income, which shows that renewable energy-based transport infrastructure gains more prominence as economies develop. The findings suggest that incorporating renewable energy sources is crucial to compensate for emissions increases.

According to the dynamic fixed effect model, transport emissions remain constant across time periods, implying that infrastructure lock-ins exist. The lagged emissions coefficient indicates that past infrastructure decisions influence current emissions to a large extent. Persistence makes eliminating carbon emissions from transportation difficult without proper planning for a considerable period of time. Incorporating renewable energy into transportation infrastructure at its early stage can reduce future emissions by preventing the infrastructure lock-ins of high-carbon emissions transportation modes.

Findings from the threshold of regression indicate that renewable energy reduces the level of transportation emission regardless of the level of income, although the impact is slightly stronger in lower-income economies. This indicates that the adoption of renewable energy infrastructure in advance results in larger reductions in emissions. Policymakers from emerging economies need to prioritize renewable transportation infrastructure ahead of time to avoid embedding carbon emission into the environment permanently. Various policies depending on the level of income can facilitate the reduction of carbon emissions from transportation sources.

The graphical representation proves the econometric results in terms of the presence of negative relationship between renewable energy use and emissions, positive correlation between economic growth and emissions and the strong persistence in case of transport emissions. Moreover, the numerical values indicate the existence of country differences and differences according to the density regimes. All these confirm the practical evidence and demonstrate the existence of structural differences between emerging economies.

Green financing is key for policymakers looking to build transport infrastructure. It provides the capital needed for sustainable transport systems. Instruments like bonds and dedicated funds make this possible. Governments and private groups can team up to reach these goals. It's especially helpful for developing nations without many resources. This gives them a way to invest in new transport systems, helping create the modern, sustainable networks we all need.

On balance I think it's safe to say that making transport carbon neutral in emerging countries needs a plan. This plan should include using energy sources having money for sustainable projects building new infrastructure and using smart transport systems. These things work together to create a way to make transport infrastructure sustainable and have low emissions in developing countries. Achieving carbon-transport needs all these parts to come together. It is a matter of using sources having finance, for sustainability overhauling infrastructure and using intelligence-based transport systems. The goal is to have transport infrastructure and low-emissions mobility in emerging and developing nations.

Overall, the findings suggest that decarbonizing transport in emerging economies requires a comprehensive strategy combining renewable energy integration, green finance, infrastructure transformation, and intelligent transport systems. Renewable energy reduces emissions; green finance enables investment, and AI-driven systems improve efficiency. Together, these elements provide a pathway toward sustainable transport infrastructure and low-carbon mobility in emerging economies.

REFERENCES

Apergis, N., & Payne, J. E. (2010). Renewable energy consumption and economic growth: Evidence from a panel of OECD countries. *Energy Policy*, *38*(1), 656–660. DOI: 10.1016/j.enpol.2009.09.002

Apergis, N., & Payne, J. E. (2014). Renewable energy, output, CO_2 emissions, and fossil fuel prices: Evidence from a nonlinear panel model. *Energy Economics*, *42*, 226–232. DOI: 10.1016/j.eneco.2014.01.003

Dinda, S. (2004). Environmental Kuznets curve hypothesis: A survey. *Ecological Economics*, *49*(4), 431–455. DOI: 10.1016/j.ecolecon.2004.02.011

Dong, K., Sun, R., & Hochman, G. (2018). Do natural gas and renewable energy consumption lead to lower carbon emission? *Renewable & Sustainable Energy Reviews*, *82*, 370–379. DOI: 10.1016/j.rser.2017.09.046

Grossman, G. M., & Krueger, A. B. (1995). Economic growth and the environment. *The Quarterly Journal of Economics*, *110*(2), 353–377. DOI: 10.2307/2118443

Hansen, B. E. (1999). Threshold effects in non-dynamic panels: Estimation, testing, and inference. *Journal of Econometrics*, *93*(2), 345–368. DOI: 10.1016/S0304-4076(99)00025-1

International Energy Agency. (2023). *The future of trucks: Implications for energy and the environment*. International Energy Agency. https://www.iea.org/reports/the-future-of-trucks

International Transport Forum. (2023). *ITF transport outlook 2023: Decarbonising freight transport*. OECD Publishing. https://www.itf-oecd.org/transport-outlook-2023

McKinnon, A. (2018). Decarbonizing logistics: Distributing goods in a low-carbon world. *Transport Reviews*, *38*(3), 295–297. DOI: 10.1080/01441647.2017.1389991

Organisation for Economic Co-operation and Development. (2021). *Decarbonising freight transport: Policy recommendations*. OECD Publishing. https://www.oecd.org/transport/decarbonising-freight-transport.htm

Our World in Data. (2024). *CO_2 and greenhouse gas emissions*. https://ourworldindata.org/co2-and-greenhouse-gas-emissions

Saboori, B., Sulaiman, J., & Mohd, S. (2014). Economic growth and CO_2 emissions in developing countries: Evidence from the environmental Kuznets curve hypothesis. *Energy Policy*, *65*, 304–311. DOI: 10.1016/j.enpol.2013.10.061

Sadorsky, P. (2009). Renewable energy consumption and income in emerging economies. *Energy Policy*, *37*(10), 4021–4028. DOI: 10.1016/j.enpol.2009.05.003

Stern, D. I. (2004). The rise and fall of the environmental Kuznets curve. *World Development*, *32*(8), 1419–1439. DOI: 10.1016/j.worlddev.2004.03.004

Timilsina, G. R., & Shrestha, A. (2009). Transport sector CO_2 emissions growth in Asia: Underlying factors and policy options. *Energy Policy*, *37*(11), 4523–4539. DOI: 10.1016/j.enpol.2009.06.009

World Bank. (2024a). *Energy use (kg of oil equivalent per capita)*. World Development Indicators. https://data.worldbank.org/indicator/EG.EGY.PRIM.PP.KD

World Bank. (2024b). *GDP (current US$)*. World Development Indicators. https://data.worldbank.org/indicator/NY.GDP.MKTP.CD

World Bank. (2024c). *Renewable energy consumption (% of total final energy consumption)*. World Development Indicators. https://data.worldbank.org/indicator/EG.FEC.RNEW.ZS

World Bank. (2024d). *Urban population (% of total population)*. World Development Indicators. https://data.worldbank.org/indicator/SP.URB.TOTL.IN.ZS

World Bank. (2024e). *World development indicators*. https://databank.worldbank.org/source/world-development-indicators

Zhang, Y., Wang, W., & Liang, S. (2021). Threshold effects of renewable energy on carbon emissions in developing economies. *Energy Economics*, *98*, 105255. DOI: 10.1016/j.eneco.2021.105255

Chapter 10
Reimagining Logistics Systems for Sustainable Supply Chain Transformation

A. Priscila
http://orcid.org/0009-0009-4733-639X
Saveetha School of Management, Saveetha Institute of Medical and Technical Sciences, Chennai, India

R. Durai Pandian
http://orcid.org/0000-0003-2932-0270
Saveetha School of Management, Saveetha Institute of Medical and Technical Sciences, Chennai, India

M. Siva Sarswathi
http://orcid.org/0009-0000-1840-495X
Saveetha School of Management, Saveetha Institute of Medical and Technical Sciences, Chennai, India

V. Selvalakshmi
Saveetha School of Management, Saveetha Institute of Medical and Technical Sciences, Chennai, India

ABSTRACT

Logistics is a major contributor to greenhouse emissions and environmental degradation which calls for a shift to a more sustainable and decarbonized model of operation. This chapter explores the significance of green logistics in the attainment of sustainable development goals, with a focus on the mediating effect of environ-

DOI: 10.4018/979-8-3373-9003-1.ch010

mental performance. This chapter presents a conceptual framework that combines eco efficient transportation, warehousing, reverse logistics and digitalization to sustainability. This is based on institutional theory, which explains how supportive policies, market forces, digitalization and firm competences reform green logistics adoption. This chapter presents real life examples of the application of sustainable logistics strategies. This chapter concludes that a supportive environment, innovation and firm competences enable logistics firms to effectively balance economic and environmental sustainability.

1. INTRODUCTION

The transition towards a low carbon transport system and sustainability has emerged at the core of the global discourse on development. The sustainability Agenda of 2030 underlines the requirement for transformative change in the systemic dimensions of the economic environment and the industry (Weiland et al., 2021). The transformative change in the factors through the achievement of SDGs need to be attained, especially those sectors which are carbon intensive (Sachs et al., 2019). As the movement of goods in the international trade and industrialization is considered as a vital part, whereas logistics industry is at the heart of the sustainability challenge.

In the context of socio technical, the constraint in the sustainability transition requires a structural change in the technological, institutional and business dimensions (Geels et al., 2017) where the conventional logistics industry, which usually relies on fossil fuel focuses on the optimization of logistics performance, needs a structural change towards a low carbon and resource efficient logistics industry. In terms of economic perspective, the embedding of sustainability into the logistics industry is not only a need for environmental improvement but also a strategic change in (Montabon et al., 2016). Emerging evidence supporting the argument that environmentally responsible logistics practices contribute favourably towards the improvement of environmental performance through the achievement of sustainability in economic level (Khan et al., 2020). However the linkage between sustainability achievement and sustainable logistics practices is complex as it requires integrative analytical tools. This chapter fills the analytical gap by exploring the contribution of green logistics practices, supported by institutional, technological and organizational drivers for the accomplishment towards sustainability to improvise the environmental progress.

This chapter provides research on green logistics and decarbonized transport systems. Firstly, to create an integrated conceptual framework by combining environmental performance, green logistics practices and Sustainable development goals which bridges the policy and operational perspectives. Secondly it underscores the environmental performance's mediating role in linking sustainability outcomes with logistics practices. Thirdly, this chapter examines the digital technologies role notably in artificial intelligence by enabling efficient low carbon logistics systems. Finally, to provide a brief explanation of comprehensive sustainable logistics transformation, the policy frameworks integrate the real world case applications and organizational capabilities.

2. RESEARCH AIM AND OBJECTIVES

This chapter aims to examines the contribution of sustainable logistics practices with the incorporation of environmental performance for attaining sustainable development to improve broader the objectives towards decarbonization in transforming the economy . This chapter is underpinned by the concept of sustainability transition (Geels et al., 2017) and aligns with the transformative goals of the SDGs (Weiland et al., 2021; Sachs et al., 2019), whereas integrated framework will be developed to connect logistics operation strategies and sustainability outcomes. The objectives of the chapter to achieve the aim are as follows:

- To analyse the contribution of green logistics to systemic sustainability transitions in transport and supply chain systems (Geels et al., 2017).
- To investigate the environmental performance's intermediate role in the linkage towards sustainable economic development and sustainable logistics (Khan et al., 2020).
- To assess the sustainability principles and logistics collaboration to ensure strategic viability (Montabon et al., 2016).
- To conceptualize a framework to connect green logistics practices, SDGs for better environmental operations. (Khan et al., 2020).

3. STRUCTURE OF THE CHAPTER

To attain a methodical and structure knowledge of the theme, this chapter is framed in a systematic manner with the following key elements:

Conceptual Frameworks: The core of this chapter is a framework that brings together green logistics and sustainable development. This framework will underscores the linkage towards green practices and the role that highlights eco-friendly transportation, digital technologies, reverse logistics and supportive policies as part of environmental performance which contributes to the attainment of SDGs.

Theoretical Framework: In this section, the theoretical perspectives from Institutional theory, Resource Based View (RBV), Stakeholder theory and Dynamic capabilities Theory support the analysis of sustainable logistics systems which help to explain the regulatory pressures, stakeholder expectations, strategic resources and organizational capabilities which influence the fostering of green supply chain strategies driven by sustainable logistics practices.

Research Methodology: The methodology approach that has been adopted in this chapter is a SLR based on the PRISMA framework consists of existing literature on sustainable supply chain operations and logistics systems. It reviewed further relevant academic articles, scholarly publications and reports to identify the core themes and evolving trends in the research on sustainable logistics practices and their environmental performance.

Managerial and Regulatory Implications: This part will provide a practical and managerial steps to add the green logistics integration into the logistics operations relies on the search from the existing research articles, practical case studies across organizations which emphasize on policy framework, adoption digital tools, organizational development in logistics operations as the major enabler to create a sustainable logistics systems.

Future Research Directions: This section identifies the opportunities for research in emerging directions such as AI, blockchain and sustainable logistics innovation and emphasis will be on research opportunities in sustainable logistics and carbon neutral transportation systems that can be achieved with the help of policy instruments for developing low carbon logistics systems.

Conclusions: The last section will summarize the key findings of the chapter as it emphasizes the need for the green logistics practices, technological innovation and supportive policy framework integration to achieve the environmental sustainability and long term supply chain resilience.

4. CONCEPTUAL FRAMEWORK

The sustainability oriented development outcomes is essential to attain environmental performance and could be achieved through green logistics practices. Energy efficient warehousing, sustainable packaging, environmentally responsible transportation and reverse logistics as these practices collectively contribute across supply chains through emissions reduction, waste minimization and improved energy efficiency. The mediating mechanism of environmental performance links the broader sustainability outcomes and green logistics practices which are aligned with global development priorities.

The conceptual framework further integrates key internal and external drivers which influence the green logistics practices adoption. For logistics adoption, external factors notably carbon market mechanisms, policy and regulatory pressures which create institutional incentives. Further, the internal capabilities, organizational competencies as well as the utilization of digital technologies like AI, data driven systems enhance environmental outcomes and operational efficiency.

Thus the framework creates a structured linkages between environmental performance, green logistics practices and sustainable development outcomes, which supports the technological and institutional enablers which facilitates the sustainable and low carbon logistics systems transition.

The below Figure 1 demonstrates the framework of the study

Figure 1. Conceptual Framework of Green Logistics and Sustainability

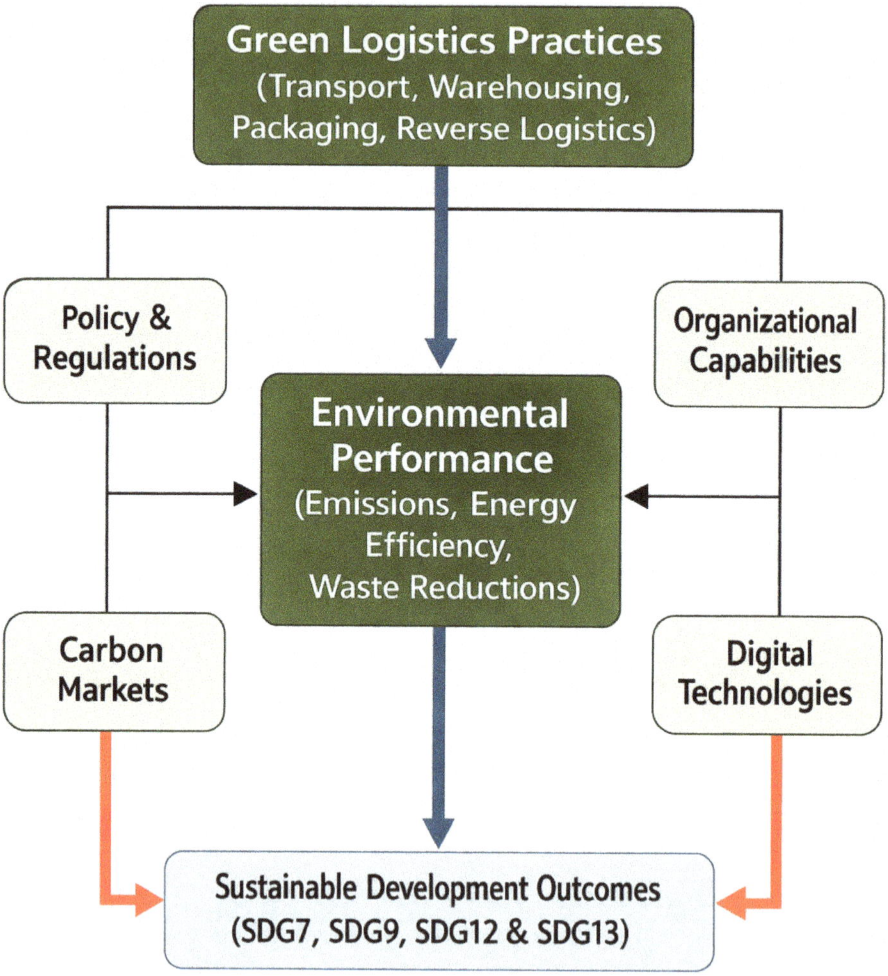

4.1 Green Logistics and Sustainable Development

Green logistics play a vital role by addressing environmental concerns in sustainable supply chain performance by eliminating carbon emissions (Lagorio et al., 2016). Transportation, warehousing and distribution logistics activities contribute efficiently to emissions requiring environmental integration (Ben Daya et al., 2019). Thus green logistics supports SDG 7, 9, 12 and 13 through responsible production and optimized energy use (Kazancoglu et al., 2023).

Therefore, green transport systems, sustainable packaging and reverse logistics practices improvise efficiency and sustainability with the contribution from digital technologies which enhance monitoring and performance (Saxena et al., 2023).

4.1.1 Evolution of Green Logistics for Decarbonization

Early Recognition and Regulatory Drivers

Green logistics first began to develop as a response to policy regulations aimed at pollution control which cause environmental damage. The companies in the early stage mainly focused on meeting emission standards, improving fuel efficiency, and managing waste more responsibly. These early measures were largely reactive, as they were implemented responding to the need in supply chain management to comply with regulations rather than a fully integrated, end to end sustainability strategy (Searcy, 2016).

Strategic Integration of Environmental Goals

Over time, sustainability has transformed its compliance activity to a key business strategy as the organizations are using sustainability goals to influence their logistics planning and decision making processes. The sustainable practices enable organizations in supply chain operations in the process of remanufacture, recycle and recover resources as alternatives (Govindan et al., 2015). These green initiatives helped organizations "close the loop" while improving environmental sustainability (Zhu et al., 2008).

Technological Advancements and Decarbonization

Significantly, technological advancements have helped organizations accelerate their journey toward a greener logistics system as these technological advancements, including the use of digital tools, route optimizations reduce fuel consumption and minimize inefficiencies in their operations (Ben Daya et al., 2019). Moreover the incorporation of Industry 5.0 technologies has helped organizations accelerate their journey toward a circular economy, including increased product traceability and resource efficiency (Kazancoglu et al., 2023). At the same time, organizations are using carbon footprint reduction methodologies to ensure decarbonization (McKinnon, 2018).

Collaborative Platforms and Policy Alignment

The collaborative platform along with policy alignment, is essential in the application of green logistics as the freight consolidation, shared transportation and urban logistics models work together to ensure the maximum load efficiency of vehicles, thus reducing emissions (Lagorio et al., 2016).In addition, global initiatives targets encourage organizations to mark emission reduction limits which align towards climate science and enhance transparency in sustainability reporting. Overall, this green logistics has become an advanced strategy that uses technology to facilitate sustainable development and decarbonised transportation networks.

Table 1. Comparison between Traditional Logistics and Green Logistics Practices

Aspect	Traditional Logistics	Green Logistics
Transportation	It relies heavily on inefficient routing and fossil fuels (Demir et al., 2014).	It use the low emission transport, modal shifts and route optimization (Fahimnia et al., 2015).
Energy Use	High energy consumption with limited efficiency measures.	Integration of sustainable energy sources optimized systems.
Warehousing	Conventional warehouse with high energy usage.	Green warehouses with energy efficient design and operations (Fahimnia et al., 2015).
Packaging	Excessive and non-recyclable packaging materials.	Sustainable and recyclable packaging solutions.
Waste Management	Limited focus on waste reduction and disposal practices (Agrawal et al., 2015).	Emphasis on waste minimization, reuse and recycling (Govindan et al., 2015).
Reverse Logistics	Minimal implementation of product return and recovery systems (Agrawal et al., 2015).	Strong integration of reverse logistics for recycling and remanufacturing (Govindan et al., 2015).
Environmental Impact	High carbon emissions and ecological footprint (Demir et al., 2014).	Reduced emissions and improved environmental performance (Fahimnia et al., 2015).
Strategic Focus	Cost and efficiency driven with limited sustainability integration.	Adoption of sustainability oriented objectives. (Fahimnia et al., 2015).

As these comparisons brings out the shift from the traditional logistics framework, which is cost based to the green logistics technique which focuses on resource efficiency and environmental aspects.

4.1.2 Sustainable Logistics and Triple Bottom Line

Sustainable logistics is a combination of economic efficiency, environmental sustainability and social responsibility incorporated directly into supply chains. It is not just about viewing merely as regulation obligations, increasingly organizations are integrating sustainability into their logistics strategies and performance metrics (Rajeev et al., 2017).

From an economic perspective, sustainable logistics increases competitive advantage and smooth supply chain operations through optimized routes, green transport modes and energy efficient warehousing. These sustainable logistics operations reduce costs and improve productivity (Yawar & Seuring, 2017). While green technology requires high capital expenditures, it ultimately reduces costs and increases supply chain resilience and lower risk of carbon regulations.

From a natural environment perspective, logistics operations generate a substantial part of greenhouse gas emissions and natural resource usage, requiring structural and organizational changes such as green transport and resource management (Abbasi & Nilsson, 2016).

4.2 Green Logistics in Transportation and Distribution

In this context, it is to limits impact towards environment; while in addition maintaining smooth and efficient transportation as it encompasses a variety of activities which includes warehousing, packaging, transportation management, and reverse logistics (Govindan, 2015). Rather than addressing a small part of a system, organizations are working to make fundamental changes to the entire system to reduce environmental impact, reduce energy consumption and minimize waste. Green road freight has been a subject of research, including fuel efficient routing, emissions planning and using alternatives to reduce carbon intensity (Demir et al., 2014). In addition, incorporating green logistics throughout the entire supply chain improves sustainability through better coordination, a more structured rollout and performance monitoring.

4.2.1 Eco Friendly Transport and Reverse Logistics

Sustainable transport aims at as improvise planning routes that consume less fuel, reducing the number of trips through load consolidation, adopting green driving habits and using the most appropriate modes of transport without limiting the efficiency towards delivery process. On the other note, the reduction of freight emissions aims at reducing the consumption of fuel while incorporating sustainability into the entire delivery strategy activities (Demir et al., 2014). However, incorporation of the above practices relies heavily on the elimination of the challenges that exists at the organizational level.

Green Warehousing Practices

Green warehousing involves conducting warehouse management in a manner which is energy efficient and environmentally friendly as the green warehousing is attainable through efficient lighting, efficient warehouse design, automated handling of materials and minimizing idle time for equipment (Agrawal, 2015). Green principles embedded in warehouse management will result in efficient use of resources, thereby improving the overall supply chain's environmental performance.

Sustainable Packaging and Distribution

Sustainable packaging and distribution is important for the environment, especially for the last mile of delivery, including the return of products as the major goal is to reduce the packaging materials, increase the recyclability of the materials which ensures that the packaging is space efficient during delivery. Smart packaging does not only protect the environment but enhances the entire delivery process efficiently (Lagorio et al., 2016).

Reverse Logistics and Circular Integration

Reverse logistics and circular integration mainly involve the handling of returned products, remanufacturing, recycling and waste recovery activities and thereby implementing circular supply chain models, companies can significantly reduce their environmental footprint which enhance the utilization of their resources. Whereas, reverse logistics systems help reduce waste and achieve sustainability (Agrawal et al., 2015).

4.3 Decarbonization for Sustainable Logistics

The integration of energy efficient and low carbon technologies are essential for making suitable transport and distribution networks. The shift towards electric mobility is considered as one of the most important developments (Queiroz et al., 2021). Therefore the commercial vehicles can significantly reduce freight related emissions as in response towards electric mobility, as the cost of ownership for the vehicles continues to improve, logistics companies see the need for the vehicles, hence the accelerated adoption of the vehicles in the logistics fleet operations. Driving habits also show that the deployment of electric vehicles at scale is possible if proper planning is made and efficient infrastructure is laid out (McKinnon, 2018). Added to this, not only electrification but also alternative forms of energy, such as hydrogen fuel, also offer promising future prospects, especially for heavy duty vehicles, as batteries may be limiting for such vehicles. Studies undertaken for transport outlook globally indicate that for actual emission reductions, structural changes in freight transport systems are necessary such as policies for change, modal shift from road to rail and overall energy transition strategies.

In fact, digitalization is helping to improve energy efficiency in logistics with the practices adopts from Industry 5.0 frameworks includes of data analytics, smart monitoring and automation to improve supply chain transparency, optimize routes and reduce overall energy consumption (Queiroz et al., 2021). At the same time, companies are increasingly factoring in environmental performance when choosing their logistics providers and making transport purchases, so sustainability is now a key consideration in logistics relationships. In some industries, rethinking logistics and distribution, especially retail has helped to clarify energy savings and improve environmental performance.

4.4 Environmental Performance in Logistics Operations

Environmental performance acts as an essential intermediary between green logistics practices and sustainable development outcomes. It can be evaluated using metrics like reduction in emissions, energy efficiency and waste minimization (Searcy, 2016). The implementation of green logistics includes sustainable packaging, optimized transportation and reverse logistics performs as an instrument in attaining improved environmental performance by reducing resource consumption and intensity (Zhu et al., 2008). As environmental performance a mediating variable which translates the sustainable operations into wider environmental, economic and social benefits for attaining long term sustainable development goals.

4.4.1 Measuring Environmental Performance in Logistics

Evaluating the environmental performance of the logistics sector is based on well-organized and well defined parameters that help in understanding the reduction in emissions, the optimized energy systems and the management of waste. The environmental accounting system in the current scenario monitors the environmental costs, carbon footprint and the utilization of resources in a way that encourages transparency in sustainability reporting.

Emissions Reduction Measurement

Carbon emission measurement is at the centre of environmental performance in logistics operations. For instance, the eco efficient transport planning and clean production has been effective in the reduction of emissions (Khan & Qianli, 2017).

In addition there is a suggestion that environmental performance is a link between green operations and overall organizational benefits (Al Ghwayeen & Abdallah, 2018).

Energy Efficiency Indicators

In the logistics domain, the indicators of energy efficiency typically involve reading the results from the fuel consumption, the energy consumption per shipment, and the improvements in the way the logistics operate. However, the incorporation of structured sustainable supply chain performance enables firms to efficiently utilize the available energy for the entire logistics chain (Wong et al., 2020). Aggressive pursuit of technology advancements, along with the support of the management, enhances the energy efficiency.

Waste Minimization Measures

The measures of reducing wastes involve the amounts of materials that can be recycled, the extent of recycling, and the reduction of packaging wastes. Aggressive pursuit of supply chain management, along with environmental management systems, enhances the performance of the management of the wastes (Weiland et al., 2021). By incorporating the indicators into the logistics performance, firms can measure the progress towards the achievement of better resource efficiency.

4.5 Environmental Performance as a Sustainability Mediator

Environmental performance acts as a bridge between green logistics and sustainable development. The sustainable practices in supply chain have been seen as it generates environmental performance benefits, which can be related to results in sustainability oriented development. Environmental pressures often encourage companies to adopt green innovation strategies and these innovations improve environmental performance. This demonstrates that environmental performance acts as a pathway connecting operational improvements with economic gains (Wong et al., 2020). Green innovation focuses on processes or products to enhance environmental results, which positively influence financial and strategic performance (Xi et al., 2019). This shows that environmental performance works as an intermediate outcome transmitting the benefits of green initiatives to overall organizational success whereas corporate sustainability and social responsibility efforts are also more effective when strong environmental performance is embedded within core strategies. Green transformational leadership improve environmental performance, thereby increasing the overall effects towards sustainability initiatives (Singh et al., 2020). Similarly it improvise the corporate progress, with environmental improvements serving as the key connecting mechanism. Thus the firm has to assimilate new knowledge and maintain proficient skills in operation will positively influence the adoption of green innovations, hence enhancing environmental performance (Aboelmaged & Hashem, 2019). This proves that environmental performance acts as a dynamic mechanism where green logistics influence sustainable development.

4.6 Green Logistics and Linkages towards SDGs

Green logistics has the reality and the direct power towards achieving several SDGs particularly SDG 7, SDG 9, SDG 12 and SDG 13. Sustainability in the movement, storage and movement of goods is the practical way to the achievement of the global SDGs.

SDG 7: Sustainable Energy Systems

To reduce the emissions arising in the field of logistics, there is a need to adopt clean and green energy as in this regard, Paris agreement and the SDG are in full support of the adoption of clean and sustainable energy, particularly in the field of energy intensive sectors, particularly the transport sector (Sachs et al., 2019). Also, the clean and green energy integration, particularly solar energy in the warehouses, has the potential to reduce the emissions in supply chain operations, by integrating the electric freight to achieve SDG 7.

SDG 9: Resilient Infrastructure and Innovation

The SDG 9 focuses on the theme which makes green logistics as the starting point for new ideas, which results in strong, forward looking infrastructure and the digitalization in supply chains, which impacts degree of transparency, resource efficiency, traceability, credibility and protection which strengthens the green industrial system (Saberi et al., 2019; Natrayan et al., 2025). Overall, the agenda for development now includes the theme of sustainable manufacturing and the modernization of infrastructure as key factors for inclusive growth. Government investments in green infrastructure and green transport modes also help to promote sustainable economic growth (Zhang et al., 2021). By integrating smart logistics systems with green transport modes, green logistics enables an industrial revolution that is compatible with SDG 9.

SDG 12: Efficient Consumption and Production

The circular economy concept is prominent which reduce amount of materials wasted and the major dynamics for product life span expansion. This concept encourages the conventional "take, make, dispose" pattern to use the available resources in a more efficient manner with reduced wastage (Kazancoglu et al., 2023). This approach of green logistics is implementing these notions into real life activities, thereby promoting the circular economy to achieve the SDG 12.

SDG 13: Climate Action

The revolution against climate change is at the heart of all sustainability endeavours in logistics. Research has reinforced the imperative which needs immediate and deeper limitations in greenhouse gas emissions. Current energy systems already lock in a large share of our future emissions, which makes it even more important to decarbonize transport as the IPCC's climate pathways involve transforming our energy, infrastructure, and industry systems to achieve climate goals (Weiland et al., 2021). By significantly reducing carbon emissions in freight and logistics, green logistics is helping to achieve climate goals under SDG 13.

Therefore, green logistics bridges the gap between aspirational sustainability targets and tangible action as it enables the uptake of clean energy, industrial innovation, sustainable production and climate mitigation, all of which bring together the threads of progress towards achieving the SDGs. In this way, it also improves overall sustainability outcomes by supporting climate change mitigation, sustainable consumption and resilient infrastructure development through low carbon transportation, sustainable resource use and transparent technologies. In addition, digitalization could strengthen supply chain resilience and transparency (Thacker et al., 2019).

4.7 Digital Transformation and AI in Sustainable Logistics

Digital technology including artificial intelligence (AI) has significantly impacted especially in the area of sustainable, environmentally friendly and carbon neutral practices in logistics sectors. Industry 5.0, which involves embracing this new industrial revolution in supply chain management, has provided greater clarity, better coordination capabilities (Queiros et al., 2021). Thus the integration of digitalization, organizations can better monitor their operations, optimized energy resources and respond towards environmental concerns and changes which is moreover better analytical tools including the use of AI, provide higher accuracy in forecasting, improving overall performance. The use of big data analytics enhances better dynamic capabilities, thus enabling better decision making including more informed business strategies (Wamba et al., 2017). The use of AI in risk analysis, along with simulation tools, has provided better resilient planning in logistics, particularly in complex situations (Ivanov et al., 2019). These tools, including big data analytics, minimize environmental concerns including the use of fuel, thus reducing carbon emissions, while the IoT has acts a influencer in attaining sustainability (Huang et al., 2025) also a significant role in enhancing these tools, injecting more intelligence into the logistics sector. IoT has helped monitor fleet, inventory and warehouses, thus enhancing greater accuracy in tracking along with better efficiency in resource usage (Ben Daya et al., 2019). Moreover, Industry 5.0 has provided better automated, integrated and optimized systems in the logistics sector. Blockchain technology has provided better transparency in the entire supply chain, thus enhancing better sustainability, including carbon emissions (Saberi et al., 2019). The use of AI integrated data analytics has provide better progress particularly during dynamic situations in logistics systems (Dubey et al., 2020).

4.7.1 Technology Driven Decisions in Sustainable Logistics

Technology supported decision making is a major catalyst for improved operational efficiency, reduced emissions and optimal resource use in sustainable logistics systems. Enhanced big data analytics support improves dynamic decision making allowing companies to better forecast, optimize and coordinate their operations (Wamba et al., 2017). Data analytics also helps logistics managers eliminate route overlaps, reduce idle times and optimize load consolidation. Thus reducing fuel consumption and operational costs. Supply chain digital twins are also major catalysts for improved decision making in logistics. Digital twins of supply chains improve scenario planning and disruption response through simulation based planning (Ivanov & Dolgui, 2021). Digital twins also facilitate proactive emission forecasting, capacity management and resilience planning. Thus, improving environmental and operational performance such as blockchain based transparency platforms are major catalysts for improved accountability and sustainability assessment in supply chain management. Blockchain based transparency platforms improve traceability and eliminate resource inefficiencies (Bai & Sarkis, 2020).

Intelligent transport systems that are emerging help directly in the mitigation of emissions. Optimization models for shared autonomous electric vehicles help in the improvement of energy scheduling and vehicle to grid integration, thus lowering the carbon footprint of freight transport where the drone based delivery infrastructure helps in the improvement of last mile delivery and it lowers the congestion emissions. On a macro systemic level, green investment and sustainable infrastructure policies help in the promotion of environmentally sound logistics practices (Zhang et al., 2021).

In summary, technology based analytics, modelling and intelligent transport systems helps in the achievement of tangible improvements in efficiency, emissions and resource optimization.

4.8 Policy and Organizational Drivers of Green Logistics

The policy mechanisms is significantly driven by sustainable logistics, including regulatory measures and internal business capabilities. Environmental regulations and carbon pricing measures create an incentive system that pushes businesses to pursue cleaner production and green innovation. Carbon taxes cap and trade schemes spur technological change in the transport and logistics industries, encouraging green innovation in the sector. Whereas, an efficient policy package that combines regulatory measures, taxes and green innovation drives green logistics adoption (Rogge & Reichardt, 2016). Carbon pricing stability is essential in mobilizing green investments in the transport sector.

On the business note, green logistics adoption is driven by factors that influence the degree to which businesses respond to policy mechanisms. HRM plays a vital part by adopting green HRM into the operations, which promotes environmental awareness and integrates green values into business operations as a responds to green business capabilities form an integrated system that drives green logistics adoption (Jabbour & De Sousa Jabbour, 2016).

4.8.1 Institutional and Market Drivers of Green Logistics

The external institutional pressures and market based instruments are crucial factors that can significantly accelerate the adoption of green logistics. Empirical evidence provides that carbon pricing can induce directed technological change towards low carbon innovation. In addition, emissions trading schemes can affect firm behaviour, operational efficiency, and environmental performance. The comparative analysis indicates that carbon pricing and emission allowance trading mechanisms can embedded environmental pricing to achieve emission reduction targets (Haites, 2018).

In addition, overall policy portfolios that combine various instruments such as regulatory policies, financial incentives, and innovation policies are essential for promoting sustainability (Rogge & Reichardt, 2016). The renewable energy and environmental policies can induce innovation, thereby promoting low carbon innovation. In addition, market based regulation of emissions not only leads to the reduction of carbon intensity but also has the potential to influence the nature of the industry by encouraging firms to improve their technologies and hence increase their competitiveness. Furthermore, a predictable carbon pricing system is important in mobilizing long term investment in a new infrastructure that is free from carbon. Thus, the institutional and market mechanisms outlined above form the external governance that promotes the transformation to sustainable logistics systems.

4.8.2 Leadership and Capabilities for Green Logistics

The green logistics integration relies on external and internal reasons includes environmental pressures, organizational capabilities and leadership styles. Green HRM is an essential component in organizational culture where the development is focused on sustainability, through the improvement of employee awareness and training in environmental issues (Jabbour & De Sousa Jabbour, 2016).

Empirical research indicates green HRM AND green supply chain practices integration makes improvement in sustainability performance, indicating the importance of employee engagement in environmental issues (Zaid et al., 2018). In summary, to strengthen operational alignment and to foster a culture of environmental responsibility as these organizational drivers aligns with the sustainability objectives for the achievement of decarbonized transport systems.

5. THEORETICAL FOUNDATIONS OF GREEN LOGISTICS ADOPTION

Sustainable logistics practices integration can be explained through an integrated theoretical lens that combines multidimensional perspectives of theories where each theory offers different, yet complementary explanation for the impact of environmental, organizational and societal forces on the transformation process of sustainable logistics.

Institutional Theory: External Regulatory Pressures

Institutional theory highlights the way firms conform to external pressures in their organizational environment. According to (DiMaggio and Powell, 2000) external pressure for organizational change include coercive, normative and mimetic pressures. For green logistics coercive pressures include environmental regulations, carbon pricing and sustainability standards. Normative pressures include professional and industry pressures, while mimetic pressures include pressures for imitating green leaders. The external pressures for conformity include regulative, normative and cognitive pillars that shape organizational behaviour (Scott, 2013). These pressures force firms in the logistics industry to adopt environmentally responsible behaviours in order to maintain organizational legitimacy and competitiveness.

Resource Based Theory (RBT): Strategic internal resources

This theory argues that for organizations, sustained competitive advantages can be achieved through its core values, scarce, imitable and non-replaceable sources (Barney, 2000). In green logistics, strategic resources include environmental expertise, digital infrastructure, green supply chain, and human resources. Organizations with the resources are better positioned for the development and implementation of eco efficient transport systems, energy management systems and reverse logistics systems.

Dynamic Capabilities: Adaptive Transformation

This theory based on earlier approach of RBT which argues that organizations can develop new ways of integrating, building and realigning internal and external processes based on changes in the organization situations (Teece, 2018). In green logistics, the dynamic capability view can be used to understand the process of organization conversion from a regulatory driven approach to green logistics to a more voluntary approach.

Stakeholder Theory: Sustainability Alignment

This theory emphasizes the companies role to respond to multiple stakeholders, which include regulatory authorities, customers, employees and communities. It is further emphasized that stakeholder engagement is vital for organizational legitimacy as the green logistics operations which are aligned with stakeholder's needs to improve environmental performance and contribute to the achievement of the Sustainable Development Goals (Harrison et al., 2015).

These theories collectively offer a broader insights into the determinants towards integration of sustainable logistics into their operations.

6. RESEARCH METHODOLOGY

In this chapter, the SLR approach is applied for achieving sustainable development outcomes by examining the green logistics role. A transparent and structured methodology was followed in the review process to ensure the rigor and reliability. The PRISMA 2020 framework has been used as the standard protocol for identifying, screening and selecting relevant studies.

An extensive research lookup was undertaken in authenticated data sources. Keywords like "green logistics", "sustainable logistics", "environmental performance", "decarbonization" and "sustainable supply chain" were employed towards diverse combinations in retrieving relevant articles. The exploration were restricted to scholarly reviewed scientific journals, conference papers and books.

The inclusion criteria centred around selecting research works that have analysed green logistics, environmental performance and sustainability implications. Articles found irrelevant, duplicates and works with insufficient methodological description were all excluded.

Selected research work was then organized according to the key thematics which include green logistics, environmental performance, digitalization and policy and organizational drivers.

The final group of selected papers was subjected to systematic analysis, which enables to create a comprehensive understanding of the connections towards the green logistics techniques and sustainable development results.

This methodology assures that the results are based on validated academic literature and serve as a strong foundation for developing a reliable basis for conceptual framework development.

The figure 2 illustrated the PRISMA framework based selection process

Figure 2. PRISMA based literature Selection Process

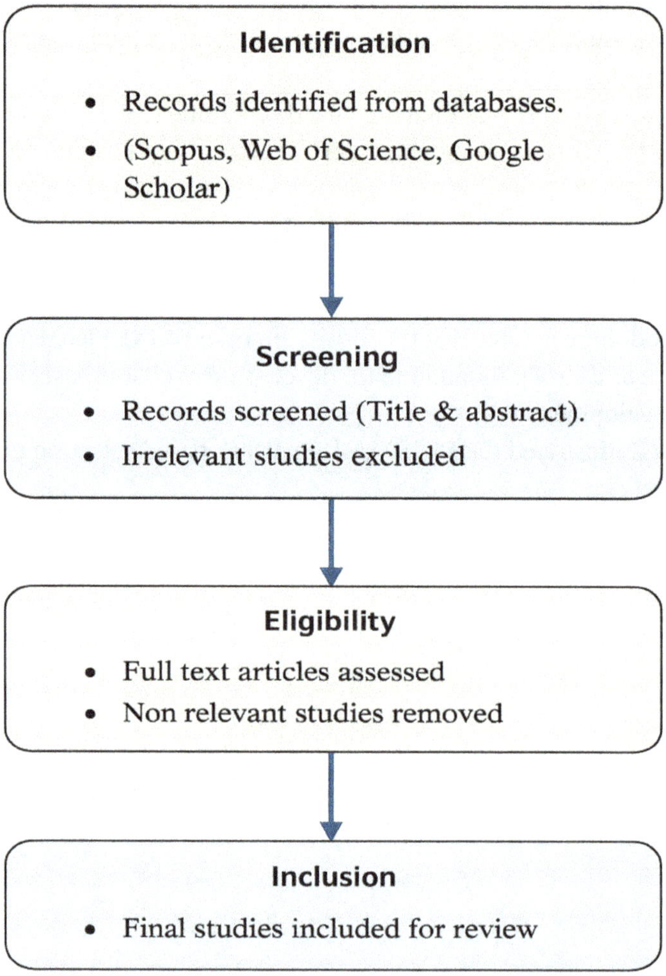

7. REAL LIFE APPLICATIONS OF GREEN LOGISTICS FRAMEWORK

Case 1: DHL Electrification and Digital Decarbonization

Background

DHL Group, an international player in the logistics industry offering freight, parcel and other related services across the globe, has made decarbonization an integral part of its strategy due to increasing environmental regulations and stakeholder pressure. As mentioned by (McKinnon, 2018) in his research on freight decarbonization, large freight companies are performing important role in the decarbonization process of the transport industry by investing heavily in technology and increasing overall efficiency.

Framework Implemented

DHL Group implemented large scale electrification strategies for its fleet, investing in sustainable aviation fuels and green warehouses to decrease the overall carbon footprint of its operations. It also implemented digital solutions for tracking and increasing overall efficiency, which is a significant step towards digital twin technology for transforming the overall logistics industry (Ivanov & Dolgui, 2021). Blockchain technology was implemented to increase transparency regarding overall carbon footprint (Saberi et al., 2019).

Outcomes

The outcomes of this strategy resulted in overall power consumption reductions and visibility of transparency regarding overall emissions within the logistics industry. This case demonstrates the effectiveness of digital technology and overall strategies implemented by the company to improve overall environmental objectives set by the global community (McKinnon, 2018).

Case 2: Maersk Low Carbon Maritime Logistics

Background

Maersk, is one among the leading global freight and logistics companies, pledged its commitment towards carbon neutral maritime transport in the wake of mounting international pressure on nations to adopt effective climate change policies. Maritime logistics has emerged as an important area for emission reduction, given its high contribution towards freight emissions (McKinnon, 2018).

Framework Implemented

The company has invested in state of the art ships propelled by green methanol and alternative fuels, along with the development of ship routes and fuel efficiency technologies The use of digital freight monitoring systems has improved the overall tracking of emissions, which is in line with the framework of an effective sustainability oriented logistics service provider (Centobelli et al., 2017).

Outcomes

The strategic investments from the company have reduced overall carbon emissions in maritime transport, while company has emerged as an industry leader in low carbon maritime transport innovation.

Case 3: UPS AI Routing and Alternative Fuel Logistics

Background

UPS operates in a congested urban logistics environment, which has increased the pressure on carbon compliance and efficiency. Research on urban logistics has highlighted the need for route rationalization and modal optimization for reducing the environmental footprint (Lagorio et al., 2016).

Framework Implemented

The organization implemented the ORION AI based smart routing solution, which optimizes routes, reduces idle time and minimizes fuel consumption. In addition, the organization has increased the usage of alternative fuels and electric vehicles, which has been integrated into the last mile operations. This has been aligned with the identified strategies for logistics sustainability for transportation service providers (Centobelli et al., 2017).

Outcome

The outcome has been the achievement of fuel savings, reduction in greenhouse gas emissions and increased efficiency for the organization.

Case 4: Walmart Sustainable Retail Logistics Integration

Background

Walmart integrates sustainability into their worldwide supply chain and retail logistics operations by understanding that their logistics operations are a significant contributor of carbon emission into their operations. Retail logistics sustainability is essential for minimizing the footprint of large scale retail logistics operations.

Framework Implemented

Walmart implemented fleet fuel efficiency programs, packaging efficiency programs, supplier sustainability scorecards and collaborative logistics networks. The implemented strategy is consistent with a structured sustainability integration framework for logistics service organizations (Centebolli et al., 2017).

Outcomes

Walmart was able to achieve improved energy efficiency, reduced carbon footprint and improved supply chain transparency and practical applications provides the commitment towards the organization and supply chain coordination mediate the relationship between the sustainability outcomes and green logistics practices.

8. MANAGERIAL AND REGULATORY IMPLICATIONS

Adoption of sustainable logistics requires a coordinated approach which combines policy support, technological innovation and organizational transformation. Based on the analysis, a number of concrete measures can be suggested for better implementation of sustainable logistics systems.

Organizations should prioritize the incorporation of low carbon logistics practices for the purpose of eliminating impact towards efficacy of operations and environment through optimized energy resources, warehouse efficiency, sustainable packaging and route optimization. The integration of digital analytics support process of logistics operations by monitoring. Further by enhancing decision making and optimize resource utilization (Wamba et al., 2017).

In context of regulatory perspective, government and regulatory bodies introduce stronger environmental regulations, carbon pricing models and incentives to adopt greener logistics technologies (Rogge & Reichardt, 2016). These approaches promote firms to adopt green initiatives and to help them achieve the aim of decarbonizing organizations more rapidly.

In terms of organizational perspective, corporations must be encouraged to develop their capabilities internally by investing in training employees, green HRM policies, leadership commitment and sustainability commitment from the management (Jabbour & Jabbour, 2016). Awareness building and cultivating a sustainable culture are very significant for achieving sustainable logistics strategies.

The incorporation of supply chain stakeholders is necessary for attaining sustainability throughout the supply chain systems. The company should consider information exchange, cooperative logistics systems and sustainability partnerships in order to minimize emissions in their operations (Centobelli et al., 2017).

Overall, the supportive policy frameworks, technological innovation and organizational commitment are required to incorporate for the successful implementation of green logistics and provides a comprehensive insights for the long term sustainable development outcomes achievement.

9. FUTURE RESEARCH DIRECTIONS

Prospective studies should focus on improving interaction between emerging smart technologies and sustainable logistics where specific areas for future studies include the incorporation process of advanced technologies in operating sustainable logistics can be explored empirically (Ivanov & Dolgui, 2021; Saberi et al., 2019). Digital technologies provide opportunities for more efficient decision making and increased transparency.

The significant area for further research are investigation of policy and market mechanisms to promote the adoption of green logistics. Future research should examine the efficacy of carbon pricing, regulatory frameworks and incentives based policies to influence organizations to adopt sustainability practices in logistics systems (Rogge & Reichardt, 2016). Comparative research across different regions give insights for the deeper policy effectiveness and the challenges in the implementation.

Additional research is required to analyse the organizational capabilities and leadership role in transforming the sustainable logistics. Quantitative research shows effects towards green HRM practices, leadership commitment and organizational culture for the performance outcomes and adoption in initiating green logistics (Zaid et al., 2018).

Furthermore, research efforts should be directed towards establishing standardized measures in logistics operations for assessing environmental performance. The absence of such standards limits the ability to conduct comparative analysis and to check sustainability progress among industries and organizations (Searcy, 2016).

In addition, there is a need for further interdisciplinary and longitudinal studies to evaluate the influence of long term green logistics activities on the outcomes of sustainable development. This research can help in obtaining a complete perspective about the changing dynamics of logistics systems evolving in response to the change in various factors like technology, environment and economic changes (Geels et al., 2017).

10. CONCLUSION

Green Logistics has emerged as an important enabler of sustainable development in core logistics and supply chain operations by integrating environmental considerations. Thus, this chapter's findings underscores the green logistics practices adoption to reduce carbon emissions and improvise environmental performance through sustainable transportation, reverse logistics and energy efficient warehousing (Govindan et al., 2015). These practices enhance the prolonged competitiveness and operational efficiency while minimizing the ecological impact.

This chapter further stresses the sustainable environmental performance's intermediary role within sustainable logistics and its outcomes. Reduction in emissions, energy efficiency and minimizing the wastes become the key drivers that determine sustainable logistics performance and enable to attain sustainable goals at the global level (Searcy, 2016). In this regard, green logistics in connection with the objectives of sustainable oriented logistics supports its shift towards low carbon and optimized energy efficient resources in supply chain management.

Further, incorporation of smart technologies has further hastened the transformation of logistics systems. These technologies aid in better decision making in real time, optimized resource usage and increased transparency and strengthen operational resilience and environmental performance (Saberi et al., 2019). In addition, policy & market mechanisms being the key enabler for ensuring the incorporation of sustainable supply chain in organizations by creating economic initiatives and regulatory coercion. Additionally, organizational capabilities, commitment of leaders and collaboration within supply chains are key enablers of sustainable logistics initiatives (Jabbour & Jabbour, 2016). Therefore, integration into technological innovations, institutional backing and internal capabilities allows organizations to maintain a balance within sustainable environment and economic performance.

Overall, sustainable logistics provides an elaborate and holistic approach by transforming logistics operations into resilient, efficient and environmentally responsible networks for attaining sustainable development.

REFERENCES

Abbasi, M., & Nilsson, F. (2016). Developing environmentally sustainable logistics: Exploring themes and challenges from a logistics service providers' perspective. *Transportation Research Part D, Transport and Environment*, *46*, 273–283. DOI: 10.1016/j.trd.2016.04.004

Aboelmaged, M., & Hashem, G. (2019). Absorptive capacity and green innovation adoption in SMEs: The mediating effects of sustainable organisational capabilities. *Journal of Cleaner Production*, *220*, 853–863. DOI: 10.1016/j.jclepro.2019.02.150

Agrawal, S., Singh, R. K., & Murtaza, Q. (2015). A literature review and perspectives in reverse logistics. *Resources, Conservation and Recycling*, *97*, 76–92. DOI: 10.1016/j.resconrec.2015.02.009

Al-Ghwayeen, W. S., & Abdallah, A. B. (2018). Green supply chain management and export performance: The mediating role of environmental performance. *Journal of Manufacturing Technology Management*, *29*(7), 1233–1252. DOI: 10.1108/JMTM-03-2018-0079

Bai, C., & Sarkis, J. (2020). A supply chain transparency and sustainability technology appraisal model for blockchain technology. *International Journal of Production Research*, *58*(7), 2142–2162. DOI: 10.1080/00207543.2019.1708989

. Barney, J. B. (2000). Firm resources and sustained competitive advantage. https://doi.org/DOI: 10.1016/S0742-3322(00)17018-4

Ben-Daya, M., Hassini, E., & Bahroun, Z. (2019). Internet of things and supply chain management: A literature review. *International Journal of Production Research*, *57*(15-16), 4719–4742. DOI: 10.1080/00207543.2017.1402140

Centobelli, P., Cerchione, R., & Esposito, E. (2017). Environmental sustainability in the service industry of transportation and logistics service providers: Systematic literature review and research directions. *Transportation Research Part D, Transport and Environment*, *53*, 454–470. DOI: 10.1016/j.trd.2017.04.032

Demir, E., Bektaş, T., & Laporte, G. (2014). A review of recent research on green road freight transportation. *European Journal of Operational Research*, *237*(3), 775–793. DOI: 10.1016/j.ejor.2013.12.033

. DiMaggio, P. J., & Powell, W. W. (2000). The iron cage revisited institutional isomorphism and collective rationality in organizational fields. https://doi.org/DOI: 10.1016/S0742-3322(00)17011-1

Dubey, R., Gunasekaran, A., Childe, S. J., Bryde, D. J., Giannakis, M., Foropon, C., Roubaud, D., & Hazen, B. T. (2020). Big data analytics and artificial intelligence pathway to operational performance under the effects of entrepreneurial orientation and environmental dynamism: A study of manufacturing organisations. *International Journal of Production Economics*, *226*, 107599. DOI: 10.1016/j.ijpe.2019.107599

Fahimnia, B., Sarkis, J., & Davarzani, H. (2015). Green supply chain management: A review and bibliometric analysis. *International Journal of Production Economics*, *162*, 101–114. DOI: 10.1016/j.ijpe.2015.01.003

Geels, F. W., Sovacool, B. K., Schwanen, T., & Sorrell, S. (2017). The socio-technical dynamics of low-carbon transitions. *Joule*, *1*(3), 463–479. DOI: 10.1016/j.joule.2017.09.018

Govindan, K., Soleimani, H., & Kannan, D. (2015). Reverse logistics and closed-loop supply chain: A comprehensive review to explore the future. *European Journal of Operational Research*, *240*(3), 603–626. DOI: 10.1016/j.ejor.2014.07.012

Haites, E. (2018). Carbon taxes and greenhouse gas emissions trading systems: What have we learned? *Climate Policy*, *18*(8), 955–966. DOI: 10.1080/14693062.2018.1492897

Harrison, J. S., Freeman, R. E., & Abreu, M. C. S. D. (2015). Stakeholder theory as an ethical approach to effective management: Applying the theory to multiple contexts. *Revista Brasileira de Gestão de Negócios*, *17*(55), 858–869. DOI: 10.7819/rbgn.v17i55.2647

Huang, S., Zhou, Y., Isleem, H. F., Tejani, G. G., & Ragab, A. E. (2025). Intelligent IoT-enabled marketing systems: Enhancing consumer sustainability engagement through perceived usefulness. *Internet of Things : Engineering Cyber Physical Human Systems*, *101797*, 101797. Advance online publication. DOI: 10.1016/j.iot.2025.101797

Ivanov, D., & Dolgui, A. (2021). A digital supply chain twin for managing the disruption risks and resilience in the era of Industry 4.0. *Production Planning and Control*, *32*(9), 775–788. DOI: 10.1080/09537287.2020.1768450

Jabbour, C. J. C., & de Sousa Jabbour, A. B. L. (2016). Green human resource management and green supply chain management: Linking two emerging agendas. *Journal of Cleaner Production*, *112*, 1824–1833. DOI: 10.1016/j.jclepro.2015.01.052

Kazancoglu, Y., Ozkan-Ozen, Y. D., Sagnak, M., Kazancoglu, I., & Dora, M. (2023). Framework for a sustainable supply chain to overcome risks in transition to a circular economy through Industry 4.0. *Production Planning and Control, 34*(10), 902–917. DOI: 10.1080/09537287.2021.1980910

Khan, S. A. R., & Qianli, D. (2017). Impact of green supply chain management practices on firms' performance: An empirical study from the perspective of Pakistan. *Environmental Science and Pollution Research International, 24*(20), 16829–16844. DOI: 10.1007/s11356-017-9172-5 PMID: 28573559

Khan, S. A. R., Zhang, Y., Kumar, A., Zavadskas, E., & Streimikiene, D. (2020). Measuring the impact of renewable energy, public health expenditure, logistics, and environmental performance on sustainable economic growth. *Sustainable Development (Bradford), 28*(4), 833–843. DOI: 10.1002/sd.2034

Lagorio, A., Pinto, R., & Golini, R. (2016). Research in urban logistics: A systematic literature review. *International Journal of Physical Distribution & Logistics Management, 46*(10), 908–931. DOI: 10.1108/IJPDLM-01-2016-0008

McKinnon, A. (2018). *Decarbonizing logistics: Distributing goods in a low carbon world.* Kogan Page Publishers.

Montabon, F., Pagell, M., & Wu, Z. (2016). Making sustainability sustainable. *The Journal of Supply Chain Management, 52*(2), 11–27. DOI: 10.1111/jscm.12103

Natrayan, L., Kaliappan, S., Bhaskarani, N., & Kasireddy, L. C. (2025, February). Enhancing Trust and Security in Digital Ecosystems with Blockchain Technology. In *2025 International Conference on Technology Enabled Economic Changes (InTech)* (pp. 1008-1013). IEEE. https://doi.org/DOI: 10.1109/InTech64186.2025.11198514

Queiroz, M. M., Pereira, S. C. F., Telles, R., & Machado, M. C. (2021). Industry 4.0 and digital supply chain capabilities: A framework for understanding digitalisation challenges and opportunities. *Benchmarking, 28*(5), 1761–1782. DOI: 10.1108/BIJ-12-2018-0435

Rajeev, A., Pati, R. K., Padhi, S. S., & Govindan, K. (2017). Evolution of sustainability in supply chain management: A literature review. *Journal of Cleaner Production, 162*, 299–314. DOI: 10.1016/j.jclepro.2017.05.026

Rogge, K. S., & Reichardt, K. (2016). Policy mixes for sustainability transitions: An extended concept and framework for analysis. *Research Policy, 45*(8), 1620–1635. DOI: 10.1016/j.respol.2016.04.004

Saberi, S., Kouhizadeh, M., Sarkis, J., & Shen, L. (2019). Blockchain technology and its relationships to sustainable supply chain management. *International Journal of Production Research, 57*(7), 2117–2135. DOI: 10.1080/00207543.2018.1533261

Sachs, J. D., Schmidt-Traub, G., Mazzucato, M., Messner, D., Nakicenovic, N., & Rockström, J. (2019). Six transformations to achieve the sustainable development goals. *Nature Sustainability, 2*(9), 805–814. DOI: 10.1038/s41893-019-0352-9

Saxena, N., Sarkar, B., Wee, H. M., Reong, S., Singh, S. R., & Hsiao, Y. L. (2023). A reverse logistics model with eco-design under the Stackelberg-Nash equilibrium and centralized framework. *Journal of Cleaner Production, 387*, 135789. DOI: 10.1016/j.jclepro.2022.135789

Scott, W. R. (2013). *Institutions and organizations: Ideas, interests, and identities*. Sage publications.

Searcy, C. (2016). Measuring enterprise sustainability. *Business Strategy and the Environment, 25*(2), 120–133. DOI: 10.1002/bse.1861

Singh, S. K., Del Giudice, M., Chierici, R., & Graziano, D. (2020). Green innovation and environmental performance: The role of green transformational leadership and green human resource management. *Technological Forecasting and Social Change, 150*, 119762. DOI: 10.1016/j.techfore.2019.119762

Teece, D. J. (2018). Business models and dynamic capabilities. *Long Range Planning, 51*(1), 40–49. DOI: 10.1016/j.lrp.2017.06.007

Thacker, S., Adshead, D., Fay, M., Hallegatte, S., Harvey, M., Meller, H., O'Regan, N., Rozenberg, J., Watkins, G., & Hall, J. W. (2019). Infrastructure for sustainable development. *Nature Sustainability, 2*(4), 324–331. DOI: 10.1038/s41893-019-0256-8

Wamba, S. F., Gunasekaran, A., Akter, S., Ren, S. J. F., Dubey, R., & Childe, S. J. (2017). Big data analytics and firm performance: Effects of dynamic capabilities. *Journal of Business Research, 70*, 356–365. DOI: 10.1016/j.jbusres.2016.08.009

Weiland, S., Hickmann, T., Lederer, M., & Schwindenhammer, S. (2021). The 2030 agenda for sustainable development: Transformative change through the sustainable development goals? *Politics and Governance, 9*(1), 90–95. DOI: 10.17645/pag.v9i1.4191

Wong, C. Y., Wong, C. W., & Boon-itt, S. (2020). Effects of green supply chain integration and green innovation on environmental and cost performance. *International Journal of Production Research, 58*(15), 4589–4609. DOI: 10.1080/00207543.2020.1756510

Yawar, S. A., & Seuring, S. (2017). Management of social issues in supply chains: A literature review exploring social issues, actions and performance outcomes. *Journal of Business Ethics*, *141*(3), 621–643. DOI: 10.1007/s10551-015-2719-9

Zaid, A. A., Jaaron, A. A., & Bon, A. T. (2018). The impact of green human resource management and green supply chain management practices on sustainable performance: An empirical study. *Journal of Cleaner Production*, *204*, 965–979. DOI: 10.1016/j.jclepro.2018.09.062

Zhang, D., Mohsin, M., Rasheed, A. K., Chang, Y., & Taghizadeh-Hesary, F. (2021). Public spending and green economic growth in BRI region: Mediating role of green finance. *Energy Policy*, *153*, 112256. DOI: 10.1016/j.enpol.2021.112256

Zhu, Q., Sarkis, J., & Lai, K. H. (2008). Green supply chain management implications for "closing the loop". *Transportation Research Part E, Logistics and Transportation Review*, *44*(1), 1–18. DOI: 10.1016/j.tre.2006.06.003

ADDITIONAL READING

Bouchery, Y., Corbett, C., Fransoo, J. C., & Tan, T. (Eds.). (2016). *Sustainable supply chains*. Springer., DOI: 10.1007/978-3-319-29791-0

Brandenburg, M., Govindan, K., Sarkis, J., & Seuring, S. (2014). Quantitative models for sustainable supply chain management: Developments and directions. *European Journal of Operational Research*, *233*(2), 299–312. DOI: 10.1016/j.ejor.2013.09.032

KEY TERMS AND DEFINITIONS

Circular Supply Chain: A model of conducting supply chain performance where the major target is to attain sustainable oriented environment with the support from circular supply chains which works to recycle and reuse of resources in environment.

Decarbonized Transport Systems: A set of systems that work to significantly reduce or totally eradicate greenhouse emissions in the environment through usage from alternative power sources in executing the logistics activities.

Digital Logistics Technologies: A set of technological platforms that work to increase the efficiency of supply chain performance with the implementation of smart technologies such as Internet of things, artificial intelligence and data analytics and blockchain technologies.

Environmental Performance: Outcomes from the activities that determine the success of strategies aimed at improving sustainability in the environment.

Green Logistics: The eco-friendly strategies in execution in the supply chain activities, including transportation, warehousing, packaging and distribution as the ultimate goal of limiting carbon footprint while improving sustainable environment.

Reverse Logistics: The process of managing the reverse movement of flows where the ultimate motive is to improvise sustainability in environment.

Sustainable Development Goals: The set of goals targeted at improving environment sustainability and was created by the United Nations to improve sustainability in the environment.

Sustainable Logistics: A model of conducting logistics activities that considers sustainable ESG factors towards the execution of sustainable logistics activities.

Compilation of References

Aamodt, A., Cory, K. S., & Coney, K. (2021). *Electrifying transit: A guidebook for implementing battery electric buses (No. NREL/TP-7A40-76932)*. National Renewable Energy Laboratory. DOI: 10.2172/1779056

Aarthi, S., Ravikumar, R. N., Sobirova, K., & Mamadiyarov, Z. (2025). Empowering a sustainable future through digital learning and the SDGs. In *Harnessing E-Learning to Create a Sustainable Future* (pp. 145–172). IGI Global Scientific Publishing., DOI: 10.4018/979-8-3373-0112-9.ch006

Abbasi, M., & Nilsson, F. (2016). Developing environmentally sustainable logistics: Exploring themes and challenges from a logistics service providers' perspective. *Transportation Research Part D, Transport and Environment*, *46*, 273–283. DOI: 10.1016/j.trd.2016.04.004

Abduljabbar, R., Dia, H., Liyanage, S., & Bagloee, S. A. (2019). Applications of Artificial Intelligence in transport: An overview. *Sustainability (Basel)*, *11*(1), 189. DOI: 10.3390/su11010189

Aboelmaged, M., & Hashem, G. (2019). Absorptive capacity and green innovation adoption in SMEs: The mediating effects of sustainable organisational capabilities. *Journal of Cleaner Production*, *220*, 853–863. DOI: 10.1016/j.jclepro.2019.02.150

Adabara, I., Olaniyi Sadiq, B., & Shuaibu, N. A., Ibrahim Danjuma, Y., & Maninti, V. (2025). Trustworthy agentic AI systems: a cross-layer review of architectures, threat models, and governance strategies for real-world deployment. *F1000Research, 14*, 905. DOI: 10.12688/f1000research.169927.1

Agbede, O. O., Akhigbe, E. E., Ajayi, A. J., & Egbuhuzor, N. S. (2021). Assessing economic risks and returns of energy transitions with quantitative financial approaches. *International Journal of Multidisciplinary Research and Growth Evaluation*, 2(1), 552–566. DOI: 10.54660/.IJMRGE.2021.2.1.552-566

Agrawal, S., Singh, R. K., & Murtaza, Q. (2015). A literature review and perspectives in reverse logistics. *Resources, Conservation and Recycling*, *97*, 76–92. DOI: 10.1016/j.resconrec.2015.02.009

Ajayi, O. O., Kurien, A., Djouani, K., & Dieng, L. (2025). Artificial intelligence for infrastructure resilience: Transportation systems as a strategic case for policy and practice. *Sustainability (Basel)*, *17*(20), 8992. Advance online publication. DOI: 10.3390/su17208992

Alamatsaz, K., Hussain, S., Lai, C., & Eicker, U. (2022). Electric bus scheduling and timetabling, fast charging infrastructure planning, and their impact on the grid: A review. *Energies*, *15*(21), 7919. DOI: 10.3390/en15217919

Alamoodi, A. H., Albahri, O. S., Deveci, M., Albahri, A. S., Yussof, S., Dinçer, H., & Sharaf, I. M. (2024). Selection of electric bus models using 2-tuple linguistic T-spherical fuzzy-based decision-making model. *Expert Systems with Applications*, *249*, 123498. DOI: 10.1016/j.eswa.2024.123498

Alawad, H., An, M., & Kaewunruen, S. (2020). Utilizing an adaptive neuro-fuzzy inference system (ANFIS) for overcrowding level risk assessment in railway stations. *Applied Sciences (Basel, Switzerland)*, *10*(15), 5156. DOI: 10.3390/app10155156

Al-Ghwayeen, W. S., & Abdallah, A. B. (2018). Green supply chain management and export performance: The mediating role of environmental performance. *Journal of Manufacturing Technology Management*, *29*(7), 1233–1252. DOI: 10.1108/JMTM-03-2018-0079

Almalioglu, Y., Turan, M., Trigoni, N., & Newman, P. (2022). Deep learning-based robust positioning for all-weather autonomous driving. *Nature Machine Intelligence*, *4*(9), 749–760. DOI: 10.1038/s42256-022-00520-5 PMID: 37790900

Altan, M. F., & Kızıltaş, M. Ç. (2020). Ulusal, bölgesel ve uluslararası bazda yüksek hızlı demiryollarının gelişimi, mevcut durumu ve yatırım planlarına dair bir derleme. *Dicle Üniversitesi Mühendislik Fakültesi Mühendislik Dergisi*, *11*(2), 715–722. DOI: 10.24012/dumf.450985

Amirah. (2024). Editorial: Smart Parking Management System using Artificial Intelligence. *Journal of Computer Science Application and Engineering (JOSAPEN)*, *2*(1), 20–23. DOI: 10.70356/josapen.v2i1.25

Ananganó-Alvarado, G., Umaña-Morel, I., & Keith-Norambuena, B. (2025). Reinforcement learning in electric vehicle energy management: A comprehensive open-access review of methods, challenges, and future innovations. *Frontiers in Future Transportation*, *6*, 1555250. DOI: 10.3389/ffutr.2025.1555250

Annice, F., & Lestari, Y. D. (2023). Proposed Design of Service Quality Performance Management System for Indonesian HSR.

Apergis, N., & Payne, J. E. (2010). Renewable energy consumption and economic growth: Evidence from a panel of OECD countries. *Energy Policy*, *38*(1), 656–660. DOI: 10.1016/j.enpol.2009.09.002

Apergis, N., & Payne, J. E. (2014). Renewable energy, output, CO_2 emissions, and fossil fuel prices: Evidence from a nonlinear panel model. *Energy Economics*, *42*, 226–232. DOI: 10.1016/j.eneco.2014.01.003

Archsmith, J., Muehlegger, E., & Rapson, D. S. (2022). Future paths of electric vehicle adoption in the United States: Predictable determinants, obstacles, and opportunities. *Environmental and Energy Policy and the Economy*, *3*, 71–110. DOI: 10.1086/717219

Arun Chakravarthy, R., Sureshkumar, C., Arun, M., & Ranjani Shree, R. S. (2025). Advancements in intelligent traffic monitoring system design for smart urban infrastructure. In *Building a Green Future Through Essential Decision-Making Competencies* (pp. 27–62). IGI Global., DOI: 10.4018/979-8-3373-0189-1.ch002

Ashmore, D. P., Pojani, D., Thoreau, R., Christie, N., & Tyler, N. A. (2018). The symbolism of 'eco cars' across national cultures: Potential implications for policy formulation and transfer. *Transportation Research Part D, Transport and Environment*, *63*, 560–575. DOI: 10.1016/j.trd.2018.06.024

Association, T. K. L. R., Nan, M.-F., Cui, Y., & Zhang, M.-Z. (2023). A study on the optimization of reverse logistics network in China's automotive industry: Focusing on abandoned cars in China. *The Korean Logistics Research Association*, *33*(3), 5–21. DOI: 10.17825/klr.2023.33.3.5

Awate, S., Larsen, M. L., & Mudambi, R. (2015). Accessing vs sourcing knowledge: A comparative study of R&D internationalization between emerging and advanced economy firms. *Journal of International Business Studies*, *46*(1), 63–86. DOI: 10.1057/jibs.2014.46

Bagloee, S. A., Tavana, M., Asadi, M., & Oliver, T. (2016). Autonomous vehicles: Challenges, opportunities, and future implications for transportation policies. *Journal of Modern Transportation*, *24*(4), 284–303. DOI: 10.1007/s40534-016-0117-3

Bai, C., & Sarkis, J. (2020). A supply chain transparency and sustainability technology appraisal model for blockchain technology. *International Journal of Production Research*, *58*(7), 2142–2162. DOI: 10.1080/00207543.2019.1708989

Bai, J., & Ru, H. (2024). Carbon emissions trading and environmental protection: International evidence. *Management Science, 70*(7), 4593–4603. DOI: 10.1287/mnsc.2023.03143

Balboni, P., & Francis, K. (2023). *Data protection as a corporate social responsibility: Integrating privacy, cybersecurity and sustainability*. Edward Elgar Publishing., DOI: 10.4337/9781035314164

Ballis, H., & Dimitriou, L. (2020). Evaluation of Reinforcement Learning traffic signalling strategies for alternative objectives: Implementation in the network of Nicosia, Cyprus. *Transport and Telecommunication Journal, 21*(4), 295–302. DOI: 10.2478/ttj-2020-0024

Barr, N. A. (2023). The evolution of substantive protection in EU international investment agreements: Taking stock of the EU's early Treaty-Making practice. *European Business Law Review, 34*(3), 415–436. DOI: 10.54648/EULR2023025

Ben-Daya, M., Hassini, E., & Bahroun, Z. (2019). Internet of things and supply chain management: A literature review. *International Journal of Production Research, 57*(15-16), 4719–4742. DOI: 10.1080/00207543.2017.1402140

Bertoni, E. (2020). Convention 108 and the GDPR: Trends and perspectives in Latin America. *Computer Law & Security Review, 40*, 105516. DOI: 10.1016/j.clsr.2020.105516

Bhandari, V., & Singh, R. (2023). Understanding India's new data protection law. Carnegie Endowment for International Peace Working Paper. https://carnegieendowment.org/research/2023/10/understanding-indias-new-data-protection-law

Bharti, M., Baswaraju, S., Nijhawan, G., Sharma, N., Kumar, A., Saleh Mashkour, M., & Nalli, N. (2024). Reduction of green house gases emission: Towards a sustainable future. *E3S Web of Conferences, 552*, 01116. DOI: 10.1051/e3sconf/202455201116

Biswas, T. K., & Das, M. C. (2019). Selection of commercially available electric vehicle using fuzzy AHP-MABAC. *Journal of The Institution of Engineers (India): Series C, 100*(3), 531-537.

Biswas, I. (2025). Relational accountability in AI-driven pharmaceutical practices: An ethics approach to bias, inequity and structural harm. *Journal of Medical Ethics*, jme-2025-110913. Advance online publication. DOI: 10.1136/jme-2025-110913 PMID: 40930712

Biswas, P. (2022). Flight price prediction: A case study. *International Journal for Research in Applied Science and Engineering Technology, 10*(6), 89–94. DOI: 10.22214/ijraset.2022.43666

Bjerkan, K. Y., Nørbech, T. E., & Nordtømme, M. E. (2016). Incentives for promoting battery electric vehicle (BEV) adoption in Norway. *Transportation Research Part D, Transport and Environment*, *43*, 169–180. DOI: 10.1016/j.trd.2015.12.002

Bland, M., Burke, M. I., & Bertolaccini, K. (2024). Taking steps toward healthy and sustainable transport investment: A systematic review of economic evaluations in the academic literature on large-scale active transport infrastructure. *International Journal of Sustainable Transportation*, *18*(3), 201–220. DOI: 10.1080/15568318.2023.2296952

Bogdanov, D., Ram, M., Aghahosseini, A., Gulagi, A., Oyewo, A. S., Child, M., Caldera, U., Sadovskaia, K., Farfan, J., Barbosa, L. S. N. S., Fasihi, M., Khalili, S., Traber, T., & Breyer, C. (2021). Low-cost renewable electricity as the key driver of the global energy transition towards sustainability. *Energy*, *227*, 120467. DOI: 10.1016/j.energy.2021.120467

Boriboonsomsin, K., Tanvir, S., & Barth, M. (2024). Modeling the impacts of low emission zone on route diversion and emissions of heavy-duty trucks: A Southern California case study. *Transportation Research Record: Journal of the Transportation Research Board*, *2678*(1), 794–805. DOI: 10.1177/03611981231172747

Boudmen, K., El ghazi, A., Eddaoudi, Z., Aarab, Z., & Rahmani, M. D. (2024). Electric vehicles, the future of transportation powered by machine learning: A brief review. *Energy Informatics*, *7*(1), 80. DOI: 10.1186/s42162-024-00379-3

Bradford, A. (2023). *Digital empires: The global battle to regulate technology*. Oxford University Press., DOI: 10.1093/oso/9780197649268.001.0001

Briand, Y., Pye, S., D'Agosto, M. de A., Goes, G. V., Schmitz-Gonçalves, D. N., Garg, A., Gupta, D., Vishwanathan, S. S., Siagian, U. W. R., Ahjum, F., & Trollip, H. (2023). Passenger transport decarbonization in emerging economies: Policy lessons from modelling long-term deep decarbonization pathways. *Climate Policy*, *23*(10), 1–21. DOI: 10.1080/14693062.2023.2194859

Burri, M., & Kugler, K. (2024). Regulatory autonomy in digital trade agreements. *Journal of International Economic Law*, *27*(3), 397–423. DOI: 10.1093/jiel/jgae025

Cadet, E., Babatunde, L. A., Ajayi, J. O., Erigh, E. D., Obuse, E., Essien, I. A., & Ayanbode, N. (2024). Developing scalable compliance architectures for cross-industry regulatory alignment. *International Journal of Scientific Research in Humanities and Social Sciences*, *1*(2), 494–524. DOI: 10.32628/IJSRSSH242556

Candia Riquelme, D. A. (2025). *Assessing innovative transport technologies and policies*. DOI: 10.5463/thesis.1257

Candio, P., & Frew, E. (2023). How much behaviour change is required for the investment in cycling infrastructure to be sustainable? A break-even analysis. *PLoS One, 18*(4), e0284634. DOI: 10.1371/journal.pone.0284634 PMID: 37075055

Cao, Y., & Zhou, M. (2024). Energy management optimization of hybrid electric vehicles based on deep learning model predictive control. *Intelligent Decision Technologies, 18*(4), 2451–2472. DOI: 10.3233/IDT-240298

Centobelli, P., Cerchione, R., & Esposito, E. (2017). Environmental sustainability in the service industry of transportation and logistics service providers: Systematic literature review and research directions. *Transportation Research Part D, Transport and Environment, 53*, 454–470. DOI: 10.1016/j.trd.2017.04.032

Chang, Q. (2024). The legal and regulatory issues of AI technology in cross-border data flow in international trade. Transactions on Economics. *Business and Management Research, 8*, 111–117. DOI: 10.62051/cyw9y102

Cha, Y., & Koo, M. G. (2020). Who embraces technical barriers to trade? the case of European REACH regulations. *World Trade Review, 20*(1), 25–39. DOI: 10.1017/S1474745620000130

Chen, B., Huang, Z., Zhang, R., Jiang, F., Liu, W., Li, H., Wang, J., & Peng, J. (2021). Adaptive slip ratio estimation for active braking control of high-speed trains. *ISA Transactions, 112*, 302–314. DOI: 10.1016/j.isatra.2020.11.027 PMID: 33293045

Chen, S., Liao, Y., Wang, F., Wang, G., Wang, L., Wang, Y., & Zhu, X. (2025). Toward the robustness of autonomous vehicles in the AI era. *Innovation (Cambridge (Mass.)), 6*(3), 100780. DOI: 10.1016/j.xinn.2024.100780 PMID: 40098668

Chen, S., Wu, J., & Zong, Y. (2020). The impact of the freight transport modal shift policy on China's carbon emissions reduction. *Sustainability (Basel), 12*(2), 583. DOI: 10.3390/su12020583

Chen, Y. (2025). A study on the allocation of funds within the global climate governance framework: Based on the interaction between green bonds and carbon markets. *International Journal of Global Economics and Management, 8*(1), 208–214. DOI: 10.62051/ijgem.v8n1.23

Ciuriak, D., & Fay, R. (2024). Trade agreements and data governance: Pathways to interoperability. Centre for International Governance Innovation Policy Brief, No. 195. https://www.cigionline.org/articles/trade-agreements-and-data-governance/

Ciuriak, D., Dadkhah, A., & Xin, D. (2023). Trade in a digital interoperability era. Brookings Institution Policy Brief. https://www.brookings.edu/articles/trade-in-a-digital-interoperability-era/

Dan, D., Ying, Y., & Ge, L. (2022). Digital twin system of bridges group based on machine vision fusion monitoring of bridge traffic load. *IEEE Transactions on Intelligent Transportation Systems*, *23*(11), 22190–22205. DOI: 10.1109/TITS.2021.3130025

Das, P. K., Bhat, M. Y., & Sajith, S. (2024). Life cycle assessment of electric vehicles: A systematic review of literature. *Environmental Science and Pollution Research International*, *31*(1), 73–89. DOI: 10.1007/s11356-023-30999-3 PMID: 38038907

Demir, E., Bektaş, T., & Laporte, G. (2014). A review of recent research on green road freight transportation. *European Journal of Operational Research*, *237*(3), 775–793. DOI: 10.1016/j.ejor.2013.12.033

Dikshit, S., Atiq, A., Shahid, M., Dwivedi, V., & Thusu, A. (2023). The use of artificial intelligence to optimize the routing of vehicles and reduce traffic congestion in urban areas. *EAI Endorsed Transactions on Energy Web*, *10*, e4. DOI: 10.4108/ew.4613

Dinda, S. (2004). Environmental Kuznets curve hypothesis: A survey. *Ecological Economics*, *49*(4), 431–455. DOI: 10.1016/j.ecolecon.2004.02.011

Dong, K., Sun, R., & Hochman, G. (2018). Do natural gas and renewable energy consumption lead to lower carbon emission? *Renewable & Sustainable Energy Reviews*, *82*, 370–379. DOI: 10.1016/j.rser.2017.09.046

Dubey, R., Gunasekaran, A., Childe, S. J., Bryde, D. J., Giannakis, M., Foropon, C., Roubaud, D., & Hazen, B. T. (2020). Big data analytics and artificial intelligence pathway to operational performance under the effects of entrepreneurial orientation and environmental dynamism: A study of manufacturing organisations. *International Journal of Production Economics*, *226*, 107599. DOI: 10.1016/j.ijpe.2019.107599

Dunning, J. H. (1988). The Eclectic Paradigm of International Production: A Restatement and Some Possible Extensions. *Journal of International Business Studies*, *19*(1), 1–31. DOI: 10.1057/palgrave.jibs.8490372

Dunning, J. H. (2000). The Eclectic Paradigm as an Envelope for Theoretical and Context-specific Theories of MNE Activity. *Business History Review*.

Efstathiou, C. I., Arunachalam, S., Arter, C. A., & Buonocore, J. (2024). Assessing the tradeoffs in emissions, air quality and health benefits from excess power generation due to climate-related policies for the transportation sector. *Environmental Research Letters*, *19*(6), 064007. DOI: 10.1088/1748-9326/ad41f1

European Commission. (2021). Commission implementing decision on standard contractual clauses for the transfer of personal data to third countries (C(2021) 3972 final). https://eur-lex.europa.eu/eli/dec_impl/2021/914/oj

European Commission. (2023). Commission implementing decision on the adequate protection of personal data under the EU-U.S. Data Privacy Framework. Official Journal of the European Union, C/2023/4745. https://commission.europa.eu/document/fa09cbad-dd7d-4684-ae60-be03fcb0fddf

European Data Protection Board (EDPB). (2021). Recommendations 01/2020 on measures that supplement transfer tools to ensure compliance with the EU level of protection of personal data (Version 2.0). https://edpb.europa.eu/our-work-tools/our-documents/recommendations/recommendations-012020-measures-supplement-transfer_en

European Environment Agency (EEA). (2025). Greenhouse gas emissions from transport in Europe. [Internet]. Available from: https://www.eea.europa.eu/en/analysis/indicators/greenhouse-gas-emissions-from-transport?activeAccordion=546a7c35-9188-4d23-94ee-005d97c26f2b

European Parliament. (2021). *Exchanges of personal data after the Schrems II judgment (Study No. 694678). Directorate-General for Internal Policies.* Policy Department for Citizens' Rights and Constitutional Affairs., DOI: 10.2861/95877

EUROSTAT. (2024). Greenhouse gas emission accounts. [Internet]. Available from: https://ec.europa.eu/eurostat/statistics-explained/index.php?title=Greenhouse_gas_emission_accounts

Eyo-Udo, N. L. (2024). Examining the integration of artificial intelligence in supply chain management from Industry 4.0 to 6.0: A systematic literature review. *Frontiers in Artificial Intelligence*, *7*, 1477044. Advance online publication. DOI: 10.3389/frai.2024.1477044 PMID: 39902380

Fahimnia, B., Sarkis, J., & Davarzani, H. (2015). Green supply chain management: A review and bibliometric analysis. *International Journal of Production Economics*, *162*, 101–114. DOI: 10.1016/j.ijpe.2015.01.003

Falanga, A., Picone, M., Greco, F. M., & Cartenì, A. (2025). A roadmap to low-carbon freight transport: A review of EU directives and regulations. *WSEAS Transactions on Power Systems*, *20*(11), 114–132. DOI: 10.37394/232016.2025.20.11

Farooq, A., Xie, M., Stoilova, S., & Ahmad, F. (2019). Multicriteria Evaluation of Transport Plan for High-Speed Rail: An Application to Beijing-Xiongan. *Mathematical Problems in Engineering*, *2019*(1), 8319432. DOI: 10.1155/2019/8319432

Feng, F., Zheng, F., Zhang, Z., & Wang, L. (2025). A framework for low-carbon container multimodal transport route optimization under hybrid uncertainty: Model and case study. *Applied Sciences (Basel, Switzerland)*, *15*(12), 6894. DOI: 10.3390/app15126894

Feng, S., Sun, H., Yan, X., Zhu, H., Zou, Z., Shen, S., & Liu, H. X. (2023). Dense reinforcement learning for safety validation of autonomous vehicles. *Nature*, *615*(7953), 620–627. DOI: 10.1038/s41586-023-05732-2 PMID: 36949337

Forsythe, C. R., Gillingham, K. T., Michalek, J. J., & Whitefoot, K. S. (2023). Technology advancement is driving electric vehicle adoption. *Proceedings of the National Academy of Sciences of the United States of America*, *120*(23), e2219396120. Advance online publication. DOI: 10.1073/pnas.2219396120 PMID: 37252977

Gao, Z., Xu, Y., Liu, X., Zhang, L., Liu, Y., & Chen, S. (2023). Electric vehicle lifecycle carbon emission reduction: A review. *Carbon Neutralization*, *2*(5), 528–550. DOI: 10.1002/cnl2.81

Ge, C., & Qin, S. (2024). Digital twin intelligent transportation system (DT-ITS)—A systematic review. *IET Intelligent Transport Systems*, *18*(7), 1165–1192. DOI: 10.1049/itr2.12539

Geels, F. W., Sovacool, B. K., Schwanen, T., & Sorrell, S. (2017). The socio-technical dynamics of low-carbon transitions. *Joule*, *1*(3), 463–479. DOI: 10.1016/j.joule.2017.09.018

Gereffi, G., & Fernandez-Stark, K. (2011). *Global Value Chain Analysis: A Primer*. Center on Globalization, Governance & Competitiveness.

Ghaffari, N., & Kimiagari, S. (2023). The Paradoxical Roles of State-Ownership in EMNE Internationalization: OFDI case. *Journal of World Trade*, *57*(4), 609–642. DOI: 10.54648/TRAD2023028

Gong, J., He, J., Cheng, C., King, M., Yan, X., He, Z., & Zhang, H. (2020). Road test-based electric bus selection: A case study of the Nanjing bus company. *Energies*, *13*(5), 1253. DOI: 10.3390/en13051253

Gosipathala, S. B. (2025). Cognitive AI-powered predictive analytics for dynamic toll pricing optimization in smart transportation networks. *International Journal For Multidisciplinary Research*, *7*(2), 57206. Advance online publication. DOI: 10.36948/ijfmr.2025.v07i02.57206

Govindan, K., Soleimani, H., & Kannan, D. (2015). Reverse logistics and closed-loop supply chain: A comprehensive review to explore the future. *European Journal of Operational Research*, *240*(3), 603–626. DOI: 10.1016/j.ejor.2014.07.012

Grossman, G. M., & Krueger, A. B. (1995). Economic growth and the environment. *The Quarterly Journal of Economics, 110*(2), 353–377. DOI: 10.2307/2118443

Gupta, D., Azizbek, I., Suxrob, P., & Abdullaeva, I. Ravshan kizi, B. M., Abdukabilovna, T. D., & Jumayev, U. (2026). Digital Hoboism. In E. Kaygisiz (Ed.), Digital Ideologies in the Age of Algorithmic Culture (pp. 307–338). IGI Global Scientific Publishing. DOI: 10.4018/979-8-3373-4531-4.ch010

Gupta, D., Xusniddin, R., Jumaniyazova, N., Sherbek, S., Rajabova, N., Shavkat, R., & Dilorom, O. (2026). Developer Confidence, Competence, and Self-Efficacy in the Age of AI. In Le, H. (Ed.), *AI Impacts on Deskilling and Reskilling Software Engineers* (pp. 27–60). IGI Global Scientific Publishing., DOI: 10.4018/979-8-3373-8450-4.ch002

Guschinsky, N., Kovalyov, M. Y., Rozin, B., & Brauner, N. (2021). Fleet and charging infrastructure decisions for fast-charging city electric bus service. *Computers & Operations Research, 135*, 105449. DOI: 10.1016/j.cor.2021.105449

Habib, S., Khan, M. M., Abbas, F., Sang, L., Shahid, M. U., & Tang, H. (2018). A comprehensive study of implemented international standards, technical challenges, impacts and prospects for electric vehicles. *IEEE Access : Practical Innovations, Open Solutions, 6*, 13866–13890. DOI: 10.1109/ACCESS.2018.2812303

Haites, E. (2018). Carbon taxes and greenhouse gas emissions trading systems: What have we learned? *Climate Policy, 18*(8), 955–966. DOI: 10.1080/14693062.2018.1492897

Han, D., & Shen, S. (2024). Deep reinforcement learning for autonomous driving with multi-scenario fusion: A unified reward function approach. In *Proceedings of the 2024 7th International Conference on Machine Learning and Machine Intelligence (MLMI)* (pp. 83-89). ACM. DOI: 10.1145/3696271.3696284

Hansen, B. E. (1999). Threshold effects in non-dynamic panels: Estimation, testing, and inference. *Journal of Econometrics, 93*(2), 345–368. DOI: 10.1016/S0304-4076(99)00025-1

Harrison, J. S., Freeman, R. E., & Abreu, M. C. S. D. (2015). Stakeholder theory as an ethical approach to effective management: Applying the theory to multiple contexts. *Revista Brasileira de Gestão de Negócios, 17*(55), 858–869. DOI: 10.7819/rbgn.v17i55.2647

Harry-Villain, L., Briand, Y., Waisman, H., Rudolph, F., Hall, C., van Asselt, H., Gjerek, M., Merkert, R., D'Agosto, M. de A., & Goes, G. V. (2025). Analyzing sectoral policies for deep decarbonization: The case of national freight transportation. *Climate Policy*, *25*(1), 1–14. DOI: 10.1080/14693062.2025.2485192

Hasan, M. A., Frame, D. J., Chapman, R., & Archie, K. M. (2021). Costs and emissions: Comparing electric and petrol-powered cars in New Zealand. *Transportation Research Part D, Transport and Environment*, *90*, 102671. DOI: 10.1016/j.trd.2020.102671

Hassan, Q., Itimad, D. J. A., Sameen, A. Z., & Salman, M. H. (2023). Hydrogen fuel cell vehicles: Opportunities and challenges. *Sustainability (Basel)*, *15*(15), 11501. DOI: 10.3390/su151511501

Hettler, B., Cordeiro, J. J., & Schuetz, P. (2024). Corporate scope 3 carbon emission reporting as an enabler of supply chain decarbonization: A systematic review and comprehensive research agenda. *Business Strategy and the Environment*, *33*(2), 1277–1299. DOI: 10.1002/bse.3486

He, Z. (2022). Battery electric bus selection based on entropy weight method and road operation test: Using nanjing bus company as an example. *Mathematical Problems in Engineering*, *2022*(1), 1696578. DOI: 10.1155/2022/1696578

High, A. (2022). Book Discussion: Response to comments by Anna High. *Asian Journal of Law and Society*, *9*(3), 526–530. DOI: 10.1017/als.2022.15

Holloway, D. (2024). Digital transformation in supply chains: Improving resilience and sustainability through AI, blockchain, and IoT. *Frontiers in Sustainability*, *6*, 1584580. Advance online publication. DOI: 10.3389/frsus.2025.1584580

Horesh, N., & Quinn, J. C. (2024). Fuel shifts reduce most of the greenhouse gas emissions from transportation in the United States. *Communications Earth & Environment*, *5*(1), 781. Advance online publication. DOI: 10.1038/s43247-024-01924-4

Huang, S., Zhou, Y., Isleem, H. F., Tejani, G. G., & Ragab, A. E. (2025). Intelligent IoT-enabled marketing systems: Enhancing consumer sustainability engagement through perceived usefulness. *Internet of Things : Engineering Cyber Physical Human Systems*, *101797*, 101797. Advance online publication. DOI: 10.1016/j.iot.2025.101797

Hu, G., Liu, Y., Liu, K., & Yang, X. (2023). Research on data-driven dynamic decision-making mechanism of mega infrastructure project construction. *Sustainability (Basel)*, *15*(12), 9219. Advance online publication. DOI: 10.3390/su15129219

Hu, H., Yuan, H., Hu, H., Xiong, S., Wang, Z., Wang, Z., & Zhou, X. (2023). How does adoption of electric vehicles reduce carbon emissions? Evidence from China. *Heliyon*, *9*(9), e20296. DOI: 10.1016/j.heliyon.2023.e20296 PMID: 37809651

Hussain, Z., Kaleem Khan, M., & Xia, Z. (2023). Investigating the role of green transport, environmental taxes and expenditures in mitigating the transport CO2 emissions. *Transportation Letters*, *15*(5), 439–449. DOI: 10.1080/19427867.2022.2065592

Ibrahum, A. D. M., Hussain, M., & Hong, J. (2024). Deep learning adversarial attacks and defenses in autonomous vehicles: A systematic literature review from a safety perspective. *Artificial Intelligence Review*, *58*(1), 11014. DOI: 10.1007/s10462-024-11014-8

Ige, O. E., & Kabeya, M. (2025). Decarbonizing the cement industry: Technological, economic, and policy barriers to CO2 mitigation adoption. *Cleanroom Technology*, *7*(4), 85. DOI: 10.3390/cleantechnol7040085

IMF. (2024). *Climate Policy and Green FDI in Emerging Market and Developing Economies*. International Monetary Fund Staff Climate Note.

India, D. P. O. (2024). Impact of the Digital Personal Data Protection (DPDP) Act on cross-border data transfers. Data Protection & Privacy Journal, 2(4), 187–204. https://www.dpo-india.com/Blogs/impact-dpdpa-cross-border/

International Energy Agency (IEA). (2020). Global CO2 emissions in transport by mode in the Sustainable Development Scenario, 2000-2070. [Internet]. Available from: https://www.iea.org/data-and-statistics/charts/global-co2-emissions-in-transport-by-mode-in-the-sustainable-development-scenario-2000-2070

International Energy Agency (IEA). (2025). The Breakthrough Agenda Report 2025. [Internet]. Available from: https://www.iea.org/reports/breakthrough-agenda-report-2025

International Energy Agency. (2023). *The future of trucks: Implications for energy and the environment*. International Energy Agency. https://www.iea.org/reports/the-future-of-trucks

International Transport Forum. (2023). *ITF transport outlook 2023: Decarbonising freight transport*. OECD Publishing. https://www.itf-oecd.org/transport-outlook-2023

International Union of Railways (UIC). (2011). Wider Benefits Of High-Speed Rail Confirmed In New Studies. [Internet]. Available from: https://www.uic.org/com/IMG/pdf/111208_high_speed_rail_study.pdf

International Union of Railways (UIC). (2018). The definition of High Speed Rail. [Internet]. Available from: https://uic.org/com/enews/nr/596-high-speed/article/the-definition-of-high-speed-rail

International Union of Railways (UIC). (2023). High-speed rail history. [Internet]. Available from: https://uic.org/passenger/highspeed/article/high-speed-rail-history

International Union of Railways (UIC). (2026). Intercity and High-Speed. [Internet]. Available from: https://uic.org/passenger/highspeed/

IPCC. (2014). Transport. In *Climate Change 2014: Mitigation of Climate Change. Contribution of Working Group III to the Fifth Assessment Report of the Intergovernmental Panel on Climate Change*. Cambridge University Press.

IRENA. (2018). *Biogas for road vehicles: Technology brief.* International Renewable Energy Agency.

Isalkar, M. A. S., & Sambhe, R. U. (2024). Artificial Intelligence in Transportation: A Review. *International Journal of Scientific Research in Science, Engineering and Technology, 11*(2), 142–146. DOI: 10.32628/IJSRSET2411212

Islam, M. S., Liu, G., Xu, D., Chen, Y., Li, H., & Chen, C. (2023). University-campus-based zero-carbon action plans for accelerating the zero-Carbon City transition. *Sustainability (Basel), 15*(18), 13504. DOI: 10.3390/su151813504

Islam, M.Master of Engineering in Civil Engineering Lamar University TX USA. (2025). Analysis of Ai-enabled Adaptive Traffic Control Systems for urban mobility optimization through intelligent road network management. *Review of Applied Science and Technology, 04*(02), 207–232. DOI: 10.63125/358pgg63

Ivanov, D., & Dolgui, A. (2021). A digital supply chain twin for managing the disruption risks and resilience in the era of Industry 4.0. *Production Planning and Control, 32*(9), 775–788. DOI: 10.1080/09537287.2020.1768450

Jabbour, C. J. C., & de Sousa Jabbour, A. B. L. (2016). Green human resource management and green supply chain management: Linking two emerging agendas. *Journal of Cleaner Production, 112*, 1824–1833. DOI: 10.1016/j.jclepro.2015.01.052

Jagiełło, A., Wołek, M., & Bizon, W. (2023). Comparison of tender criteria for electric and diesel buses in Poland—Has the ongoing revolution in urban transport been overlooked? *Energies, 16*(11), 4280. DOI: 10.3390/en16114280

Jia, J., Jin, G. Z., & Wagman, L. (2021). The short-run effects of the General Data Protection Regulation on technology venture investment. *Marketing Science, 40*(4), 661–684. DOI: 10.1287/mksc.2020.1271

Jorgenson, D. W., Goettle, R. J., Ho, M. S., & Wilcoxen, P. J. (2018). The welfare consequences of taxing carbon. *Climate Change Economics (Singapore)*, *09*(01), 1840013. DOI: 10.1142/S2010007818400134

Jusić, M. (2022). The application of GDPR in blockchain technology. *Journal of Emerging Technologies in Accounting*, *19*(1), 47–59. DOI: 10.2308/JETA-2020-065

K&L Gates. (2023). New EU-U.S. Data Privacy Framework—Reliable solution for transatlantic data transfers or gateway to Schrems III? Global Privacy & Data Security Law Blog. https://doi.org/DOI: 10.5281/zenodo.8142367

Kaewunruen, S., AbdelHadi, M., Kongpuang, M., Pansuk, W., & Remennikov, A. M. (2023). Digital twins for managing railway bridge maintenance, resilience, and climate change adaptation. *Sensors (Basel)*, *23*(1), 252. Advance online publication. DOI: 10.3390/s23010252 PMID: 36616851

Kaneti, V. R., Yamini, B., Nagarajan, S., Adaikkammai, A., Anto Gracious, L. A., Siva Subramanian, R., & Girija, P. (2025). Smart transportation systems and sustainable urban mobility. In *Revolutionizing Urban Development and Governance With Emerging Technologies* (pp. 261–288). IGI Global., DOI: 10.4018/979-8-3373-1375-7.ch009

Karthick, K., Ravivarman, S., & Priyanka, R. (2024). Optimizing electric vehicle battery life: A machine learning approach for sustainable transportation. *World Electric Vehicle Journal*, *15*(2), 60. DOI: 10.3390/wevj15020060

Kazancoglu, Y., Ozkan-Ozen, Y. D., Sagnak, M., Kazancoglu, I., & Dora, M. (2023). Framework for a sustainable supply chain to overcome risks in transition to a circular economy through Industry 4.0. *Production Planning and Control*, *34*(10), 902–917. DOI: 10.1080/09537287.2021.1980910

Keiser, D., Lade, G. E., & Rudik, I. (2018). Air pollution and visitation at US national parks. Science Advances, 4(7), eaat1613. DOI: 10.1126/sciadv.aat1613

Kelly, A. (2024). Impact of artificial intelligence on supply chain optimization. *The Journal of Supply Chain Management*, *60*(2), 234–256. DOI: 10.1111/jscm.12298

Khan, M., Raza, M. A., Abbas, G., Othmen, S., Yousef, A., & Jumani, T. A. (2024). Pothole detection for autonomous vehicles using deep learning: A robust and efficient solution. *Frontiers in Built Environment*, *9*, 1323792. DOI: 10.3389/fbuil.2023.1323792

Khan, S. A. R., & Qianli, D. (2017). Impact of green supply chain management practices on firms' performance: An empirical study from the perspective of Pakistan. *Environmental Science and Pollution Research International*, *24*(20), 16829–16844. DOI: 10.1007/s11356-017-9172-5 PMID: 28573559

Khan, S. A. R., Zhang, Y., Kumar, A., Zavadskas, E., & Streimikiene, D. (2020). Measuring the impact of renewable energy, public health expenditure, logistics, and environmental performance on sustainable economic growth. *Sustainable Development (Bradford)*, *28*(4), 833–843. DOI: 10.1002/sd.2034

Khong, T. D., Tong, Y. D., & Bui, L. T. H. (2023). Cost-benefit analysis and model preference of public transportation in Can Tho City, Vietnam. *Sustainability (Basel)*, *15*(9), 7247. DOI: 10.3390/su15097247

Kidokoro, Y. (2010). Revenue recycling within transport networks. *Journal of Urban Economics*, *68*(1), 46–55. DOI: 10.1016/j.jue.2010.02.001

Kim, N. S., Janic, M., & van Wee, B. (2009). Trade-off between carbon dioxide emissions and logistics costs based on multiobjective optimization. *Transportation Research Record: Journal of the Transportation Research Board*, *2139*(1), 107–116. DOI: 10.3141/2139-13

Knights, V., Petrovska, O., & Prchkovska, M. (2024). Enhancing smart parking management through machine learning and AI integration in IoT environments. In *Navigating the Internet of Things in the 22nd Century - Concepts, Applications, and Innovations [Working Title]*. IntechOpen. DOI: 10.5772/intechopen.1006490

Kopytsia, V. O., & Kvyetnyy, R. N. (2025). Analysis of approaches to improving intelligent parking management technologies. *Optoelectronic Information-Power Technologies*, *49*(1), 157–167. DOI: 10.31649/1681-7893-2025-49-1-157-167

Körner, M. F., Bauer, D., Keller, R., Rösch, M., Schlereth, A., Simon, P., Bauernhansl, T., & Fridgen, G. (2025). Bridging carbon data's organizational boundaries: Toward automated data sharing in sustainable supply chains. *Electronic Markets*, *35*(1), 13. Advance online publication. DOI: 10.1007/s12525-025-00779-7

Kotlars, A., Hudenko, J., Jurgelane-Kaldava, I., Stankevičienė, J., Gailis, M., Kukjans, I., & Batenko, A. (2025). Transitioning to hydrogen trucks in small economies: Policy, infrastructure, and innovation dynamics. *Sustainability (Basel)*, *17*(24), 11272. DOI: 10.3390/su172411272

Kumar, K. B. N., Pratyusha, D., Sravanthi, B., & Reddy, E. J. (2024). Recent AI applications in electrical vehicles for sustainability. *SSRG International Journal of Mechanical Engineering*, *11*(3), 50–64. DOI: 10.14445/23488360/IJME-V11I3P106

Kušić, K., Schumann, R., & Ivanjko, E. (2023). A digital twin in transportation: Real-time synergy of traffic data streams and simulation for virtualizing motorway dynamics. *Advanced Engineering Informatics, 55*, 101858. Advance online publication. DOI: 10.1016/j.aei.2022.101858

Lagorio, A., Pinto, R., & Golini, R. (2016). Research in urban logistics: A systematic literature review. *International Journal of Physical Distribution & Logistics Management, 46*(10), 908–931. DOI: 10.1108/IJPDLM-01-2016-0008

Latham & Watkins. (2023). India's Digital Personal Data Protection Act 2023 vs. the GDPR: A comparison. Data Protection & Privacy Practice, White Paper Series. https://www.lw.com/admin/upload/SiteAttachments/Indias-Digital-Personal-Data-Protection-Act-2023-vs-the-GDPR-A-Comparison.pdf

Lee, M. (2020). An analysis of the effects of artificial intelligence on electric vehicle technology innovation using patent data. *World Patent Information, 63*, 102002. DOI: 10.1016/j.wpi.2020.102002

Lefèvre, J., Briand, Y., Pye, S., Tovilla, J., Li, F., Oshiro, K., Waisman, H., Cayla, J.-M., & Zhang, R. (2021). A pathway design framework for sectoral deep decarbonization: The case of passenger transportation. *Climate Policy, 21*(1), 93–106. DOI: 10.1080/14693062.2020.1804817

Liimatainen, H., Hovi, I. B., Arvidsson, N., & Nykänen, L. (2015). Driving forces of road freight CO2 in 2030. *International Journal of Physical Distribution & Logistics Management, 45*(3), 260–285. DOI: 10.1108/IJPDLM-10-2013-0255

Lin, P.-C., & Bai, H.-J. (2024). Emissions intensity comparisons and consumption-based CO2 accounting of transportation services. *Maritime Economics & Logistics, 26*(1), 131–150. DOI: 10.1057/s41278-023-00259-9

Lin, S., Fang, X., Lin, F., Yang, Z., & Wang, X. (2018). Reliability of rail transit traction drive system-A review. *Microelectronics and Reliability, 88*, 1281–1285. DOI: 10.1016/j.microrel.2018.07.037

Liu, D., Wang, J., Xu, L., Zhang, H., & Tan, X. (2025). Comparison of energy consumption and carbon emissions of high-speed rail with other transportation modes from life cycle perspective: A case of Beijing-Shanghai. *Research in Transportation Business & Management, 59*, 101278. DOI: 10.1016/j.rtbm.2024.101278

Liu, L., Hwang, T., Lee, S., Ouyang, Y., Lee, B., Smith, S. J., Yan, F., Daenzer, K., & Bond, T. C. (2015a). Emission projections for long-haul freight trucks and rail in the United States through 2050. *Environmental Science & Technology, 49*(19), 11569–11576. DOI: 10.1021/acs.est.5b01187 PMID: 26368392

Liu, P., & Mu, D. (2015). Evaluating sustainability of truck weight regulations: A system dynamics view. *Journal of Industrial Engineering and Management*, *8*(5). Advance online publication. DOI: 10.3926/jiem.1593

Liu, S., & Putro, U. S. (2024). Passenger service satisfaction evaluation of Jakarta-Bandung high-speed railway. *European Journal of Business and Management Research*, *9*(4), 115–126. DOI: 10.24018/ejbmr.2024.9.4.2432

Liu, Z., Gang, L., Yu, B., & Zhang, H. (2022). The routing problem for school buses considering accessibility and equity. *Transportation Research Part D, Transport and Environment*, *107*, 103299. DOI: 10.1016/j.trd.2022.103299

Li, X., & Cheng, Z. (2022). Does high-speed rail improve urban carbon emission efficiency in China? *Socio-Economic Planning Sciences*, *84*, 101308. DOI: 10.1016/j.seps.2022.101308

Li, Y., & Zhang, W. (2023). Traffic flow digital twin generation for highway scenario based on radar-camera paired fusion. *Scientific Reports*, *13*(1), 642. Advance online publication. DOI: 10.1038/s41598-023-27696-z PMID: 36635372

Liyanage, S., Abduljabbar, R., & Dia, H. (2025). Machine learning traffic flow prediction models for smart and sustainable traffic management. *Infrastructures*, *10*(7), 155. DOI: 10.3390/infrastructures10070155

Lv, Z., Li, Y., Feng, H., & Lv, H. (2022). Deep learning for security in digital twins of cooperative intelligent transportation systems. *IEEE Transactions on Intelligent Transportation Systems*, *23*(9), 16666–16675. DOI: 10.1109/TITS.2021.3113779

Macharis, C., & Nocera, S. (2019). The future of freight transport. *European Transport Research Review*, *11*(1), 21. Advance online publication. DOI: 10.1186/s12544-019-0359-3

Mahale, Y., Kolhar, S., & More, S. A. (2025). A comprehensive review on artificial intelligence driven predictive maintenance in vehicles: Technologies, challenges and future research directions. *Discover Applied Sciences*, *7*(4), 243. DOI: 10.1007/s42452-025-06681-3

Mahmoodian, M., Shahrivar, F., Setunge, S., & Mazaheri, S. (2022). Development of digital twin for intelligent maintenance of civil infrastructure. *Sustainability (Basel)*, *14*(14), 8664. Advance online publication. DOI: 10.3390/su14148664

Mandala, V., Surabhi, S. N. R. D., Kommisetty, P. D. N. K., Kuppala, B. M. S. R., & Ingole, R. (2024). *Towards carbon-free automotive futures: Leveraging AI and ML for sustainable transformation*. Educational Administration Theory and Practices., DOI: 10.53555/kuey.v30i5.3474

Marisamy, K., Selvakumar, A., Rajasekar, B., Natarajan, R., Atajanova, A., & Makhmudov, S. (2025). Smart logistics integrating AI, IoT, blockchain, and Robotics for a sustainable Future. In *Emerging Trends in Smart Logistics Technologies* (pp. 73–104). IGI Global Scientific Publishing., DOI: 10.4018/979-8-3373-2434-0.ch003

Mathiesen, L., & Mæstad, O. (2004). Climate policy and the steel industry: Achieving global emission reductions by an incomplete climate agreement. *The Energy Journal (Cambridge, Mass.)*, *25*(4), 91–114. DOI: 10.5547/ISSN0195-6574-EJ-Vol25-No4-5

Matthan, R. (2023). Understanding India's new data protection law: An analysis. Carnegie Endowment for International Peace Working Paper. https://carnegieendowment.org/research/2023/10/understanding-indias-new-data-protection-law

Maume, P. (2023). The Regulation on Markets in Crypto-Assets (MICAR): Landmark codification, or first step of many, or both? *European Company and Financial Law Review*, *20*(2), 243–275. DOI: 10.1515/ecfr-2023-0014

McKinnon, A. (2018). *Decarbonizing logistics: Distributing goods in a low carbon world*. Kogan Page Publishers.

McKinnon, A. (2018). Decarbonizing logistics: Distributing goods in a low-carbon world. *Transport Reviews*, *38*(3), 295–297. DOI: 10.1080/01441647.2017.1389991

McLeod, S., & Browne, M. (2023). Planning for the sustainability of freight and logistics. *European Journal of Transport and Infrastructure Research*. https://doi.org/DOI: 10.18757/ejtir.2023.23.3.6145

Millard-Ball, A., & Schipper, L. (2011). Are we reaching peak travel? Trends in passenger transport in eight industrialized countries. *Transport Reviews*, *31*(3), 357–378. DOI: 10.1080/01441647.2010.518291

Mohsen, M. M., & Mohsen, M. (2025). Reducing emissions through AI-driven multimodal transport optimization in IoT-connected environments. *International Journal of Energy Research*, *2399288*(1), 2399288. Advance online publication. DOI: 10.1155/er/2399288

Montabon, F., Pagell, M., & Wu, Z. (2016). Making sustainability sustainable. *The Journal of Supply Chain Management*, *52*(2), 11–27. DOI: 10.1111/jscm.12103

Moraga, A., de Curtò, J., de Zarzà, I., & Calafate, C. T. (2025). AI-driven UAV and IoT traffic optimization: Large language models for congestion and emission reduction in smart cities. *Drones (Basel)*, *9*(4), 248. DOI: 10.3390/drones9040248

Mulholland, E., & Rodríguez, F. (2022). *The rapid deployment of zero-emission buses in Europe*. International Council on Clean Transportation.

Namchimplee, K., Inohae, T., & Saengsathien, A. (2025). Multimodal transport efficiency in agricultural supply chains: A case study of rail-road integration in Thailand's sugar logistics. *Acta Logistica, 12*(4), 615–626. DOI: 10.22306/al.v12i4.696

Natrayan, L., Kaliappan, S., Bhaskarani, N., & Kasireddy, L. C. (2025, February). Enhancing Trust and Security in Digital Ecosystems with Blockchain Technology. In *2025 International Conference on Technology Enabled Economic Changes (InTech)* (pp. 1008-1013). IEEE. https://doi.org/DOI: 10.1109/InTech64186.2025.11198514

Naumov, S., Keith, D. R., & Sterman, J. D. (2023). Accelerating vehicle fleet turnover to achieve sustainable mobility goals. *Journal of Operations Management, 69*(1), 36–66. DOI: 10.1002/joom.1173

Nehiba, C. (2024). Electric vehicle usage, pollution damages, and the electricity price elasticity of driving. *Journal of Environmental Economics and Management, 124*, 102915. DOI: 10.1016/j.jeem.2023.102915 PMID: 39022448

Nix, J. (2022). Cities Are Buying More Electric Buses, But an EU Deadline Is Needed. [Internet]. Available from: https://www.transportenvironment.org/discover/cities-are-buying-more-electric-buses-but-an-eu-deadline-is-needed

Nonomura, K., Hiekata, K., Nishino, N., & Nakashima, T. (2023). Evaluation of Feebate by multi-agent simulation for policy making in the complex international maritime transport. In *Advances in Transdisciplinary Engineering*. IOS Press., DOI: 10.3233/ATDE230653

OECD. (2002). Strategies to reduce greenhouse gas emissions from road transport: Analytical methods, organization for economic co-operation and development. https://www.itf-oecd.org/sites/default/files/docs/02greenhousee.pdf

OECD. (2020). *International Regulatory Cooperation: Policy Brief.* Organisation for Economic Co-operation and Development.

Oecd. (2022). OECD Framework for the Classification of AI systems. OECD Digital Economy Papers. Regulation (EU) 2016/679 of the European Parliament and of the Council of 27 April 2016 on the protection of natural persons with regard to the processing of personal data and on the free movement of such data, and repealing Directive 95/46/EC (General Data Protection Regulation). Official Journal of the European Union, L 119/1. https://eur-lex.europa.eu/eli/reg/2016/679/ojDOI: 10.1787/20716826

Organisation for Economic Co-operation and Development. (2021). *Decarbonising freight transport: Policy recommendations*. OECD Publishing. https://www.oecd.org/transport/decarbonising-freight-transport.htm

Orlov, A. (2017). Distributional effects of higher natural gas prices in Russia. *Energy Policy*, *109*, 590–600. DOI: 10.1016/j.enpol.2017.07.047

Oteri, O. J., Onukwulu, E. C., Igwe, A. N., Ewim, C. P.-M., Ibeh, A. I., & Sobowale, A. (2023). Artificial Intelligence in product pricing and revenue optimization: Leveraging data-driven decision-making. *International Journal of Multidisciplinary Research and Growth Evaluation*, *4*(1), 842–851. DOI: 10.54660/.IJMRGE.2023.4.1-842-851

Our World in Data. (2024). *CO_2 and greenhouse gas emissions*. https://ourworldindata.org/co2-and-greenhouse-gas-emissions

Oyewale, K., & Bassey, K. E. (2024). Climate action and social equity: Mitigation strategies and carbon credits. *World Journal of Advanced Research and Reviews*, *24*(2), 187–201. DOI: 10.30574/wjarr.2024.24.2.3325

Peng, M. W., Wang, D. Y., & Jiang, Y. (2008). An institution-based view of international business strategy: A focus on emerging economies. *Journal of International Business Studies*, *39*(5), 920–936. DOI: 10.1057/palgrave.jibs.8400377

Peng, M. W., Wang, J. C., Kathuria, N., Shen, J., & Welbourne Eleazar, M. J. (2023, June). Nishant Kathuria, Shen J., Eleazar M. J. W. (2023). Toward an institution-based paradigm. *Asia Pacific Journal of Management*, *40*(2), 353–382. Advance online publication. DOI: 10.1007/s10490-022-09861-6

Petrović, N., Jovanović, V., Marković, S., Marinković, D., & Nikolić, B. (2025). Multi-criteria decision-making approach for choising e-Bus for urban public transport in the city of Niš. *Acta Technica Jaurinensis*, *18*(1), 1–8. DOI: 10.14513/actatechjaur.00758

Picone, M., Falanga, A., Henke, I., Greco, F. M., & Carteni, A. (2025). Decarbonizing road transport: A systematic review of methods and models for emission impact assessment. *WSEAS Transactions on Environment and Development*, *21*(56), 674–688. DOI: 10.37394/232015.2025.21.56

Pinchasik, D. R., Hovi, I. B., Mjøsund, C. S., Grønland, S. E., Fridell, E., & Jerksjö, M. (2020). Crossing borders and expanding modal shift measures: Effects on mode choice and emissions from freight transport in the Nordics. *Sustainability (Basel)*, *12*(3), 894. DOI: 10.3390/su12030894

Pithale, R. K.Rohit Kashinath Pithale. (2025). The economics of public transport in Mumbai: A critical analysis of inefficiencies and policy failures. *International Journal For Multidisciplinary Research*, *7*(1), 37881. Advance online publication. DOI: 10.36948/ijfmr.2025.v07i01.37881

Pretis, F. (2022). Does a carbon tax reduce CO2 emissions? Evidence from British Columbia. *Environmental and Resource Economics*, *83*(1), 115–144. DOI: 10.1007/s10640-022-00679-w

Puzio, E., Drożdż, W., & Kolon, M. (2025). The role of intelligent transport systems and smart technologies in urban traffic management in Polish smart cities. *Energies*, *18*(10), 2580. DOI: 10.3390/en18102580

Queiroz, M. M., Pereira, S. C. F., Telles, R., & Machado, M. C. (2021). Industry 4.0 and digital supply chain capabilities: A framework for understanding digitalisation challenges and opportunities. *Benchmarking*, *28*(5), 1761–1782. DOI: 10.1108/BIJ-12-2018-0435

Rajeev, A., Pati, R. K., Padhi, S. S., & Govindan, K. (2017). Evolution of sustainability in supply chain management: A literature review. *Journal of Cleaner Production*, *162*, 299–314. DOI: 10.1016/j.jclepro.2017.05.026

Rapson, D. S., & Muehlegger, E. (2023a). Global transportation decarbonization. *The Journal of Economic Perspectives*, *37*(3), 163–188. DOI: 10.1257/jep.37.3.163

Rapson, D. S., & Muehlegger, E. (2023b). The economics of electric vehicles. *Review of Environmental Economics and Policy*, *17*(2), 274–294. DOI: 10.1086/725484

Ravikumar, R. N., & Aarthi, S. (2025a). AI-driven digital twins and autonomous operations for sustainable logistics and procurement. In *Advances in Computational Intelligence and Robotics* (pp. 65–100). IGI Global Scientific Publishing. DOI: 10.4018/979-8-3373-7006-4.ch003

Ravikumar, R. N., & Aarthi, S. (2025b). Human-AI synergy for organizational resilience. In *Advances in Computational Intelligence and Robotics* (pp. 287–322). IGI Global Scientific Publishing. https://doi.org/DOI: 10.4018/979-8-3373-7416-1.ch011

Ravikumar, R. N., & Aarthi, S. (2025c). Intelligent logistics. In *Advances in Computational Intelligence and Robotics* (pp. 217–248). IGI Global Scientific Publishing. DOI: 10.4018/979-8-3373-7006-4.ch008

Ravikumar, R. N., & Aarthi, S. (2025). AI-driven governance. In *Advances in Computational Intelligence and Robotics* (pp. 343–372). IGI Global Scientific Publishing., DOI: 10.4018/979-8-3373-3760-9.ch012

Ravikumar, R. N., & Aarthi, S. (2025b). Artificial Intelligence and IoT integration in supply chains. In *Leveraging Technology and Renewable Energy for Sustainable Supply Chains* (pp. 1–32). IGI Global Scientific Publishing., DOI: 10.4018/979-8-3373-3790-6.ch001

Ren, H. (2025). Optimization method of electric vehicle energy system based on machine learning. *Frontiers of Mechanical Engineering*, *11*, 1597558. DOI: 10.3389/fmech.2025.1597558

Rennert, K., Errickson, F., Prest, B. C., Rennels, L., Newell, R. G., Pizer, W., Kingdon, C., Wingenroth, J., Cooke, R., Parthum, B., Smith, D., Cromar, K., Diaz, D., Moore, F. C., Müller, U. K., Plevin, R. J., Raftery, A. E., Ševčíková, H., Sheets, H., & Anthoff, D. (2022). Comprehensive evidence implies a higher social cost of CO2. *Nature*, *610*(7933), 687–692. DOI: 10.1038/s41586-022-05224-9 PMID: 36049503

Reserve Bank of India (RBI). (2025). *Census on Foreign Liabilities and Assets of Indian Direct Investment Entities*.

Richey, R. G.Jr, Chowdhury, S., Davis-Sramek, B., Giannakis, M., & Dwivedi, Y. K. (2023). Artificial intelligence in logistics and supply chain management: A primer and roadmap for research. *Journal of Business Logistics*, *44*(4), 532–549. DOI: 10.1111/jbl.12364

Rodrigues, A. L., & Seixas, S. R. (2022). Battery-electric buses and their implementation barriers: Analysis and prospects for sustainability. *Sustainable Energy Technologies and Assessments*, *51*, 101896. DOI: 10.1016/j.seta.2021.101896

Rogge, K. S., & Reichardt, K. (2016). Policy mixes for sustainability transitions: An extended concept and framework for analysis. *Research Policy*, *45*(8), 1620–1635. DOI: 10.1016/j.respol.2016.04.004

Rout, C., Li, H., Dupont, V., & Wadud, Z. (2022). A comparative total cost of ownership analysis of heavy duty on-road and off-road vehicles powered by hydrogen, electricity, and diesel. *Heliyon*, *8*(12), e12417. DOI: 10.1016/j.heliyon.2022.e12417 PMID: 36593823

Rozkrut, M., Kucharski, A., Nermend, K., & Waśniewski, J. (2025). The governmental hand in the algorithmic age: Policy levers, challenges, and implications in shaping artificial intelligence skills. In *Intelligent Management and Artificial Intelligence: Trends, Challenges, and Opportunities, Vol.1* (pp. 557–582). Wydawnictwo Naukowe Uniwersytetu Szczecińskiego. DOI: 10.18276/978-83-8419-028-9-38

Saberi, S., Kouhizadeh, M., Sarkis, J., & Shen, L. (2019). Blockchain technology and its relationships to sustainable supply chain management. *International Journal of Production Research*, *57*(7), 2117–2135. DOI: 10.1080/00207543.2018.1533261

Saboori, B., Sulaiman, J., & Mohd, S. (2014). Economic growth and CO_2 emissions in developing countries: Evidence from the environmental Kuznets curve hypothesis. *Energy Policy*, *65*, 304–311. DOI: 10.1016/j.enpol.2013.10.061

Sachs, J. D., Schmidt-Traub, G., Mazzucato, M., Messner, D., Nakicenovic, N., & Rockström, J. (2019). Six transformations to achieve the sustainable development goals. *Nature Sustainability*, *2*(9), 805–814. DOI: 10.1038/s41893-019-0352-9

Sadorsky, P. (2009). Renewable energy consumption and income in emerging economies. *Energy Policy*, *37*(10), 4021–4028. DOI: 10.1016/j.enpol.2009.05.003

Sahoo, A. P. (2025). Revolutionizing eCommerce: AI-powered dynamic pricing strategies. *World Journal of Advanced Research and Reviews*, *26*(2), 4194–4201. DOI: 10.30574/wjarr.2025.26.2.2070

Sahoo, L. K., & Varadarajan, V. (2025). Deep learning for autonomous driving systems: Technological innovations, strategic implementations, and business implications - a comprehensive review. *Complex Engineering Systems*, *5*(1), 11. DOI: 10.20517/ces.2024.83

Sahu, P. K., Pani, A., & Santos, G. (2022). Freight traffic impacts and logistics inefficiencies in India: Policy interventions and solution concepts for sustainable city logistics. *Transportation in Developing Economies*, *8*(2), 31. Advance online publication. DOI: 10.1007/s40890-022-00161-8

Saki, S., & Soori, M. (2024). Artificial intelligence, machine learning and deep learning in advanced transportation systems, a review. *Multimodal Transportation*, *4*(2), 100242. DOI: 10.1016/j.multra.2025.100242

Sang, L. T., Ravikumar, R. N., Aarthi, S., & Ben, T. L. (2025). Optimizing sales and inventory performance using AI and business intelligence in POS environments. In *Advances in Computational Intelligence and Robotics* (pp. 259–290). IGI Global Scientific Publishing. DOI: 10.4018/979-8-3373-4392-1.ch011

Santos, G., Maoh, H., Potoglou, D., & von Brunn, T. (2013). Factors influencing modal split of commuting journeys in medium-size European cities. *Journal of Transport Geography*, *30*, 127–137. DOI: 10.1016/j.jtrangeo.2013.04.005

Sarker, T., & Serieux, J. (2022). The impact of reverse technology spillover on environmental performance in India. *Journal of Management Sciences*.

Saxena, N., Sarkar, B., Wee, H. M., Reong, S., Singh, S. R., & Hsiao, Y. L. (2023). A reverse logistics model with eco-design under the Stackelberg-Nash equilibrium and centralized framework. *Journal of Cleaner Production*, *387*, 135789. DOI: 10.1016/j.jclepro.2022.135789

Schrems, M. (2020). Data Protection Commissioner v Facebook Ireland Limited and Maximillian Schrems (Case C-311/18). Court of Justice of the European Union. https://curia.europa.eu/juris/liste.jsf?num=C-311/18

Scott, W. R. (2013). *Institutions and organizations: Ideas, interests, and identities*. Sage publications.

Searcy, C. (2016). Measuring enterprise sustainability. *Business Strategy and the Environment, 25*(2), 120–133. DOI: 10.1002/bse.1861

Shafique, M., Azam, A., Rafiq, M., & Luo, X. (2022). Life cycle assessment of electric vehicles and internal combustion engine vehicles: A case study of Hong Kong. *Research in Transportation Economics, 91*, 101112. DOI: 10.1016/j.retrec.2021.101112

Shafique, M., & Luo, X. (2022). Environmental life cycle assessment of battery electric vehicles from the current and future energy mix perspective. *Journal of Environmental Management, 303*, 114050. DOI: 10.1016/j.jenvman.2021.114050 PMID: 34872799

Singh, S. K., Del Giudice, M., Chierici, R., & Graziano, D. (2020). Green innovation and environmental performance: The role of green transformational leadership and green human resource management. *Technological Forecasting and Social Change, 150*, 119762. DOI: 10.1016/j.techfore.2019.119762

Song, J., He, G., Wang, J., & Zhang, P. (2022). Shaping future low-carbon energy and transportation systems: Digital technologies and applications. *IEnergy, 1*(3), 285–305. DOI: 10.23919/IEN.2022.0040

Song, L., Chen, C., & Lin, F. (2025). AI algorithmic pricing for online platforms: A literature review. *Advances in Economics. Management and Political Sciences, 196*(1), 125–139. DOI: 10.54254/2754-1169/2025.BJ24935

Sresakoolchai, J., & Kaewunruen, S. (2023). Railway infrastructure maintenance efficiency improvement using deep reinforcement learning integrated with digital twin based on track geometry and component defects. *Scientific Reports, 13*(1), 2439. Advance online publication. DOI: 10.1038/s41598-023-29526-8 PMID: 36765166

Sroczyński, A., & Czyżewski, A. (2023). Road traffic can be predicted by machine learning equally effectively as by complex microscopic model. *Scientific Reports, 13*(1), 14523. Advance online publication. DOI: 10.1038/s41598-023-41902-y PMID: 37666950

Stern, D. I. (2004). The rise and fall of the environmental Kuznets curve. *World Development, 32*(8), 1419–1439. DOI: 10.1016/j.worlddev.2004.03.004

Sun, D., Sampene, A. K., & Asante, D. (2023). An investigation on the role of electric vehicles in alleviating environmental pollution: Evidence from five leading economies. *Environmental Science and Pollution Research International*, *30*(7), 18244–18259. DOI: 10.1007/s11356-022-23386-x PMID: 36208376

Sun, T. Q., Liu, Y., Fu, X., & Rogers, J. (2025). Global innovation cooperation and governance: Evidence from China. *Science & Public Policy*, *52*(3), 436–437. DOI: 10.1093/scipol/scae089

Sutikno, T., & Purnama, H. S. (2025). The smart e-bike ecosystem integrates internet of things and artificial intelligence. *Computer Science and Information Technology*, *6*(3), 307–314. DOI: 10.11591/csit.v6i3.p307-314

Szczepański, E., Żochowska, R., Izdebski, M., & Jacyna, M. (2025). Decision-making problems in urban transport decarbonization strategies: Challenges, tools, and methods. *Energies*, *18*(15), 3970. DOI: 10.3390/en18153970

Tasdemir, B. D., & Ayan, M. A. (2025). Driving to Future Integrating Digital Transformation to Sustainable Transportation. In *Developing Dynamic and Sustainable Supply Chains to Achieve Sustainable Development Goals* (pp. 91–120). IGI Global Scientific Publishing. DOI: 10.4018/979-8-3693-6284-6.ch004

Teece, D. J. (2018). Business models and dynamic capabilities. *Long Range Planning*, *51*(1), 40–49. DOI: 10.1016/j.lrp.2017.06.007

Thacker, S., Adshead, D., Fay, M., Hallegatte, S., Harvey, M., Meller, H., O'Regan, N., Rozenberg, J., Watkins, G., & Hall, J. W. (2019). Infrastructure for sustainable development. *Nature Sustainability*, *2*(4), 324–331. DOI: 10.1038/s41893-019-0256-8

Timilsina, G. R., & Shrestha, A. (2009). Transport sector CO_2 emissions growth in Asia: Underlying factors and policy options. *Energy Policy*, *37*(11), 4523–4539. DOI: 10.1016/j.enpol.2009.06.009

Toorajipour, R., Sohrabpour, V., Nazarpour, A., Oghazi, P., & Fischl, M. (2020). Artificial intelligence in supply chain management: A systematic literature review. *Journal of Business Research*, *122*, 502–517. DOI: 10.1016/j.jbusres.2020.09.009

Tran, D. H., & Choi, W. (2017). Design of a high-efficiency wireless power transfer system with intermediate coils for the on-board chargers of electric vehicles. *IEEE Transactions on Power Electronics*, *33*(1), 175–187. DOI: 10.1109/TPEL.2017.2662067

TrustArc. (2024). How the Schrems II decision changed privacy law. Privacy Compliance Resources. https://trustarc.com/resource/schrems-ii-decision-changed-privacy-law/

Tsekouras, G. E., Chatzisavvas, K. C., Triantos, D., Mitsikas, G., Christopoulos, L., & Dialynas, E. (2024). AI-driven predictive maintenance in modern maritime transport—Enhancing operational efficiency and reliability. *Applied Sciences (Basel, Switzerland), 14*(20), 9439. DOI: 10.3390/app14209439

Ucar, A., Karakose, M., & Kırımça, N. (2024). Artificial intelligence for predictive maintenance applications: Key components, trustworthiness, and future trends. *Applied Sciences (Basel, Switzerland), 14*(2), 898. DOI: 10.3390/app14020898

UNCTAD. (2025). *World Investment Report 2025*. United Nations.

UNESCAP. (n.d.). *Outward Foreign Direct Investment (OFDI) Toolkit: Know-how and technology*.

United Nations Economic Commission for Europe (UNECE). (2024). White paper on data governance for trade facilitation. United Nations. https://unece.org/sites/default/files/2024-11/WhitePaper-DataGovernanceTradeFacilitation.pdf

van den Bijgaart, I., Gerlagh, R., & Mattauch, L. (2023). Healthy climate, healthy bodies: Optimal fuel taxation and physical activity. *Economica, 90*(360), 1233–1261. DOI: 10.1111/ecca.12497

van Dijk, J., Farsi, M., & Weber, S. (2021). Travel mode choices in a greening market: The impact of electric vehicles and prior investments. *Transportation Research Record: Journal of the Transportation Research Board, 2675*(11), 1205–1218. DOI: 10.1177/03611981211025279

Van Ooijen, I., & Vrabec, H. U. (2019). Does the GDPR enhance consumers' control over personal data? An analysis from a behavioural perspective. *Journal of Consumer Policy, 42*(1), 91–107. DOI: 10.1007/s10603-018-9399-7

Venkatesh, N. H., & Raslavičius, L. (2024). A National Innovation System concept-based analysis of autonomous vehicles' potential in reaching zero-emission fleets. *Technologies, 12*(2), 26. DOI: 10.3390/technologies12020026

Vezyroglou, K., & Siokis, F. (2025). Pricing in the sharing economy—A hybrid approach leveraging econometrics, machine learning, and artificial intelligence. *Information (Basel), 16*(6), 450. DOI: 10.3390/info16060450

Villegas-Ch, W., Govea, J., & Jaramillo-Alcazar, A. (2023). Advances in the optimization of vehicular traffic in smart cities: Integration of blockchain and computer vision for sustainable mobility. *Sustainability (Basel), 15*(22), 15736. DOI: 10.3390/su152215736

Vleugel, J. M., & Bal, F. (2018). Regional goods delivery: How to reduce its CO 2-, NO x- and PM 10- emissions? *International Journal of Energy Production and Management*, *3*(4), 338–347. DOI: 10.2495/EQ-V3-N4-338-347

von Malmborg, F. (2025). At the controls: Politics and policy entrepreneurs in EU policy to decarbonize maritime transport. *The Review of Policy Research*, *42*(5), 1243–1276. DOI: 10.1111/ropr.12609

Wamba, S. F., Gunasekaran, A., Akter, S., Ren, S. J. F., Dubey, R., & Childe, S. J. (2017). Big data analytics and firm performance: Effects of dynamic capabilities. *Journal of Business Research*, *70*, 356–365. DOI: 10.1016/j.jbusres.2016.08.009

Watson, I., Ali, A., & Bayyati, A. (2022). Energy efficiency of high-speed railways. *Advances in Environmental and Engineering Research*, *3*(4), 1–22. DOI: 10.21926/aeer.2204055

Wei, H., Xu, N., Zhang, H., Zheng, G., Zang, X., Chen, C., Zhang, W., Zhu, Y., Xu, K., & Li, Z. (2019). CoLight: Learning network-level cooperation for traffic signal control. In *Proceedings of the 28th ACM International Conference on Information and Knowledge Management* (pp. 1913-1922). ACM. DOI: 10.1145/3357384.3357902

Weiland, S., Hickmann, T., Lederer, M., & Schwindenhammer, S. (2021). The 2030 agenda for sustainable development: Transformative change through the sustainable development goals? *Politics and Governance*, *9*(1), 90–95. DOI: 10.17645/pag.v9i1.4191

Winkler, L., Pearce, D., Nelson, J., & Babacan, O. (2023). The effect of sustainable mobility transition policies on cumulative urban transport emissions and energy demand. *Nature Communications*, *14*(1), 2357. Advance online publication. DOI: 10.1038/s41467-023-37728-x PMID: 37095105

Wong, C. Y., Wong, C. W., & Boon-itt, S. (2020). Effects of green supply chain integration and green innovation on environmental and cost performance. *International Journal of Production Research*, *58*(15), 4589–4609. DOI: 10.1080/00207543.2020.1756510

Woody, M., Stolper, S., Vaishnav, P., & Keoleian, G. A. (2024). Vehicle scrappage policies for transportation decarbonization. *Environmental Research: Energy*, *1*(3), 033002. DOI: 10.1088/2753-3751/ad63aa

World Bank. (2024). *Global Economic Prospects: Strategic Frameworks for Development*.

World Bank. (2024a). *Energy use (kg of oil equivalent per capita)*. World Development Indicators. https://data.worldbank.org/indicator/EG.EGY.PRIM.PP.KD

World Bank. (2024b). *GDP (current US$)*. World Development Indicators. https://data.worldbank.org/indicator/NY.GDP.MKTP.CD

World Bank. (2024c). *Renewable energy consumption (% of total final energy consumption)*. World Development Indicators. https://data.worldbank.org/indicator/EG.FEC.RNEW.ZS

World Bank. (2024d). *Urban population (% of total population)*. World Development Indicators. https://data.worldbank.org/indicator/SP.URB.TOTL.IN.ZS

World Bank. (2024e). *World development indicators*. https://databank.worldbank.org/source/world-development-indicators

World Meteorological Organization (WMO). (2022). Provisional state of the global climate 2022. [Internet]. Available from: https://wmo.int/publication-series/provisional-state-of-global-climate-2022

Wu, D., Zheng, A., Yu, W., Cao, H., Ling, Q., Liu, J., & Zhou, D. (2025). Digital twin technology in transportation infrastructure: A comprehensive survey of current applications, challenges, and future directions. *Applied Sciences (Basel, Switzerland)*, *15*(4), 1911. Advance online publication. DOI: 10.3390/app15041911

Wu, Y., & Zhang, R. (2023). Evaluation model for a port hinterland intermodal freight network considering environmental impacts and capacity constraints. *Transportation Research Record: Journal of the Transportation Research Board*, *2677*(2), 462–478. DOI: 10.1177/03611981221107008

Xu, X., Kamboj, P., Almutairi, S., Gertin, T., Arora, A., Hejazi, M., & Center, K. A. P. S. and R. (2025). *Decarbonizing road freight transportation in Saudi Arabia*. King Abdullah Petroleum Studies and Research Center. DOI: 10.30573/KS--2025-DP10

Yalçıntaş, D. (2022). Invoking the nullity of non-compete agreements in Employment Law: A comparison of Turkish and Belgian law. *International Journal of Comparative Labour Law and Industrial Relations*, *38*(3), 331–358. DOI: 10.54648/IJCL2022015

Yan, B., Yang, F., Qiu, S., Wang, J., Cai, B., Wang, S., Zaheer, Q., Wang, W., Chen, Y., & Hu, W. (2023). Digital twin in transportation infrastructure management: A systematic review. *Intelligent Transportation Infrastructure*, *2*, liad024. Advance online publication. DOI: 10.1093/iti/liad024

Yao, Q., Zhu, S., & Li, Y. (2022). Green vehicle-routing problem of fresh agricultural products considering carbon emission. *International Journal of Environmental Research and Public Health*, *19*(14), 8675. DOI: 10.3390/ijerph19148675 PMID: 35886525

Yao, R., Tripathi, S., Bayen, A., & Poolla, K. (2025). Big-data empowered traffic signal control could reduce urban carbon emission. *Nature Communications*, *16*(1), 1701. DOI: 10.1038/s41467-025-56701-4 PMID: 40016199

Yawar, S. A., & Seuring, S. (2017). Management of social issues in supply chains: A literature review exploring social issues, actions and performance outcomes. *Journal of Business Ethics*, *141*(3), 621–643. DOI: 10.1007/s10551-015-2719-9

Zaid, A. A., Jaaron, A. A., & Bon, A. T. (2018). The impact of green human resource management and green supply chain management practices on sustainable performance: An empirical study. *Journal of Cleaner Production*, *204*, 965–979. DOI: 10.1016/j.jclepro.2018.09.062

Zhang, D., Mohsin, M., Rasheed, A. K., Chang, Y., & Taghizadeh-Hesary, F. (2021). Public spending and green economic growth in BRI region: Mediating role of green finance. *Energy Policy*, *153*, 112256. DOI: 10.1016/j.enpol.2021.112256

Zhang, H., Xue, B., Li, S., Yu, Y., Li, X., Chang, Z., Wu, H., Hu, Y., Huang, K., Liu, L., Chen, L., & Su, Y. (2023). Life cycle environmental impact assessment for battery-powered electric vehicles at the global and regional levels. *Scientific Reports*, *13*(1), 7952. DOI: 10.1038/s41598-023-35150-3 PMID: 37193809

Zhang, T., Chen, X., Yu, Z., Zhu, X., & Shi, D. (2018). A Monte Carlo simulation approach to evaluate service capacities of EV charging and battery swapping stations. *IEEE Transactions on Industrial Informatics*, *14*(9), 3914–3923. DOI: 10.1109/TII.2018.2796498

Zhang, Y., Wang, W., & Liang, S. (2021). Threshold effects of renewable energy on carbon emissions in developing economies. *Energy Economics*, *98*, 105255. DOI: 10.1016/j.eneco.2021.105255

Zhao, R., Li, Y., Fan, Y., Gao, F., Tsukada, M., & Gao, Z. (2024). A survey on recent advancements in autonomous driving using deep reinforcement learning: Applications, challenges, and solutions. *IEEE Transactions on Intelligent Transportation Systems*, *25*(12), 19482–19503. DOI: 10.1109/TITS.2024.3452480

Zhao, X., Ma, X., Chen, B., Shang, Y., & Song, M. (2022). Challenges toward carbon neutrality in China: Strategies and countermeasures. *Resources, Conservation and Recycling*, *176*, 105959. DOI: 10.1016/j.resconrec.2021.105959

Zhao, Z., & Chen, J. (2025). Application of artificial intelligence technology in the economic development of urban intelligent transportation system. *PeerJ. Computer Science*, *11*, e2728. DOI: 10.7717/peerj-cs.2728 PMID: 40134871

Zhu, L., Liu, Z., & Jian, W. (2023). Contribution assessment of carbon tax on the reduction of freight corridor carbon emissions through modal shift. *Transportation Research Record: Journal of the Transportation Research Board*, *2677*(10), 167–179. DOI: 10.1177/03611981231160538

Zhu, Q., Sarkis, J., & Lai, K. H. (2008). Green supply chain management implications for "closing the loop". *Transportation Research Part E, Logistics and Transportation Review*, *44*(1), 1–18. DOI: 10.1016/j.tre.2006.06.003

About the Contributors

Mohamed Amine Frikha is an Assistant Professor at King Faisal University. He holds a Ph.D. from the University of Sfax, Tunisia, specializing in logistics, transport economics, and sustainability. His research focuses on topics such as goods clearance, international transactions, and improving the efficiency of logistics systems. With expertise in the economic and environmental aspects of transportation, Dr. Frikha aims to contribute to the development of sustainable global supply chains. His work combines academic insights with real-world applications to enhance the efficiency and sustainability of international trade and logistics.

***

Anorgul Ashirova is working as an Associate Professor at the Department of General Professional Sciences, Mamun University, Khiva, Uzbekistan

Shoyimkulov Asror is affiliated with the Department of Information Technology and Exact Sciences at Termez University of Economics and Service, Termez, Uzbekistan. He is engaged in academic teaching and research in the areas of information technology, computational sciences, and applied digital technologies. His academic interests include software development, data analysis, and the application of modern computing techniques to solve practical problems in science and industry. Through his teaching and scholarly activities, he contributes to the development of students' technical skills and analytical abilities. He is also involved in academic collaborations, research projects, and knowledge dissemination through scholarly publications and conferences, supporting the advancement of information technology education and research.

Deepak Gupta is a distinguished academician with over 20 years of teaching experience and expertise in Computer Science and Engineering. He holds a Ph.D. in Computer Engineering and has an extensive research portfolio, including many international journal papers, multiple conference proceedings, and several books. His research interests span machine learning, artificial intelligence, and data mining. Currently, Dr. Gupta serves as an Associate Professor and Head of Department of CSE (Emerging Branches) at ITM Gwalior, MP, India. He has also contributed significantly to the field through patents and copyrights and actively engages as a reviewer, conference chair and editor.

Gautam Jha is a finance researcher and undergraduate student pursuing a Bachelor of Business Administration (BBA) with a specialization in Finance and Digital Marketing. His academic work focuses on financial markets, sustainable finance, emerging market investment strategies, and macro-financial dynamics. He has contributed to several academic publications, including book chapters indexed in international academic databases, with research covering topics such as fintech ecosystems, startup financing, green finance, and sectoral investment dynamics in emerging economies. His current research interests include green finance, sustainable transport infrastructure investment, yield curve dynamics, and the role of financial markets in economic transitions. Alongside academic research, he works on equity research, financial modeling, and valuation analysis through his independent platform The Valuation House, where he publishes market insights and valuation frameworks. His work integrates academic research with practical financial analysis to explore real-world investment and policy implications.

Sena Kumcu is a research assistant in the Department of Industrial Engineering at Gazi University (Türkiye). She holds both a Master's and a PhD degree in Industrial Engineering from Gazi University. During her PhD studies, she was a visiting PhD student at the University of Padova (Italy), where she conducted research on carbon capture and storage (CCS) supply chain optimization. Her research interests include mathematical modelling, network optimization, supply chain management, and decarbonization technologies.

Abdusamatov Mamayusup is a faculty member in the Department of Accounting and Statistics at Termez University of Economics and Service, Termez, Uzbekistan. He is engaged in teaching and academic research in the areas of financial accounting, management accounting, and applied statistics. His scholarly interests include quantitative methods for economic analysis, financial data interpretation, and evidence-based decision-making in organizational and public-sector contexts. He actively contributes to curriculum development and student mentoring, with an emphasis on strengthening analytical competencies and practical skills. His work supports the integration of statistical reasoning into accounting education and economic research.

Vijaishree Pandey, a distinguished academician and legal professional, serves as the President of the Artificial Intelligence for Women's Empowerment and Representation Council, spearheading initiatives at the intersection of law, technology, and gender equality. Experienced and accomplished academician with a demonstrated history of working in the legal services industry and a passion for research and publication. Her expertise in Human Rights and IPRs and had undergone trainings related to Artificial Intelligence. She has worked in collaboration with jails, orphanages, schools, and RWAs, aiming to provide legal aid and basic legal rights. Her leadership skills, coupled with her dedication to professional ethics and academic excellence, have earned her the respect of her peers and students alike. Her dedication to social causes is evident through her involvement in legal aid programs, advocacy efforts, and community outreach initiatives. Beyond academia, Dr. Pandey is a sought-after resource person and guest speaker, lending her expertise to various institutions and organizations. Her expertise spans across various domains, coupled with her leadership acumen and commitment to women's empowerment. As the President of the Artificial Intelligence for Women's Empowerment and Representation Council, Dr. Pandey spearheads initiatives aimed at bridging the gender gap in AI and fostering inclusivity. Her research prowess is evidenced by a prolific publication record, comprising numerous papers, chapters, and books on diverse legal topics. She has also been an active participant in conferences, seminars, and webinars, contributing to the advancement of legal scholarship and continuously expanding her knowledge and professional network. With an extensive portfolio including multiple paper publications in reputed national and international journals, workshops, book chapters in edited books, and conference presentations, she has established a strong presence in the academic community. Experienced Legal Professional with a strong background in Web 4.0 and Artificial Intelligence. She is skilled in analysing complex legal cases and providing innovative solutions. Proficient in applying cutting-edge technology to the legal field, effectively utilizing AI tools to streamline processes and enhance efficiency. She has developed a deep understanding of the intersection between technology and law, with a focus on leveraging AI advancements to improve access to justice. Looking ahead, her goal is to continue making significant contributions to the legal field and to establish myself as a leading expert and thought leader in the field of law while also mentoring and inspiring the next generation of scholars. She is driven, meticulous, and committed to fostering academic excellence.

Kurbonov Jasurbek Pozilovich serves as the Dean of the Faculty of Economics at Alfraganus University, Tashkent, Uzbekistan. He is actively involved in academic leadership, teaching, and research in the fields of economics, finance, and economic development. His scholarly interests include economic policy, financial management, and the application of modern analytical approaches to economic systems and business environments. In his role as dean, he contributes to the development of academic programs, research initiatives, and international collaborations that strengthen the quality of higher education. Through his academic and administrative work, he supports the advancement of economic education and the professional development of students and researchers in Uzbekistan.

Duraipandian R. is a Principal in the Saveetha School of Management at Saveetha University, with many years of teaching experiences.

Sukanya R. holds a Ph.D. in Finance from CHRIST (Deemed to be University), specializing in Outward Foreign Direct Investment (FDI) from India. Since 2022, she has served as an Assistant Professor in the Department of Commerce at CHRIST. Her research interests include key areas such as Outward FDI, globalization, internationalization, and urbanization. Her work also focuses on financial services, consumer satisfaction, food security, and sustainability. She aims to inform policies that promote economic growth, environmental awareness, and social responsibility. Her research provides valuable insights into the intersections between economic development and sustainability. With a strong background in globalization and economic development, Dr. Sukanya contributes to academic discourse on these critical issues. She collaborates widely and has published extensively on these topics. Her work is dedicated to advancing knowledge and shaping sustainable development strategies.

Ravikumar R. N. is an experienced academician with over 13+ years of teaching and research expertise across institutions in India, the UAE, and the Maldives. He currently serves as an Assistant Professor at Marwadi University, Rajkot, specializing in Machine Learning, Recommender Systems, and AI-driven applications in healthcare and security. He holds a Ph.D. in Machine Learning and Recommender Systems from Amity University, Jaipur, a Master of Engineering in CSE from VMRF University, Salem, and a Bachelor of Engineering in CSE from Anna University. He also has a MiniMBA from the Swiss eLearning Institute. Dr. Ravikumar has authored more than 8+ multiple SCIE/Scopus-indexed journal articles, 25+ IEEE/Springer conference papers, and co-authored a book on Artificial Intelligence. He has also published 9 patents and contributed 85+ book chapters in emerging domains such as Federated Learning, Blockchain, and Digital Twins for IGI Global, Wiley and Springer publisher. He actively mentors students through initiatives like the Research Activities Club (RAC) and Student Research Internship Training (SRIT), promoting innovation and research culture.

Aarthi S. is a dedicated Assistant Professor in Computer Science with over six years of teaching experience. She is currently pursuing her Ph.D. at Marwadi University, Gujarat, and holds an M.Phil. and MCA from Bharathiar University, Tamil Nadu. Throughout her academic career, Aarthi has specialized in programming languages such as C++, Java, and C, and contributed to research in recommender systems and AI-related data privacy. She has published journal articles, contributed to book chapters, and actively participated in technical workshops. Known for her student mentorship and engagement in academic events, Aarthi remains committed to fostering innovation and excellence in computer science education.

Turdiev Abdullo Sagdullaevich is an Associate Professor in the Department of Finance at Alfraganus University, Tashkent, Uzbekistan. He is actively involved in teaching, research, and academic development in the fields of finance, banking, and economic management. His scholarly interests include financial systems, investment strategies, corporate finance, and the application of modern analytical methods in economic decision-making. Through his academic work, he contributes to enhancing financial literacy and professional competencies among university students. He also participates in research collaborations, academic conferences, and scholarly publications, supporting the advancement of financial education and research in higher education institutions.

Jakhongir Shaturaev is an Associate Professor working in the Department of International Cooperation at Termez University of Economics and Service, Termez, Uzbekistan.

Muzaffar Shojonov is a researcher and faculty member in the Department of Information Technology at Urgench State University, Urgench, Uzbekistan. His professional interests include information systems, software engineering, and applied IT for education and public services. He participates in collaborative projects and conferences and contributes to publications addressing practical and theoretical aspects of computing.

Mukimov Askar Shukhratovich is an Associate Professor in the Department of Digital Technologies at Alfraganus University, Tashkent, Uzbekistan. His academic and research interests focus on digital technologies, information systems, data analytics, and the application of modern computing solutions in education and industry. He is actively involved in teaching and scholarly activities that promote the development of students' technical skills in programming, information technology, and digital innovation. His work emphasizes the integration of advanced digital tools, emerging technologies, and data-driven approaches to address contemporary technological challenges. Mukimov Askar Shukhratovich also contributes to academic discussions related to digital transformation, information technology management, and the advancement of technology-based education. Through his teaching and research engagement, he aims to support the development of skilled professionals capable of contributing to modern digital ecosystems and technological innovation.

Sheetal Singh is a seasoned legal academic with over 15 years of experience in teaching, research, and academic administration. Currently serving as Assistant Professor at the School of Law, CHRIST (Deemed to be University), Delhi NCR Campus, she previously held senior faculty roles at Amity Law School, Noida, where she also founded the Amity Legal Aid Cell. She holds a Ph.D. in Law from Amity University and is UGC-NET qualified, with expertise spanning Family Law, Criminal Law, Constitutional Law, Property Law, and Human Rights. Dr. Singh has guided more than 150 LLB and LLM dissertations and supervises Ph.D. research on gender justice and victimology. Her scholarly contributions include chapters in edited volumes published by Thomson Reuters, CRC Press, Springer, and Cambridge Scholars Publishing, covering topics such as media law, reproductive rights, cybersecurity, and comparative constitutional analysis. She has presented papers at national and international conferences, delivered guest lectures, and organized seminars and workshops on legal education, gender sensitization, and human rights. Her administrative roles include serving as Head of Department, Program Coordinator, and member of various university committees such as IQAC, Moot Court, and Placement. Widely recognized for her commitment to legal education and interdisciplinary research, Dr. Singh continues to contribute meaningfully to academia and social justice initiatives.

Rituraj Sinha is an Assistant Professor at the School of Law, CHRIST (Deemed to be University), Delhi NCR. He holds a Ph.D. from Guru Gobind Singh Indraprastha University and an LL.M. from NALSAR. With prior teaching experience at Amity Law School and IMS Unison University, he also practiced as an advocate in Delhi. His academic interests include Corporate Law, gender justice, intellectual property rights, and the legal dimensions of emerging technologies. He has contributed to reputed journals and international conference volumes and actively mentors students in research and legal scholarship.

Shashank Solanki is a legal researcher and corporate governance professional working at the intersection of law, technology, and environmental policy. He has authored and co-authored over 40 book chapters, mostly published or accepted in Scopus-indexed volumes by IGI Global, Springer, Elsevier, Taylor & Francis, and Wiley. His research focuses on AI regulation, cybersecurity, climate resilience, quantum computing ethics, and digital forensics, adopting a multidisciplinary approach to global governance and innovation. Professionally, Solanki has interned with top law firms including Shardul Amarchand Mangaldas & Co., Karanjawala & Co., and Singhania & Partners LLP, among many others, and has collaborated with Hon'ble Justice Ashok Bhushan at the NCLAT. He has presented at international conferences, contributed to policy dialogues, and held leadership roles in legal aid initiatives, demonstrating a commitment to academic excellence and social impact.

Jabbarov Umarbek is affiliated with the Department of Accounting and Business Administration at Mamun University, Khiva, Uzbekistan. He is engaged in academic teaching and research in the fields of accounting, business management, and financial administration. His academic interests include financial reporting, managerial accounting, business strategy, and modern practices in organizational management. Through his teaching and scholarly activities, he contributes to developing students' understanding of accounting systems and effective business decision-making. He also participates in academic collaborations and research initiatives aimed at strengthening professional education in accounting and business administration and supporting the advancement of business studies in higher education.

Vijeta Verma is an Assistant Professor at the School of Law, CHRIST (Deemed to be University), Delhi NCR. She holds a Ph.D. in Law from Mewar University and an LL.M. from Amity University, Noida. With over a decade of academic experience, she has previously served as an Assistant Professor at JIMS Engineering Management & Technical Campus and Ideal Institute of Management & Technology. Her research interests lie in Constitutional Law, Human Rights, and Gender Justice. At CHRIST, she actively contributes as the Faculty Convenor for various academic committees and has been a key organizer of national and international legal conferences.

Index

A

Active Transport 247, 249, 251, 257, 258, 259, 261, 263, 267, 268, 269, 270
AI-Enabled Logistics 44, 45, 70
Artificial Intelligence 1, 2, 4, 6, 9, 10, 14, 18, 19, 21, 25, 27, 28, 29, 30, 31, 34, 35, 40, 45, 77, 78, 79, 85, 94, 97, 99, 108, 136, 144, 148, 167, 171, 173, 174, 180, 208, 210, 213, 214, 216, 217, 219, 220, 221, 224, 226, 227, 234, 238, 240, 242, 243, 244, 282, 283, 304, 307, 315, 326, 339, 342
Autonomous Driving 2, 4, 5, 10, 11, 12, 13, 25, 26, 28, 29, 30, 31

B

Blockchain Technology 78, 327, 333, 338, 340, 341

C

Carbon Emissions 22, 36, 45, 59, 62, 82, 85, 96, 98, 99, 101, 104, 141, 145, 152, 153, 154, 155, 156, 171, 173, 184, 214, 258, 263, 270, 271, 282, 284, 286, 290, 302, 303, 304, 305, 306, 307, 308, 311, 319, 320, 326, 327, 334, 337
Carbon Emissions Reduction 141
Circular Economy 87, 100, 104, 178, 201, 203, 319, 325, 326, 340
Climate Policy Effectiveness 282
Cost-Benefit Analysis 16, 186, 247, 248, 259, 261, 271, 272
Cross-Border Data Governance 34, 36, 39, 41, 42, 45, 47, 55, 61, 63, 68, 70, 74

D

Data-Driven Infrastructure 173, 177, 203, 210
Decarbonization 1, 3, 6, 10, 16, 22, 27, 30, 31, 34, 36, 38, 41, 61, 70, 77, 83, 85, 86, 100, 107, 108, 109, 113, 114, 115, 116, 117, 118, 119, 120, 121, 122, 123, 124, 125, 126, 127, 128, 129, 130, 131, 132, 133, 134, 135, 136, 137, 138, 139, 140, 145, 151, 152, 159, 173, 174, 175, 177, 178, 187, 191, 202, 203, 204, 206, 208, 209, 210, 213, 214, 215, 216, 217, 218, 219, 220, 222, 224, 227, 228, 229, 230, 232, 233, 234, 235, 236, 237, 238, 244, 247, 248, 249, 251, 252, 253, 254, 255, 256, 257, 258, 262, 263, 265, 266, 267, 268, 270, 276, 277, 278, 279, 281, 282, 283, 291, 303, 304, 305, 306, 307, 315, 319, 320, 322, 331, 333
Decarbonized Transport 1, 2, 4, 5, 21, 24, 84, 85, 86, 173, 203, 314, 329, 342
Decision Making 40, 137, 319, 326, 327, 335, 336, 337
Deep Reinforcement Learning 4, 7, 10, 12, 13, 15, 29, 30, 183, 209
Digital Trade 34, 35, 37, 38, 39, 42, 44, 54, 55, 56, 64, 65, 67, 68, 69, 70, 71, 72, 73, 74, 75, 76
Digital Twins 34, 46, 143, 173, 174, 175, 176, 177, 178, 180, 181, 182, 183, 184, 185, 187, 188, 189, 191, 193, 197, 198, 199, 200, 201, 202, 203, 204, 206, 209, 243, 327

E

Economic Signals 213, 215, 216, 218, 219, 220, 221, 222, 223, 224, 226, 227, 228, 233, 234, 236, 237, 238, 244, 245
Electric Buses 147, 148, 152, 153, 154, 155, 156, 157, 158, 159, 166, 167, 169, 171, 172, 302, 303
Electric Vehicles 1, 2, 6, 7, 8, 9, 10, 17, 20, 28, 31, 86, 99, 101, 144, 148, 150, 151, 155, 167, 170, 172, 191, 209, 247, 249, 250, 252, 255, 270, 271, 272, 276, 306, 322, 327, 334
Emerging Economies 55, 81, 82, 83, 84,

87, 88, 90, 98, 102, 103, 104, 106, 107, 111, 114, 128, 191, 192, 208, 258, 270, 275, 277, 282, 284, 286, 293, 297, 302, 303, 306, 307, 308, 309, 311
Energy Management Systems 6, 9, 330
Environmental Kuznets Curve 277, 279, 280, 286, 288, 289, 290, 310, 311
Environmental Performance 35, 85, 86, 89, 90, 106, 111, 161, 214, 217, 218, 219, 238, 252, 254, 255, 305, 313, 314, 315, 316, 317, 320, 322, 323, 324, 325, 328, 330, 331, 336, 337, 338, 340, 341, 343
Environmental Upgrading 87, 89
ESG Compliance 64

G

Green Finance 90, 95, 106, 275, 277, 278, 281, 283, 301, 302, 304, 307, 309, 342
Green Transportation 100, 151

H

High-Speed Railway 164, 171
Hydrogen Fuel Cell Vehicles 247, 255, 271

L

Life-Cycle Assessment 247, 272
Logistics Emissions 74
Low-Carbon Mobility 148, 149, 219, 228, 234, 238, 239, 245, 247, 249, 259, 261, 263, 267, 273, 309

M

Machine Learning 1, 2, 4, 5, 6, 7, 8, 9, 14, 15, 17, 18, 19, 21, 24, 25, 27, 28, 29, 30, 31, 35, 46, 94, 136, 167, 174, 177, 180, 181, 183, 193, 194, 198, 201, 210, 211, 218, 219, 221, 227, 242, 244, 266
Market Behavior 113, 119, 123, 125, 126, 127, 134, 140

O

Outward FDI 81, 91, 103

P

Policy Instruments 115, 116, 118, 120, 122, 123, 125, 127, 135, 145, 191, 216, 224, 249, 256, 262, 316
Predictive Analytics 2, 40, 44, 48, 51, 58, 60, 61, 85, 174, 206, 218, 219, 235, 241, 305
Predictive Maintenance 1, 3, 4, 19, 20, 25, 26, 29, 30, 46, 62, 63, 67, 68, 74, 85, 174, 177, 180, 197, 203, 211, 305
Public Transit 18, 31, 184, 191, 196, 197, 199, 247, 257, 258, 261, 264, 265, 267, 295

R

Regulatory Conditioning 102
Regulatory Interoperability 39, 59, 71, 72
Renewable Energy 3, 6, 9, 10, 22, 31, 83, 86, 91, 93, 95, 96, 97, 98, 99, 100, 101, 102, 104, 144, 148, 151, 167, 169, 171, 177, 185, 189, 199, 254, 275, 276, 277, 278, 279, 280, 281, 282, 284, 285, 286, 288, 289, 290, 291, 292, 293, 301, 302, 303, 304, 306, 307, 308, 309, 310, 311, 328, 340
Reverse Logistics 141, 314, 315, 316, 319, 320, 321, 322, 323, 330, 337, 338, 339, 341, 343
Reverse Spillovers 81, 82, 87, 102, 103
Risk-Based Governance 40
Road and Freight Transport 113, 114, 115, 116, 117, 118, 119, 120, 123, 124, 128, 133, 137, 139, 140, 145

S

Selection Criteria 124, 147, 156, 161, 162, 167, 168
Smart Infrastructure 97, 211
Social Cost Of Carbon 5, 247, 248, 249, 273
Sustainability Governance 36, 40, 64

Sustainability Regulation 34, 38
Sustainable Mobility 2, 26, 30, 96, 101, 143, 210, 257, 258, 272, 303, 304
Sustainable Supply Chains 78, 86, 144, 172, 342
Sustainable Transportation 25, 29, 31, 104, 149, 152, 168, 172, 173, 177, 189, 270, 276, 277, 278, 279, 337
Sustainable Transport Infrastructure 281, 309

T

Threshold Regression 277, 282, 286, 287, 288, 291, 303, 307
Total Cost Of Ownership 10, 188, 247, 253, 267, 271, 273
Transport Decarbonization 30, 107, 108, 114, 116, 117, 118, 119, 124, 126, 127, 128, 131, 145, 208, 214, 216, 220, 222, 224, 227, 228, 234, 235, 255, 256, 262, 263, 265, 266, 267, 268, 270, 282, 283, 291, 304

U

Urban Transportation 14, 15, 18, 149, 152, 153, 155, 159, 166, 167, 184, 303

www.ingramcontent.com/pod-product-compliance
Lightning Source LLC
LaVergne TN
LVHW080907300926
849162LV00003B/583
9798337390031